PREVENTING CHILDHOOD DISORDERS, SUBSTANCE ABUSE, AND DELINQUENCY

Ray DeV. Peters
Robert J. McMahon
editors

BANFF INTERNATIONAL BEHAVIORAL SCIENCE SERIES

SAGE Publications
International Educational and Professional Publisher
Thousand Oaks   London   New Delhi

For information address:

SAGE Publications, Inc.
2455 Teller Road
Thousand Oaks, California 91320
E-mail: order@sagepub.com

SAGE Publications Ltd.
6 Bonhill Street
London EC2A 4PU
United Kingdom

SAGE Publications India Pvt. Ltd.
M-32 Market
Greater Kailash I
New Delhi 110048 India

Printed in the United States of America

Library of Congress Cataloging-in-Publication Data

Preventing childhood disorders, substance abuse and delinquency /
  editors, Ray DeV. Peters, Robert J. McMahon.
    p. cm. — (Banff international behavioral science series; v. 3)
    Includes bibliographical references and index.
    ISBN 0-7619-0014-4 (cloth: acid-free paper). —
ISBN 0-7619-0015-2 (pbk.: acid-free paper)
    1. Conduct disorders in children—Prevention. 2. Conduct
disorders in adolescence—Prevention. 3. Children—Substance use.
4. Teenagers—Substance use. 5. Substance abuse—Prevention.
I. Peters, Ray DeV., 1942- . II. McMahon, Robert J. (Robert
Joseph), 1953- . III. Series.
RJ506.C65P735 1996
618.92′8582—dc20   96-4477

        98 99 10 9 8 7 6 5 4 3 2

Sage Production Editor: Vicki Baker

This volume is dedicated to
the memory of our deceased parents

Paul D. and Pauline H. Peters
and
Robert J. McMahon, Jr.

Contents

Preface

The chapters in this volume are the work of a collection of experienced scientist-practitioners in the field of childhood disorders, substance abuse, and delinquency. The central theme of the volume is prevention and early intervention approaches to dealing with these important social problems.

A long tradition of research in the behavioral and social sciences exists describing myriad etiological factors that contribute to the manifestation of childhood and adolescent problems. Also, there exists an extensive literature concerning a variety of treatment approaches to child and adolescent psychological and social problems, and much exciting work in this area continues, particularly in the context of developing empirically validated treatments (see, for example, Weisz, 1996; Weisz, Weiss, Han, Granger, & Morton, 1995). However, despite whatever successes these treatment interventions may have with seriously disordered children, there is a growing recognition that there are simply not enough individuals trained in these procedures to make a significant impact on the prevalence of these disorders (e.g., Albee, 1982; Offord, 1987; Peters, 1988).

Consequently, there has been increased interest in the past decade in approaches to these major social and emotional disorders in children that are designed to prevent the onset of disorder or to deal with problematic behaviors when they first appear. This volume presents theories and practices of leading-edge prevention and early intervention programs with children from birth through adolescence.

Following an introductory overview chapter by Coie, the volume is organized in a developmental or chronological fashion with the first chapters describing interventions with very young children and their families. Subsequent chapters address issues and interventions with elementary school children, "transition" or preadolescent children, and finally, adolescents. Although the volume is organized around the age of the focal children, there is also a strong emphasis on involving parents, schools, and the community in most of the intervention programs.

The volume represents a collection of current prevention and early intervention approaches selected to be of interest to academics, other researchers, and students in the behavioral sciences as well as to those involved in direct intervention with children and adults, such as social workers, clinical psychologists, psychiatrists, and other mental health professionals. Finally, given the timely nature of the topic, the volume should be of substantial interest to policymakers at the state or provincial and national levels who are searching for more effective and efficient large-scale intervention approaches to dealing with social and behavioral problems in children and adolescents.

A major issue running throughout the volume, and indeed, throughout the field itself, is the definition of different approaches to prevention. Historically, the concept of prevention has developed from the fields of disease, public health, and epidemiology. The first attempt to identify different categories of prevention activities appeared in a working group report of the Commission on Chronic Illness (1957), which proposed a distinction between *primary* prevention, which is practiced prior to the biological origin of the disease, and *secondary* prevention, which is practiced after the disease can be recognized but before it has caused suffering and disability. Somewhat later, a third class of prevention activities was proposed by Leavell and Clark (1965)—namely, *tertiary* prevention, which is practiced after suffering or disability from the disease is being experienced with the goal of preventing further deterioration.

In a chapter on prevention in child and adolescent psychiatry, Graham (1994) has commented,

> By convention, three types of preventive activity are recognized (Henderson, 1988). Primary prevention involves intervention that *reduces the incidence* of disorder. Secondary prevention comprises treatment that *reduces the duration* of the disorder, and tertiary prevention covers rehabilitative activity that *reduces the disability* arising from an established disorder. (p. 815, italics added)

This tripartite division of prevention activities has been criticized by several writers. Gordon (1983) argues that it does not distinguish between preventive interventions that have different epidemiologic justifications and require different strategies for optimal use. He claims that the classification scheme is an artifact of the earlier mechanistic conceptions of health and disease that do not apply easily to more complex, multifactorial causal models of physical disease and mental disorders.

Bower (1987) suggests that secondary and tertiary prevention constitute contradictions in terms, because they do not represent prevention per se but various forms of treatment and rehabilitation. He argues that only primary prevention should be called prevention.

A similar point is made by Peters (1990), who argues that the term *prevention* should be reserved for those interventions that attempt to reduce the incidence or onset of a problem, disorder, or disease in individuals who do not show any sign of the disorder in question and suggests that the term *early intervention* replace secondary prevention, and *treatment/rehabilitation* replace tertiary prevention.

Finally, Gordon (1983) has proposed a further division of prevention or primary prevention interventions into three categories: *universal* preventive interventions, and two types of *targeted* preventive interventions. Universal (or populationwide) preventive strategies are designed to reach all individuals of a particular age in a specified area or setting (for example, all 0- to 2-year-old children in a particular community or all children attending a particular primary school). *Selective* preventive interventions are one form of targeted strategies and are implemented with individuals who are considered to be at risk for developing a particular disease or disorder based on specified biological, psychological, or social factors external to the targeted individuals. Examples include children living in families on social assistance and children of drug-abusing or divorced parents. *Indicated* preventive interventions are a second type of targeted strategies designed to reach individuals considered to be at risk for a particular disorder by virtue of specified current characteristics of the individuals themselves, so-called internal factors, such as low-birth-weight babies or children experiencing peer relationship difficulties.

A recent publication on the prevention of mental disorders by the Institute of Medicine (IOM, 1994) advocates the adoption of a modification of Gordon's distinction between the three types of universal and targeted prevention strategies. All three types of preventive interventions are represented in the current volume, in addition to promotion strategies such as those discussed by Peters (1988, 1990). Also, discussions of advantages and disadvantages of each of these intervention approaches appear throughout the volume.

In the opening chapter, Coie introduces a conceptual framework of prevention in the context of violence and antisocial behavior. In a discussion of some of the most important considerations in designing preventive interventions for violent and antisocial behavior, Coie argues against a universal or populationwide strategy in favor of a targeted approach that attempts to select participants on the basis of identified risk factors. Coie notes that there is some recognition of the difficulty in distinguishing between primary and secondary prevention with children who are at high risk for problems such as antisocial behavior. He claims that those children who are at risk for later violence or antisocial behavior are those who show some form of antisocial behavior at school entry. He thus advocates an indicated strategy of prevention. This emphasis on *preventing* later serious antisocial behavior by working with young children who are identified as *currently showing* less serious antisocial behavior underscores the definitional conundrum that continues to plague the field of prevention.

Coie is one of the members of the Conduct Problems Prevention Research Group (CPPRG), which is currently funded by the National Institute of Mental Health and the Center for Substance Abuse Prevention to implement a multisite trial of a prevention program for antisocial children, known as the Fast Track Program. The details of this project are presented in later chapters, but in his opening chapter, Coie describes the developmental model that the CPPRG has employed in planning and implementing their intervention strategies with antisocial children beginning at the entry to elementary school. The model elegantly encapsulates a broad range of factors that have been identified in previous research as contributing to the development of antisocial behavior in children beginning as young as 2 to 3 years of age through to the expression of delinquency in adolescence.

In Chapter 2, Peters and Russell describe a type of universal prevention initiative titled the Better Beginnings, Better Futures Project. The project has three major goals: (a) to prevent serious social, emotional, behavioral, physical, and cognitive problems in young children; (b) to promote the social, emotional, behavioral, physical, and cognitive development of these children; and (c) to enhance the abilities of socioeconomically disadvantaged families and communities to provide for their children.

The focus is on children to the age of 8 years old, living in socioeconomically disadvantaged communities and neighborhoods in Ontario. These communities are being funded to provide services tailored to local circumstances for 4 years of implementation. The children, families, and demonstration communities will be followed until the children reach their mid-20s to see if this type of early childhood education and family support model has made a difference in life span development and community development for children, families, and high-risk neighborhoods.

In many ways, this model in unique because it focuses on child, family, and community factors. In the Better Beginnings, Better Futures Project, the neighborhood or community is considered to be high risk. All children and families living within a designated neighborhood or community are eligible to take part in any of the programs; that is, the intervention is universal but within a high-risk community. The purpose of the project is to strengthen children and their families as well as the local community itself. In this sense, the project is designed to foster three aspects of human development: child development, family development, and community development.

One of the most salient differences between the Better Beginnings Project and other models is the requirement for meaningful, significant parent and community leader involvement in decision making. During the first year of local development, this characteristic of the model came to mean that the Steering Committee and each major subcommittee of the local project needed to have a membership of at least 50% parents or other community residents. It became equally clear that although the requirement for 50% local representation was important, what really made this level of participation possible was the transfer of real decision-making power to these committees. The participants on these committees wrote the job descriptions, delegated the hiring committees, decided salary levels, and decided the amount of funding to go to each component of the model (e.g., child care, home visiting, community safety). The transfer of this level of control and responsibility to parents and other community members has the potential of empowering community residents who, individually and collectively, may have felt little control over their lives and the lives of their children.

In the third chapter, Pizzolongo describes the Comprehensive Child Development Program (CCDP), an innovative effort put forth by the Administration on Children, Youth and Families (ACYF) and established by Congress in 1988. CCDP is based on an extensive history of research and programmatic efforts in early-intervention programs for young children and their families who are part of the low-income population of the United States. These programs, of which CCDP is now a part, have focused on alleviating the pressing problems faced by low-income families, including inadequate housing, health care and nutrition, family breakup, teenage pregnancy, lack of positive role models and growth experiences for children, and poor educational attainment and employment prospects. These problems often lead to crime or welfare dependency. This chapter provides information on the history and program features of the CCDP as well as an overview of early intervention studies and other programs that attempt to enhance the strengths of low-income families and their children and diminish the problems that they face.

In Chapter 4, Bierman, Greenberg, and the CPPRG provide a description of part of the Fast Track Program, which is based on the developmental model described earlier by Coie. Fast Track is a multisite demonstration project involved in the development, implementation, and evaluation of a comprehensive, multicomponent prevention program targeting children at risk for conduct disorders. Seven integrated components make up the program. This chapter focuses on three components: (a) a universal prevention curriculum used by teachers, (b) a targeted social skill training group program, and (c) a peer-pairing program, all designed to build social skills and enhance positive peer relationships. The chapter begins with an overview of the social skill deficits associated with conduct disorders and targeted in Fast Track.

The content and structure of the social skill training components used in the Fast Track Program are then described. The ways in which the Fast Track social skill training programs attempt to address the needs of children with conduct problems and the interpersonal contexts in which their social skills are developing are elaborated. Across both the universal (classroom-based) and targeted (high-risk group-based) levels of intervention, the procedures used to promote competencies in six social skill domains are described. These domains include (a) social participation, (b) prosocial behavior, (c) communication skills, (d) self-control, (e) regulating oneself in rule-based interactions, and (f) social problem-solving skills. In the last section of the chapter, special issues in the implementation of social skill training programs with children who exhibit multiple conduct problems are discussed.

The chapter by McMahon, Slough, and the CPPRG is a continuation of the description of the Fast Track Program, emphasizing the three program components that focus on the family context: (a) parent groups, (b) parent-child relationship enhancement, and (c) home visiting. The parent group component focuses on four specific content areas: (a) the development of positive family-school relationships, (b) parental self-control (i.e., anger control), (c) the development of reasonable and appropriate expectations for the child, and (d) parenting skills to increase positive parent-child interaction and decrease the occurrence of acting-out behaviors. Prior to focusing on parenting skills, parents learn how to maintain their self-control when faced with frustrating child behavior and to develop expectations for their children's behavior that are realistic and appropriate for their children's developmental level. These skills are viewed as necessary to the learning and mastery of various parenting skills to facilitate positive parent-child interactions and to decrease inappropriate child behaviors.

At the conclusion of each parent group, the parents and children meet together for parent-child sharing time. The primary goal is to foster positive parent-child relationships through the promotion of positive interchanges between parents and children. A variety of cooperative activities, games, crafts, and joint reading activities are employed. A second goal of this component is to provide an opportunity for parents to practice the new skills that they learned in the parent group with their children with supervision and support from Fast Track staff.

The home-visiting component of Fast Track is intended to serve a variety of functions. First, it provides an opportunity for the development of a positive relationship between the Fast Track staff member and the family members. Second, the home visits provide yet another opportunity to promote the generalization of parenting skills to the natural environment. Third, the home visits can promote effective parental support for the children's school adjustment through the encouragement and support of parent-child reading activities, parental monitoring and assistance with the child's homework assignments, and discussion regarding effective parent-teacher communication and teamwork to assist the child in meeting his or her academic and social goals. Fourth, the home visits provide an opportunity to promote parental problem-solving and coping skills concerning the stressors that affect many of these families. The ultimate goal is to foster parental feelings of empowerment and efficacy and to decrease the risk of fostering dependency on Fast Track staff. The chapter concludes with a discussion of implementation issues that have arisen in the course of developing and applying the family-focused program components.

The chapter by Lochman and Wells begins with an overview of developmentally oriented preventive intervention projects. The importance of a clear conceptual model for the intervention is stressed. This model can include an understanding based on current empirical work of the risk factors that predict later disorder and of the mediating and moderating factors that influence how the projected trajectory for the disorder manifests itself. One central model describing the occurrence and development of aggressive behavior is a social-cognitive or social information-processing model. This model has been derived from research over the past 15 years that has documented that aggressive children are hyperattentive to hostile social cues, have hostile attributional biases, have social problem-solving deficits involving a relative lack of verbal assertion and compromise solutions, and expect that aggressive behavior will have relatively positive outcomes for them.

Based on this model of social-cognitive difficulties, an intervention known as the Anger Coping program was developed. This program focuses on aggressive children's difficulties in social perspective taking, awareness of arousal, use of self-instructional inhibiting abilities, and social problem solving. This preventive intervention is school based and consists of 18 weekly group sessions. A series of four programmatic outcome studies has found that in comparison to untreated or comparison treatment conditions, children who have participated in the Anger Coping program have reductions in independently observed off-task behavior, reductions in parent- or teacher-rated aggression, and improvements in self-esteem in the month after treatment.

Lochman and Wells' current work on the Coping Power program is an extension of the Anger Coping program that is longer in duration and that incorporates the family as well. The child and parent components of this more comprehensive intervention are described. The chapter concludes with a discussion of implementation issues with teachers, peers, and family members.

Cunningham begins Chapter 7 by reviewing the research literature that indicates that externalizing or Disruptive Behavior Disorders (Attention-deficit Hyperactivity Disorder, Oppositional Defiant Disorder, and Conduct Disorder) are among the most prevalent, persistent, and vexing of the early childhood problems referred to children's mental health centers. Although these disorders reflect the complex interplay of genetic factors, parental psychopathology, marital interactions, family functioning, peer relationships, educational experiences, and larger socioeconomic variables, parenting is almost universally considered to play a mediating role in either their emergence, maintenance, or longer-term developmental course. Parent training programs designed to teach more effective child management strategies have emerged as an important component in more comprehensive prevention and intervention programs for this population.

In this chapter, Cunningham describes the design and evaluation of the Community Parent Education (COPE) program's large group, neighborhood-based parent training courses. To increase the availability of parent training, this program shifted from individual or small-group programs to courses capable of accommodating from 25 to 35 participants. To increase accessibility and improve use among high-risk families, courses are advertised widely, scheduled at day and evening times, conducted at conveniently located neighborhood schools and community centers, and equipped with an on-site volunteer child care service. To enable large groups of parents to participate actively in the problem-solving discussions, modeling exercises, and role-playing activities that represent the critical skill-building components of individual programs, much of the work of the course is accomplished in five-member subgroups, in which parents review the successful application of new strategies to problems at home, rehearse new skills, and formulate homework goals.

Recently completed trials comparing large, community-based courses with more clinic-based individual programs suggest that, in addition to a substantial improvement in cost-effectiveness, large groups improved use among socioeconomically disadvantaged parents, immigrants, and families of children with more severe problems. Parents participating in larger groups reported greater reduction in child management problems, better maintenance of gains at 6-month follow-ups, and better problem-solving skills.

In Chapter 8, Prinz and Miller continue the discussion of parent training and family involvement in interventions for children at risk for conduct disorder. These authors claim that despite moderate success rates with childhood antisocial behavior, the greatest stumbling block for family-based interventions has been insufficient engagement of parents. Indications of inadequate engagement include sporadic attendance, missed appointments (both canceled and uncanceled), tardiness to sessions, failure to complete "homework" assignments, limited or counterproductive involvement in sessions, and ultimately, premature dropout.

Four major domains have been identified as having a strong impact on parental engagement: (a) the therapeutic process, (b) personal constructs, (c) intervention characteristics, and (d) situational demands and constraints. Prinz and Miller describe ways of addressing each of these four domains to foster more successful parental engagement. They conclude by observing that intervention research on parental engagement is important but is not without its share of major challenges. In a free society, people have a right to choose not to participate, even to their own or their children's detriment. Furthermore, the collection of attrition data, or even the expectation of attrition, is not always compatible with the aims of community programs or grant-funding agencies. Nonetheless, progress in the evolution of interventions for childhood conduct problems depends in part on researchers themselves staying engaged in the tackling of problems associated with parental engagement and attrition.

In Chapter 9, Dishion, Andrews, Kavanagh, and Soberman begin by noting that problem behavior in children is highly situational, ebbing and flowing as a function of context and development. Thus, it is unlikely that a single course of intervention will likely result in a permanent solution. They suggest that a dental model of prevention may be helpful as a guiding metaphor for preventing child and adolescent problem behavior. Just as preventive interventions for tooth decay are needed throughout the life span, preventive interventions are needed throughout childhood (ages 0 to 18). Like a dental model, intervention is necessarily individualized and may consist of both treatment and prevention, depending on the vulnerabilities and protective factors at each stage of development.

The Adolescent Transitions Program (ATP) is an evolving menu of intervention and assessment resources that was conceptualized under such a framework. ATP is intended as an intervention for high-risk youth, formulated on the basis of a social interactional model for the development of antisocial behavior in childhood and problem behavior in adolescence. There are two basic intervention targets: the parents (parent focus) and the young adolescents (teen focus). Group interventions with the parents seek to improve parent family management skills; interventions with the youth aim at developing self-regulation of problem behavior. The two curricula are designed to parallel each other, and skill development exercises frequently include parent-child activities.

Dishion and colleagues conclude their chapter by noting that problem behavior has stability across development and within context. Knowledge of early antisocial antecedents, long-term sequelae, and negative outcomes provides a guidance in the preventive procedures necessary for young adolescents and their parents. Dishion and colleagues propose that regular checkups provide a nonstigmatizing mechanism for assessing levels of "decay" and gathering the necessary resources across contexts to prevent further deterioration and eventual loss of these youth to our society.

Significant progress has been made over the past decade in developing effective strategies for preventing substance abuse among adolescents. No one has contributed more to this research knowledge than Botvin. In Chapter 10, Botvin presents a conceptual model that incorporates what is known about causes and developmental progressions of drug abuse. He then describes a cognitive-behavioral prevention approach based on this model called Life Skills Training, which was developed to (a) affect drug-related expectancies, (b) teach skills for resisting social influences to use drugs, and (c) promote the development of general personal self-management and social skills. The Life Skills Training program consists of 15 class periods of roughly 45 minutes each. The background and rationale for the Life Skills Training approach to drug abuse prevention is discussed, intervention materials are described, and the research studies testing its efficacy are summarized. This is a universal or primary prevention intervention that has been tested on several different populations of adolescents in school settings.

In Chapter 11, Kumpfer, Molgaard, and Spoth review the research on family risk and protective factors that influence delinquency and drug abuse in youth, identify principles of effective family intervention models, and describe promising family-focused intervention models for use with special populations. This is followed by a description of the theoretical underpinnings, development, implementation process and results of various forms of the Strengthening Families Program. This is a family-focused, selective prevention intervention that has been tailored for special populations at high risk for substance abuse and delinquency, such as children of substance abusers, children being removed from the home because of child abuse and neglect, and low-income rural and urban parents of different ethnic groups. The chapter concludes with a presentation of research methods and a summary of several outcome studies evaluating the effectiveness of the Strengthening Families program.

In Chapter 12, Tremblay, Mâsse, Pagani, and Vitaro describe the long-term outcomes of a group of adolescents who had been involved in a longitudinal-experimental study aimed at understanding the development of aggressive kindergarten boys in Montreal and also to test the effectiveness of an early intervention strategy. The emphasis in the chapter is on the early intervention program that was designed to attenuate early aggressive behavior and to prevent later delinquency involvement. The program was planned in the early 1980s when parent training and child social skills training were proposed as alternative approaches to the treatment of aggressive early elementary school-age children and early adolescents. These two intervention components were carried out with a group of highly aggressive, low-socioeconomic-status boys for a period of 2 years while they were between the ages of 7 and 9. These boys have now been followed for 6 years after program termination to the age of 15, along with two control groups of aggressive boys. The results indicated significant long-term impacts of the intervention program on a variety of adolescent behaviors, including gang membership, substance abuse, self-reported delinquency, and police arrests of self and friends. The chapter concludes with a discussion of the successes and limitations of this early intervention approach to aggressive behavior and suggestions for improvement in future program planning.

In Chapter 13, Spoth and Redmond cite the recent report on the prevention of mental disorders by the IOM (1994) as providing a framework for preventive intervention research that can be productively applied to rural populations. The *preventive intervention research cycle* presented by the IOM articulates several phases of research. The application of the prevention intervention research cycle to rural populations described in this chapter follows the same sequence as the phases. Consistent with the problem identification and knowledge base review phases of the prevention intervention research cycle, the chapter begins with a review of the need for prevention research targeting rural families (Phase 1) and a brief summary of family-related etiological factors, including recent rural family research conducted at their center (Phase 2). An overview of project procedures and rural implementation strategies is then given (Phases 3 and 4). Finally, the chapter illustrates studies used during Phases 3 and 4 to examine rural family characteristics influencing response to project recruitment strategies and to project interventions.

In the concluding chapter, Offord presents a critical review of this volume and the field of prevention of childhood mental disorders in general. His review examines the quality of research designs, the multicomponent nature of many preventive interventions, type of evaluation measures, and the adequacy of replication. The parallel between these criteria of judging quality and those employed by the American Psychological Association's

Division 12 Task Force on Promotion and Dissemination of Psychological Procedures (1995) is examined. Following the review of existing prevention efforts, Offord identifies a number of outstanding issues that need to be addressed: (a) issues in developmental epidemiology concerning risk factors, (b) the advantages and disadvantages of universal versus targeted prevention programs, (c) the role of descriptive versus experimental epidemiology, and (d) issues of program dissemination and maintenance, including cost, feasibility, whether or not a program is imposed, and reliance on exceptional people. These issues represent important challenges for the field of prevention in the coming years.

REFERENCES

Albee, G. W. (1982). Preventing psychopathology and promoting human potential. *American Psychologist, 37,* 1043-1050.

Bower, E. M. (1987). Prevention: A word whose time has come. *American Journal of Orthopsychiatry, 57,* 4-5.

Commission on Chronic Illness. (1957). *Chronic illness in the United States* (Vol. 1; published for the Commonwealth Fund). Cambridge, MA: Harvard University Press.

Gordon, R. S. (1983). An operational classification of disease prevention. *Public Health Reports, 98,* 107-109.

Graham, P. (1994). Prevention. In M. Rutter, E. Taylor, & L. Hersov (Eds.), *Child and adolescent psychiatry* (3rd ed., pp. 815-828). Oxford, UK: Blackwell Scientific Publications.

Institute of Medicine. (1994). *Reducing risks for mental disorders: Frontiers for preventive intervention research.* Washington, DC: National Academy Press.

Leavell, H. R., & Clark, E. G. (1965). *Preventive medicine for a doctor in his community: An epidemiological approach* (3rd ed.). New York: McGraw-Hill.

Offord, D. R. (1987). Prevention of behavioral and emotional disorders in children. *Journal of Child Psychology and Psychiatry, 25,* 9-20.

Peters, R. DeV. (1988). Mental health promotion in children and adolescents: An emerging role for psychology. *Canadian Journal of Behavioural Science, 20,* 389-401.

Peters, R. DeV. (1990). Adolescent mental health promotion: Policy and practice. In R. J. McMahon & R. DeV. Peters (Eds.), *Behavior disorders of adolescence: Research, intervention, and policy in clinical and school settings* (pp. 207-223). New York: Plenum.

Task Force on Promotion and Dissemination of Psychological Procedures. (1995). Training on and dissemination of empirically validated psychological treatments. *The Clinical Psychologist, 48,* 3-23.

Weisz, J. R. (1996, March). *Empirically validated treatments for children and adolescents: Criteria, problems and prospects.* Paper presented at the 28th Banff International Conference on Behavioural Science, Banff, AB.

Weisz, J. R., Weiss, B., Han, S., Granger, D. A., & Morton, T. (1995). Effects of psychotherapy with children and adolescents revisited: A meta-analysis of treatment outcome
studies. *Psychological Bulletin, 117,* 450-468.

The Banff Conferences
on Behavioural Science

This volume is one of a continuing series of publications sponsored by the Banff International Conferences on Behavioural Science. We are pleased to join Sage Publications in bringing this series to an audience of practitioners, investigators, and students. The publications arise from conferences held each spring since 1969 in Banff, Alberta, Canada, with papers representing the product of deliberations on themes and key issues. The conferences serve the purpose of bringing together outstanding behavioral scientists and professionals in a forum where they can present and discuss data related to emergent issues and topics. As a continuing event, the Banff International Conferences have served as an expressive "early indicator" of the developing nature and composition of the behavioral sciences and scientific applications to human problems and issues.

Because distance, schedules, and restricted audience preclude wide attendance at the conferences, the resulting publications have equal status with the conferences proper. Presenters at each Banff Conference are required to write a chapter specifically for the forthcoming book, separate from their presentation and discussion at the conference itself. Consequently, this volume is not a set of conference proceedings. Rather, it is an integrated volume of chapters contributed by leading researchers and practitioners who have had the unique opportunity of spending several days together presenting and discussing ideas prior to preparing their chapters.

Our "conference of colleagues" format provides for formal and informal interactions among all participants through invited addresses, workshops, poster presentations, and conversation hours. When combined with sight-seeing expeditions, cross-country and downhill skiing, and other recreations in the spectacular Canadian Rockies, the conferences have generated great enthusiasm and satisfaction among participants. The Banff Centre, our venue for the conferences for many years, has contributed immeasurably to the success of these meetings through its very comfortable accommodation, dining, and conference facilities. The following documents conference themes over the past 28 years.

1969 I
Ideal Mental Health Services

1970 II
Services and Programs for Exceptional Children and Youth

1971 III
Implementing Behavioural Programs for Schools and Clinics

1972 IV
Behaviour Change: Methodology, Concepts, and Practice

1973 V
Evaluation of Behavioural Programs in Community, Residential, and School Settings

1974 VI
Behaviour Modification and Families and Behavioural Approaches to Parenting

1975 VII
The Behavioural Management of Anxiety, Depression, and Pain

1976 VIII
Behavioural Self-Management Strategies, Techniques, and Outcomes

1977 IX
Behavioural Systems for the Developmentally Disabled
    A. School and Family Environments
    B. Institutional, Clinical, and Community Environments

1978 X
Behavioural Medicine: Changing Health Lifestyles

1979 XI
Violent Behaviour: Social Learning Approaches to Prediction,
Management, and Treatment

1980 XII
Adherence, Compliance, and Generalization in Behavioural Medicine

1981 XIII
Essentials of Behavioural Treatments for Families

1982 XIV
Advances in Clinical Behaviour Therapy

1983 XV
Childhood Disorders: Behavioural-Developmental Approaches

1984 XVI
Education in "1984"

1985 XVII
Social Learning and Systems Approaches to Marriage and the Family

1986 XVIII
Health Enhancement, Disease Prevention, and Early Intervention:
Biobehavioural Perspectives

1987 XIX
Early Intervention in the Coming Decade

1988 XX
Behaviour Disorders of Adolescence: Research, Intervention,
and Policy in Clinical and School Settings

1989 XXI
Psychology, Sport, and Health Promotion

1990 XXII
Aggression and Violence Throughout the Lifespan

1991 XXIII
Addictive Behaviours Across the Lifespan: Prevention, Treatment,
and Policy Issues

1992 XXIV
State of the Art in Cognitive-Behaviour Therapy

We would especially like to thank Philomene Kocher for her diligence in preparing the manuscript for publication and Valerie Angus for her secretarial services. Also, we would like to acknowledge the expert guidance and support that we received from C. Terry Hendrix, Jim Nageotte, Nancy Hale, and Vicki Baker at Sage Publications. It has been a pleasure working with them. While preparing this volume, Ray Peters was on the faculty of Queen's University and Bob McMahon was on the faculty of the University of Washington. The assistance and support of these institutions is gratefully acknowledged.

—Ray DeV. Peters

—Robert J. McMahon

1

Prevention of Violence and Antisocial Behavior

JOHN D. COIE

The problem of violence has been dominant in the public mind for the past few years. In part, this is because of the steady increase in criminal offending, generally over the past 30 years (Moffitt, 1993), but it is also because there is evidence that the seriousness of aggression and antisocial behavior among adolescents has accelerated. Fox and Pierce (1994) report that homicide arrests doubled among 15- and 16-year-olds over the period from 1986 to 1991 without any population increase in the number of youth of this age. In a theoretical article on the causes of adolescent conduct problems, Moffitt provided graphs for uniform crime statistics that illustrate the marked increase in adolescent crimes during the period from 1937 to 1983.

Adding to the problem of increased violence rates among adolescents is the fact that there is little evidence of the long-term efficacy of most current treatment programs for antisocial youth (Kazdin, 1987). Furthermore, there is no indication that incarceration has been an effective constraint on subsequent offending (Brennan & Mednick, 1992). These sobering facts have

AUTHOR'S NOTE: Support by Grants R01 MH 39140 and K05 MH 00797 from the Prevention Branch of the National Institute of Mental Health is gratefully acknowledged.

led a number of panels of experts (Institute of Medicine, 1994; National Institute of Mental Health, 1993) to the conclusion that much more emphasis in public policy should be placed on early prevention programs.

Prevention as a strategy for reducing the prevalence of mental health problems is an idea that has been prominent for more than 30 years (Caplan, 1964), but it has not yet been translated into public policy to any significant extent. Only 1% of the U.S. national budget for health, for example, is devoted to prevention research or to funding prevention trials (Martin, 1994). Thus, it is not surprising that the thought of solving the problem of violence through early prevention programs is but an unproven promise. In the past few years, the National Institute of Mental Health has funded several large prevention trials that have been designed to reduce adolescent antisocial behavior problems (e.g., Conduct Problems Prevention Research Group [CPPRG], 1992). These field trials have several important features that distinguish them from earlier projects with high-risk youth. One of the purposes of this chapter is to demonstrate the logical connections between these newer approaches to prevention and conclusions that can be drawn from a growing body of developmental and epidemiological research (e.g., Reid, 1993) on the problems of youthful aggression and antisocial behavior.

The conceptual framework for prevention has changed from the earlier days when primary prevention was considered the best hope for reducing disorder in our society. There is now some recognition of the difficulty in distinguishing between primary and secondary prevention with children who are at high risk for problems such as antisocial behavior. Robins (1966), for example, notes that it is rare to find an antisocial adolescent or young adult who has not exhibited some form of these problems in the childhood years. This means that the best way to identify those children who may be at risk for violence or antisocial behavior later in life is to determine whether they have displayed some form of childhood antisocial behavior. If this is the most logical way to define the target group for preventing antisocial activity, however, then it becomes virtually impossible to plan for primary prevention in this area because the essence of primary prevention is to prevent even the early signs of disorder. For this and other reasons, many of those investigators involved in trying to prevent antisocial problems have abandoned the distinction between primary and secondary prevention programs. The Institute of Medicine (1994) report on prevention advocates the adoption of a modification of Gordon's (1983) trilevel distinction between universal, selective, and indicated preventive interventions. Universal strategies attempt to reach population-based groups such as total school populations or children in a particular grade level. Selective interventions are targeted for those at risk of developing disorder on the basis of biological, psychological, or social factors. Indicated interventions are targeted for those who qualify as being at risk for serious antisocial behavior in later life by virtue of their own current behavior but who do not qualify as disordered. In the case of targeted interventions, the goal is to reduce the impact of risk factors operating on the high-risk child and to enhance the influence of protective factors on this child. The choice of adopting a universal versus a targeted strategy for preventing serious antisocial behavior is currently a matter of some controversy in the field.

To begin a prevention trial for youth who are at risk for violence or antisocial behavior, it is first necessary to formulate research-based answers to a number of basic questions. Not to do so is to risk engaging substantial amounts of human effort and money on an undertaking based primarily on good intentions and intuition. The first and most obvious of these questions is who should be the targets of a preventive intervention trial? To answer this question, we must be able to identify those characteristics of children, their families, or their environments that reliably predict adolescent violence and other antisocial behavior. Furthermore, the level of predictability must be sufficiently high as to justify the expense and effort that would be required to conduct an adequate intervention. Obviously, there is a trade-off between the accuracy of prediction and the relative efficiency and effectiveness of the proposed intervention. It is easier to point out examples of disorder in which some predictors are known but do not provide sufficient power to justify a targeted intervention. Robins (1966), for example, found that truancy was a reliable predictor of adult alcoholism. The magnitude of the difference in incidence rate for the target population (11%) versus the rate of alcoholism in the general population (8%) would not seem to justify a targeted prevention trial for alcoholism with truant youth. These same data from the Robins study provide a cautionary note on the way prediction data are analyzed. Robins found that 75% of all alcoholics in her sample had been truant in their youth. By contrast, only 26% of her control sample of nondisordered adults had been truant. This dramatic difference in rates when the data are analyzed backward from adult outcomes is misleading given the follow-forward differences of 8% and 11%. Thus, care must be taken to identify the risk rates associated with childhood characteristics when the data are analyzed prospectively with the nonindex childhood comparison group.

Timing is a second consideration in the identification of a target group for prevention trials. In most cases, the level of predictability increases as the interval between the point of prediction and the point of outcome decreases. If the interval is too short, however, the predictive advantage may be relatively worthless. Using the developmental model of violence and antisocial behavior that is outlined in this chapter, it will be clear that a series of risk factors, rather than any single factor, seem to escalate the probability of risk for such outcomes. Thus, predictability increases with age, but this increased predictive efficiency reflects the operation of factors in the child and between the child and the environment that will pose a serious challenge to intervention planning. The goal, then, is to find a point in development at which prevention efforts have some hope of success and, at the same time, the identification of those at risk is reasonably accurate (Coie, Watt, et al., 1993).

There are several important factors that determine the plausibility of preventive interventions. The first is access to the high-risk population. To address the problem of preventing violence, it is necessary to have effective screening of a broad-scale sample of the child population in high-crime areas. Schools are a logical place to select a child sample because a grade-level sample is reasonably representative of the community of children of that age. On the other hand, some types of information are not easy to obtain within a school context (e.g., parental crime records) even though they might add significantly to the prediction process. Thus, there are often trade-offs between access and accuracy of screening.

Another plausibility factor involves the motivation of the high-risk group to participate in the intervention. If a school-based sample is to be recruited for a prevention trial and parents are to be invited to participate, it needs to be possible to phrase that invitation in terms that resonate with parental motivations for themselves and their children. Closely related to this motivational issue, but reflective of the earlier point that certain developmental processes can solidify risk status, is the point that if an intervention is to be successful, the critical factors that place a child at risk must be amenable to change at the time of intervention. For example, sometimes parents are reluctant to seek help for a seriously aggressive child; they wait until the child has reached an age at which they have very little leverage for controlling that child (Stouthamer-Loeber, Loeber, Van Kammen, & Zhang, in press).

Thus, in planning for the effective prevention of antisocial behavior, it is necessary to be able to identify a target population that is reliably at risk but amenable to intervention. It is also important to time the intervention in terms of life events or transitions that would lead individuals or social systems to be willing to participate in the intervention.

Although these are important preconditions for successful prevention planning, it is important to know why the target population is at risk. Sometimes the connections between risk factors and outcome may seem obvious (e.g., the link between early oppositional behavior and later delinquency), but it is important to understand the developmental process that connects these two points. Not all high-risk youth become antisocial adults. In fact, it has been difficult for developmental epidemiologists to establish more than 50% accuracy in the long-term prediction of violence. This fact suggests that there are important mediating factors involved in the development of antisocial behavior. A good understanding of these mediating processes can provide the ideas for shaping the intervention program. What follows is a synthesis of current research on the development of antisocial individuals.

A DEVELOPMENTAL MODEL OF RISK
FOR ADOLESCENT ANTISOCIAL BEHAVIOR

There is a useful distinction between two different pathways to adolescent delinquency that has been made by Moffitt (1993) and Patterson, Reid, and Dishion (1992). This distinction emerges from some speculations about age-related patterns of antisocial activity. When either uniform crime statistics or self-reported antisocial acts are plotted by age, there is a sharp increase in the frequency of delinquent acts at early adolescence (Moffitt, 1993). This high level of antisocial acts peaks between ages 15 and 17 and then decreases in the early adult years. Both Moffitt and Patterson et al. have argued that there is a group of children who begin their antisocial careers as early as ages 6 to 8 and continue to exhibit antisocial behavior into their adult years. Patterson et al. referred to them as "early starters," and Moffitt uses the term *life-course persisters* to recognize that these are the youth at greatest risk for adult criminality. This group also accounts for some of the increased volume of delinquency seen in adolescence; much of this increase, however, is thought to be due to a second group, the "late starters," who begin to exhibit antisocial activity primarily in early adolescence and discontinue it as they move into jobs and marriages. Although it is important to consider both groups in prevention terms, the early starters represent a much greater problem for society in the long run and more is known about them from a

Preschool to School Transition

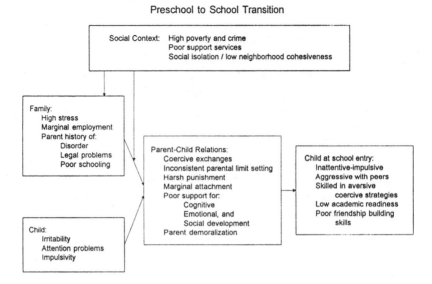

Figure 1.1. Social Context, Family and Child Factors That Establish Early Risk for Antisocial Behavior

research standpoint. The bulk of this chapter will describe what is known about the development of early starting antisocial youth. Figure 1.1 outlines the developmental sequence prior to school entry.

Loeber and colleagues (1993) have demonstrated that children who will become violent adolescents can be identified with reasonable reliability as early as age 7. Children at this age who display aggressive, disruptive, and oppositional behavior both at home and at school have a 50% likelihood of committing violent antisocial acts in adolescence. Less is known about the developmental period from birth to school entry than about the school-age years for these children, but the majority of children who are irritable, inattentive, and impulsive at ages 2 or 3 will show the kind of early childhood behavior problems that Loeber and colleagues use as the major risk criteria at this age (Bates, Bayles, Bennett, Ridge, & Brown, 1991; Campbell, Breaux, Ewing, & Szumowski, 1986).

These same children most often come from families experiencing high stress and instability. The sources of stress can be multiple—some coming from neighborhood and economic factors and some from the social history of the parents. Poverty, parent psychopathology or criminality, divorce, and parental conflict are all family factors that are predictive of child conduct problems (Dodge, Bates, & Pettit, 1990; McGee, Silva, & Williams, 1984; Offord, 1982; Offord, Alder, & Boyle, 1986; Richman, Stevenson, & Graham, 1982; West & Farrington, 1973). These family conditions, combined with child characteristics such as impulsivity, create a negative parent-child socialization circumstance. In this kind of situation, parents often resort to the use of harsh physical punishment and are inconsistent in the way they set limits for their children. Patterson (1982) described this pattern of interaction between parent and child as a coercive cycle in which parent and child escalate the level of their aversive behavior toward each other during discipline encounters. Often, the child's whining and refusals to comply are rewarded by a cessation of parental demands, thus reinforcing the child's noncompliance (Snyder & Patterson, 1995). At other times, the parent concludes the episode with abusive behavior toward the child. In this way, the child is both exposed to violent models of behavior and is reinforced for the skilled use of aversive behavior.

Parents can become demoralized by these child-rearing experiences and by the social isolation that accompanies poverty, marital separation, and lack of social support (Dumas & Wahler, 1983; Webster-Stratton, 1990). As a consequence of this demoralization, parents of skillfully aversive children are less likely to interact with them and provide the kind of supportive activities that promote academic readiness, emotional control, and other social skills (Greenberg, Kusche, & Speltz, 1991). This leaves the high-risk child poorly prepared for the social and academic demands of school. Greenberg et al. have argued that the same deficits in language development that lead to poor reading readiness also can undermine the child's ability to label strong emotional reactions and develop the cognitive skills for self-monitoring and regulating these negative feelings.

This potent combination of child, family, and social context factors leaves the young child poorly equipped to enter school with any real chance of success. Figure 1.2 summarizes the escalating sequence of risk factors that evolves across the school years. Not surprisingly, the same children who come to school with well-developed capacities for aggression and noncompliance (Lochman & CPPRG, 1995) are also inadequately prepared to learn to read, which is the most significant learning task of the early school years (Maughan, Gray, & Rutter, 1985). The inattentiveness of early childhood that characterizes some of these children further compounds their difficulties in learning at school (Meltzer, Levine, Karniski, Palfreg, & Clarke, 1984;

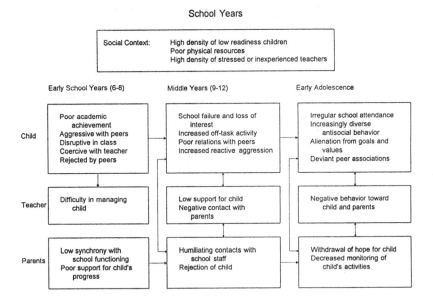

Figure 1.2. The Process of Escalating Risk Across the School Years

Moffitt, 1990). In addition to the problems of inattentiveness and poor reading readiness, aggressive children have been found to show cognitive deficits in the social domain. These social-cognitive deficits are thought to be responsible for their aggressiveness with peers because they lack nonaggressive solutions for solving disagreements and often jump to conclusions about the hostile intentions of peers (Dodge et al., 1990; Dodge, Pettit, McClaskey, & Brown, 1986).

Another characteristic of many of the high-risk youth at school entry is that they do not have adequate family support for good behavior and academic performance in school. Often, their parents did not do well in school or their parents' experience in dealing with the school staff regarding older siblings was accusatory and inconclusive. Thus, there is a lack of synchrony between the parents' approaches to preparing the children for school and the school's expectations and requirements for these children. This lack of synchrony further undermines the child's potential to do well in school (Comer, 1980).

A further handicap for many high-risk children at early school entry is that they attend schools serving many other children like themselves (Rutter,

Maughan, Mortimore, Ouston, & Smith, 1979). This high density of poorly prepared children makes the instructional task much more difficult for the teachers of high-risk children and can cause these teachers to fall into patterns of inconsistent discipline, verbal abuse, and coercive interactions with the children. Ironically, these patterns reenact the home experience of high-risk youth and reinforce the aversive behaviors that are so problematic for these children.

Many of the deficits that mark the high-risk youth at school entry will continue to be present as these children move on through elementary school. Their initial lack of reading readiness will likely result in poor academic performance, and this will become a source of embarrassment for them. Their aggressive and disruptive behavior may cause them to be socially rejected by their peers (Ladd, Price, & Hart, 1990). If rejection continues across several years of school, the high-risk children will begin to receive even poorer treatment from peers because of the expectations peers have of them and the social stigma of being rejected (Dodge, 1989; Hymel, Wagner, & Butler, 1990; Li, 1985). In turn, the high-risk youth will increase their mistrust of peers and be even more likely to react to them with aggression (Dodge & Coie, 1987).

The social relations problems of aggressive, rejected children are not limited to their peers. They also are less likely than other classmates to be supported by their teachers (Campbell, 1991; Dodge, Coie, & Brakke, 1982). These problems with teachers often set in motion a series of parent-teacher meetings that are painful and humiliating for the parents. Perhaps because of the child's academic and behavioral difficulties (and the negative meetings with teachers during the elementary school years), and because of their own continuing aversive encounters with their children, some parents of aggressive youth also begin to reject them (Patterson & Bank, 1989; Patterson, DeBaryshe, & Ramsey, 1989).

Thus, as high-risk children approach the transition to middle school or junior high school, they are likely to have had a history of poor school performance and poor social relations with classmates and to have received low levels of personal support from either their parents or their teachers. Relative to their classmates, they are more frequently aggressive with peers and are aggressive in ways that can lead peers to avoid conflict with them (Coie, Dodge, Terry, & Wright, 1991). As a consequence of being rejected by teachers, peers, and parents, high-risk youth may become alienated from the values and standards of society (Hawkins & Weis, 1985). One result of this alienation from conventional sources of social support is that high-risk youth are apt to join with other early adolescents like themselves (Cairns, Cairns, Neckerman, Gest, & Gariepy, 1988). These deviant peer associations, in turn, may serve to promote adolescent delinquency above and beyond that which would be predictable from earlier individual histories of aggressive and antisocial behavior (Coie, Terry, & Lochman, 1993).

The transition in middle school or junior high school in early adolescence is itself an additional stress factor for many youth because of the changing structure of teaching arrangements (Eccles, Midgley, & Adler, 1984) and peer associations. The youth who have followed the risk progression outlined previously are vulnerable to a variety of negative outcomes, including school failure and dropping out of school (Cairns, Cairns, & Neckerman, 1989), and psychological problems such as depression (Capaldi, 1991, 1992). Although they are also more likely to engage in substance use (Elliott, Huizinga, & Ageton, 1985), this usually follows the onset of other serious antisocial activities (Tolan & Loeber, 1993). The fact that the same developmental model can be described for youth who are at risk for multiple forms of disorders and negative adolescent outcomes is itself an important factor in prevention planning (Coie, Watt, et al., 1993), because the low base rate for many disorders reduces the potential impact of prevention designs that focus on a single negative outcome.

IMPLICATIONS OF THE DEVELOPMENTAL MODEL FOR PREVENTION

The preceding brief and overly simplified description of the developmental history of highly aggressive youth provides some important directions for any serious attempt to prevent adolescent violence and antisocial behavior. First, this developmental model suggests that we can identify the children most likely to engage in antisocial activity in adolescence as early as age 6 or 7. These children can be identified by their aggressive, disruptive, and noncompliant behavior in the home and school settings. Two factors are critical to this selection criterion. The first is that the children exhibit diverse forms of misbehavior in early childhood. The second is that they misbehave in more than one social context.

A second lesson from this developmental model is that there are clear advantages to implementing programs for the early prevention of aggression and antisocial behavior. The picture of development previously described reflects a downward spiral of events that propel high-risk children toward adolescent violence and antisocial behavior. The probability of each negative event is conditional on the preceding series of events. Each step in this spiral makes it more likely the child will become enmeshed in a sequence of accumulating risk. For this reason, successful prevention efforts will be more difficult to attain with children who are at later points in the sequence. The model suggests, for example, that the early school years are a time when the cognitive, social, and emotional deficits of high-risk youth can easily translate into academic and social failure experiences that set the child on a trajectory toward more serious consequences. Some of these consequences involve social expectancies on the part of teachers and peers that add to the difficulties in adaption for high-risk children. Early prevention trials have the potential advantage of sparing the high-risk child the added handicap of these negative expectations.

A third implication of the model is that risk is not a static characteristic of individual children or families but rather is a developmental process. The model articulates a set of mediating factors that transform an irritable or inattentive toddler into a delinquent adolescent. Early risk factors create an environment conducive to dysfunctional behavior. Risk factors set in motion the mediating processes that eventuate in serious antisocial activity. These mediating processes are the key to prevention planning because they identify factors to be altered and they specify the points in life when intervention with a given mediating factor may have the greatest impact (Dodge, 1993; McMahon, 1994). The model suggests, for example, that entry into elementary school is an optimal point for selecting high-risk children for a targeted preventive intervention. Entry into school is a time when we can reliably establish risk status among children (Lochman & CPPRG, 1995). It is also a time when nearly all children are accessible for this kind of screening procedure. Because school entry is an important transition in the lives of young children and their parents, parents are likely to be responsive to a prevention program that provides some promise of helping children make a better adjustment to school. Thus, three important aspects of prevention planning can be realized at this transition point.

Although school entry is one important point of intervention for preventing chronic antisocial behavior, a case can be made for intervening earlier. Reid (1993) argued that an analysis of the risk factors operating in the preschool phase suggests that the most direct approach to prevention would be to teach parents more effective and less punitive early discipline methods. The problem lies in identifying those preschoolers whose parents would benefit from this training. Several successful prevention programs for preschoolers have been implemented that did involve parents but did not focus their screening on parents themselves. For example, in the High/Scope Perry Preschool project (Weikart & Schweinhart, 1992), children were selected on the basis of their intelligence test scores at age 3 or 4 and their parents' years of schooling and employment status. Although the program emphasized a developmentally appropriate curriculum, a key feature was the partnership of teachers and parents that included weekly home visits in which effective adult-child activities were modeled. The long-term (age 19) evaluation of arrests and adolescent problems for this moderate-sized study ($N = 123$) provides encouragement for other preschool projects in which early screening of children and parents is feasible.

We now consider those factors at school entry that would seem to be the most logical focus for intervention. In this way, we can attempt to translate the developmental model into a prevention design. First, high-risk children seem to lack certain critical skills in the academic, social, and emotional domains. These skill deficits lead to failure in the school and the peer systems. Reading preparedness is one very critical skill. The ability to recognize strong feelings in one's self and others is a second important skill because it can lead to the development of the capacity to modulate one's own behavioral response. Being able to resolve disagreements with peers without jumping to aggressive solutions is another significant skill for elementary school. Being able to follow the rules of the classroom and of the peer play setting without attempting to coerce peers and adults with aversive behavior is another important skill. These are just some of the implications of the developmental model that can help us design a child-focused component to any well-conceived prevention plan.

Concerning family, we know that parents need to acquire discipline techniques that are effective in obtaining compliance without modeling the use of threat and bodily injury for their children. Parents need to be able to talk to their children about strong feelings (their own and the child's) so that children acquire the basic mechanisms of self-control. Obviously, parents need to be able to model self-control for their children. To achieve this, parents may need some of the same kinds of skill training as their children, but it also may be the case that they need support in coping with the life stress that accompanies poverty, living in dangerous neighborhoods, and having disrupted families. Parents also need to know how they can support the development of their children's academic skills and need to find activities with their children that can be a source of mutual pleasure.

A third focus of prevention planning involves the school context itself. Many high-risk youth attend schools that are poorly equipped to serve them. Part of the problem is the density of other high-risk children in these schools, and part of the problem involves teacher preparation. Inadequate school facilities are also a factor. Teachers who are confronted with a high ratio of inadequately prepared students must have help in preparing these children to learn. Part of this readiness training relates directly to the academic tasks, but it is equally essential that these young children be prepared for the social and emotional demands of the school setting. They must be able to make friends, be part of a group, and be able to respond appropriately to the instructions of their teachers. It is also clear from the developmental model that an important prevention concern is with building a trusting and co-operative relationship between the parents of high-risk children and the children's teachers. This alliance building must begin before serious problems with the child require the teacher to request a conference with parents. Once problems have emerged, the probability that such a conference will turn into an exchange of accusations increases markedly, and teachers will soon find that these parents will not attend conferences when asked.

Finally, we see that our prevention plan must be focused on the multiple systems that support the child, namely the family, the school, and peers. The prototypical pattern of risk is one that involves an impulsive or irritable child being raised by unskilled and highly stressed parents in a neighborhood containing many antisocial role models and served by inadequate schools. It is hard to say that any one factor is responsible for youthful delinquency. Similarly, it is not likely that intervention in any one domain will be successful in taking the child out of a negative life trajectory and putting that child on a more adaptive course. Simultaneous changes in parenting, child behavior, and peer or school influences may be what are needed for successfully deflecting a child from deviant activities.

When considering a framework for intervention, it is also clear that much of what the child requires directly is belated socialization. Many high-risk children have been inadvertently trained to use aversive behavior to get what they need or want. Although threats, whining, or the use of physical force are not behaviors that will endear the high-risk child to adults or peers, these behaviors often have high immediate payoff. Thus, it can be very difficult to help a child unlearn these strategies and adopt more prosocial behaviors. We have also seen that high-risk children often lack the ability to monitor their feelings and delay their immediate reactions to anger or disappointment. Helping them develop these new abilities is also a form of resocialization because it must be accomplished in the context of situational demands for greater maturity than the child is capable of providing. Unfortunately, this can make the relearning experience more difficult and more embarrassing.

This same point about new learning may be true for the parents of high-risk youth as well. Stouthamer-Loeber, Loeber, Van Kammen, et al. (in press) found that age of mother at the birth of her child was a significant risk factor for serious delinquency. Not only do young mothers have less preparation for the parenting task, but if they had problems of behavioral control as children themselves (Caspi, Elder, & Bem, 1987), they are likely to continue to have these problems as mothers. Because this is so, it is not likely that this resocialization process will take place quickly. A long-range plan is therefore required—one that considers the sequence in which social, emotional, and cognitive skills can be best acquired. Parents and children will need time to unlearn maladaptive behaviors and acquire new skills. Short-term programs or programs that are not tailored to the developmental needs of the high-risk child will not be adequate. The more deprived and chaotic the family circumstances, the more important it is to think of prevention as a continuous process with timely checkpoints for determining whether the child, family, and school are moving on course toward more normal functioning.

In this chapter, we have limited our discussion of youthful violence to the early starting antisocial youth. Much less is known about the late-starter group than the early starters. Moffitt (1993) speculates that the late starters engage in delinquent acts in imitation of the early starters. Whether this is true is hard to say as yet, but there is no shortage of role models for violence and risk-taking activity in the media presentations that children are exposed to in today's culture. In those middle schools marked by high violence, we have found a disturbing pattern to the relation between peer status and individual aggressiveness across the early adolescent years (Coie, Terry, Zakriski, & Lochman, 1995). As late as the fourth and fifth grades, this relation is a negative one. Aggressive children are generally not well liked in elementary school. In middle school, this begins to change. In the schools we studied, there was no significant negative correlation between peer status and aggression among sixth graders, and by eighth grade the relation had become significantly positive. This suggests that adolescent peer values are changing with respect to violence. A reputation for aggression can be a social asset in many of the middle schools in our studies—other things being equal. We do not know how this has come about or how generalizable it is to all middle schools and junior high schools. Our findings do indicate that we cannot focus exclusively on the early-starter group if we are to make a serious effort to prevent youthful violence. We must find a way to have impact on the values and norms for behavior in the general population of early adolescents. This is a level of prevention thinking for which we do not yet have a good developmental model.

If, as a society, we are to come to terms with the increasing severity of violent and antisocial behavior among American youth, we will have to develop prevention programs for both the early starters and the late starters. Each group provides a part of the social context for the other, and the net effect is to promote higher levels of hostile expectations and violent behavior. Early prevention activities with high-risk youth must be coupled with serious attempts to reduce the more general societal attitudes toward violence, particularly the acceptability of intimidation and angry posturing that seems to pervade so many levels of social influence that bear on our developing children. This will be a formidable task, but it is one that cannot be avoided if we are to survive as a civilized society.

REFERENCES

Bates, J. E., Bayles, K., Bennett, S. D., Ridge, B., & Brown, M. M. (1991). Origins of externalizing behavior problems at eight years of age. In D. J. Pepler & K. H. Rubin (Eds.), *The development and treatment of childhood aggression* (pp. 93-120). Hillsdale, NJ: Lawrence Erlbaum.

Brennan, P., & Mednick, S. (1992, May). *Punishment and subsequent criminal behavior: Report on the Danish birth cohort.* Paper presented at the biennial meeting of the Society for Life History Research, Philadelphia.

Cairns, R. B., Cairns, B. D., & Neckerman, H. J. (1989). Early school dropout: Configurations and determinants. *Child Development, 60,* 1437-1452.

Cairns, R. B., Cairns, B. D., Neckerman, H. J., Gest, S. D., & Gariepy, J. L. (1988). Social networks and aggressive behavior: Peer support or peer rejection? *Developmental Psychology, 24,* 815-823.

Campbell, S. B. (1991). Longitudinal studies of active and aggressive preschoolers: Individual differences in early behavior and outcome. In D. Cicchetti & S. L. Toth (Eds.), *Internalizing and externalizing expressions of dysfunction: Rochester symposium on developmental psychopathology* (Vol. 2, pp. 67-90). Hillsdale, NJ: Lawrence Erlbaum.

Campbell, S. B., Breaux, A. M., Ewing, L. J., & Szumowski, E. K. (1986). Correlates and prediction of hyperactivity and aggression: A longitudinal study of parent-referred problem preschoolers. *Journal of Abnormal Child Psychology, 14,* 217-234.

Capaldi, D. M. (1991). Co-occurrence of conduct problems and depressive symptoms in early adolescent boys: I. Familial factors and general adjustment at grade 6. *Development and Psychopathology, 4,* 277-300.

Capaldi, D. M. (1992). Co-occurrence of conduct problems and depressive symptoms in early adolescent boys: II. A 2-year follow-up at grade 8. *Development and Psychopathology, 4,* 125-144.

Caplan, G. (1964). *Principles of preventive psychiatry.* New York: Basic Books.

Caspi, A., Elder, G. H., & Bem, D. J. (1987). Moving against the world: Life-course patterns of explosive children. *Developmental Psychology, 23,* 308-313.

Coie, J. D., Dodge, K. A., Terry, R., & Wright, V. (1991). The role of aggression in peer relations: Analysis of aggression episodes in boys' play groups. *Child Development, 62,* 812-826.

Coie, J. D., Terry, R., & Lochman, J. (1993, November). *Changing social networks and their impact on juvenile delinquency.* Paper presented at the annual meeting of the American Society for Criminology, Phoenix, AZ.

Coie, J. D., Terry, R., Zakriski, A., & Lochman, J. (1995). Early adolescent social influences on delinquent behavior. In J. McCord (Ed.), *Coercion and punishment in long-term perspectives* (pp. 229-244). New York: Cambridge University Press.

Coie, J. D., Watt, N. F., West, S. G., Hawkins, J. D., Asarnow, J. R., Markman, H. J., Ramey, S. L., Shure, M. D., & Long, B. (1993). The science of prevention: A conceptual framework and some directions for a national research program. *American Psychologist, 48,* 1013-1022.

Comer, J. P. (1980). *School power.* New York: Free Press.

Conduct Problems Prevention Research Group. (1992). A developmental and clinical model for the prevention of conduct disorders: The FAST Track program. *Development and Psychopathology, 4,* 509-527.

Dodge, K. A. (1989). Enhancing social relationships. In E. J. Mash and R. A. Barkley (Eds.), *Behavioral treatment of childhood disorders* (pp. 222-244). New York: Guilford.

Dodge, K. A. (1993). The future of research on the treatment of conduct disorder. *Development and Psychopathology, 5,* 311-319.

Dodge, K. A., Bates, J. E., & Pettit, G. S. (1990). Mechanisms in the cycle of violence. *Science, 250,* 1678-1683.

Dodge, K. A., & Coie, J. D. (1987). Social information processing factors in reactive and proactive aggression in children's peer groups. *Journal of Personality and Social Psychology, 53,* 1146-1158.

Dodge, K. A., Coie, J. D., & Brakke, N. P. (1982). Behavior patterns of socially rejected and neglected preadolescents: The roles of social approach and aggression. *Journal of Abnormal Child Psychology, 18,* 389-409.

Dodge, K. A., Pettit, G. S., McClaskey, C. L., & Brown, M. (1986). Social competence in children. *Monographs of the Society for Research in Child Development, 51*(2, Serial No. 213).

Dumas, J. E., & Wahler, R. G. (1983). Predictors of treatment outcome in parent training: Mother insularity and socioeconomic disadvantage. *Behavioral Assessment, 5,* 301-313.

Eccles, J. E., Midgley, C. M., & Adler, T. (1984). Age-related changes in the school environment: Effects on achievement motivation. In J. P. Nicholls (Ed.), *The development of achievement motivation* (pp. 283-331). Greenwich, CT: JAI.

Elliott, D. S., Huizinga, D., & Ageton, S. S. (1985). *Explaining delinquency and drug use.* New York: Guilford.

Fox, J. A., & Pierce, G. (1994, January). American killers are getting younger. *USA Today,* pp. 24-26.

Gordon, R. (1983). An operational definition of prevention. *Public Health Reports, 98,* 107-109.

Greenberg, M. T., Kusche, C. A., & Speltz, M. (1991). Emotional regulation, self control and psychopathology: The role of relationships in early childhood. In D. Cicchetti & S. L. Toth (Eds.), *Internalizing and externalizing expressions of dysfunction: Rochester symposium on developmental psychopathology* (Vol. 2, pp. 21-66). Hillsdale, NJ: Lawrence Erlbaum.

Hawkins, J. D., & Weis, J. G. (1985). The social development model: An integrated approach to delinquency prevention. *Journal of Primary Prevention, 6,* 73-95.

Hymel, S., Wagner, E., & Butler, L. J. (1990). Reputational bias: View from the peer group. In S. R. Asher & J. D. Coie (Eds.), *Peer rejection in childhood* (pp. 156-186). New York: Cambridge University Press.

Institute of Medicine. (1994). *Reducing risks for mental disorders: Frontiers for preventive intervention research.* Washington, DC: National Academy Press.

Kazdin, A. E. (1987). Treatment of antisocial behavior in children: Current status and future directions. *Psychological Bulletin, 102,* 187-203.

Ladd, G. W., Price, J. M., & Hart, C. H. (1990). Preschoolers' behavioral orientations and patterns of peer contact: Predictive of peer status. In S. R. Asher & J. D. Coie (Eds.), *Peer rejection in childhood* (pp. 90-115). New York: Cambridge University Press.

Li, A. K. F. (1985). Early rejected status and later social adjustment: A 3-year follow-up. *Journal of Abnormal Child Psychology, 13,* 567-577.

Lochman, J. E., & Conduct Problems Prevention Research Group (CPPRG). (1995). Screening of child behavior problems for prevention programs at school entry. *Journal of Consulting and Clinical Psychology, 63,* 549-559.

Loeber, R., Wung, P., Keenan, K., Giroux, B., Stouthamer-Loeber, M., Van Kammen, W. B., & Maughan, B. (1993). Developmental pathways in disruptive child behavior. *Development and Psychopathology, 5,* 103-133.

Martin, S. (1994, June). Behavioral factors essential, Elder informs conference. *APA Monitor,* p. 9.

Maughan, B., Gray, G., & Rutter, M. (1985). Reading retardation and antisocial behavior: A follow-up into employment. *Journal of Child Psychology and Psychiatry, 26,* 741-758.

McGee, R., Silva, P. A., & Williams, S. (1984). Perinatal, neurological, environmental, and developmental characteristics of seven year old children with stable behavioral problems. *Journal of Child Psychology and Psychiatry, 25,* 573-586.

McMahon, R. J. (1994). Diagnosis, assessment, and treatment of externalizing problems in children: The role of longitudinal data. *Journal of Consulting and Clinical Psychology, 62,* 901-917.

Meltzer, L. J., Levine, M. D., Karniski, W., Palfreg, J. S., & Clarke, S. (1984). An analysis of the learning style of adolescent delinquents. *Journal of Learning Disabilities, 17,* 600-608.

Moffitt, T. E. (1990). Juvenile delinquency and Attention Deficit Disorder: Boys' developmental trajectories from age 3 to age 15. *Child Development, 61,* 893-910.

Moffitt, T. E. (1993). Adolescence-limited and life-course persistent antisocial behavior: A developmental taxonomy. *Psychological Review, 100,* 674-701.

National Institute of Mental Health. (1993). *The prevention of mental disorders: A national research agenda.* Bethesda, MD: Author.

Offord, D. R. (1982). Family backgrounds of male and female delinquents. In J. Gunn &
    D. P. Farrington (Eds.), *Delinquency and the criminal justice system* (pp. 129-151).
    New York: John Wiley.
Offord, D. R., Alder, R. J., & Boyle, M. H. (1986). Prevalence and sociodemographic
    correlates of conduct disorder. *American Journal of Social Psychiatry, 6*, 272-278.
Patterson, G. R. (1982). *Coercive family process.* Eugene, OR: Castalia.
Patterson, G. R., & Bank, C. L. (1989). Some amplifying mechanisms for pathologic
    processes in families. In M. Gunnar & E. Thelen (Eds.), *Systems and development:
    Symposia on child psychology* (pp. 167-210). Hillsdale, NJ: Lawrence Erlbaum.
Patterson, G. R., DeBaryshe, B. D., & Ramsey, E. (1989). A developmental perspective on
    antisocial behavior. *American Psychologist, 44*, 329-335.
Patterson, G. R., Reid, J. B., & Dishion, T. J. (1992). *Antisocial boys.* Eugene, OR: Castalia.
Reid, J. B. (1993). Prevention of conduct disorder before and after school entry: Relating
    interventions to developmental findings. *Development and Psychopathology, 5*, 243-
    262.
Richman, N., Stevenson, J., & Graham, P. J. (1982). *Preschool to school: A behavioural study.*
    London: Academic Press.
Robins, L. N. (1966). *Deviant children grown up: A sociological and psychiatric study of
    sociopathic personality.* Baltimore, MD: Williams & Wilkins.
Rutter, M., Maughan, B., Mortimore, P., Ouston, J., & Smith, A. (1979). *Fifteen thousand
    hours: Secondary schools and their effects on children.* Cambridge, MA: Harvard
    University Press.
Snyder, J. J., & Patterson, G. R. (1995). Individual differences in social aggression: A test of
    a reinforcement model of socialization in the natural environment. *Behavior Therapy,
    26*, 371-391.
Stouthamer-Loeber, M., Loeber, R., Farrington, D. P., Zhang, Q., Van Kammen, W., &
    Maguin, E. (in press). The double edge of protective and risk factors for delinquency:
    Interrelations and developmental patterns. *Development and Psychopathology.*
Stouthamer-Loeber, M., Loeber, R., Van Kammen, W., & Zhang, Q. (in press). Uninterrupted
    delinquent careers: The timing of parental help-seeking and juvenile court contact.
    Studies on Crime and Crime Prevention.
Tolan, P. H., & Loeber, R. (1993). Antisocial behavior. In P. H. Tolan & B. J. Cohler (Eds.),
    Handbook of clinical research and practice (pp. 307-331). New York: John Wiley.
Webster-Stratton, C. (1990). Stress: A potential disruptor of parent perceptions and family
    interaction. *Journal of Clinical Child Psychology, 19*, 302-312.
Weikart, D. P., & Schweinhart, L. J. (1992). High/Scope preschool program outcomes. In
    J. McCord & R. E. Tremblay (Eds.), *Preventing antisocial behavior* (pp. 67-86). New
    York: Guilford.
West, D. J., & Farrington, D. P. (1973). *Who becomes delinquent?* London: Heinemann
    Educational.

2

Promoting Development and Preventing Disorder

THE BETTER BEGINNINGS, BETTER FUTURES PROJECT

RAY DeV. PETERS

CAROL CRILL RUSSELL

D ue to better sanitation, improved nutrition, and more effective curative medicine, the health of children throughout the world has shown consistent improvement over the past 100 years and continues to show increased improvement in the most recent decades (Doll, 1983). As a result, the majority of chronic disorders affecting children and adolescents in developed countries consist largely of psychological, social, and educational problems (Graham, 1985).

Survey studies indicate that the prevalence of mental health problems among children aged 4 to 16 in developed countries is between 10% and 20%

AUTHORS' NOTE: Address correspondence to Ray DeV. Peters, Department of Psychology, Queen's University, Kingston, Ontario K7L 3N6, Canada.

(Institute of Medicine, 1989; Offord, 1985; Offord, Boyle, & Racine, 1991), and there is reason to believe that similar rates exist in developing countries (World Health Organization, 1977).

Despite the increased awareness of the severity of these problems among children and adolescents, as well as the resultant long-term personal, social, and financial costs (Robins, 1978), there are limited resources for dealing with them. Mental health needs receive little attention in health education programs, and available methods focus almost exclusively on the remediation or treatment of specific disorders despite the fact that these procedures are extremely expensive and have been consistently criticized as providing "too little too late for too few" (Advisory Committee on Children's Services, 1990; Sax, Cross, & Silverman, 1988).

The ultimate success of therapeutic procedures for various types of childhood and adolescent disorders is currently the focus of a substantial amount of empirical research. The difficulty of trying to deal effectively with these problems by concentrating exclusively on those children who show substantial deviations from normal psychosocial development remains. Regardless of the ultimate success of therapeutic interventions, the number of individuals who manifest disordered behavior is too large to be dealt with effectively by the current mental health care system in industrialized countries and it is an impossible task for developing countries in which the number of trained professionals available to deliver therapeutic services is so small that only an extremely small percentage of mentally disordered children and adolescents can be seen.

A striking example of this last point is provided in the recent large-scale epidemiological survey of mental health problems in children and adolescents in Ontario, Canada, conducted by Offord, Boyle, and colleagues (Boyle et al., 1987; Offord et al., 1987). It was found that only one of six children between the ages of 4 and 16 who were suffering from major internalizing and externalizing disorders had been in contact with a mental health or social service agency in the past 6 months, and only one third had ever received any special educational programming. Thus, in a relatively well-resourced country such as Canada, and in a province that prides itself on its child and adolescent mental health service system, even if therapeutic procedures were 100% effective (a highly optimistic view of psychotherapy with children and adolescents) only a small percentage of disordered youth would receive such services and the overall impact on the incidence and prevalence of such disorders would be minimal. The impact of psychotherapeutic procedures in countries with even more limited professional resources would be virtually nonexistent. Given this state of affairs, there has been increased interest in approaches to mental health care that emphasize prevention and health promotion (Health & Welfare Canada, 1986, 1988; Long, 1986; Peters, 1988; Price, Cowan, Lorion, & Ramos-McKay, 1989).

It has been said that "no major disease in the history of mankind has been conquered by therapists and rehabilitation methods alone, but ultimately only through prevention" (Dubos, 1959, p. 44). Such an analysis certainly seems to apply to psychosocial disorders of children and adolescents. During the past decade, there has been an expanding concern with methods and programs that have as their focus the prevention of social, behavioral, and emotional problems in children and adolescents (Coie et al., 1993; Kessler & Goldston, 1986; Long, 1986; Ontario Ministry of Community and Social Services, 1989; Price et al., 1989).

In this chapter, we describe a community-based prevention program that is designed to contribute to the growing literature on effective prevention approaches to children's mental health.

THE BETTER BEGINNINGS, BETTER FUTURES PROJECT

The Better Beginnings, Better Futures Project has three major goals: (a) to prevent serious social, emotional, behavioral, physical, and cognitive problems in young children; (b) to promote the social, emotional, behavioral, physical, and cognitive development of these children; and (c) to enhance the abilities of socioeconomically disadvantaged families and communities to provide for their children.

The Better Beginnings, Better Futures Project is funded by three Ontario provincial ministries (Community and Social Services, Health, and Education and Training) as well as the Federal Department of Indian and Northern Affairs and Heritage Canada. Better Beginnings is the first long-term prevention policy research demonstration project of its kind in Canada.

The focus is on children up to the age of 8 years old living in 11 socioeconomically disadvantaged communities-neighborhoods in Ontario. These communities are being funded to provide services tailored to local circumstances for 4 years of implementation. The children, families, and demonstration communities will be followed until the children reach their mid-20s to see if this type of early childhood education and family support model has made a difference in life span development and community development for children, families, and high-risk neighborhoods.

BACKGROUND

The Better Beginnings, Better Futures Project had its origin in the Ontario Ministry of Community and Social Services. As mentioned previously, the 1983 Ontario Child Health Study (Offord et al., 1987) revealed that one in six children had an identifiable emotional or behavioral disorder, and it also identified that children living in families that received social assistance or who lived in subsidized housing were at much greater risk for these problems. This is not an unusually high percentage of children with emotional and behavioral disorders, and the risk factors are common to other childhood problems such as child welfare and young offenders. Other surveys of the Western world show similar rates of psychiatric problems and similar risk factors. Nonetheless, given the drain on families and public funds of trying to address significant problems after they are fully developed, the ministry became more committed than ever to prevention.

In 1988, the ministry released a consultation paper, *Investing in Children: New Directions in Child Treatment and Child and Family Intervention* (Ontario Ministry of Community and Social Services, 1988), that documented the importance of prevention with high-risk populations. Also in 1988, the ministry set aside $1.8 million per year for as long as necessary to investigate the short- and long-term effectiveness of a prevention model.

Technical Advisory Group

In the spring of 1988, the ministry convened a 25-member interdisciplinary technical advisory group to recommend a prevention model that had the greatest potential to prevent problems in child development for children living in economically disadvantaged communities and neighborhoods. The group consisted of key program directors and researchers from across the province. Each member was well respected in an area of expertise, including education, public health, social work, psychology and psychiatry, epidemiology, community development, infant development, and child care. Thus, the technical advisory group was able to bring varied disciplines and perspectives to their task of developing a prevention model. The group examined the literature and unpublished prevention program reports in three areas: (a) perinatal prevention programs, such as maternal and infant nutrition supplements and holistic home visiting; (b) preschool and child care prevention programs, such as Head Start and family resource centers; and (c) school-based prevention programs, such as social skills training and ecological school models.

The technical advisory group also examined the literature and unpublished reports on two additional topics: (a) community involvement, including community empowerment and community development, and (b) research emphasizing the implementation of high-quality, multisite, longitudinal evaluation procedures with prevention programs.

The findings from this review and the description of the recommended model were published by the Ministry of Community and Social Services in the November 1989 book *Better Beginnings, Better Futures: An Integrated Model of Primary Prevention of Emotional and Behavioral Problems.* This document captured the attention of more than 8,000 professionals, researchers, community groups, and parents. In addition to presenting a bibliography, this report summarizes the literature and outlines the Better Beginnings prevention model. The model recommended by the technical advisory group as having the greatest promise of preventing problems in child development consisted of the following seven major characteristics:

1. The model must be based on known effective prevention programs. Infant home-visiting programs, such as those demonstrated by Olds, Henderson, Tatelbaum, and Chamberlin (1986), were identified as being successful in preventing child abuse, in particular, but also in reducing subsequent unplanned pregnancies and in increased self-esteem and employment of mothers. The reviewers examined the evidence for both nurse home visitors and trained lay home visitors and found support for both approaches.

The reviewers also examined high-quality child care programs. Although the Head Start program as well as the well-documented Perry Preschool model (Berrueta-Clement, Schweinhart, Barnett, Epstein, & Weikart, 1984; Consortium for Longitudinal Studies, 1983; Lazar & Darlington, 1982) were examples of group-based preschool programs that increased cognitive development and physical health, the reviewers acknowledged that not all families want this type of child care or are able to obtain it. In addition, only 15% of children are in licensed child care. Thus, to become preventive at the local level, it was thought to be important to support high-quality child care of various types. The funding for Better Beginnings was not able to support the start-up of additional preschool programs but was able to enhance existing group-based care to become high quality. The funding was able to support additional high-quality child care such as drop-in centers, Moms and Tots groups, toy-lending libraries, increased training and other informal supports, improved physical facilities, and materials for mothers and other home care providers.

Finally, the reviewers examined ecological school models such as that demonstrated by Comer (1985) in low-income urban primary schools. It was felt that key elements of these models would also be successful in Ontario primary schools; this, therefore, became the third type of known effective prevention program to serve as a basis for the Better Beginnings model.

2. The model must be ecological. Successful prevention programs understand that the child lives in the family and the family in the community, so components of successful programs address the wholeness of the child and environment (Bronfenbrenner, 1979, 1987). Therefore, strategies that focus on individual children must be integrated with strategies that improve each part of the environment within which the children spend their time—homes, child care, neighborhoods, and schools.

3. The model must be tailored to meet local needs and desires. Risk factors and protective factors vary from community to community—for example, some communities have high rates of teen pregnancy; some communities are bedroom communities and parents are employed out of the community from dawn to dusk, thus requiring before and after school programs; and some communities have mothers that are isolated and in need of support. Therefore, successful models will vary from community to community depending on local needs and desires.

4. The model must be comprehensive. Most economically disadvantaged communities will need a variety of prevention programs to address the needs and strengths of the neighborhood. Single-focus programs in a multirisk community cannot prevent poor child development.

5. The model must be of high quality. Successful programs have high-quality management and administrative approaches. The staff has enough

time set aside for planning and preparation, there is good supervision and the staff is well trained, people are paid well for the work they do, and there are funds for needed supplies and equipment.

6. The model must be integrated. Successful prevention programs link with other programs, schools, and community activities. This requires developing common goals, objectives, and collaborative plans for sharing human, financial, and material resources.

7. The model must have meaningful, significant parent and community resident involvement. This was one of the most neglected areas of research on successful prevention programs. Nonetheless, the concept of community, family, and parent empowerment was strong, and the ecological model of healthy child development certainly supports parent and community resident involvement. Therefore, the technical advisory group recommended that this become an important part of the Better Beginnings model. They recommended this involvement be meaningful and significant rather than token and that it happen during program planning as well as implementation.

It is interesting to note the similarity between these characteristics of successful programs identified by the technical advisory group and other recent attempts to summarize major findings in this area (e.g., Ounce of Prevention Fund, 1994; Schorr, 1988). It appears that there is an emerging consensus on the characteristics of successful prevention and promotion programs with disadvantaged youth and families. The Better Beginnings, Better Futures Project program model was designed to incorporate and evaluate many of these characteristics.

THE BETTER BEGINNINGS, BETTER FUTURES PROJECT MODEL

There are two types of the Better Beginnings model currently being implemented. In one type, prenatal and infant development programs integrate with preschool programs for children from conception to age 4. In the second type of Better Beginnings model, the preschool programs integrate with primary school programs for children between the ages of 4 and 8. Families and community residents also identify other program components important for healthy child development in their neighborhoods. Such components include support groups, family planning, child development education, drop-in centers, and recreation programs.

A Communitywide Ecological Model

In many ways, this model is unique because it focuses on child, family, and community factors. In the Better Beginnings, Better Futures Project, it is the neighborhood or community that is considered to be high risk. All children and families living within a designated neighborhood or community are eligible to take part in any of the programs—that is, the intervention is universal but within a high-risk community. The purpose of the project is to strengthen children and their families as well as the local community itself. In this sense, the project is designed to foster three aspects of human development: child development, family development, and community development.

Local Responsibility

Another major characteristic of the Better Beginnings project is the degree of shared responsibility for implementing and measuring the effect of the model. The model is decentralized to seven urban neighborhoods and five First Nations scattered throughout Ontario. The government provides a supervisor-coordinator to assist in implementing the model, and an interministerial government committee reviews the projects regularly. This gives the government hands-on experience in implementing the model that could assist in translating the model into policy if the model proves successful. In addition, the research coordination unit works with each community to develop appropriate research methods and tools.

It is the local steering committees and subcommittees, however, that tailor the model to meet local needs and desires. These committees work with local resources to determine what needs to be enhanced, what needs to be added, where duplication can be eliminated, and how services and community members can work more closely together to promote positive development, prevent poor outcomes, and enhance the abilities of the neighborhoods to provide for their own residents. Thus, the power for implementation of both the program and research is shared among the local communities, the government committee, and the research coordination unit. It is not driven by local communities alone, by the government alone, nor by researchers alone.

Significant Parent-Community Involvement

One of the most salient differences between the Better Beginnings project and other models is the requirement for meaningful, significant parent and community leader involvement in decision making. During the first year of local development, this characteristic of the model came to mean that the steering committee and each major subcommittee of the local project needed to have a membership of at least 50% parents or other community residents. It became equally clear that although the requirement for 50% local resident representation was important, what really made this level of participation possible was the transfer of real decision-making power to these committees. The participants on these committees wrote the job descriptions, delegated the hiring committees, decided salary levels, and decided the amount of funding to go to each component of the model (e.g., child care, home visiting, and community safety). The transfer of this level of control and responsibility to parents and other community members has the potential of empowering community residents who may have individually and collectively felt little control over their lives and the lives of their children.

In summary, in comparison with other prevention and early intervention models that typically address one or two risk factors intensely, the Better Beginnings project addresses multiple factors less rigorously. The assumption on which the Better Beginnings model rests is that there are many pathways to health or disorder, and people experience the pathways at various intensities and at different times in their lives. The Better Beginnings model assumes that in addition to the prevention programs that have been shown to be successful in preventing poor outcomes, there are local risk and protective factors that can be addressed to develop healthier children. The programs and approaches to address these local factors may be of equal importance to the programs that have already demonstrated effectiveness in prevention (e.g., infant home visiting, high-quality child care, and ecological school programs).

It is equally clear that it should be possible for prevention programs with demonstrated effectiveness to be brought into harmony with one another and with local needs and desires. This will have the advantage of addressing multiple risk factors. At the time of the review of prevention models for Better Beginnings, most early childhood models lasted only 2 years at most. By combining infant home visiting, high-quality child care, and an ecological early elementary school model, an overall prevention approach is being implemented for children from conception through at least early primary school.

By expanding the fundamental tenets of the early successful prevention models to include (a) integration of services, (b) high-quality and meaningful significant parent and community leader involvement, and (c) tailoring the programs and additional services to meet the needs and desires of the community, the model has the advantage of addressing multiple factors rather than one or two factors intensely. In the high-risk neighborhoods where the Better Beginnings model is being demonstrated, this may be particularly important. Forces such as neighborhood violence, collective demoralization, sheer boredom, and welfare dependency can undermine the best programs focusing solely on child and family factors.

Provincial and Federal Funding

In 1989, the Better Beginnings, Better Futures model was accepted by the Ministry of Community and Social Services as the model with which to launch its longitudinal prevention policy research demonstration project. The model also came to be financially supported by the Ministry of Education to prevent poor school performance; by the Ministry of Health to prevent poor physical development in children and poor mental health of mothers; by the Federal Department of Indian and Northern Affairs because Natives had been requesting this type of holistic, community-based prevention model; and by the Federal Secretary of State to support the model in a francophone community.

Total provincial and federal funding for the first several years of the project has averaged approximately $7 million per year.

Community Selection Process

The Ontario government released a request for proposals in the spring of 1990. The first step in applying for the Better Beginnings project was designed to ensure that potential program sponsors had a minimal level of integration already in place and were prepared to implement the local project in a low-income, high-risk community. Proposal development grants of approximately $5,000 were awarded to 55 initial applicants to offset expenses incurred in gathering information, obtaining expertise, administrative support, and community involvement. The second step was a full proposal describing the local model, community plans for meaningful and significant involvement of community residents, integration of services, and high-quality programming.

Forty-eight proposals were submitted in July 1990 and reviewed by a 15-member proposal review panel with expertise in implementing health, education, and social service programs in economically disadvantaged communities. The top 25 proposals were considered by the panel, which met in person with local proposing groups. Nine selected communities were announced on January 29, 1991. Since that time, 2 additional communities have been added, resulting in a total of 11 Better Beginnings research sites.

Project Organization

The Better Beginnings, Better Futures Project is composed of three major partners: community research sites, consisting of project coordinators, project staff, parents and community residents, service providers, and educators, established under local sponsorship in 11 Ontario communities; a government committee consisting of representatives from the cofunding ministries and departments; and a research coordination unit consisting of a core team of academic researchers and locally hired site researchers in each of the communities.

Community Research Sites

The major responsibilities of the 11 Better Beginnings, Better Futures communities are to develop and implement high-quality prevention and promotion programs for young children and their families. These programs are to be characterized by meaningful, significant involvement of community residents in all aspects of program development and implementation and by integration of existing and new services for children and families.

Of the 11 selected communities, 8 are implementing prenatal and preschool models for children from birth to age 4. Neyaashiinigmiing (located near Wiarton), Long Lake No. 58 and Ginoogaming (near Geraldton), Walpole Island (situated near Wallaceburg), and Wauzhushk Onigum (located near Kenora) are First Nation communities that are implementing prenatal and preschool prevention models. Urban projects for children in the 0- to 4-year-old age range include Willow Road neighborhood in Guelph, the north end community in Kingston, the Toronto neighborhood of Regent Park and Moss Park, and the community of Albion, Heatherington, Fairlea, and Ledbury in southeast Ottawa.

Cornwall, with a significant francophone population, has developed a preschool and primary school prevention model for children between the ages of 4 and 8 in four elementary school areas. The Highfield School neighborhood of Etobicoke is ethnically diverse with more than 40 languages spoken in the homes of students attending the local junior school. They, too, have developed a preschool and primary school prevention project. Within Sudbury, children from the Flour Mill/le Moulin a Fleur and Donovan neighborhoods participate in their preschool and primary school prevention model. Although the majority of residents in the Sudbury neighborhoods are Canadian-born anglophones and francophones, 14% of the people living in this community speak a language other than French or English as their first language, and 1 child in 10 is Native.

Program Activities

The specific Better Beginnings program activities differ from community to community. They can be described, however, as generally using the following major categories:

1. Home visiting—all projects for the 0- to 4-year-olds include home visiting to families in which the primary strategy is to support families during pregnancy and infancy. Home visitors are trained lay professionals who assist the families to meet basic needs, answer questions about child development, and link with services and community resources.
2. Classroom enrichment—all projects for the 4- to 8-year-olds include enrichment of the classroom or formal education experience of the child. This includes a variety of components, such as multicultural facilitation, social skills training, academic support, and reducing the child-teacher ratio.
3. Child care enrichment—all projects supplement the child care already in place in the community. Enrichment can take the form of additional staff, resources, drop-in centers for at-home child care providers, toy-lending libraries, and so on.

4. Other child-focused programs—these programs are tailored to each community's needs and desires for healthy child development. Examples include play groups, breakfast programs, heritage language classes, and so on.

5. Family and parent-focused programs—these programs are tailored to each community's needs and desires for program experiences supporting healthy parenting and family functioning. These programs include activities such as parent training and parent support groups.

6. Community-focused programs—these programs focus on creating new resources in the community, experiences and activities for community members at large, initiatives focused directly on improving the quality of life in the community, activities focused on increasing cross-cultural awareness and sensitivity, enhancing cross-cultural relations, and increasing cultural pride. These programs include activities such as improving neighborhood safety, antiracism workshops, community celebrations, and community theater.

7. Community healing—these approaches are established in First Nation communities and are designed to cultivate an understanding and appreciation of Native culture or to address a variety of community issues, such as substance abuse and family violence associated with a loss of cultural identity, or both. Activities include traditional healing, Nechi training, and naming ceremonies.

Government Committee

This committee consists of approximately 15 representatives from the cofunding and cost-sharing partners of the Better Beginnings, Better Futures Project: the Ontario Ministries of Community and Social Services, Health and Education, the Federal Department of Indian and Northern Affairs, and the Secretary of State. Also, the Ontario Prevention Clearinghouse provides an ex officio member.

The purpose of the committee is to provide guidance, support, advice, monitoring, coordination, and approval for the Better Beginnings project to (a) funding ministries and departments, (b) the 11 research communities, and (c) the research coordination unit. The committee representatives also report the basic findings of the project back to senior management in government.

The Children's Services Branch of the Ministry of Community and Social Services is responsible for central staff support to the project as well as administrative and financial coordination of the Better Beginnings project. The branch provides a project design coordinator for the project who is responsible for the overall design and implementation of the program and research. The two positions of site supervisor-coordinators are cofunded by all ministries. These positions are responsible for the financial and administrative coordination and implementation of the Better Beginnings model in the 11 communities. The urban site supervisor-coordinator works with the 7 diverse neighborhoods in large municipalities, and the Native site supervisor-coordinator works with the First Nation Better Beginnings projects.

The government committee has 15 members. There are subcommittees for each of the 11 demonstration communities. The site subcommittees are responsible for approving the contract, budget, and local model and verifying that the Better Beginnings model is adhered to in the demonstration. There are also several research subcommittees: budget, economic analysis, child development, program model development, comparison communities, and research ethics. The comprehensiveness of the scope of research, as well as the problems of implementing research in communities that are extremely cynical about the possibility of research to improve daily life, have required innovation and sensitivity at almost every step of the research. The government committee has also worked closely with the communities and the researchers to develop research procedures that do not compromise confidentiality or freedom of information or both.

Research Coordination Unit

To facilitate comparable research across the selected research sites, the government has funded a research coordination unit (RCU). In the spring of 1990, a separate request for proposals was issued by the Ontario government to form a research coordination unit for the Better Beginnings, Better Futures Project.

A multidisciplinary consortium of researchers sponsored by the Social Program Evaluation Group at Queen's University, the Center for Social Welfare Studies at Wilfrid Laurier University, and the Department of Family Studies at the University of Guelph was awarded the contract to form the research coordination unit and began operation on September 1, 1990.

The RCU is establishing comparable research among the sites and will follow children beginning prenatally or at 4 years of age through to their 20s. Gathering information on a community-based demonstration project requires a collaborative relationship between the researchers and the program directors as well as the community leaders and the program participants. Therefore, although the RCU has ultimate responsibility for the design and implementation of the research, collaborative relationships with each site have been formed.

RESEARCH OVERVIEW

RCU Organizational Structure and Responsibilities

The RCU consists of a core research team and research director, site research teams, central support staff, and advisers.

Core Research Team and Research Director

The core research team has primary responsibility for making decisions about all aspects of the research design and measurement plans, oversees the implementation of the research, and maintains a centralized database at Queen's University. The core team consolidates the key research credentials required by the project—that is, quantitative and qualitative research expertise; familiarity with child care, primary school, and social service programming; knowledge of key research areas (child, family, and community); costs and cost-effectiveness; program evaluation; and experience with multidisciplinary research.

The research director is a member of the core research team and is responsible for ensuring high-quality research for the entire Better Beginnings project, integrating research activities, and maintaining communication with the government committee.

Community Research Teams

Site Liaisons. Each of the community research sites has a designated core team member who functions as a liaison between the research coordination unit and the site.

Site Researchers. Each Better Beginnings community has a site researcher who helps develop and implement research activities. The site researchers are employed by the RCU core team and work collaboratively with their site liaisons. The RCU has worked with each community to select local site researchers. In several of the communities, research assistants have also been hired to work with the site researchers.

The role of the site researcher in the Better Beginnings, Better Futures Project is unique and challenging. On one hand, the site researcher, a member of the RCU, carries out the research and evaluation plans in an objective and impartial manner. On the other hand, as a member of the research team operating in (and often living in) the community, the site researcher is expected to attend site meetings, carry out extensive consultation with community members about the research plans, and develop close communication with community residents and project staff, especially project coordinators.

Local Research Committees. Each community has formed a research committee or research advisory group composed of residents and service providers along with members of the local RCU research team. These groups provide a consistent forum to discuss research activities and review research reports.

Central Support Staff. In addition to the research director, there are four support staff located in the central RCU offices at Queen's University. These positions include research coordinator, programmer analyst, research associate, and secretary. The staff assist in developing research protocols; training field staff; handling the research budget; receiving, cleaning, and storing research data; drafting reports; and providing administrative, technical, and secretarial support.

RCU Advisers. Given the breadth of research required to evaluate the Better Beginnings model, the research coordination unit is strengthened by the advice and consultation of technical and subject area advisers. Although the core team membership is intentionally small to maximize communication and efficiency, there are more than 30 senior researchers participating as advisers to the RCU.

These advisers have agreed to donate time varying between 3 and 10 days per year for the duration of the project. As members of the academic research community, these advisers have expressed a keen interest in the Better Beginnings project and a willingness to contribute their expertise to ensure high-quality social policy research.

The subject area advisers represent the areas of maternal-child health, child development, family functioning, community health, community development, education, epidemiology, school organization and performance, child care and preschool programs, Native research, multicultural research, and poverty research.

The technical advisers offer expertise in research design, program evaluation, cost accounting and management or organizational development, economic analysis, database design, analysis and management, and research ethics.

RESEARCH QUESTIONS,
DESIGN, AND MEASUREMENT PLANS

The research component of the Better Beginnings, Better Futures Project addresses three general questions: Is the Better Beginnings model effective? What structures and processes are associated with project results? Is the Better Beginnings model affordable?

In developing the research plans, the RCU established a broad consultation process. In each Better Beginnings community, the RCU site researchers and site liaisons consult with neighborhood residents, service agency personnel, educators, and project staff members. These discussions have often occurred in meetings of local research committees that have been established to facilitate community-level review and feedback concerning RCU research plans and reports.

In addition to these community consultations, the government committee systematically reviews all research plans. Finally, a Better Beginnings research ethics review committee at Queen's University, consisting of several university researchers and community representatives, ensures that all research procedures meet acceptable ethical standards.

Is the Model Effective? Outcome Evaluation

Each community is developing and implementing programs designed to address the three major project goals of preventing major long-term problems in young children, promoting the development of these children, and strengthening the ability of the community to respond effectively to the needs of the children and their families.

The first research objective is to determine the size of the program effects in each community and across the various communities. This outcome research entails collecting information on a wide range of child, family, and community characteristics on an ongoing basis so that both short- and long-term project effects can be determined. Several types of comparison-group designs are being integrated into the research plan to determine program outcome effects. The first of these designs entails the collecting of baseline information early in the project and collecting the same data 4 years later to determine changes in child, family, and community functioning during the Better Beginnings project implementation.

Baseline Measures

This information was collected from children and their families who lived in Better Beginnings neighborhoods and were at the upper age limit of the longitudinal group currently being followed. These children were too old to be a direct focal group of the programs in the study; therefore, they provided baseline measures for each community against which the characteristics of children and families will be compared after 4 years of Better Beginnings program involvement. The baseline cohorts were 4-year-old children in communities with the birth to 4-year-old model, and the baseline cohorts were 8-year-old children in Better Beginnings communities that elected the model for children of ages 4 to 8.

The procedures and measures for collecting baseline information were developed in consultation with community and government representatives during the early years of the project, and these data were collected in each of the seven urban demonstration communities in 1992 and 1993. Collection of baseline measures in the First Nation communities began 1 year later.

The baseline measures consist of a parent interview, child measures, teacher reports, and existing community data.

Parent Interview. Because of the key position of parents concerning knowledge about children, families, and the neighborhood in which they live, an extensive parent interview was developed, field tested, and discussed in each community and with the government committee. This resulted in numerous revisions to the parent interview form. It was then used in collecting the baseline data by RCU researchers with parents of 4- and 8-year-old children.

The interview covers a wide variety of topics and concepts about the child's development and behavior, including dietary intake; parent and family characteristics; use of health, education, and social services; and perceptions of neighborhood and community characteristics.

All questions in the interview were read to the parent by a trained RCU researcher to reduce literacy concerns. The interview is available in both Ontario's official languages and several other languages that are spoken by a substantial percentage of families in multicultural Better Beginnings communities.

On average, the interview requires approximately 2 hours to complete. Full parental consent is required, and confidentiality of information is ensured by the RCU. The parent is paid $25 for participating in the interview.

Child Measures. Baseline information was also collected directly from the 4- and 8-year-old children concerning various aspects of their development including language, problem solving, physical growth, attention, and memory. For the 8-year-olds, information on reading and mathematics skills as well as self-concept was also collected.

This information is meaningful only in describing the development and characteristics of groups of children and families. It cannot be used to draw conclusions about individuals. If parents expressed concerns to the researcher about their children, themselves, or their families, they were encouraged to contact a local agency in which individual assessments or services could be provided.

The information was collected from the children by RCU researchers either in the home or in their school. As with all parts of the research, parent consent was required before any information was collected from the child. It took approximately 90 minutes to collect this information.

Teacher-Provided Information on the Child. In addition to the parent interview and child measures, information was collected about various aspects of the child's behavior, skills, and development from his or her teacher where possible. The measures used for this aspect of the research have been adapted from other studies carried out in Ontario schools or from measures currently employed by several boards of education.

Existing Community Data. The fourth source of baseline data is information about various characteristics of the Better Beginnings neighborhoods collected from existing records of local organizations and agencies, such as public health units, hospitals, child welfare agencies, school boards, and police files. Some of the data are available from Statistics Canada.

The final set of "community indicators" is currently under review. Some examples being considered, however, are child abuse cases reported, children taken into custody or made wards of child welfare agencies, number of individuals and families receiving unemployment insurance and social assistance, hospital emergency room use, birth weights, juvenile and adult court referrals, police crime reports, school attendance figures, and number of children requiring specialized school services.

The baseline information was collected during late 1992 and 1993. In 4 years, the same type of information will be collected from children and their families who have been living in the Better Beginnings neighborhoods to get an indication of change within each of the project communities.

Longitudinal Research Groups

After the baseline information was collected, the RCU began to focus attention on a group of children in each community who were at the bottom of the program age range. This meant identifying children in the younger cohort communities as soon as possible after their mothers become pregnant, and identifying children in the older cohort communities who were 4 years old.

This group of children and their families constitute the "longitudinal research group" because it is planned that they will be involved in the research throughout the duration of the Better Beginnings project and then followed for another 20 years to determine long-term effects of the project.

In the younger cohort communities, the longitudinal research group consists of all children born in 1994. In the older cohort communities, the longitudinal research group is all children who were born in 1989. These are all the children who were 4 years old in 1993 and therefore old enough to begin junior kindergarten in September 1993.

The decision to focus on these groups of children was based on the fact that Better Beginnings programs in each community required some time to become organized and implemented. By the fall of 1993, all program components were to be fully implemented.

Information on the children and families of the longitudinal research groups will be collected approximately once each year over the 4 years of the project. The measures to be employed will be similar to those used in the baseline in that they will cover a broad range of child, family, and community characteristics and development. Of course, the specific measures will vary to reflect the age and developmental level of the children.

The developmental changes in the longitudinal research group and in the community over a 4-year period and a comparison at the end of that time with the baseline measures will provide important information relevant to the research question regarding the effects of the Better Beginnings project.

Program Participation Patterns

Another aspect of the research design involves program participation patterns of the longitudinal research group in the Better Beginnings communities. The programs being implemented are open to all birth to 4- or 4- to 8-year-old children and their families living in the designated Better Beginnings neighborhoods. Some families will choose to participate in many of the available program activities, some in only a few, and some will not participate at all.

From a research point of view, it will be important to know which children and families participate in which program activities and how frequently. By systematically collecting this information, it will be possible to relate changes in children and families over time to their participation in various aspects of the local Better Beginnings, Better Futures programs.

If the programs are effective, it is expected that children and families who are more involved will show more positive changes than those who are less involved.

Comparison Communities

Some changes that occur in Better Beginnings communities may result from factors other than the project—for example, from major fluctuations in the economy or changes in government funding of children and family services. To determine the effects of these more general factors, the RCU is also collecting information from children and families living in communities that are similar to those involved in the Better Beginnings project but not receiving project funding.

For this aspect of the research design to yield appropriate information, it is important that the comparison communities be as similar as possible to the Better Beginnings demonstration communities in terms of socioeconomic factors, size, ethnic and cultural composition, child development, and so on.

After the comparison communities were selected, longitudinal research groups of children born in 1989 and 1994 and their families were involved in the research. The information being collected in these comparison communities is the same as that collected in the Better Beginnings neighborhoods. This allows for a determination of how developmental change in children, families, and communities involved in the Better Beginnings project differs from that of those not involved in the project under similar general economic and societal conditions. This information will be collected at regular intervals not only during the 4 years of project funding but also for an additional 20 years to document both short-term as well as much longer-term answers to the question, is the Better Beginnings model effective?

What Structures and Processes
Are Associated With Project Results?
Project Development and Program Model Research

This question has been overlooked in many demonstration projects. There has been little documentation of the structure, processes, activities, and organization of the programs that are associated with positive outcomes for children. In the Better Beginnings project, investigating project development and program implementation at the local project level is an important research objective.

During the first several years of the project, this research concentrated on describing how the individual communities developed and implemented child development programs that adhered to the major characteristics of the Better Beginnings model—high-quality programs developed with meaningful local resident participation and involving the integration of existing and new child and family services.

Information about program development is collected by the RCU site researchers and site liaisons in a number of ways including attending committee meetings of the local Better Beginnings project and taking extensive field notes on the content of these discussions. Also, the researchers review project documents, such as committee minutes, newsletters, and project descriptions, and make field notes on these documents. Finally, interviews and focus groups are held with community residents, service providers, and project staff on specific topics relevant to the development and implementation of the local program model. Notes are also kept by the researchers on these interviews.

All these notes are routinely entered into a computer database and the content of these notes is coded into a variety of categories using a software package called Ethnograph. The coding categories cover various aspects of the Better Beginnings project, including the local program model, the organizational structure of the local project, the involvement of community residents and service providers in decision making, relations with the government, staffing issues, and research procedures and issues.

The field notes are kept in a confidential file by the local researchers. This information is the basic data that are used to write specific reports about how the local projects were developed and how they are being implemented. The content of these project development-program model reports is discussed in each community and also with the government committee before any report is undertaken.

These reports allow the RCU to give feedback to each community that may be of value in improving their program model, inform government policymakers about program development, provide information to other communities that may wish to develop similar prevention programs, and generate knowledge and theory concerning prevention programs, service integration, and community involvement.

The topics of the first of these project development-program model qualitative reports have been (a) proposal development, (b) resident participation, (c) service provider involvement, and (d) program model.

The proposal development report describes how the local communities generated their original proposals for the Better Beginnings competition during the spring and summer of 1990. The resident participation report examines how residents of the local Better Beginnings communities were involved in project organization and decision making during the first several years. The service provider involvement report is concerned with describing how individuals from local agencies became involved in project decision making and the contributions being made by the agencies to program activities. The program model report describes the various program activities and resources being implemented in each Better Beginnings community.

Other topics to be addressed in future reports include the local organizational structures that have been developed for decision making in each community and a report of the personal experiences associated with the Better Beginnings project from the perspective of program participants, staff, committee members, children, and representatives from local service agencies.

Report Preparation Procedures

The basic procedures being followed by the RCU in preparing these reports are described in the following sections.

Report Framework. A tentative framework for a particular report is developed by the RCU. This framework, including the proposed content and questions to be addressed in the report, is then discussed with the government committee and also with each Better Beginnings community steering committee or research committee or both. Based on the feedback from these consultations, the final report framework is established.

Draft Site Report. The RCU researchers review the information in their field notes, hold interviews with relevant individuals, and prepare a draft of the report. This report must preserve individual confidentiality. This draft is reviewed by the local Better Beginnings committee for accuracy of content. This is an important point because it means that all information to be included in the report is reviewed at the local level.

Cross-Site Report. All draft site reports are sent to the central RCU office where a "cross-site report" is written incorporating the major findings from each individual site report. The cross-site report, like the draft site reports, is written in such a way as to ensure that no individual or agency can be identified.

The draft of the cross-site report is sent to each community for review and comment to ensure that the information is consistent with their individual site reports. The cross-site report is also reviewed by members of the government committee.

After the feedback from these reviews is integrated into the cross-site report, it becomes a public document of the RCU and is circulated widely.

Although this is a very time-consuming process, it has been developed by the RCU to address concerns about community understanding of research information and reports that leave the community.

The RCU researchers are collecting and coding the project development-program model information and preparing reports on an ongoing basis throughout the project. RCU researchers review the purpose and procedures for this aspect of the research on a regular basis with members of local Better Beginnings committees.

Is the Better Beginnings, Better Futures Model Affordable? Economic Analysis

A major inadequacy of public policy research in general, and prevention in particular, has been the lack of attention to program costs. Often, the issue has been ignored. When addressed, costs have almost always been computed retrospectively. This has resulted in broad inferences and assumptions that are less accurate and objective than prospective studies. Therefore, the third research objective is to investigate the costs of the Better Beginnings, Better Futures model from the commencement of funding and throughout the program and longitudinal follow-up.

The economic analysis will examine whether the programs are worthwhile given all the effects as well as the costs incurred. This approach will permit justification of replication, with or without modification, in terms of the costs. Therefore, it is necessary to monitor costs closely and tie them to major components of the program.

To monitor project costs in a way that minimizes the amount of financial accounting required while at the same time permitting an accurate description of real costs in each site, the RCU has worked closely with the government committee and site representatives in developing a cost accounting format. These costs are collected using a common accounting system and software at each site.

The costs include both direct costs in terms of dollars and also indirect costs of operating the programs, such as volunteer time and donated space, so-called "opportunity" costs.

These costs are broken down into the major components of the program model in each community, such as home visiting, child-focused programs, family and parent-focused programs, community-focused programs, classroom enrichment, and community healing.

Collecting these cost data in an ongoing way and relating them to project outcome effects and benefits will yield information relevant to questions concerning how affordable the Better Beginnings, Better Futures model would be to replicate in other communities.

CONCLUSION

Treatment and rehabilitation approaches to mental health care have relied predominantly on a definition of mental health that emphasizes health as the absence of disease. Most prevention approaches have adopted the same definition in that mental health is considered to be present if mental illness or disorder is successfully prevented. In this sense, both approaches have adopted a pathology or disease model of mental health. On the other hand, health promotion approaches, such as the Better Beginnings, Better Futures

Project, adopt what might be referred to as an "educational model" of health. An educated person is generally defined in terms of the presence of particular skills, types of knowledge, and attitudes—depending on the age or developmental level, the ability to think critically and systematically, the ability to solve novel problems in an efficient and effective way, and eventually a willingness to take responsibility for one's own learning. The educational system is expected to actively encourage these skills, attitudes, and capabilities in all youth. An educated person is not defined as one who does not evidence a learning disorder or disability. All children are actively encouraged to develop new skills and expand existing ones.

Health promotion adopts a similar approach to physical, mental, and social well-being. All youth are actively encouraged to learn skills and attitudes toward health that will influence their physical and psychosocial development. In being provided with such learning experiences, certain children will inevitably be identified as requiring more intensive learning experiences, more extensive attention, and, in extreme cases, highly expensive treatment and residential services for them to effectively learn these skills and attitudes in the same way that some children who experience difficulty in reading often receive assessment and remediation services. Thus, two major functions can be addressed by broad-based mental health promotion programs: (a) enhancing the physical, social, and mental well-being of all youth and (b) providing an efficient and effective means of identifying youth who require more intensive early intervention or treatment services. From this perspective, what is required at present is a change or expansion in the model of how mental health is conceptualized—that is, a shift from a disease elimination model that underlies many approaches to treatment to one that incorporates the more proactive, promotional characteristics of an educational or learning model (Peters, 1990).

Who is responsible for providing these psychosocial learning experiences to youth? First and foremost in our society, that responsibility rests with parents. Many parents, however, do not have the knowledge, skills, interests, or orientation that allow them to be as effective as they could be. Also, youth who appear to suffer the most from poor mental health often have parents who are extremely ill prepared to teach their children. To argue that it is only the parents who should bear responsibility for psychosocial education is to deny this reality. Certainly, much more effort should be placed on teaching parents to be more effective in fostering the development of their children and also on providing parents with social and emotional support in their child-rearing efforts. To do more than provide lip service to the notion of child mental health promotion, however, more resources than those that can be provided by parents will be required.

In addition to the family, the school is the most influential setting in which youth learn about themselves, others, and society at large. Relationships with teachers and peers are extremely powerful influences not only on cognitive and academic development but also on psychosocial development. As such, the school setting has enormous potential for systematic health promotion activities and screening for more intensive prevention and treatment interventions. For preschool children whose parents require support in promoting effective psychosocial development, nursery schools and day care facilities offer one potential focus for mental health activities. Currently, however, many children who are most in need of such attention are not involved in routine day care. Reaching this preschool group with a comprehensive range of mental health services is a challenge that has been identified in a number of reviews of children's mental health services. For younger children and their parents, effective and comprehensive mental health services may be provided through the public health system and community organizations such as churches or more informal parent support groups. Also, general medical practitioners and pediatricians represent a potentially powerful resource for providing mental and physical health and education activities to a large percentage of the population.

Although the challenge of developing and implementing such mental health promotion programs may appear overwhelming, we believe that the Better Beginnings, Better Futures Project provides a good model for combining community development processes with effective educational approaches to children's mental health.

REFERENCES

Advisory Committee on Children's Services. (1990). *Children first.* Toronto, Canada: Queen's Printer for Ontario.

Berrueta-Clement, J., Schweinhart, L. J., Barnett, W. S., Epstein, A. S., & Weikart, D. P. (1984). *Changed lives: The effects of the Perry Preschool Program on youths through age 19.* Ypsilanti, MI: High/Scope Press.

Boyle, M. H., Offord, D. R., Hofmann, H. G., Catlin, G. P., Byles, J. A., Cadman, D. T., Crawford, J. W., Links, P. S., Rae-Grant, N. I., & Szatmari, P. (1987). Ontario Child Health Study: I. Methodology. *Archives of General Psychiatry, 44,* 826-831.

Bronfenbrenner, U. (1979). Contexts of child rearing: Problems and prospects. *American Psychologist, 34,* 844-850.

Bronfenbrenner, U. (1987). The ecology of the family as a context for human development: Research perspectives. *Developmental Psychology, 22,* 723-742.

Coie, J. D., Watt, N. F., West, S. G., Hawkins, J. D., Asarnow, J. R., Markman, H. J., Ramey, S. L., Shore, M. B., & Long, B. (1993). The science of prevention: A conceptual framework and some directions for a national research program. *American Psychologist, 48,* 1013-1022.

Comer, J. P. (1985). The Yale-New Haven primary prevention project: A follow-up study. *Journal of the American Academy of Child Psychiatry, 24,* 154-160.

Consortium for Longitudinal Studies. (1983). *As the Twig is Bent. . . .* Hillsdale, NJ: Lawrence Erlbaum.

Doll, R. (1983). Prospects for prevention. *British Medical Journal, 286,* 445-453.

Dubos, R. (1959). *Mirage of health.* Garden City, NY: Doubleday.

Graham, P. (1985). Psychology and health of children. *Journal of Child Psychology and Psychiatry, 26,* 333-347.

Health and Welfare Canada. (1986). *Achieving health for all: A framework for health promotion.* Ottawa, Ontario: Minister of Supply and Services Canada.

Health and Welfare Canada. (1988). *Mental health for Canadians: Striking a balance.* Ottawa, Ontario: Minister of Supply and Services Canada.

Institute of Medicine. (1989). *Research on children and adolescents with mental, behavioral, and developmental disorders: Mobilizing a national initiative.* Washington, DC: National Academy Press.

Kessler, M., & Goldston, S. E. (Eds.). (1986). *A decade of progress in primary prevention.* Hanover, NH: University Press of New England.

Lazar, I., & Darlington, R. (1982). Lasting effects of early education: A report from the Consortium for Longitudinal Studies. *Monographs of the Society for Research in Child Development, 47*(2-3, Serial No. 195).

Long, B. L. (1986). The prevention of mental-emotional disabilities: A report from a National Mental Health Association Commission. *American Psychologist, 41,* 825-829.

Offord, D. R. (1985). Child psychiatric disorders: Prevalence and perspectives. *Psychiatric Clinics of North America, 8,* 637-652.

Offord, D. R., Boyle, M. H., & Racine, Y. A. (1991). Epidemiology of behavioral and emotional disorders of adolescence: Implications for treatment, research and policy. In R. J. McMahon & R. DeV. Peters (Eds.), *Behavior disorders of adolescence: Research, intervention, and policy in clinical and school settings* (pp. 13-26). New York: Plenum.

Offord, D. R., Boyle, M. H., Szatmari, P., Rae-Grant, N. I., Links, P. S., Cadman, D. T., Byles, J. A., Crawford, J. W., Munroe Blum, H., Byrne, C., Thomas, H., & Woodward, C. A. (1987). Ontario Child Health Study: II. Six-month prevalence of disorder and rates of service utilization. *Archives of General Psychiatry, 44,* 832-836.

Olds, D. L., Henderson, C. R., Tatelbaum, R., & Chamberlin, R. (1986). Improving the delivery of prenatal care and outcomes of pregnancy: A randomized trial of nurse home visitation. *Pediatrics, 77,* 16-28.

Ontario Ministry of Community and Social Services. (1988). *Investing in children: New directions in child treatment and child and family intervention.* Toronto, Canada: Queen's Printer for Ontario.

Ontario Ministry of Community and Social Services. (1989). *Better Beginnings, Better Futures: An integrated model of primary prevention of emotional and behavioral problems.* Toronto, Canada: Queen's Printer for Ontario.

Ounce of Prevention Fund. (1994). *A head start on Head Start: Effective birth-to-three strategies.* Chicago: The Ounce of Prevention Fund.

Peters, R. DeV. (1988). Mental health promotion in children and adolescents: An emerging role for psychology. *Canadian Journal of Behavioural Sciences, 20,* 389-401.

Peters, R. DeV. (1990). Adolescent mental health promotion: Policy and practice. In R. J. McMahon & R. DeV. Peters (Eds.), *Behavior disorders of adolescence: Research, intervention, and policy in clinical and school settings* (pp. 207-223). New York: Plenum.

Price, R., Cowan, E., Lorion, R., & Ramos-McKay, J. (1989). The search for effective prevention programs: What we learned along the way. *American Journal of Orthopsychiatry, 59,* 49-58.

Robins, L. (1978). Sturdy childhood predictors and adult antisocial behavior: Replications from longitudinal studies. *Psychological Medicine, 8,* 611-612.

Sax, L., Cross, T., & Silverman, N. (1988). Children's mental health: The gap between what we know and what we do. *American Psychologist, 43,* 800-807.

Schorr, L. B. (1988). *Within our reach: Breaking the cycle of disadvantage.* New York: Anchor.

World Health Organization. (1977). *Child mental health and psychosocial development* (WHO Tech. Rep. No. 613, report of a WHO expert committee). Geneva: Author.

3

The Comprehensive Child
Development Program and Other
Early Intervention Program Models

PETER J. PIZZOLONGO

The Comprehensive Child Development Program (CCDP) is an innovative effort put forth by the U.S. Administration on Children, Youth and
Families (ACYF) and was established by the U.S. Congress in 1988. CCDP
is based on an extensive history of research and programmatic efforts in early
intervention programs for young children and their families who are part of
the low-income population of the United States. These programs, of which
CCDP is now a part, have focused on alleviating the pressing problems faced
by low-income families, including inadequate housing, health care and
nutrition, family breakup, teenage pregnancy, lack of positive role models
and growth experiences for children, and poor educational attainment and
employment prospects (ACYF, 1994; Hubbell et al., 1991). These problems
often lead to crime or welfare dependency.

This chapter will provide information on the history and program features
of the CCDP as well as an overview of early intervention studies and other

AUTHOR'S NOTE: Address correspondence to Peter J. Pizzolongo, CSR Incorporated,
Suite 200, 1400 Eye Street NW, Washington, D.C. 20005.

programs that attempt to enhance the strengths of low-income families and their children and diminish the problems that they face.

OVERVIEW OF EARLY
INTERVENTION STUDIES AND PROGRAMS

Most educators, social workers, psychologists, and others who work with low-income families and their children have two basic understandings as a foundation for their work: (a) that systematic differences in intellectual ability, physical skills (to a certain extent), and temperament are clearly related to child rearing, and (b) that, although some children from economically and socially deprived environments do succeed as self-sufficient adults, and other children who are given many advantages do not succeed, the social condition of poverty has profound effects on children's development (Stone & Church, 1984).

Bridging these understandings are the professionals who engage in intervention programs—intervening in the lives of young children directly and through work with their parents and others who provide primary nurturance to the children. Interventionists have goals that address the problems of poverty (or, at a minimum and more realistically, a segment of the problems of poverty) such as those espoused by Project Head Start to bring about a greater degree of social competence in children of low-income families (ACYF, 1984), by the Center for Successful Child Development, also known as the Beethoven Project, to promote the healthy growth and development of children from before birth through age 5 and to prepare them for achievement in the public school (Hubbell et al., 1991), or by the University of Colorado's Parent-Infant Project to support low-income parents of infants to lead to better mother-child interaction (Dawson et al., 1991).

To address these problems, interventionists must begin with a picture of the end result—the target that they hope to facilitate families working toward. Useful tools for formulating the picture of the end result can be found in the work of Bradley and Caldwell (1976, 1977, 1979), White and associates (White, 1975; White & Watts, 1973), and Alison Clarke-Stewart (1978).

Bradley and Caldwell's (1976, 1977, 1979) work demonstrated the complexity of activities and attitudes found in households that produce children who succeed. Using an instrument called the Home Observation for Measurement of the Environment, Bradley and Caldwell defined favorable and less favorable family settings along the following dimensions:

a. Stimulation through toys, games, and reading materials
b. Language stimulation
c. Properties of the physical environment, such as safety, cleanliness, cheerfulness, pleasantness of outdoor surroundings, and spaciousness
d. Pride, affection, and warmth
e. Stimulation of academic behavior (color naming, rhymes, spatial vocabulary, counting, word recognition)
f. Modeling and encouraging socially mature behavior
g. Variety of stimulation (music, art materials, outings, and the like)
h. The sparing use of physical punishment

White and associates (White, 1975; White & Watts, 1973) have provided information regarding the characteristics of competent mothers and competent children—information that can further the picture of the end result that interventionists can find useful. These studies have demonstrated that competent mothers produce competent children. Competent mothers are those who enjoy being with their children and who (a) are available when needed, (b) structure the environment in keeping with children's interests and capacities, and (c) respond verbally to their children's preverbal signals.

Less competent mothers are prone to overwhelming children with unwanted attention or not giving their children enough time. Children's competence was defined according to the following characteristics (White, 1975; White & Watts, 1973):

a. Are well developed cognitively and socially
b. Show planning and persistence in their activities
c. Make their feelings known
d. Are effective in getting the attention and the help of adults

Clarke-Stewart's (1978) work, using home observations and tests, describes the interactions between mothers and their 9- to 18-month-old children. Competent children, at 18 months, were defined as possessing the following traits (Clarke-Stewart, 1978):

a. Intellectual ability
b. Language skill
c. Adaptability to new situations
d. Positive emotions
e. Strong attachment to their mothers

Competent mothers were defined as being warm and loving, as stimulating and enriching, and as responsive to their infants' behaviors. Less competent mothers were observed spending more time attending to their infants' physical needs. They also restricted their infants' activities (Clarke-Stewart, 1978).

With this picture of competent mothers and children, interventionists have moved on to investigate—and use—the principles of enrichment programs that grew largely out of the War on Poverty programs of the late 1960s and early 1970s. These principles (Bronfenbrenner, 1974) are as pertinent today as they were 20 years ago: (a) it is essential to involve parents as deeply as possible in enrichment programs, (b) programs should begin with children as young as possible, and (c) programs should continue well into the school years.

Furthermore, interventionists can investigate—and use—the philosophies and practices underlying the genre of programs on which most intervention programs are based, which are categorized as community-based family support and education programs, home visitation and case management, and the developmentally appropriate practices of early childhood education programs.

Community-Based Family Support and Education Programs

Community-based family support and education programs normally include the following features (Weiss & Halpern, 1990):

a. They provide information, guidance and feedback, practical assistance, and emotional support in a goal-oriented framework.
b. They provide sustained support to young families, interacting with them regularly over a period of months or years.
c. They focus on both enhancing parenting and attending to the intra- and extrafamilial forces impinging on parenting.

  d. They provide a secure, accepting climate in which young parents can share
     and explore child-rearing goals, beliefs, and concerns.
  e. They often strive to promote or strengthen informal support ties among young
     families in the community.
  f. They often advocate on behalf of the population served for improved services
     and other institutional supports.
  g. It is viewed as the programs' responsibility to reach out to families who are
     unwilling or unable to seek support themselves and to nurture their capacity
     to accept and use support.

Family support and education programs are part of a community system
of "preventively oriented helping services." These programs often supplement or fill the gaps or both in meeting families' total needs that are left by
other service programs with more limited goals.

Home Visitation and Case Management

Intervention programs often use home visitation for providing a variety
of services; the services provided vary according to the model that each
program follows. The practice of visiting families in the home is based on
several assumptions (Wasik, Bryant, & Lyons, 1990):

  a. Parents are usually the most consistent and caring people in the lives of their
     young children, and the home is the most important setting for the child.
  b. Parents can learn positive, effective ways of responding to their children if
     they are provided with support, knowledge, and skills.
  c. For parents to respond effectively and positively to their children, their own
     needs must be met.

Based on these assumptions, five principles guide the work of staff who
are using a home-visit model to meet children's and families' needs:

  a. Family support should enhance the ability of families to work toward their
     own goals and deal effectively with their own problems.
  b. Home-based intervention should be individualized based on an assessment of
     the social, psychological, cultural, educational, economic, and physical or
     health characteristics of the family.
  c. A home visitor must be responsive to the immediate needs of families as well
     as to their long-term goals.

d. A helping relationship should be a collaboration between the home visitor and the family members.

e. The family should be recognized as a social system, understanding that intervention efforts directed at one individual within the family can influence other family members and can influence the overall functioning of the family.

Many home-visit model programs include the use of the system of case management for service identification and provision. Case management places the responsibility for service planning and delivery, as well as system coordination, on the case managers and the family to develop a service plan that ensures access to needed services. Case management activities also allow program staff to monitor service delivery, advocate for clients' needs, and evaluate service outcomes (CSR, Incorporated, 1993).

Case management functions are varied. Most case managers are responsible for recruiting families to participate in programs and for determining families' eligibility for participation. Case management includes the conduct of needs assessments for the family, individual adult family members, and children. On the basis of these needs assessments, case managers help families identify short- and long-term goals, desired outcomes, and activities that lead to the outcomes. Case management procedures also include developing service plans that match family needs to resources, services, or benefits and connecting these services to the long- and short-term goals. Case management can include program staff providing direct services, such as counseling or crisis intervention, brokering for services, and helping to educate parents through information dissemination and other types of activities. Lastly, case management involves an assessment of (i.e., tracking) how the service plan is implemented, what quality of service has been provided to the family, and how the family has progressed in attaining its goals.

In home-visitation programs that include parent education and experiences for young children in addition to case management, program staff must recognize that they are not child educators; they are adult educators who work with the child through the parents (ACYF, 1993). The focal point of the home visit is providing information to parents on what and how to teach their child. Parents then learn to teach children on their own, and, as they become more skillful with using teaching techniques, they can generalize these skills to teach in different settings, with a variety of materials, without the aid of the home visitor.

A feature of home-visitation programs is the use of the home as a learning environment. Home visitors primarily help parents understand how to use home materials and their family routines as opportunities for children to learn concepts, practice new skills, and explore feelings. Home visitors often supplement materials found in the home with agency-purchased consumable supplies for the families to use during the year, such as construction paper, glue, paste, and crayons. In addition, home visitors may supplement home materials with toys, puzzles, and games for specific activities with a child to meet a child's individual needs, to complete a developmental screening or assessment, or to amuse children while home visitors and parents work together.

Developmentally Appropriate Practice

In both home-based and center-based models, intervention programs often include the tenets of developmentally appropriate practice (DAP) in their services for children and families. DAP is based on the dimensions of age appropriateness and individual appropriateness (Bredekamp, 1987). Age appropriateness involves the universal, predictable sequences of growth and change that occur during the first 9 years of life in all domains of development—physical, emotional, social, and cognitive. Knowledge of children's development within this age span provides a framework for adults who work with young children to plan appropriate experiences. Individual appropriateness indicates that each child is a unique person with an individual pattern and timing of growth, as well as individual personality, learning style, and family background. Adults who work with young children must be responsive to individual differences, match children's abilities to experiences provided, and challenge each child's interest and understanding.

In addition to these features of DAP, group programs for children consider the effects of group size and child-staff ratios on quality. Children in smaller groups are more verbal, more involved in activities, less aggressive, and make the greatest gains in standardized tests of learning and vocabulary. Ideal group sizes are 6 to 8 for 0- to 12-month-olds, 6 to 12 for 12- to 30-month-olds, 10 to 14 for 30- to 36-month-olds, and 14 to 20 for 3- to 5-year-olds (National Association for the Education of Young Children, 1991). Children in classrooms with better child-staff ratios (i.e., fewer children and more adults) are more likely to receive more appropriate caregiving and experience more developmentally appropriate activities. Better ratios range from 3:1 for infants to 10:1 for 5-year-olds.

The Head Start Home-Based Program Option

An early intervention program that includes many of the features noted in the previous section is the home-based program option of Project Head Start. In 1972, the U.S. Office of Child Development (OCD), now ACYF, funded 16 communities to demonstrate how a home-based approach could provide comprehensive Head Start services to parents as the primary educators of their own children (ACYF, 1993). In 1973, OCD made the Head Start home-based program option available to all Head Start agencies. Grantees that implement the home-based option must (a) provide one home visit per week per family (a minimum of 32 home visits per year) lasting for a minimum of 1.5 hours each; (b) provide, at a minimum, 2 group socialization activities per month for each child (a minimum of 16 group socialization activities each year); (c) make up planned home visits or scheduled group socialization activities that were canceled by the grantee or by program staff when this is necessary to meet the minimum number of visits required; (d) allow staff sufficient employed time to participate in preservice training, to plan and set up the program at the start of the year, to close the program at the end of the year, to maintain records, and to keep component and activities plans current and relevant; and (e) maintain an average caseload of 10 to 12 families per home visitor with a maximum of 12 families for any individual home visitor (Final Rule on Head Start Staffing Requirements and Program Options, 1992).

The key elements of the Head Start home-based program option are

a. meeting the Head Start Program Performance Standards in the home-based option;
b. establishing and maintaining partnerships with parents;
c. using the home as a learning environment;
d. basing work with families on the family needs assessment and the child's developmental profile;
e. using information to develop individualized short- and long-term goals;
f. encompassing all the Head Start component areas (education, health-nutrition- mental health, social services, and parent involvement) in working with families;

g. individualizing services with families; and

h. receiving support from supervisors, component coordinators, and other Head Start team members (Pizzolongo & Thomas, 1993).

THE COMPREHENSIVE
CHILD DEVELOPMENT PROGRAM

CCDP was authorized by the 1988 Comprehensive Child Development Centers Act, Sections 2501-2504 of Public Law 100-297 ("the act") (ACYF, 1994). Under the act, the Department of Health and Human Services (DHHS) funded 24 projects for a 5-year period, beginning in fiscal years (FYs) 1989 and 1990, at a total annual cost of $25 million. Management at the federal level is the responsibility of DHHS's Head Start Bureau, ACYF.

Subsequently, under Title VIII of the Augustus F. Hawkins Human Services Reauthorization Act of 1990, the CCDP authorization was extended through 1994 and increased to $50 million per year beginning in FY 1991. The FY 1994 appropriation for CCDP was $46.8 million. Also, an additional 10 centers were funded beginning in 1992 and 1993.

The 34 CCDP projects are located in the 10 DHHS regions. These projects serve large urban, metropolitan, and rural communities. The grantees that administer these projects comprise a wide range of organizations, including community action agencies, hospitals, health agencies, universities, and municipalities.

The goals of CCDP are (a) to prevent educational failure by addressing the medical, psychological, institutional, and social needs of infants, young children, and their parents; (b) to reduce the likelihood that young children will be caught in a cycle of poverty; and (c) to prevent welfare dependency and promote self-sufficiency and educational achievement.

To achieve these goals, CCDP projects are designed to encourage intensive, comprehensive, integrated, and continuous support services. These services address the physical, social, emotional, and intellectual development of children from birth to compulsory school age, as well as the support needed by parents and other family members. To be eligible for CCDP, families must have an income below the poverty line, have an unborn child or a child under the age of 1, and agree to participate for 5 years. (Note, however, that all family members receive services.)

CCDP projects vary in the approaches they undertake to meet the program goals. All CCDP projects, however, must

a. intervene as early as possible in the child's life;
b. involve the whole family, including all preschool children in the family;
c. provide comprehensive services to address a wide range of needs;
d. provide continuous services from birth to compulsory school age; and
e. use services available locally and avoid duplication.

The services that CCDP projects provide are described in the following section.

Case Management

Agency staff and participants complete a Family Needs Assessment (FNA) within 90 days of the family's enrollment and update the FNA for each family every 6 months. The FNA update reflects the current needs of families.

Agency staff and participants also complete a service plan for each family member within 90 days of the family's enrollment and update the service plan every 3 months. The service plan update reflects the family members' current goals and proposed activities. For a young child, the service plan update includes current information regarding his or her early childhood education intervention (i.e., home or center based).

Case managers refer and broker services and resources for families to the extent identified in the family member service plan. All families receive a biweekly case management home visit. The case management home visit includes the following activities: a services' checklist review, assessment of progress toward goal achievement, brokering services, and other appropriate case management activities. Case managers and parents jointly plan home visits, which are based on family member service plans. The project uses a system for making parents aware of all required services.

Home visits are based on a plan that delineates goals and activities to achieve the goals; the plan is updated with the parent at the conclusion of each visit, and activities conducted are documented. Each family's and family member's progress toward goals is monitored and documented during each home visit. Case managers help parents to be aware of their goals and their progress toward achieving goals. Families receive assistance with social services, including securing adequate housing and income support. Staffings and case conferences are held on a regularly scheduled basis, such as once per week or biweekly.

Parent Education, Early Childhood Education, and Early Intervention

Developmental screenings and assessments are completed by the project or another agency for all children under compulsory school age in the program family. The assessments are completed within 6 months after the screening and updated annually thereafter (i.e., entered into the Management Information System). Ongoing assessment procedures are used for planning activities and intervention strategies and include systematic observation and documentation of children's behavior, the use of standardized instruments and developmental checklists, collections of children's work over time (portfolios), and other methods that complete a profile for each child in the cognitive, physical, and socioemotional domains.

Based on the findings of the screening and assessment, an individual development plan (IDP) is written for all children under compulsory school age in the program family. The IDP is updated every 6 months. Children who are at risk or developmentally delayed have timely access to an intervention program. Each program uses appropriate developmental curriculum materials, and staff members who implement the curriculum are trained on its use.

A developmentally appropriate child development experience is provided for each CCDP family member under school age each week. If these experiences are center based, they are provided at least three times per week and meet the Head Start Program Performance Standards. If home based, they are provided at least once per week. Home-based intervention focuses on the primary caregiver as the primary educator of the child. Home visitors work directly with parents, encourage and facilitate interaction between parents and child, and ensure that the focus of the home visit is providing information on infant-child development and parenting to the parents. Parents work directly with the child, and home visitors encourage and support the parents and, at times, model appropriate interactions. Agencies that use a combination model (home- and center-based interventions) for providing early childhood education plan a minimum number of class sessions and corresponding number of home visits. These experiences are coordinated and based on children's IDPs.

Home visitors help parents to understand how to use home materials and their family routines as opportunities for children to learn concepts, practice new skills, and explore feelings. Home visitors supplement materials found in the home with agency-purchased consumable supplies for the families to use during the year, which may include construction paper, glue, paste, crayons, and children's scissors. Parents are trained to be their child's teacher. For families whose children receive no home-based early childhood education intervention (i.e., all children are in center-based settings that meet or exceed the Head Start Program Performance Standards), the CCDP project provides parenting education through center- or home-based training. Projects may provide parenting classes and support groups as part of their adult education curriculum. Drop-in care is available for families who need this service.

Health

Children. Comprehensive health screenings for children are completed within 90 days of the child's enrollment. Immunizations current with the Centers for Disease Control schedule for the child's age are available, brokered, and monitored. Well-baby and well-child care current with the American Academy of Pediatrics schedule are available, brokered, and monitored. Acute health care is available. Project staff are aware of proper procedures to follow in cases of serious illness or injury to a child. Therapeutic mental health care is available (as appropriate).

Adults. Prenatal and postpartum care are available, brokered, and monitored. Routine and acute health care are provided as needed. Preventive mental health activities, which facilitate parents' motivation toward achieving economic and social self-sufficiency, are provided, such as support groups, parent appreciation days, special assessment visits from the mental health coordinator, and so on. Therapeutic mental health care is available (as appropriate). Substance abuse education and treatment are provided or brokered as needed.

WIC (Women, Infants, and Children) eligibility or other nutritious food sources or both are available, brokered, and monitored. Staff is trained to work with individuals addicted to alcohol and other drugs, including identification, prevention, and providing services to abusers in treatment and recovery.

Child Care

Child care for all children, regardless of age, is available and accessible to any parent requesting it when the primary caregiver(s) is in training or working. Child care centers, family child care homes, and child development centers meet state licensing and registration standards or certification and all Head Start Performance Standards.

Adult Education

Training in health care, nutrition, stress reduction, budgeting, and other life skills is provided to participating adults. This training may be provided through CCDP center-based or home-visit training or through a contracting-interagency agreement if the training is accessible to parents and procedures have been established to monitor the training. Adult literacy education, GED (general equivalency diploma) education, and postsecondary education are available to all program families. Linkages and referrals for adult education are established.

Support groups and other expert- and peer-led support programs are provided by the CCDP project or through linkages with other community agencies or both. Specific efforts to increase male participation or involve males in the program are made. The CCDP project facilitates opportunities for parent ownership of the program and for parent empowerment. The CCDP project provides administrative support for the parent council(s).

Vocational Education and Training

Vocational training, employment counseling, and job training and placement are available to all program families. Linkages with major employers and agencies for jobs for family members are established.

Administration of the Program

Interagency Requirements. Agreements exist with all relevant community agencies.

Transportation. Adequate transportation is provided to all family members to ensure access to core services, including parent education programs and meetings, child care, and health care visits.

Resources. Emergency resources are included in the CCDP project budget and made available in a timely manner for families needing assistance. The primary intent of this fund is short-term crisis intervention, with a limited number of grants to families for one-time emergency needs, such as home repair (a broken window in winter) or baby care supplies (in the event of unexpected and unavoidable break in income, etc.). The purpose of the emergency fund is to offer assistance to families, with no strings attached, for legitimate, one-time emergencies. CCDP projects may also use funds to help families not in crisis move toward economic self-sufficiency by establishing a loan fund or through grants to families for purchasing books for college classes, for repairing an automobile so that a family member can begin employment, or to meet other educational or vocational needs.

Advisory Board. Each program has an advisory board that actively participates in the important aspects of the project and meets at least quarterly (committees should meet more frequently) with representatives from program parents, agencies, and experts representing the services the project provides, as well as community and significant local employers and businesses who can bring the perspective of private industry to the CCDP project.

Management and Personnel Supervision. The CCDP project receives support from its sponsoring agency that can include (a) collaboration between the CCDP and grantee agency administration toward the development of an ongoing strategic planning process; (b) in-kind contribution of facilities, personnel, and training programs; and (c) priority in referrals of CCDP participants for programs administered by the grantee. The CCDP project maintains good relations with the community, in which community citizens and agency personnel view the CCDP project as a primary provider of family support and education program services, as a source of expertise in comprehensive programming, and as a provider of referrals that receive priority for referrals by community agencies.

The ethnic distribution of staff is representative of the population served by the CCDP project. The staff communication system includes staff meetings, case conferences, staffings, and other methods that ensure an appropriate flow of information. Staff responsibilities are clearly documented and understood, and they receive appropriate training for their positions.

CCDP project records are maintained in a way that is integrated, complete, functional, and, when appropriate, confidential. The CCDP project's organizational framework is functional, and space and facilities are appropriate for the services provided.

Evaluation of the CCDP

The legislation authorizing CCDP requires a continuing evaluation of CCDP projects to determine their effectiveness in achieving stated goals, their impact on related programs, and their structure and mechanisms for delivery of services. To meet this legislative mandate, ACYF awarded two contracts: CSR, Incorporated, is conducting a feasibility analysis, process evaluation, and cost study of initial CCDP projects, and Abt Associates is assessing the program's impact on children and families. The evaluations are now in progress. An interim report based on data collected when families had been in the program for 2 years or less was submitted to Congress in May 1994 (ACYF, 1994). A final report will be prepared in 1996 after the end of the grant period.

CONCLUSION

Intervention programs for young children and their families have demonstrated that the characteristics of "successful environments" for young children and their families who are members of the low-income population in the United States can be achieved. These environments include such features as stimulation through toys, games, and reading materials; language stimulation; safety, cleanliness, cheerfulness, pleasing outdoor surroundings, and spaciousness; pride, affection, and warmth among family members; stimulation of academic behavior; modeling and encouraging socially mature behavior; a variety of stimulation (music, art materials, outings, etc.); and the sparing use of physical punishment. Furthermore, interventionists can investigate and use the philosophies and practices underlying the genre of programs on which most intervention programs are based, which are categorized as community-based family support and education programs, home visitation and case management, and the developmentally appropriate practices of early childhood education programs. Two effective community-based family support and education programs in the United States that include the components of case management and home visiting and that employ developmentally appropriate practices in their services for children are the Head Start home-based program option and the CCDP.

REFERENCES

Administration on Children, Youth and Families. (1984). *Head Start program performance standards* (45-CFR 1304). Washington, DC: Author.

Administration on Children, Youth and Families. (1993). *The Head Start home visitor handbook.* Washington, DC: Author.

Administration on Children, Youth and Families. (1994). *Comprehensive Child Development Program—A national family support demonstration: Interim report to Congress and executive summary.* Washington, DC: Author.

Bradley, R., & Caldwell, B. (1976). The relations of infants' home environments to mental and test performance at fifty four months: A follow-up study. *Child Development, 47,* 1172-1174.

Bradley, R., & Caldwell, B. (1977). Home Observation for Measurement of the Environment: A validation study of screening efficiency. *American Journal of Mental Deficiency, 81,* 417-420.

Bradley, R., & Caldwell, B. (1979). Home Observation for Measurement of the Environment: A revision of the preschool scale. *American Journal of Mental Deficiency, 84,* 235-244.

Bredekamp, S. (Ed.). (1987). *Developmentally appropriate practice in early childhood programs serving children from birth through age 8.* Washington, DC: National Association for the Education of Young Children.

Bronfenbrenner, U. (1974). *A report on longitudinal evaluations of preschool programs. 2: Is early intervention effective?* Arlington, VA: Computer Microfilm International Corp. ERIC Reports.

Clarke-Stewart, A. (1978). Recasting the lone stranger. In J. Glick & K. A. Clarke-Stewart (Eds.), *Studies in social and cognitive development: The development of social understanding* (Vol. 1). New York: Gardner.

CSR, Incorporated. (1993). *Case management curriculum.* Washington DC: Author (draft manuscript).

Dawson, P., Robinson, J., Butterfield, P., van Doorninck, W., Gaensbauuer, T., & Harmon, R. (1991). Supporting new parents through home visits: Effects on mother-infant interaction. *Topics in Early Childhood Special Education, 10*(4), 29-44.

Final Rule on Head Start Staffing Requirements and Program Options—45 CFR Part 1306. (1992, December). *Federal Register, 57,* 58084-58096.

Hubbell, R., Cohen, E., Halpern, P., DeSantis, J., Chaboudy, P., Titus, D., DeWolfe, J., Kelly, T., Novotney, L., Newbern, L., Baker, D., & Stec, R. (1991). *Comprehensive Child Development Program—A national family support demonstration: First annual report.* Washington, DC: CSR, Incorporated, and Information Technology International.

National Association for the Education of Young Children. (1991). *Accreditation criteria and procedures of the National Academy of Early Childhood Programs* (Rev. ed.). Washington, DC: Author.

Pizzolongo, P., & Thomas, J. (1993). *User's guide for a partnership with parents.* Washington, DC: Administration on Children, Youth and Families.

Stone, J., & Church, J. (1984). *Childhood and adolescence—A psychology of the growing person.* New York: Random House.

Wasik, B., Bryant, D., & Lyons, C. (1990). *Home visiting: Procedures for helping families.* Newbury Park, CA: Sage.

Weiss, H., & Halpern, R. (1990). *Community-based family support and education programs: Something old or something new?* New York: National Center for Children in Poverty.

White, B. (1975). *The first three years of life.* Englewood Cliffs, NJ: Prentice Hall.

White, B., & Watts, J. (1973). *Experience and environment: Major influences on the development of the young child.* Englewood Cliffs, NJ: Prentice Hall.

4

Social Skills Training in
the Fast Track Program[1]

KAREN L. BIERMAN

MARK T. GREENBERG

CONDUCT PROBLEMS PREVENTION
RESEARCH GROUP

The Fast Track Program is a multisite prevention research project involved in the development and evaluation of a comprehensive, multicomponent preventive intervention. Key program goals include promoting the competencies of children at risk for conduct disorders (Conduct Problems Prevention Research Group [CPPRG], 1992). The program involves a series of controlled field trials currently under way in four areas of the United States that were selected to represent a range of geographical areas and demographic characteristics—rural Pennsylvania; Seattle, Washington; Durham, North Carolina; and Nashville, Tennessee.

AUTHORS' NOTE: This work was supported in part by National Institute of Mental Health Grants R18MH48043, R18MH50951, R18MH50952, and R18MH50953. The Center for Substance Abuse Prevention also has provided support for Fast Track through a memorandum of agreement with the NIMH. Support has also come from the Department of Education Grant S184U30002 and NIMH Grants K05MH00797 and K05MH01027.

At each of these sites, three cohorts of children have been identified as at risk for the development of conduct disorders based on teacher and parent ratings of behavior problems in kindergarten (see CPPRG, 1992, for details). During the first year of the program, participating schools were matched on size, ethnic composition, and economic disadvantage (e.g., percentage of children eligible for free or reduced-priced lunch) and were randomly assigned to the intervention or control condition. Hence, depending on the child's school in first grade, half of the families of high-risk children were recruited into the intervention, and the others continued to participate in a developmental study that composed the comparison group.

In this chapter and in Chapter 5, the intervention activities of the Fast Track Program are described. The total program involves a 6-year span of prevention activities, covering the important developmental transitions of school entry and the transition to middle school; this chapter and Chapter 5 focus on the school entry intervention conducted at the first- and second-grade levels. The program is composed of seven integrated components, including parent training, home visiting, parent-child relationship enhancement, and academic tutoring, as well as three components focused on strengthening social-cognitive skills, emotional regulation capabilities, and interpersonal competencies of high-risk children. This chapter will focus on the latter three components—a universal prevention curriculum used by teachers, a social skill training group program for targeted high-risk children, and a peer-pairing program, all designed to build social skills and enhance positive peer relationships. In Chapter 5, the parent-focused components are described. This chapter is organized into three sections: (a) an overview of the social skill deficits associated with conduct disorders that are targeted in the Fast Track Program, (b) a description of the structure and content of the social skill training intervention components, and (c) special issues in the implementation of social skill training groups with conduct-problem children.

SOCIAL SKILL DEFICITS
ASSOCIATED WITH CONDUCT PROBLEMS

Poor peer relations frequently co-occur with conduct problems (McMahon & Wells, 1989) and predict later school maladjustment, juvenile delinquency, and referral for mental health services (Parker & Asher, 1987). Aggressive behavior is one primary cause of the poor peer relations of conduct-problem children (see Coie, Dodge, & Kupersmidt, 1990), but not all aggressive children are rejected. Aggressive children who become rejected typically show a range of conduct problems, including disruptive, hyperactive, and disagreeable behaviors as well as physical aggression. In addition, many show concurrent inattention, insensitivity, and social anxiety (Bierman, Smoot, & Aumiller, 1993). Hence, social skill training programs designed for children at risk for conduct disorder must focus on more than simply the reduction of aggressive behaviors; they must also address the interpersonal, cognitive, and emotional deficits (or distortions) posited to contribute to this broader array of social adjustment problems.

A number of theorists have described the child characteristics and family and peer interaction patterns that contribute to the "early starter" pattern of conduct disorder (see CPPRG, 1992; Loeber, 1990; Patterson, 1982). Hence, only a brief review will be provided here focused on the experiences that influence children's social development and, accordingly, have important implications for the design of remedial interventions.

Family Experiences

Several investigators have postulated that the quality of the parent-child attachment during infancy and early childhood may affect the development of the child's emotional regulation capabilities and behavioral control as well as serve as a "template" or model for the child's later expectancies and affect in interpersonal relationships (see Greenberg, Speltz, & DeKlyen, 1993). In caregiving relationships characterized by unpredictability and nonresponsiveness, child affective reactions of anxiety, anger, or ambivalence may become part of a set of generalized expectations for other interpersonal relationships. Corresponding behavioral reactions in social situations may include withdrawal and avoidance or, alternatively, intrusive and demanding behaviors. In this latter case, intrusive, high-rate social behaviors may serve both to express anger or anxiety and to create predictability and responsivity in interpersonal interactions by creating demand characteristics that cannot be easily ignored (Jacobvitz & Sroufe, 1987). In contrast, when caregivers are able to provide consistent and supportive responses to children at times of emotional distress, children may learn to model and internalize or self-generate the comfort that initially was provided by an external agent. In addition, caregivers may help the child develop the cognitive and verbal skills to recognize and discuss their feelings and thereby better regulate their emotional arousal (Greenberg, Kusche, & Speltz, 1991).

Parental discipline practices have also been linked conclusively with the development of child conduct problems. Patterson (1982) provides an eloquent description of the ways in which inconsistent and punitive discipline strategies can lead to escalating cycles of coercive interaction in which parents and children model and reinforce each other for increasingly aversive interpersonal demands. Exposure to and participation in coercive family interactions may have several negative developmental effects. One effect is to train the child in a style of interpersonal interaction that includes aggressive, oppositional, and coercive behavior that, if generalized to peer interactions, may lead to alienation and counteraggression. In addition, exposure to high rates of hostile interactions is demoralizing for children and parents, contributing to feelings of depression, anxiety, and anger. Finally, coercive family interactions appear to affect the development of social cognitions in a negative fashion. Dodge, Bates, and Pettit (1990) found that several of the deficits and biases in social perceptions and social problem-solving skills that characterize aggressive children are predictable from early family experiences such as overly harsh discipline practices. For example, aggressive children often make impulsive, incomplete, and inaccurate social judgments and show deficits in social problem-solving skills (Dodge, Pettit, McClaskey, & Brown, 1986; Lochman, 1987). Perhaps reflecting modeling of negative family interactions and deficits in positive prosocial instruction and support, these kinds of social-cognitive deficits and distortions may contribute to adjustment difficulties in peer interaction situations.

Peer Experiences and School Contexts

Although family interactions appear to have an important impact on children's development of social competence, it is important to recognize that the behavior problems exhibited by children in home and school settings show only a moderate correspondence, with cross-setting correlations averaging only $r = .27$ (Achenbach, McConaughy, & Howell, 1987). Hence, as children move from family to school peer interaction settings, there are both positive opportunities for adaptation and new challenges that can elicit new or additional adaptational failures.

The social interactional demands in the school peer group setting differ from those of the parent-child relationship. To sustain interactive and reciprocal play, children need to attend positively to play partners, show cooperative and agreeable behaviors, and communicate clearly, establishing a "common ground" in play and conversational focus (Gottman, 1983; Hartup, 1983). In addition, the more complex, rulebound games of older children require an ability to follow rules, understand one's role in a group, and negotiate conflicts effectively. Most children learn to inhibit physical aggression in their peer interactions rather quickly, and those children who continue to show high rates tend to be rejected by their peers (Coie et al., 1990).

Infrequent positive peer interactions may directly precipitate or increase inadequacies in social adaptation. That is, in naturalistic interactions, peers act as teachers, models, and sources of reinforcement and emotional support, facilitating the development of children's social competencies, such as cooperation and negotiation skills, aggression control, communication skills, and perspective-taking abilities (Hartup, 1983; Ladd & Asher, 1985). Children who have few opportunities for positive peer interactions because of either inadequate contextual support or peer avoidance and ostracism may miss out on these learning opportunities, leading to greater deficits in interactional skills (Coie et al., 1990).

Peer responses can also become detrimental when these responses serve to reinforce or elicit aggressive or inappropriate behavior. Peers may inadvertently reinforce aggressive behavior, for example, by attending to it or complying with the aggressor's demands (Klein & Young, 1979). Negative peer responses can elicit and lead to escalations in aggressive interactions because aggressive children often believe that counteraggression will terminate aversive peer treatment (Asarnow, 1983; Perry, Perry, & Rasmussen, 1986). A negative spiral can ensue when victimized peers become proactively counteraggressive, developing negatively biased attitudes and expectations for rejected children and treating these children differently (and more aversively) than they treat their well-accepted peers (see Hymel, Wagner, & Butler, 1990). Negative peer experiences may thus promote or exacerbate the development of asocial goals and negatively biased interpersonal expectations.

The likelihood that peer influences will contribute to the negative escalation of behavior problems in school is increased in classrooms that contain a high proportion of children with aggressive propensities (Kellam et al.,

1991). Unfortunately, high-risk children often attend schools in which there is a high density of other high-risk children (Rutter, Maughan, Mortimore, Ouston, & Smith, 1979), creating a difficult teaching environment and an increased exposure to the modeling and escalation of conduct problems. In addition, children who are particularly stressed cognitively and behaviorally by the academic demands of school, such as children with attentional deficits or hyperactive behaviors, may be at increased risk for negative interactional experiences in the school setting (Moffitt & Silva, 1988; Richman, Stevenson, & Graham, 1982). Over time, teachers tend to become less positive and less contingent in their reactions to problematic students, which makes these teachers less effective at managing problematic behaviors or teaching new social skills (Strain, Lambert, Kerr, Stagg, & Lenkner, 1983).

Summary

Child characteristics, family relationships, peer interactions, and school experiences can all contribute to the development of deficits or distortions that negatively affect social adaptation. The social adjustment difficulties of children at risk for conduct disorder are often complex and include behavioral features (e.g., excessive displays of aggressive, oppositional, or intrusive and disruptive behaviors and deficient displays of prosocial and cooperative behaviors), affective features (e.g., negative expectations for interpersonal relationships and easily aroused feelings of anxiety, anger, or ambivalence in interpersonal contexts), and cognitive features (e.g., impulsive and inaccurate perceptions, negatively biased evaluations, and inadequate or aggression-prone problem-solving skills). In addition, the child's social success is not determined by these features alone; it is also determined by the characteristics of the social partners (peers, teachers, and parents) with whom the child interacts.

Correspondingly, social skill training interventions need to address the behavioral, social-cognitive, and affective-motivational aspects of children's social adjustment. In addition, interventions need to address the interpersonal contexts in which social behaviors and peer interactions are taking place. That is, social partnerships must become a focus of intervention as well as the target children because it is in the context of ongoing relationships that the child's working models continue to develop and have the potential to change. The following section describes the ways in which the Fast Track social skill training programs were designed to address these needs.

COMPONENTS OF THE FAST TRACK
SOCIAL SKILLS TRAINING PROGRAMS

The Fast Track social skill training programs contain both universal and selective levels of intervention (Mrazek & Haggerty, 1994). The universal intervention is a primary prevention strategy directed at all first-grade children in targeted schools and designed to strengthen the competencies needed for successful adaptation to school and thus to prevent the emergence of school adjustment difficulties. The selective levels of intervention are aimed at children who demonstrated behavior problems in kindergarten and thus were considered at risk for school adjustment problems in first grade and beyond. In the Fast Track Program, the universal and selective interventions complement each other, with all children receiving some social skill training in the classroom and at-risk children receiving additional in-school and extracurricular social skill training and social support.

At school entry (Grades 1 and 2), children are struggling with the new demands of sustained behavioral control in the classroom, social interactions with a large peer group, and demands for academic performance. Across both universal and selective levels of intervention, six skill domains are addressed: (a) social participation (e.g., joining in, paying attention, and being part of a group); (b) prosocial behavior (e.g., cooperating, sharing, taking turns, and helping); (c) communication skills (e.g., expressing one's point of view and feelings clearly and listening to another's point of view); (d) self-control (e.g., inhibiting impulsive reactivity in the face of frustration and negative arousal and taking the time to think about an appropriate response); (e) regulating oneself in rule-based interactions (e.g., following rules in the classroom and in games with peers); and (f) social problem-solving skills (e.g., identifying problems, generating and evaluating solutions, and making and executing a plan). The ways in which these target skill domains are addressed in the content and structure of each level of intervention are described in the following sections.

The Universal Intervention

At the universal level of intervention, classroom teachers are trained by the Fast Track staff (educational coordinators) in the implementation of the Promoting Alternative Thinking Strategies (PATHS) Curriculum (Greenberg & Kusche, 1993; Kusche & Greenberg, 1994). Previously designed for special education populations, this multiyear (first through fifth grade) classroom prevention program was adapted to fit the needs of regular education students in high-risk schools for the Fast Track Program. The program is "universal" in that it is taught by classroom teachers and directed at the entire classroom. The goals are to (a) enhance the skills of all children in the classroom; (b) improve the manageability and positivity of the classroom climate by increasing the compliance and on-task behavior of all children, thus reducing the distractions that may stimulate inappropriate behavior of risk children; and (c) create a positive classroom climate by increasing peer and teacher support for the display of self-control and nonaggressive solutions to peer problems. Previous research involving controlled field trials with regular education, special needs, and deaf students (Greenberg & Kusche, 1993; Greenberg, Kusche, Cook, & Quamma, in press; Kusche, 1991) has found that the use of the PATHS Curriculum has significantly increased the children's ability to understand social problems, develop effective alternative solutions, decrease the percentage of aggressive and violent solutions, and increase the children's understanding and recognition of emotions. In all three samples of children, teachers reported significant improvements in children's behavior on skills targeted by PATHS (self-control, emotional understanding, thinking before acting, and use of effective conflict resolution strategies). In studies with special education children, PATHS led to significant decreases in self-reported sadness and depression, decreases in teacher reports of internalizing problems, and increases in teacher reports of social competence (e.g., frustration tolerance and positive peer relations).

In the version of the PATHS Curriculum adapted for use in the Fast Track Program for first and second graders, about one third of the lessons focus on skills related to the increase of positive social behavior (e.g., social participation, prosocial behavior, and communication skills). For example, there are lessons on friendship and how to make and sustain friendships, manners, taking turns and sharing in games, expressing the child's viewpoint, and listening to others. In addition, positive behaviors are elicited and reinforced during the course of each lesson. For example, during each PATHS lesson, one child (selected on a rotating basis) serves as the teacher's helper (the "PATHS Kid of the Day"). At the end of the lesson, these children receive compliments from classmates, the teacher, and themselves.

Another one third of the lessons focus on skills related to the inhibition and redirecting of inappropriate behaviors (e.g., lessons targeting skills related to self-control and emotion regulation). As a basic step toward self-control, PATHS focuses on teaching young children to recognize the internal and external cues of affect and to label them with appropriate terms. Often, young children do not recognize the differences between their feelings and behaviors, and they lack the verbal skills needed to appropriately express feelings. Without the verbal skills needed to inhibit, express, and redirect negative arousal, school frustrations may lead to explosive or disruptive behaviors. In the PATHS program, children are taught a vocabulary to talk about their feelings at school. In a series of lessons, feeling words are identified along with descriptions of the kinds of situations that may elicit the feeling, descriptions of the external cues to recognize that feeling in others and the internal cues to identify that feeling in oneself. Additional lessons seek to help children understand the difference between feelings and behaviors. They are taught that "feelings are OK, but behaviors can be OK or not OK." Appropriate and inappropriate behavioral responses are discussed. For example, if children are feeling upset or frustrated by their peers or their work at school, they are taught that it is appropriate to talk with the teacher about those feelings, but it is not appropriate to behave in an aggressive or disruptive manner. As with other skills in PATHS, the teaching of feelings involves a generalization technique, "feeling faces," which is used to promote the student's new knowledge and skills throughout the classroom day. After each emotion concept is introduced, the children personalize their own feeling faces for that affect; these faces are small cards with idealized line drawings of the affect that are kept on the student's desks. The faces allow the children to communicate their feelings with minimal difficulty throughout the day, and they facilitate the children's understanding about how feelings change (e.g., children can physically "change" their feeling faces in a concrete manner when they become aware of a change in their internal emotional state). Teachers have their own set of feeling faces and use them as models for their students. Teachers are encouraged to promote generalization at the beginning and at the end of the day, after recesses, and after lunchtime by suggesting that the children evaluate how they feel and display the appropriate face(s).

Finally, one third of the lessons in the first- and second-grade PATHS program focus on social problem-solving skills. A "control signals poster," using a traffic light to illustrate a three-step model of problem solving, is introduced into each classroom. Children are taught that when they are in a situation that they find upsetting or frustrating (such as a playground conflict or difficult work situations), the first step toward effective problem solving is to "go to the red light" to stop and think before they act. Children are taught to tell themselves to "stop" just as they would at a traffic stoplight. Before they take an action, they should "take a long, deep breath," calm down, and "say the problem and how they feel." Once the children identify the problem, they can move to the yellow light to "make a plan," considering first the possible solutions and then selecting the best option. The next step is to "try the plan" at the green light and evaluate the effectiveness of that plan, recycling through the problem-solving steps if the plan proves ineffective. In addition to scripted lessons that teach children these steps to problem solving, teachers are instructed in the method for holding classroom problem-solving meetings, which are designed to help children use the problem-solving steps to address the problems currently facing them in their classroom.

The PATHS Curriculum is taught by teachers two or three times each week. Each lesson provides teachers with a list of the goals for the session, the materials needed, and a suggested script, including ideas for introducing key issues and guiding class discussions, follow-up practice activities, or role plays. Typically, skill concepts are presented via direct instruction, discussion, modeling stories, or video presentations. Discussion and role-playing activities follow, giving children a chance to practice the skill and teachers a chance to monitor the level of understanding and skill attained by each class. Although a standard script describes each lesson, teachers are encouraged to adapt the lessons and to adjust the level of presentation and amount of practice as dictated by the responsivity and developmental level of each class.

Although the lessons form an important part of the PATHS program, teachers are instructed in and encouraged to generalize their use of PATHS concepts across the school day and to other settings of the school outside the classroom. This sort of generalization is deemed an essential part of PATHS to help children become adept at using the skills in their ongoing school and peer interactions. In particular, teachers are encouraged to help children identify their feelings, communicate clearly with others, use self-control strategies, and apply the three steps of problem solving when frustrations, challenges, and interpersonal problems occur at school. Each classroom has a mailbox in which students can submit written problems or concerns that will then be discussed in problem-solving meetings.

Attempts are also made to generalize concepts to the home situation. The curriculum includes frequent parent updates on curriculum content and suggestions for ways parents can promote their children's growing competence. Regular home activities are designed to help children engage their parents in cooperatively completing drawings or stories related to curriculum components.

Educational coordinators observe PATHS lessons on a weekly basis and have a weekly consultation time with each teacher to discuss both PATHS and more general issues in classroom management. On an as-needed basis, educational coordinators also consult with teachers regarding strategies for the effective management of disruptive behavior of individual children who are having particular difficulties adapting to the demands of the classroom (e.g., establishing clear rules and directions; providing positive and corrective feedback for appropriate behavior; and applying reprimands, time-out, or response cost procedures contingent on the occurrence of problematic behavior).

The Selective Interventions
for High-Risk Children

Although universal interventions can be quite effective, children with severe behavior problems may fail to benefit from this level of intervention alone. Hence, the Fast Track Program includes a second level of more intensive remedial intervention for those children most at risk for conduct problems—a series of extracurricular social skill training friendship groups and corresponding school-based peer-pairing sessions.

Friendship Groups. The friendship group program targets the same skills as the PATHS program and uses the same cues and labels (such as the control signals poster and fair play rules) to support social skill development. In the friendship group setting, however, there is a more intense focus on remediating deficits in prosocial and play skills (Bierman, Miller, & Stabb, 1987; Ladd, 1981; Oden & Asher, 1977) as well as extended practice employing self-control, anger coping, and interpersonal problem-solving skills in the context of peer interactions (Coie & Krehbiel, 1990; Lochman, Burch, Curry, & Lampron, 1984). Skills are arranged in a developmental sequence. For example, the program begins with an emphasis on participation, communication, and emotional expression—skills designed to foster the identification of common ground and friendship initiation among members. Then, behavioral inhibition, anger management, and cooperative play skills are introduced to strengthen the ability of group members to associate cooperatively with each other. The third phase of the program focuses on the understanding of reciprocity in relationships. Fair play concepts are introduced (e.g., taking turns, following rules, and refraining from teasing) along with basic negotiation skills. Finally, the more advanced skills needed to maintain friendships, including attending to feedback, giving feedback, avoiding retribution, and using interpersonal problem-solving skills to work through conflicts, are presented in later skill training sessions. The program is organized in a way that provides synchrony and integration with the classroom PATHS program. For example, as feeling words or social skill concepts are introduced in PATHS, these same words and concepts are incorporated into the group program. Just as in the PATHS program, the control signals poster is used as the framework for teaching social problem-solving skills and for processing conflicts as they emerge in group interactions.

Following a standard format for coaching programs (see Ladd, 1985), each session is focused on a set of target skills. Various forms of skill presentation are used to help children form a solid mental picture of the principles and examples of target skills. To foster children's interest and comprehension, multiple media, including modeling videotapes, stories, puppet shows, and coach role plays, are used to present skills concepts. Skills are practiced in the context of both structured activities (e.g., child role plays and puppet shows, focused board games, and guided peer interactions) and naturalistic peer interactions (e.g., dramatic play and group games). In recognition of the short attention spans of many young children with conduct problems, initial practice activities are often brief and engaging activities such as "partner challenges" that require the cooperative interaction of dyads to complete.

By second grade, many groups are ready for practice activities that require more sustained focus and interaction. Projects that have meaning and challenge for the children and are characterized by superordinate goals (e.g., requiring the cooperative interaction of all team members to achieve), such as cooperative cooking projects or team-focused physical challenges, become increasingly important foci of the program. In addition, "free play" periods are included to allow children to practice naturalistic peer activities, including shared fantasy and competitive game play. During practice activities, coaches cue skilled performance and provide feedback to group members to increase children's recognition of cause-and-effect relations linking their behavior to peer responses and to foster increasingly child-generated (self-regulated) use of targeted skills in peer interactions.

Structure and Organization of the Friendship Groups. In first grade, friendship groups of five or six children meet weekly for 22 weeks during the year and are run by the educational coordinators and coleaders. These groups are embedded in 2-hour "enrichment program" sessions, which families attend together, held at local elementary schools. During the initial hour, children meet in friendship groups while parents meet in parent training groups. Following these training sessions, children and parents spend half an hour together in parent-child sharing time, and parents observe a tutor working with their child on academic skills for half an hour (see Chapter 5, this volume). Siblings are cared for in a separate part of the program during these sessions. The same basic format characterizes the groups during second grade. Groups, however, meet biweekly rather than weekly (for 14 sessions during the year), groups may be somewhat larger (e.g., six or seven children), and friendship group sessions are 90 minutes in duration. In second grade, some children have "graduated" out of the need for academic tutoring; hence, tutoring is no longer conducted during the extracurricular enrichment sessions.

Structure and Organization of Peer-Pairing Sessions. Although group sessions held outside of the school day have the advantage of allowing integration with the parent training, parent-child sharing time, and academic tutoring components of the Fast Track Program, they have the potential disadvantage of limiting generalization. Hence, a second aspect of the selective level of the social skill training program was developed to promote the generalization of positive social skills to the school setting and to increase the likelihood that these skills would be observed and responded to positively by classroom peers. Previous research has suggested that including classmates in social skill training sessions and cooperative group activities with target children is an effective method of changing classmate behavior and attitudes toward rejected children (Bierman, 1986; Bierman & Furman, 1984). The peer-pairing component of the Fast Track social skills training program uses this strategy. In the peer-pairing program that runs parallel to the friendship group program, each target child has a weekly half-hour guided play session during the school day with a classroom peer. (Classmate partners rotate during the course of the school year.) In these sessions, the dyad completes activities (games and art and crafts activities) designed to allow the target child to display improved social skills to the classroom peer and to foster mutually rewarding exchanges between the target child and a variety of classmates. In addition, social problem-solving skills are cued, and children are encouraged to use their skills to negotiate win-win solutions to their conflicts. These sessions are run by tutors who also work with target children on academic skills during the school day, with training and supervision provided by Fast Track educational coordinators.

Academic Tutoring. In addition to the social skill training children receive in the Fast Track Program, academic tutoring is provided to support the development of reading skills during the initial school years. Learning difficulties and academic failure frequently accompany social and behavioral problems at school and lead to poor adjustment outcomes (Moffitt, 1990). Hence, academic tutoring is provided to all identified high-risk children during their first-grade year and occurs parallel to the peer-pairing and friendship group sessions. Paraprofessionals selected for their ability to work well with high-risk children are identified and receive 40 hours of training. They are trained to administer an individualized tutoring program that emphasizes a phonics-based, mastery-oriented approach toward the development of initial reading skills (Wallach & Wallach, 1976). This program is designed to promote phonemic awareness skills in young children who might otherwise have difficulty learning to read, and it has been demonstrated to bring low-readiness children from disadvantaged backgrounds up to grade-expected reading skill levels in the first year of school. The paraprofessional tutors are also trained in positive behavioral support strategies designed to promote the development of the social and self-control skills the children need for successful adaptation at school. By using the same paraprofessionals to provide tutoring in reading skills and to direct the peer-pairing sessions, both of which occur in the school setting, high-risk children are provided with a supportive adult who they see on a regular basis throughout the year. Tutors work with children three times each week for half-hour sessions outside the classroom (two for reading and one for peer pairing). In addition, tutors have a third tutoring session with children during the extracurricular program in first grade (the 2-hour weekly session that includes the parent training group and child friendship group) so that parents can observe and model the work the tutor is doing to help their children with reading skills. After the first-grade year, academic tutoring is continued on an as-needed basis for those children who continue to struggle with reading skills.

SPECIAL ISSUES IN THE MANAGEMENT OF SKILL TRAINING SESSIONS

The design of an effective curriculum is important to the impact of both universal and selective interventions. The management of the social skill training sessions, however, may be equally important. The nature of the interpersonal exchanges that occur may be important for the long-term generalization of treatment gains particularly in the friendship group and peer-pairing sessions, which allow children multiple opportunities for practicing new social strategies and receiving positive support and corrective feedback (Bierman, 1986). That is, generalization may be greatest when the children have experienced positive responses to their skillful behaviors, have come to feel interested in and competent with these new behaviors, and have come to believe that these behaviors will, in fact, enable them to achieve positive interpersonal outcomes in naturalistic peer settings. Conversely, replacing old behavioral habits may require reducing the kinds of interpersonal exchanges in which those habits emerged and had adaptive value.

Three key features in the processing of the intervention sessions may help to promote corrective interpersonal experiences and corresponding adjustments to the social self-system: (a) the provision of an interpersonal climate that is positively responsive to appropriate behavior and does not allow coercive escalations in response to aggressive behaviors; (b) the provision of information that helps children identify the cause-and-effect relationships between their behavior and the interpersonal responses they receive, helping children to develop positive control beliefs about nonaggressive strategies; and (c) the use of interpersonal support strategies that encourage children to internalize a view of themselves as prosocial and likable individuals.

Avoiding Coercion and
Promoting Positive Responsivity

The creation of a positive and supportive interpersonal climate and the avoidance of coercive escalations can be difficult in a therapeutic group consisting of children with conduct problems. Research suggests that "difficult to manage" children who engage in high rates of oppositional and intrusive behavior often elicit high rates of commands and prohibitions from parents, teachers, and peers. Paradoxically, commands and prohibitions may increase the resistant and aggressive behaviors displayed by oppositional children as they seek to "escape" from or terminate these control attempts. In peer interactions, coercive exchanges can escalate quickly, leading both to unpleasant behavioral exchanges and to negative interpersonal attitudes among group members. One way to reduce or avoid this sort of negative escalation is to have in place a set of consequences that cannot be manipulated by behavioral escalations—for example, a token economy or response-cost system in which the positive and negative consequences for various behaviors are set. Although often effective and sometimes needed, this sort of external control can have the disadvantage of limiting the generalization of treatment gains in interpersonal situations in which similar external controls are not in place. A second strategy that can serve to reduce interpersonal escalation is to keep children isolated or limit interaction during group sessions. The likelihood that children can learn how to modify their interpersonal interactions if they do not have the opportunity to practice interactions in the context of intervention, however, remains questionable.

A third way to reduce or avoid negative escalations relies on the skill of the group therapist to structure the group and to support children in ways that enhance their ability to feel secure and in control of positive social outcomes without resorting to negative or coercive strategies. Oppositional, resistant behaviors often emerge when children feel that they are being forced to do something that they do not want to do or when they are trying to elicit and maintain the attention and responsivity of another. By structuring a session in a manner that is inviting, supportive, and nonthreatening, group leaders can reduce the extent to which a child's oppositional behavior is triggered. A typical group of first-grade children at risk for conduct disorder might contain a number of children who have short attention spans, poor impulse control, and difficulty controlling their arousal level. Many of these children may balk at "sit and talk" activities and prefer more active modes of learning. The particular activities that are selected, the pacing of the group, and the ways in which materials and space are organized and used can all affect the extent to which these children can sustain their positive engagement and avoid oppositional or disruptive behavior. It is important to have a clear structure for children, to select games and activities that are interesting and engaging for the children, and to avoid periods of unoccupied or unstructured time, distracting materials, and skill presentations that exceed the verbal and cognitive skills of the participating children. Reducing the size of the group and increasing the availability of adult support can also be used to reduce the level of developmental challenge in a peer interaction setting. In the Fast Track friendship group program, educational coordinators are encouraged to adjust the curriculum, as needed, to maintain a level of challenge that is achievable for the children, thus reducing the likelihood that disruptive and oppositional "escape" behaviors will be elicited. As children begin to show capabilities for more extended interactions and more complex tasks, the developmental level of the group is increased accordingly.

In addition, fundamental principles of positive behavioral management are employed. Educational coordinators are trained to use commands only as needed, to give clear commands, to focus on the desired behavior rather than the undesired behavior whenever possible, and to avoid exhibiting irritable or angry affect. In addition, educational coordinators are trained to give frequent praise, to give specific praise, to ignore inappropriate behaviors when possible, to praise positive models, and to maintain a positive and supportive orientation toward children. When aggressive or destructive behavior does occur, educational coordinators are trained to use time-out along with strategies designed to de-escalate negative arousal (e.g., using a quiet voice and calm affect).

Enhancing Positive Control Beliefs

In addition to these features of the adult-child interactions that take place in the therapy groups, group leaders must closely attend to the influence that peer interchanges have on the behaviors and feelings of group members. For example, in one previous study, the positive responsivity of peer partners in a skill training program was one of the strongest predictors of long-term improvement (Bierman, 1986). Children need to be able to influence the behaviors that other peers direct toward them. Positive strategies will be used only if, in the child's experience, they have been successful in attaining positive results (whereas other strategies have not). High-rate or aggressive behaviors can be quite successful in the short run (terminating unwanted behavior from others or attaining an immediate goal) and can be triggered as a defensive strategy if a child feels threatened by others in the group. Only when children have had experiences in which they found that they could control positive social outcomes for themselves with alternative responses are these responses likely to be applied in naturalistic peer settings when adult and external controls are not present.

Unfortunately, the immediate concrete rewards of aggressive behaviors may be more salient to young children than the social or interpersonal consequences. For example, consider the issue of going first in a game. By grabbing the game, taking the dice, or pushing the partner out of the way, a child can get to be first. By engaging in the prosocial behavior (e.g., taking turns being first or throwing the dice to see who goes first), the child has only a 50-50 chance of going first. If short-term, instrumental gains are considered alone, the aggressive response is the more effective. It is only if the child can see and he or she cares about the longer-term, interpersonal consequences (e.g., keeping vs. losing companionship) that the prosocial response is better, and it is only if the child has the faith that the partner will return this prosocial behavior (e.g., let him or her go first the next time) that the prosocial behavior does not appear simply to promote victimization.

One step toward modifying children's control beliefs is taken when group coaches help children recognize the interpersonal impact of their negative behaviors on others by eliciting feedback from peers. For example, if a child grabs the dice, the coach might stop the action and cue the children to discuss the conflict using a prompt, such as "Oh, just a minute. I wonder how Jimmy feels about you taking the dice like that?" or "Hmm, I think we might have a problem to solve here. Jimmy, can you say how you feel about Jane taking the dice?" This method of guidance allows the perpetrator of an insensitive social behavior to get immediate feedback about the effects of his or her behavior on another and to take corrective action before the conflict escalates. In contrast to an alternative adult-controlled intervention (e.g., the adult simply taking the dice and saying "No grabbing"), this type of interpersonal processing helps children to develop better causal reasoning about their interactions and encourages self-regulation.

In addition, it may be helpful for group leaders to be sensitive to the anxieties that often accompany intrusive or aggressive social behavior. That is, for children who have experienced interpersonal environments in which hostile treatment occurs frequently and unexpectedly, it may be self-protective to become wary of others and to take an offensive stand interpersonally

(Dodge et al., 1990). Unfortunately, this sort of aggressive attitude may elicit counteraggression from others, leading to a self-fulfilling cycle of animosity. To counter this self-defensive and offensive mind-set, it may be particularly important for group leaders to provide reassurance rather than blame when they are helping children consider alternatives to aggressive behaviors. For example, in the grabbing dice example used previously, the group leader could maintain a calm and supportive voice tone and might help the perpetrator identify his or her own motives (e.g., "You're worried that you won't get a turn" or "You want to go first") and label the problem (e.g., "So, our problem is to think of a fair way to decide who goes first—so you both get a chance to go first today") rather than simply chastising the child (e.g., "Grabbing isn't nice"). From this vantage point, conflicts that arise in the course of group interaction are viewed as learning opportunities that, with appropriate adult guidance, can help children gain an understanding of and competence in the skills needed to maintain mutually rewarding relationships (Selman et al., 1992).

The use of the social problem-solving steps in group planning and processing can also support children's development of positive control beliefs. For example, before an activity or game is begun, educational consultants lead the children in a planning session to help them anticipate and negotiate how they will work together to complete the activity. In initial sessions, this planning process is typically short (e.g., "What would be a fair way to divide the snack?" "How shall we decide which game to play?") and children are taken through the problem-solving steps of listening to each other's ideas and then deciding on a solution that is mutually agreeable. In later sessions, the group planning becomes more complex—for example, children are helped to plan the ways in which they will share the tasks and work together to complete a cooking project or tackle a physical challenge. These exercises help children develop confidence in their ability to influence others with verbal expression and provide a foundation of experiences in which negotiating and cooperating with others led to an exciting and rewarding interaction.

Encouraging Self-Regulation

As mentioned previously, external controls (such as token reinforcement or response-cost systems) are often effective in suppressing unwanted behaviors but may have effects that are limited to situations in which the external control systems are in place. One goal of social skill training programs is to promote generalization by promoting internalized self-regulatory systems. The establishment of behavioral control is a critical issue in groups of conduct-problem children and the risks of negative interpersonal escalation have already been described. In some cases, elaborate external control systems may be needed to maintain a positive climate for skill training. One intervention goal, however, is to minimize the need for external controls and to increase the effectiveness of children's self-regulatory systems so that they become more effective at managing their own behavior in the interpersonal interactions that occur in the intervention sessions (as well as later in naturalistic settings).

In the Fast Track social skill training program, educational consultants are trained in the use of "inductive" behavior management strategies that are designed to encourage the child's use of self-regulation. These group processing strategies are designed to cue and support children's comfort with and motivation for skillful behaviors. Induction strategies are designed to minimize adult and external control of children's behavior (whenever possible) and encourage children to self-regulate in appropriate ways. Some induction strategies serve to provide the child with cues about the behavior that is desired. For example, if a child begins to show disruptive or inattentive behaviors, the educational consultant might praise children in the group who are exhibiting the desired behavior (thus identifying appropriate role models), direct the child's attention to a constructive task to be done (thus eliciting a desirable motivational framework), and praise behaviors that represent a movement toward the desired behavior (thus reinforcing appropriate attempts and increasing the likelihood of continuing attempts).

Other induction strategies serve to provide the child with interpersonal support and feedback. For example, the coach might respond to a child who begins to engage in disruptive behavior by providing supportive physical contact (e.g., an arm around the shoulder or a hand on the knee) to help the child refocus his or her attention. The way in which suggestions are worded can also make a difference in the impact they have on children. Commands that focus on the behavior that the adult wants from the child may trigger oppositional reactions from a child, increasing the need for external control. Alternatively, comments that identify ways in which a particular behavior might be rewarding or beneficial for a particular child are more likely to elicit self-regulation attempts. For example, suppose a group is moving to a table to work on a project and one child refuses to accompany the group. The "command" response might be to tell the child that they must come to the table now or face some sort of consequence. Alternatively, in an inductive approach, the coach sitting at the table with the project and game box might begin to wonder aloud about the project: "I'm really curious to see what sort of game we have for today, aren't you? Squeeze in close. I'll open the box." By talking softly to the children at the table and making a mystery of the task, the coach may stimulate the curiosity of the wayward child and thus draw him or her in. Once the child has moved toward the group, praise can be used to support this self-regulated behavior. Although adults must be careful not to unwittingly reinforce oppositional behavior with attention and support, coaches can make general comments to the group at large that are designed to encourage the wayward child to join the group. For example, the coach might point out the fun and positive interactions that await children who join the group: "That project sure looks neat to me. It looks like the kids at the table are really having fun with it. They'd probably have more fun with another person there. If someone else wanted to join, it looks like he or she could have fun too."

In general, inductive cues are designed to help children identify the ways in which the desired behaviors would lead to positive outcomes for them or help them avoid negative outcomes. For example, if children are resisting a request to join a circle, instead of restating the command or giving a reprimand, the leader might point out "I'm worried that if we don't start our circle we won't have time for the game I brought" or "I'm worried that if you don't listen, you won't know how to play this game." Similarly, if a child were pushing another, the adult might replace a straightforward command (e.g., "You need to keep your hands to yourself") with a statement that informs the child about the interpersonal consequences of the behavior (e.g., "I'm worried that if you are pushing people like that, they are not going to want to sit next to you anymore."). By stating cues as concerns, the adult "stays on the child's side," avoiding a power play and providing the child with information the child can use to make more effective interactional choices.

CONCLUSIONS

This chapter has focused on the three social skill training components used during the early elementary school years in the Fast Track Program to address the social developmental needs of children at risk for conduct disorder. The multilevel structure of intervention includes a universal school-based prevention curriculum for all children in high-risk schools, a focused friendship group program targeting children at particularly high risk, and a peer-pairing program to enhance generalization of intervention gains to peer interactions at school. The content of each social skill training component is based on developmental and clinical research documenting the behavioral, social-cognitive, and affective-motivational deficits and distortions that characterize children with conduct problems. In the implementation of the social skill training groups, a set of strategies have been developed to promote "corrective" peer interactions and support children's internalization of positive social orientations and control beliefs.

From a developmental standpoint, conduct disorder is multiply determined. Effective prevention efforts must be comprehensive in nature and extend over the formative years (Kazdin, 1987). Hence, the social skill training programs described in this chapter are embedded within a larger program that also includes a focus on improving parenting, parent-teacher relationships, and child academic skills. In Chapter 5, the family-focused components of the Fast Track Program at the school entry intervention phase are described.

The Fast Track Program is designed to continue intervention into the later elementary school years when the transition into middle school marks a second important developmental risk point for the escalation of conduct disorders. The structure and focus of the program shift somewhat in these later years to address the developmental issues and additional risk factors for conduct problems that emerge in preadolescence. For example, in fourth grade, social skill training groups are supplemented with a mentor program that is designed to support the preadolescents' development of a positive sense of self and a positive orientation toward recreational activities and prevocational interests that can be shared with nondeviant peers.

One of the long-term goals of the Fast Track Program is to determine the effects of sustained, comprehensive, and integrated prevention activity. It is hoped that by addressing multiple socialization contexts (family and school), focusing on multiple skill domains (social, emotional, and cognitive-academic), and continuing intervention support across the elementary and preadolescent years significant reductions in conduct disorders and significant improvements in adaptive outcomes will be attained.

NOTE

1. Members of the CPPRG (in alphabetical order) are Karen L. Bierman (Pennsylvania State University), John D. Coie (Duke University), Kenneth A. Dodge (Vanderbilt University), Mark T. Greenberg (University of Washington), John E. Lochman (Duke University), and Robert J. McMahon (University of Washington).

REFERENCES

Achenbach, T. M., McConaughy, S. H., & Howell, C. T. (1987). Child/adolescent behavioral and emotional problems: Implications of cross-informant correlations for situational specificity. *Psychological Bulletin, 101,* 213-232.

Asarnow, J. (1983). Children with peer adjustment problems: Sequential and nonsequential analyses of school behaviors. *Journal of Consulting and Clinical Psychology, 51,* 709-717.

Bierman, K. L. (1986). Process of change during social skills training with preadolescents and its relation to treatment outcome. *Child Development, 57,* 230-240.

Bierman, K. L., & Furman, W. (1984). The effects of social skills training and peer involvement on the social adjustment of preadolescents. *Child Development, 55,* 151-162.

Bierman, K. L., Miller, C. M., & Stabb, S. (1987). Improving the social behavior and peer acceptance of rejected boys: Effects of social skill training with instructions and prohibitions. *Journal of Consulting and Clinical Psychology, 55,* 194-200.

Bierman, K. L., Smoot, D. L., & Aumiller, K. A. (1993). Characteristics of aggressive-rejected, aggressive (non-rejected) and rejected (non-aggressive) boys. *Child Development, 64,* 139-151.

Coie, J. D., Dodge, K. A., & Kupersmidt, J. (1990). Peer group behavior and social status. In S. R. Asher & J. D. Coie (Eds.), *Peer rejection in childhood* (pp. 17-59). New York: Cambridge University Press.

Coie, J. D., & Krehbiel, G. K. (1990). Adapting intervention to the problems of aggressive and disruptive rejected children. In S. R. Asher & J. D. Coie (Eds.), *Peer rejection in childhood* (pp. 309-337). New York: Cambridge University Press.

Conduct Problems Prevention Research Group. (1992). A developmental and clinical model for the prevention of conduct disorder: The Fast Track Program. *Development and Psychopathology, 4,* 509-528.

Dodge, K. A., Bates, J. E., & Pettit, G. S. (1990). Mechanisms in the cycle of violence. *Science, 250,* 1678-1683.

Dodge, K. A., Pettit, G. S., McClaskey, C. L., & Brown, M. (1986). Social competence in children. *Monographs of the Society for Research in Child Development, 51*(2, Serial No. 213).

Gottman, J. M. (1983). How children become friends. *Monographs of the Society for Research in Child Development, 48*(3, Serial No. 201).

Greenberg, M. T., & Kusche, C. A. (1993). *Promoting social and emotional development in deaf children: The PATHS Project.* Seattle: University of Washington Press.

Greenberg, M. T., Kusche, C. A., Cook, E. T., & Quamma, J. P. (in press). Promoting emotional competence in school-aged children: The effects of the PATHS Curriculum. *Development and Psychopathology.*

Greenberg, M. T., Kusche, C. A., & Speltz, M. (1991). Emotional regulation, self-control and psychopathology: The role of relationships in early childhood. In D. Cicchetti & S. Toth (Eds.), *Rochester symposium on developmental psychopathology: Internalizing and externalizing expressions of dysfunction* (Vol. 2, pp. 21-56). Hillsdale, NJ: Lawrence Erlbaum.

Greenberg, M. T., Speltz, M. L., & DeKlyen, M. (1993). Toward a conceptual model for understanding the early development of disruptive behavior problems. *Development and Psychopathology, 5,* 191-213.

Hartup, W. W. (1983). Peer relations. In E. M. Hetherington (Ed.), *Socialization, personality and social development* (Handbook of Child Psychology, Vol. 4, pp. 103-196). New York: John Wiley.

Hymel, S., Wagner, E., & Butler, L. J. (1990). Reputational bias: View from the peer group. In S. R. Asher & J. D. Coie (Eds.), *Peer rejection in childhood* (pp. 156-186). Cambridge, UK: Cambridge University Press.

Jacobvitz, D., & Sroufe, L. A. (1987). The early caregiver-child relationship and Attention Deficit Disorder with hyperactivity in kindergarten: A prospective study. *Child Development, 58,* 1488-1495.

Kazdin, A. E. (1987). Treatment of antisocial behavior in children: Current status and future directions. *Psychological Bulletin, 102,* 187-203.

Kellam, S. G., Werthamer-Larsson, L., Dolan, L. J., Brown, C. H., Mayer, L. S., Rebok, G. W., Anthony, J. C., Laudolff, J., Edelsohn, G., & Wheeler, L. (1991). Developmental epidemiology based preventive trials: Baseline modeling of early target behaviors and depressive symptoms. *American Journal of Community Psychology, 19,* 563-584.

Klein, A. R., & Young, R. D. (1979). Hyperactive boys in their classroom: Assessment of teacher and peer perceptions, interactions, and classroom behaviors. *Journal of Abnormal Child Psychology, 7,* 425-442.

Kusche, C. A. (1991, April). *Improving classroom behavior and emotional understanding in special needs children: The effects of the PATHS curriculum.* Paper presented at the Society for Research in Child Development, Seattle, WA.

Kusche, C. A., & Greenberg, M. T. (1994). *The PATHS curriculum.* Seattle, WA: Developmental Research and Programs.

Ladd, G. (1981). Effectiveness of a social learning method for enhancing children's social interaction and peer acceptance. *Child Development, 52,* 171-178.

Ladd, G. W. (1985). Documenting the effects of social skill training with children: Process and outcome assessment. In B. Schneider, K. Rubin, & J. Ledingham (Eds.), *Children's peer relations: Issues in assessment and intervention* (pp. 243-269). New York/Berlin: Springer-Verlag.

Ladd, G. W., & Asher, S. R. (1985). Social skill training and children's peer relations: Current issues in research and practice. In L. L'Abate & M. Milan (Eds.), *Handbook of social skill training* (pp. 219-244). New York: John Wiley.

Lochman, J. E. (1987). Self and peer perceptions and attributional biases of aggressive and nonaggressive boys in dyadic interactions. *Journal of Consulting and Clinical Psychology, 55,* 404-410.

Lochman, J. E., Burch, P. R., Curry, J. F., & Lampron, L. B. (1984). Treatment and generalization effects of cognitive-behavioral and goal-setting interventions with aggressive boys. *Journal of Consulting and Clinical Psychology, 52,* 915-916.

Loeber, R. (1990). Development and risk factors of juvenile antisocial behavior and delinquency. *Clinical Psychology Review, 10,* 1-41.

McMahon, R. J., & Wells, K. C. (1989). Conduct disorders. In E. J. Mash & R. A. Barkley (Eds.), *Treatment of childhood disorders* (pp. 73-134). New York: Guilford.

Moffitt, T. E. (1990). Juvenile delinquency and Attention Deficit Disorder: Boys' developmental trajectories from age 3 to age 15. *Child Development, 61,* 893-910.

Moffitt, T. E., & Silva, P. A. (1988). Self-reported delinquency, neuropsychological deficit, and history of Attention Deficit Disorder. *Journal of Abnormal Child Psychology, 16,* 553-569.

Mrazek, P. J., & Haggerty, R. J. (Eds.). (1994). *Reducing risks for mental disorders: Frontiers for preventive intervention research.* Washington, DC: National Academy Press.

Oden, S., & Asher, S. R. (1977). Coaching children in social skills. *Child Development, 48,* 495-506.

Parker, J. G., & Asher, S. R. (1987). Peer relations and later personal adjustment: Are low-accepted children at risk? *Psychological Bulletin, 102,* 357-389.

Patterson, G. R. (1982). *Coercive family process.* Eugene, OR: Castalia.

Perry, D. G., Perry, L. C., & Rasmussen, P. (1986). Cognitive social learning mediators of aggression. *Child Development, 57,* 700-711.

Richman, N., Stevenson, J., & Graham, P. J. (1982). *Preschool to school: A behavioural study.* London: Academic Press.

Rutter, M., Maughan, B., Mortimore, P., Ouston, J., & Smith, A. (1979). *Fifteen thousand hours: Secondary schools and their effects on children.* Cambridge, MA: Harvard University Press.

Selman, R. L., Schultz, L. H., Nakkula, M., Barr, D., Watts, C., & Richmond, J. B. (1992). Friendship and fighting: A developmental approach to the study of risk and prevention of violence. *Development and Psychopathology, 4,* 529-558.

Strain, P. S., Lambert, D. L., Kerr, M. M., Stagg, V., & Lenkner, D. A. (1983). Naturalistic assessment of children's compliance to teacher's requests and consequences for compliance. *Journal of Applied Behavior Analysis, 16,* 243-249.

Wallach, M. A., & Wallach, L. (1976). *Teaching all children to read.* Chicago: University of Chicago Press.

5

Family-Based Intervention in the Fast Track Program[1]

ROBERT J. McMAHON

NANCY M. SLOUGH

CONDUCT PROBLEMS PREVENTION
RESEARCH GROUP

As noted in Chapter 4 by Bierman, Greenberg, and the Conduct Problems Prevention Research Group (CPPRG), Fast Track is a multisite, collaborative study that is investigating the efficacy of a comprehensive intervention designed to prevent the development of serious conduct problems in young at-risk children. The project is being conducted at four sites in the United

AUTHORS' NOTE: This work was supported by National Institute of Mental Health Grants R18 MH48043, R18 MH50951, R18 MH50952, and R18 MH50953. The Center for Substance Abuse Prevention has also provided support for Fast Track through a memorandum of agreement with the NIMH. This work was also supported in part by Department of Education Grant S184U30002 and NIMH Grants K05MH00797 and K05MH01027. The authors express their appreciation to the following individuals for their invaluable assistance in the development, implementation, and refinement of the family-based components of Fast Track in Grades 1 and 2: the clinical supervisors at each site—Richard Plut, Sheila Peters, and Donna-Marie Winn; the family coordinators, especially Walterine French, Mary Kratz, and Mary Jo

States that represent urban, suburban, and rural communities. Children are identified as being at high risk on the basis of both parent and teacher reports of high levels of disruptive behavior and other conduct problems in kindergarten (Lochman & CPPRG, 1995). The intervention begins in Grade 1 and continues through Grade 6. There are, however, two periods of intensive intervention: the transition to elementary school (first and second grade) and the transition into middle school (fifth and sixth grade). This chapter focuses on the school entry intervention that takes place in Grades 1 and 2. Whereas Chapter 4 described the social skills training and reading tutoring components of the Fast Track intervention, in this chapter we will focus on the family-based components: (a) a parenting skills group, (b) a parent-child relationship enhancement group, and (c) a home-visiting program.

The chapter is organized into three sections: (a) a brief discussion of the conceptual and empirical bases of these components, (b) a description of the content and structure of each of the family-based components, and (c) a discussion of the issues involved in the initial recruitment of families and the maintenance of their involvement in Fast Track.

CONCEPTUAL AND EMPIRICAL BASES
OF THE FAMILY-BASED COMPONENTS

Parenting Behavior

The role of parenting behavior in the development and maintenance of conduct problems, especially during the preschool and early school-age years, has been the focus of much research (for reviews, see Loeber & Stouthamer-Loeber, 1986; Rothbaum & Weisz, 1994). It has been well established that the parents of children with conduct problems demonstrate more critical and commanding behaviors toward their children (i.e., they are more coercive and controlling), have less positive involvement with their children, have more punitive and inconsistent disciplinary practices, and are less effective monitors of their children's behavior (McMahon & Estes, in

Stoddard; and Julie Olsen. We are indebted to Carolyn Webster-Stratton for the use of selected videotaped vignettes from *The Parents and Children Series* parenting skills program and to David Hawkins and Richard Catalano for allowing us to adapt their curriculum materials for some parent group sessions. Correspondence should be addressed to Robert J. McMahon, University of Washington, Department of Psychology, Box 351525, Seattle, WA 98195-1525.

press). Such parenting practices account for greater explanatory variance than do other variables, such as child temperament or socioeconomic status (Loeber & Stouthamer-Loeber, 1986; Olweus, 1980). The magnitude of the association between parenting behavior and child conduct problems has been shown to increase at about the time children begin school (Rothbaum & Weisz, 1994).

Social learning-based parent training programs have been predicated on the assumption that such parenting practices are key factors in the development and maintenance of child conduct problems. Several reviews have documented the efficacy of this approach to intervening with children with conduct problems and their families, especially during the preschool and early school-age years (e.g., McMahon & Wells, 1989; Miller & Prinz, 1990; Patterson, Dishion, & Chamberlain, 1993). Family-based interventions that occur with children of this age can be viewed as preventative in nature in that they attempt not only to alleviate current child conduct problems but also to decrease the likelihood that children will develop the more serious conduct problems that are characteristic of later stages in the "early starter" progression of conduct problems (McMahon, 1994; Reid, 1993). Although the evidence for both immediate and longer-term effects of family-based intervention has been encouraging, this approach to intervention has been less successful with families that present with multiple concomitant problems (see below) (Miller & Prinz, 1990).

Family-School Partnership

Once children start school, risk factors over and above those related to the family begin to play an important role in the maintenance of conduct problems (CPPRG, 1992a; Reid, 1993). These factors include the child's own academic readiness and abilities, the child's interactions with teachers and peers, and the context of the school itself. A primary basis for difficulties in the acquisition of basic academic skills (especially reading) appears to be coexisting attentional problems (i.e., Attention-Deficit Hyperactivity Disorder) (Hinshaw, 1992). In addition, parents of children with conduct problems may be less likely to provide adequate amounts of cognitive stimulation and support for academic performance and good behavior in school, which can contribute to low levels of academic readiness at school entry and academic and social difficulties during the school years (Comer, 1980; Rutter & Giller, 1983). There has been an increased recognition of the potential value of incorporating material into social learning-based parent training programs that address the academic needs of school-aged children with conduct problems (CPPRG, 1992a; Reid, 1993). A key factor in children's success in school has been shown to be active, positive parental involvement in the child's education, both with respect to fostering cognitive development and by fostering academic socialization (i.e., the attitudes and motives that are essential for learning at school) (Bempechat, 1990). Parental involvement can be manifested by parental behavior (e.g., attending open houses or participating in a parent-teacher conference), by personal involvement (i.e., the child's affective sense that the parent cares about and enjoys dealing with the child's school and learning-related activities), and by cognitive-intellectual involvement (e.g., providing learning materials or reading to the child) (Grolnick & Slowiaczek, 1994). Research has documented a number of potential benefits of parental involvement in family-school partnerships (Greenwood & Hickman, 1991). For the child, these include higher attendance, academic achievement, and self-esteem; more positive perceptions of the classroom and the school climate; increased readiness to do homework; improved behavior in the classroom; more academically related time with parents; and higher educational aspirations. For the parent, benefits include increased satisfaction with teachers, more positive attitudes toward the school, and higher educational aspirations.

"Multiproblem" Aspect of Families

Not only do parents of conduct-problem children engage in less effective parenting behaviors, they are also at risk for increased levels of personal (e.g., depression, anxiety, or antisocial personality) and interparental (marital conflict and violence or single-parent status) distress (McMahon & Estes, in press; Webster-Stratton, 1990). They also seem to experience higher frequencies of stressful events both of a minor and of a more significant nature, such as unemployment or poverty (Patterson, 1983; Webster-Stratton, 1990). Many parents of conduct-problem children tend to be quite isolated from friends, neighbors, and the community. Wahler (Wahler, 1980; Wahler & Dumas, 1984) has labeled this pattern as "insularity." Wahler and colleagues have documented maternal perceptions of high levels of coercive interactions between these parents and other relatives and helping agency representatives as well as perceptions of low levels of positive interactions with friends.

These various forms of stress and distress affecting parents often co-occur, further increasing the likelihood of disrupted parenting practices (Sanders & Markie-Dadds, 1992). For example, a single parent who has just lost his or her job, is moderately depressed, and who perceives himself or herself as socially isolated is likely at significant risk for being less able to engage in effective parenting practices with his or her children. These same stressors have also been shown to be related to premature termination (i.e., dropout) from parent training programs (Kazdin, 1990; McMahon, Forehand, Griest, & Wells, 1981) as well as less improvement in treatment and failure to maintain gains once treatment has ended (e.g., Dadds, Schwartz, & Sanders, 1987; Dumas & Wahler, 1983).

Summary

There are a number of implications of the preceding discussion for preventively oriented, family-based interventions. First, it is paramount that parents of children with conduct problems acquire more positive and less punitive discipline strategies and apply them in a more consistent manner. Second, because of the multiple risk factors operating in multiple settings once the child begins school, family-based interventions must focus not only on parental discipline strategies but also on ways to foster the children's social-cognitive development and academic achievement (CPPRG, 1992a; Reid, 1993). Thus, family-based interventions should focus on the development of a positive family-school partnership in which parents become active participants in their children's education by learning how to provide support for their children's cognitive development and academic socialization. Third, many children with conduct problems reside in families that are characterized by high levels of stress and disorganization. It is essential that interventions address these personal, interpersonal, and extrafamilial stressors if significant parental participation in the intervention and maintenance of effects are to occur (Dunst, Trivette, & Deal, 1989; Miller & Prinz, 1990).

DESCRIPTION OF COMPONENTS

Parent Group

Content. The overarching goal of the family-based components of Fast Track is to help parents help their children succeed in school. This goal is defined quite broadly to include academic success as well as success in personal and social contexts. The breadth of these goals is exemplified in the learning challenges for the children that are the focus of the various parent group sessions. The learning challenges for Grades 1 and 2 are learning to read (Grade 1 only), learning to follow rules, learning to get along with others, learning to feel good about themselves, and learning to be more self-reliant (Grade 2 only).

There are four primary content areas in the parent group that focus on the development of (a) a positive family-school relationship, (b) parental self-control, (c) reasonable and developmentally appropriate expectations for the child's behavior, and (d) parenting skills to increase positive parent-child interaction and to decrease the occurrence of acting-out behaviors.

Because of the primary importance of children getting off to a good start in school, much of the material concerning the development of a positive family-school relationship is placed in the first half of the academic year. In addition, we hypothesized that this overt focus on school-related goals and activities early on in the program might facilitate parental involvement in, and commitment to, Fast Track, and that we would be less likely to encounter resistance when the focus of the parent group sessions shifted to behavior management skills later in the year. The focus of this part of the curriculum is to increase parental involvement in and encouragement of the child's learning both at home and at school, increase regular parental communication with the child about school, and establish positive communication and relationships between the parents and their children's teachers. Topics addressed in these sessions include how to talk with children about school, engaging in regular parent-child reading sessions (during Fast Track activities and at home), setting up a system of regular communication between the teacher and parent concerning the child's performance at school (we often use a daily school-home notebook), encouraging learning-related behaviors at home, and learning appropriate ways to assist children with homework assignments. Various in-session and home practice activities are included to increase the parents' familiarity and comfort in interacting with their children's teachers and with school-related activities, such as helping their children with homework assignments.

Teachers attend portions of the parent group sessions three or four times each year. During these visits, they talk with the parents about their classroom routines, preferred methods of school-home communication, and the academic skills that the children will be covering during that part of the academic year. Parents are given the opportunity to share general information about their children with the teacher through the use of a worksheet that includes items such as "My child likes books about . . . " and "One positive thing about my child that you may not know is. . . ." Shortly after these initial teacher visits to the parent group, each parent also makes a brief observational visit to his or her child's classroom accompanied by a Fast Track staff member. For many parents, this is the first time that they have entered a school building since their own schooling. At the end of the school year, teachers attend part of a celebration session with the children and families.

Prior to focusing on parenting skills related to discipline, parents learn how to (a) maintain their self-control when faced with frustrating child behavior, and (b) develop expectations for their children's behavior that are reasonable and appropriate for their children's developmental level. These skills are viewed as necessary prerequisites to the learning and mastery of various parenting skills to facilitate positive parent-child interactions and to decrease inappropriate child behaviors. If a parent is angry to the point of losing control or has unrealistic expectations concerning the child's behavior, then the probability of an inappropriate parent response is increased. Parents first learn to identify the behavioral, cognitive, and affective cues that indicate that they are becoming angry through the use of an anger thermometer. We use a three-step anger management strategy that is adapted from one developed by Hawkins et al. (1988). Parents are taught to interrupt themselves ("Stop—identify your feelings"), reduce their anger using any of a variety of anger control strategies (e.g., taking a deep breath or counting silently to 10), and then reward themselves for staying in control.

Material concerning the development of reasonable and developmentally appropriate expectations for child behavior was developed and incorporated into the curriculum when we discovered that many of our parents had quite unrealistic expectations for what their first or second grader could reasonably be expected to do (Kendziora & O'Leary, 1992). For example, one parent was quite frustrated and angry that her 7-year-old child had difficulty getting himself up in the morning, preparing his own breakFast, and then getting to the school bus on time by himself. Separate sessions in first and second grade are devoted to a discussion of the physical, social, behavioral, and cognitive capabilities of children in that age range. Although the extensive range of individual differences within these age groups is acknowledged, the purpose of these sessions is to provide parents with a developmentally appropriate context for viewing their children's behavior.

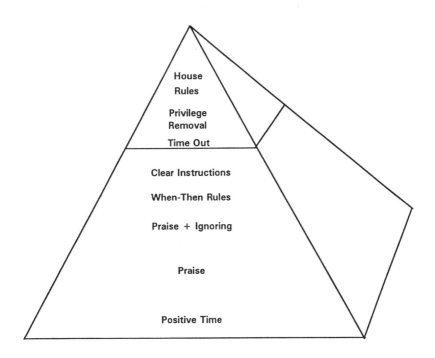

Figure 5.1. The Discipline Pyramid

The majority of parent group sessions in Grades 1 and 2 are concerned with the teaching of parenting skills to enhance positive parent-child interaction and to decrease the occurrence of conduct-problem behaviors. The skills are ones that are commonly taught in social learning-based parent training programs (Miller & Prinz, 1990). The skills taught in the Fast Track parent group, however, are most closely derived from the well-validated program presented in Forehand and McMahon (1981), with additional material drawn from the group-based program developed by Webster-Stratton (1987). The skills are taught in a hierarchical manner using the Discipline Pyramid depicted in Figure 5.1. The skills are arranged into two clusters: those that are designed to increase positive, appropriate behaviors and those that are designed to decrease inappropriate child behaviors. As can be seen in Figure 5.1, the former cluster occupies a large area at the base of the pyramid and is viewed as the foundation of good parenting skills. As such, these skills are intended to receive the most frequent use. Parents are first

TABLE 5.1   The Problem-Solving Approach

Calm down
  Use the Anger Control Technique if necessary

Define the problem
  "What is the problem?"

What are my expectations?
  "What is the positive behavior that I want my child to do?"
  ("Is this realistic?")

Select strategy from the Discipline Pyramid
  "What should I do?"
    —Right now?
    —In the longer term?

---

taught a variety of methods for spending positive time with children (such as instruction in appropriate play behaviors) and the Child's Game, which is a form of child-directed play that is an integral part of many social learning-based parent training programs (Forehand & McMahon, 1981). Parents then learn strategies such as praise, differential attention (praise plus ignoring), when-then rules ("When you finish your homework, then you can watch TV."), and clear instructions. The second cluster of parenting skills contains fewer skills and occupies a smaller area of the Discipline Pyramid, consistent with the idea that these strategies work best when they are used relatively infrequently. The skills that are taught here include a time-out procedure based on that employed by Forehand and McMahon (1981), privilege removal, and the use of house rules (e.g., "You are not allowed to hit. If you do, you will go immediately to time-out.")

The skills on the Discipline Pyramid are taught in a hierarchical manner beginning with the skills in the bottom part of the pyramid. By the end of Grade 1, parents have been exposed to most of the skills on the pyramid. A major focus of the parent group sessions in Grade 2 is teaching the parents a protocol for selecting the most appropriate strategies from the Discipline Pyramid when they are faced with a child-rearing issue. This protocol, which is referred to as the problem-solving approach, consists of four steps (see Table 5.1). The parent first maintains or regains self-control using the anger control technique described previously. The parent then defines the problem and recasts it in terms of a preferred alternative positive child behavior that is developmentally appropriate and realistic. Only then does the parent select an appropriate strategy or strategies from the Discipline Pyramid, using the most positive action needed to get the desired child behavior. Parents are also taught to make the distinction between dealing with a particular conflict situation or inappropriate behavior that is occurring at that moment and taking steps to deal with that same situation in a more proactive manner in the future.

Structure. A typical parent group is composed of 5 to 7 parents, although at any given session there may be as few as 2 or 3 or as many as 9 or 10 parents. The primary parenting figures in the children's lives are targeted for participation in the parent group. In most cases, that is the biological mother with or without participation by her partner (e.g., the child's father or stepfather or the mother's boyfriend). Because of a myriad of caretaking arrangements in our Fast Track families, however, we have active and ongoing participation from stepparents, grandparents, aunts, uncles, and even teenage and adult-age siblings.

The parent group sessions are conducted by a family coordinator and, in most cases, a coleader. (See CPPRG, 1992a, for a description of Fast Track staffing.) The coleader assists the family coordinator in running the group, especially by serving as a role-play partner and by providing feedback to parents during various exercises.

The number and length of parent group sessions varies in first and second grade. In first grade, there are 22 sessions, each of which is 60 minutes in duration. In second grade, there are 14 sessions, each of which lasts 90 minutes. The first-grade sessions are held on a weekly basis throughout the school year, whereas the second-grade sessions are held biweekly. Sessions typically begin a few weeks after the start of the school year (i.e., early to mid-September) and are finished around the middle of April. Parent group sessions are embedded within 2-hour "enrichment program" sessions that also include parent-child sharing time (see below), the children's friendship group, and, in Grade 1, 30-minute reading tutoring sessions (see Chapter 4, this volume). In the summer, there are monthly meetings with parents and children that are social in nature and that do not involve formal curricula.

A typical parent group session begins with a brief informal social time. The first task at the beginning of the parent group is usually a review of the home practice exercise that was assigned at the conclusion of the previous session. The bulk of the session is concerned with presentation of the new topic. Family coordinators employ a wide variety of teaching methods during the parent group. These include some didactic presentation of material, group discussion and exercises, posters and handouts, and demonstration of various skills either through role plays presented by the family coordinator and her (all family coordinators are female) coleader or through videotaped vignettes of parent-child interaction. With respect to the latter, we have employed selected vignettes from *The Parents and Children Series* (Webster-Stratton, 1987) to illustrate various teaching points. After the skill has been demonstrated, then parents are given role-play tasks and exercises to give them firsthand experience with the procedure. They often receive more direct supervised practice with their own children in the parent-child sharing time session that immediately follows the parent group (see below). At the end of the session, there is a brief closing section in which the home-practice exercise is assigned, the nature of the upcoming parent-child sharing time is briefly described, and an overview of the next parent group session is presented.

Parent-Child Sharing Time

Content. At the conclusion of each parent group, the parents and children meet together for parent-child sharing time. There are two goals of this component of Fast Track. The primary goal is to foster positive parent-child relationships through the promotion of positive, cooperative verbal behavior and nonverbal interchanges between parents and children. As noted previously, parent-child relationships in families with conduct-problem children are often characterized by coercive, highly unpleasant interactions. To interrupt this negative pattern and to provide an alternative, families participate in a variety of cooperative activities, games, and crafts; they also participate in joint reading activities. With respect to the former, examples include the regular use of a reciprocal complimenting exercise between parents and children, parental implementation of the Child's Game, and games designed to enhance the children's self-esteem. The activities and games that occur during parent-child sharing time often have direct ties to social skills that the children have been learning in the Promoting Alternative Thinking Strategies (PATHS) Curriculum and the friendship group (see Chapter 4, this volume), providing one method for increasing cross-setting generalization. They also provide an opportunity to expose the parents to the social skills that the children have been learning in the other components of Fast Track. For example, there are activities designed to facilitate children's identification and expression of feelings; other activities focus on the use of social problem-solving skills.

There is also a heavy emphasis on joint reading activities during parent-child sharing time. The family coordinator usually begins the session by gathering the children and parents around her while she reads a short book. The theme of the story typically relates to one that the children have been working on in PATHS or friendship group. Each child sits with his or her parent on the floor while the story is being read, thus providing another opportunity for close positive physical contact between parents and children. It is hypothesized that this exposure to enjoyable yet meaningful children's literature will not only foster the children's interest in reading but that it will also encourage parents to engage in similar reading activities with their children at home (and thus complement the more formal reading tutoring component of the Fast Track intervention). Children and parents have access to appropriate reading material through a small collection of books that each family coordinator has available for brief loan to the families.

The second goal of parent-child sharing time is to provide an opportunity for parents to practice the new skills that they learned in the parent group with their children with appropriate support and supervision from Fast Track staff members. It also provides the children with the opportunity to learn the new strategies that their parents will be using with them at home. Examples include the use of the Child's Game (mentioned earlier), differential attention, when-then rules, clear instructions, and time-out.

Structure. Each parent-child sharing time session occurs immediately after the conclusion of the parent group and children's friendship group and lasts 30 minutes. A typical session would begin with the family co-ordinator (or coleader) reading a book to the children and parents. At the conclusion of the story, a complimenting exercise would be conducted in which each child gives his or her parent a compliment concerning something that the parent has said or done over the past day or two. The parents then reciprocate by complimenting their children. Finally, parent-child dyads would engage in an activity designed to facilitate the generalization of skills either that the children have been learning in PATHS or friendship group or that the parents have been learning in the parent group. The coleader assists the family coordinator in conducting this activity and by providing feedback to parents and children.

Home Visiting

Content. The home-visiting component of Fast Track is intended to serve a variety of functions. First, it provides an opportunity for the family coordinator to familiarize herself with the entire family system (as well as various support systems) as an important step toward the development of a positive relationship with the family. Many of these families have had negative experiences with helping professionals in the past, and we have found that it often may take several months to a year or longer to establish a mutual relationship based on trust. Second, the home visits provide an opportunity to promote the generalization of newly acquired parenting skills to the home. The family coordinator can review material from the parent group or go over material from a missed session, provide supervised practice of skills in the home setting, and assist in the individualization of material from the parent group to the family's needs. Third, the home visits can promote effective parental support for the child's school adjustment through the encouragement and support of parent-child reading activities, parental monitoring and assistance with the child's homework assignments, and discussion regarding effective parent-teacher communication and teamwork to assist the child in meeting his or her academic and social goals.

The fourth goal of the home-visiting component is to promote parent problem solving, coping, and goal setting as means of dealing with the myriad of stressful life events (e.g., marital conflict, substance abuse, social isolation, and housing and employment issues) that these families often experience (McMahon & Estes, in press; Sanders & Markie-Dadds, 1992). We employ a problem-solving approach to dealing with such issues developed by Wasik and colleagues (Wasik, Bryant, & Lyons, 1990) in home visiting with economically disadvantaged families. The family coordinator works with the parent to identify family or life situation stressors that may be impeding effective parenting and to generate alternative solutions to deal with those stressors. Increasing the parent's knowledge and utilization of available community resources is viewed as one way in which the parent may become more self-sufficient and successful in dealing with these stressors. The ultimate goals of this problem-solving approach are to foster parental feelings of empowerment and self-efficacy (Dunst et al., 1989) and to decrease the risk of fostering dependency on Fast Track staff (a risk that seems inherent if the staff were to assume responsibility for those decisions). This empowerment process is one that must necessarily unfold over time as the parent becomes progressively more competent in dealing with these situations. We view the role of the family coordinator during these home visits as one that should change over time: " 'doing for,' then 'doing with,' and finally, 'cheering on' " (Wasik et al., 1990, p. 68).

Structure. The frequency of home visits is highest in Grade 1. During the first year of the program, family coordinators make biweekly home visits and weekly phone contact with each family. In Grade 2, home visits are expected to occur somewhat less frequently, with phone contacts still occurring on a weekly basis. These are average expectations; the actual frequency of contact varies tremendously within and across families over time depending on the type and severity of issues facing families. The typical caseload for an individual family coordinator ranges from 15 to 20 families.

RECRUITMENT OF FAMILIES AND MAINTENANCE OF INVOLVEMENT

Multiproblem families, especially those with conduct-problem children, are notoriously difficult to involve in family-based interventions (Kumpfer, 1991; Sanders & Markie-Dadds, 1992; and Chapter 8, this volume). Furthermore, approximately 30% of families that begin intervention have been shown to drop out prior to the completion of treatment in published studies of parent training interventions (Forehand, Middlebrook, Rogers, & Steffe, 1983). Kumpfer noted a number of common barriers to parental involvement that can be factors in recruitment and attrition issues. These include costs, transportation, child care, time, lack of knowledge about or interest in parent training, lack of program ownership, cultural differences between providers and parents, and fear or distrust of social service agencies.

Given that the family-based components of Fast Track are much broader, more intensive, and last for significantly longer periods of time than the typical 8- to 12-session course of parent training, we were especially concerned about the initial recruitment of our families and maintenance of their involvement in the program. The fact that these families typically had multiple problems, were not self-referred, and would be provided with a preventive intervention rather than treatment per se further increased our concerns about recruitment and maintenance.

Recruitment

We have attempted a sustained effort to encourage involvement with every family. This has led to the development of very active outreach efforts. Recruitment of families into the Fast Track intervention is typically initiated by the family coordinators a week or so prior to the start of first grade. Prior to this recruitment contact, families have had two significant contacts with Fast Track research staff: a brief telephone interview in which they completed a behavior problem checklist concerning their child and a 2.5- to 3-hour home visit consisting of separate parent and child interviews and a 30-minute observation of parent-child interaction. Because these assessments were presented in the context of the longitudinal, developmental aspects of the project (see CPPRG, 1992a), there was no mention of any intervention-related activities. In the initial recruitment contact, the family coordinator tells the parent that a program designed to help children get off to a good start in first grade is in place at the child's school. The family coordinator then states that, given the parent's concerns about the child's behavior at the phone interview and the home visit and the concerns of the child's kindergarten teacher, it seems that this program might be appropriate for this child. The program is described to the parent, and he or she is invited to attend an informal information meeting about Fast Track at the child's school. This meeting is attended by the principal, first-grade teachers, and Fast Track staff who work with children attending that school. Some current Fast Track parents also attend the meeting. The meeting is intended not only to inform potential participants about Fast Track but also to provide an initial demonstration of the close working relationship between Fast Track staff and school personnel and to give parents a sense of the long-term commitment that school and Fast Track staff bring to the project.

One of the more innovative strategies that we have adopted to facilitate involvement in Fast Track and parental participation in the enrichment program is to hire parents as paid staff members. The rationale is that parents know their children better than either the teachers or Fast Track staff and, by virtue of their role as parents, are in an optimal position to be primary agents of change. In addition, our goal is to develop a partnership with these parents, many of whom might never participate in more traditional treatment-oriented mental health services. Hiring them as staff members is a concrete manifestation of our commitment to such a partnership. Participation in the activities in the parent group and parent-child sharing time is viewed as a form of in-service training for these parents. Each family is paid $15 (i.e., $7.50 per hour) for each enrichment program session that they attend.

Although most parents agree from the initial invitation to participate and become involved immediately, some parents are quite wary of us initially, whereas others are reluctant to see that their children are having behavioral difficulties. Given our preventive focus, the fact that these are not referred clients, and because we do not want to turn off a family by coming on too strongly, families begin to attend the program at different time frames and with differing levels of initial participation. For example, some parents gave consent for their children to participate in Fast Track, but they declined initially to become involved in the family-based components. In both situations, Fast Track staff recontact the families a few weeks after school has started to see whether they would like to change their decision. In some cases, behavioral difficulties encountered by the child during the first few weeks of school provide the impetus for the families to become involved in the Fast Track intervention. Further contacts with eligible but nonparticipating families are made throughout the school year.

Maintenance of Family Involvement

Once parents have agreed to participate, a number of strategies have been developed to facilitate participation and involvement in the family-based intervention components of Fast Track. The enrichment program sessions are held in a location that is both nearby and familiar to the parents—the child's school. The sessions are scheduled at times that are convenient for most parents. Most sessions are scheduled for Saturday mornings or afternoons, but there are a number of groups that meet on weekday evenings or on afternoons after school. Transportation to and from the sessions is provided for families that request it.

A potential obstacle to attendance at the parent group sessions is the parents' need to provide care for other children in the family who are not direct participants in Fast Track. To counter that issue, we provide a sibling care program that is concurrent with the 2-hour enrichment program session. This program is typically held in the school gymnasium and is supervised by paid hourly and volunteer staff. There are a variety of games and activities for the children as well as ample opportunities for free play.

As noted previously, parents are hired as staff members and paid for their attendance at enrichment program sessions. This financial incentive has proven to be a powerful motivator for many families, especially at the initial stages of their involvement in Fast Track. Although the financial incentive continues to be important for some families, our sense is that other factors that are more integral to the intervention itself come into play and become increasingly important as the family becomes more comfortable with the intervention and the Fast Track staff and begins to experience some success.

One way in which we have attempted to enhance the comfort level of the parents has been our attempt to match the ethnicity of our staff with that of our families to as great an extent as possible. For example, a parent group that is composed primarily of African American parents will in most cases be led by a family coordinator who is also African American. We believe that such matching leads to increased feelings of comfort with a concomitantly greater willingness to participate actively in the parent group and an increased receptivity to suggestions by the family coordinator. Preliminary analyses suggest that this may indeed be the case (Orrell, Pinderhughes, & Valente, 1995).

Another factor that appears to exert an increasing influence over time is the social support that develops among group members. As noted previously, many of these parents can be characterized as insular and as having low levels of social support. As such, the social interactions with other parents that occur during the enrichment program become very reinforcing for these parents. It has been very gratifying to see the development of positive affiliations develop among group members over time. Many individual group members see each other socially, and there have been multiple examples of spontaneous help giving from one parent to another concerning issues of personal support, child care, transportation, and so on.

Preliminary Evidence

These efforts to enhance recruitment and participation in the family-based components of the Fast Track intervention have led to significant success. For example, in our first cohort, 94% of the families participated regularly in Fast Track during the first grade (CPPRG, 1993). Parents attended, on average, 15.2 (69.1%) of the 22 parent group and parent-child sharing time sessions. Family coordinators completed an average of 11.9 home visits to each family over the 22-week intervention period (at least 11 were recommended) and made an average of 21.1 telephone contacts per family (at least

11 were recommended). Thus, parents averaged a total of 48.2 contacts with intervention staff during Grade 1.

There was a highly skewed distribution of participation in the parent group. Six percent ($n = 10$) of the parents attended three or fewer sessions, whereas the remaining parents attended, on average, 73% of the sessions. Nonparticipation and absences by parents were related to school transfers (although participation was encouraged even after school departures), parental employment, family crises, and parent resistance. Families who did not attend a particular enrichment program session still had contact with individual staff members through home visits and phone calls in the hope of decreasing the likelihood that parents might miss upcoming sessions because they had fallen behind. The 10 parents who did not regularly attend the parent group still received substantial contact with intervention staff, receiving an average of 9.2 home visits and 11.5 telephone contacts from family coordinators. The generally high level of participation by our families is very exciting because principals, teachers, and others had warned us that it would be nearly impossible to get many of these parents involved or to have them stay involved. Furthermore, parental ratings of the individual components of the intervention obtained at the end of the first year indicated general satisfaction with the services provided by the intervention, including the family-based components (CPPRG, 1992b). In addition, 93% of the parents reported the support provided by Fast Track staff to be of "much help."

CONCLUSIONS

In summary, this chapter has focused on the three family-based components in the Fast Track Program as they are implemented during the transition to elementary school phase of the intervention (i.e., Grades 1 and 2). These interventions are a parent group, a parent-child interaction enhancement component (parent-child sharing time), and a home-visiting component. These family-based components are closely integrated with each other as well as with the other Fast Track intervention components. A series of strategies have been developed and implemented to facilitate the recruitment of families into the intervention and to maintain their involvement.

It is essential that the Fast Track intervention reflect the changing nature of conduct problems and their associated risk factors as the children move through elementary school and prepare for the transition into middle school (CPPRG, 1992a; Sanders & Markie-Dadds, 1992). This has implications for both the content and the structure of the family-based intervention components. There will be decreased emphasis on parenting strategies, such as differential attention and time-out, and an increased emphasis on strategies such as parental monitoring, communication and problem-solving skills, and negotiation and contracting. Significant developmental issues, such as sexual behavior, exposure to alcohol and other drugs, and the increased salience of the peer group, will be the focus of parent group discussions as well as serve as the context for implementation of the parenting skills described previously. There will be additional sessions that focus specifically on issues related to the transition to middle school. These sessions will be held in the semesters just prior to, and immediately after, the transition. Attendance of the children at some of the parent group sessions in the later years is also being considered.

In conclusion, it is hypothesized that the family-based components of Fast Track will serve as prime focal points for the instigation of adaptive change in the children with a concomitant decrease in conduct-problem behaviors and a decreased probability of continued progression to more serious conduct problems. Our experience to date has been that treating parents with respect, involving them as partners in dealing with their children's conduct-problem behavior and family-related stressors, using developmentally appropriate curricula, and providing them with the opportunity for a variety of successful experiences interacting with their children have resulted in very high levels of participation, involvement, and satisfaction. Our hope is that this, in conjunction with the other components of the Fast Track intervention, will lead to meaningful and long-term improvements in the lives of these children and their families.

NOTE

1. Members of the CPPRG (in alphabetical order) are Karen L. Bierman (Pennsylvania State University), John D. Coie (Duke University), Kenneth A. Dodge (Vanderbilt University), Mark T. Greenberg (University of Washington), John E. Lochman (Duke University), and Robert J. McMahon (University of Washington). Nancy Slough is based at the University of Washington.

REFERENCES

Bempechat, J. (1990). *The role of parental involvement in children's academic achievement: A review of the literature.* New York: ERIC Clearinghouse on Urban Education.

Comer, J. P. (1980). *School power.* New York: Free Press.

Conduct Problems Prevention Research Group. (1992a). A developmental and clinical model for the prevention of conduct disorders: The FAST Track program. *Development and Psychopathology, 4,* 509-527.

Conduct Problems Prevention Research Group. (1992b). *Multisite prevention of conduct disorders.* Grant proposal submitted to the National Institute of Mental Health.

Conduct Problems Prevention Research Group. (1993). Effects of intervention on children at high risk for conduct problems. In J. D. Coie (Chair), *A multisystem approach to preventing conduct problems.* Symposium conducted at the meeting of the Society for Research in Child Development, New Orleans, LA.

Dadds, M. R., Schwartz, S., & Sanders, M. R. (1987). Marital discord and treatment outcome in behavioral treatment of child conduct disorders. *Journal of Consulting and Clinical Psychology, 55,* 396-403.

Dumas, J. E., & Wahler, R. G. (1983). Predictors of treatment outcome in parent training: Mother insularity and socioeconomic disadvantage. *Behavioral Assessment, 5,* 301-313.

Dunst, C. J., Trivette, C. M., & Deal, A. (1989). *Enabling and empowering families: Principles and guidelines for practice.* Cambridge, MA: Brookline.

Forehand, R., & McMahon, R. J. (1981). *Helping the noncompliant child: A clinician's guide to parent training.* New York: Guilford.

Forehand, R., Middlebrook, J., Rogers, T., & Steffe, M. (1983). Dropping out of parent training. *Behaviour Research and Therapy, 21,* 663-668.

Greenwood, G. E., & Hickman, C. W. (1991). Research and practice in parent involvement: Implications for teacher education. *Elementary School Journal, 91,* 279-287.

Grolnick, W. S., & Slowiaczek, M. L. (1994). Parents' involvement in children's schooling: A multidimensional conceptualization and motivational model. *Child Development, 65,* 237-252.

Hawkins, J. D., Catalano, R. F., Brown, E. O., Vadasy, P. F., Roberts, C., Fitzmahan, D., Starkman, N., & Ransdell, M. (1988). *Preparing for the drug (free) years: A family activity book.* Seattle, WA: Comprehensive Health Education Foundation.

Hinshaw, S. P. (1992). Externalizing behavior problems and academic underachievement in childhood and adolescence: Causal relationships and underlying mechanisms. *Psychological Bulletin, 111,* 127-155.

Kazdin, A. E. (1990). Premature termination from treatment among children referred for antisocial behavior. *Journal of Child Psychology and Psychiatry, 31,* 415-425.

Kendziora, K. T., & O'Leary, S. G. (1992). Dysfunctional parenting as a focus for prevention and treatment of child behavior problems. In T. H. Ollendick & R. J. Prinz (Eds.), *Advances in clinical child psychology* (Vol. 15, pp. 175-206). New York: Plenum.

Kumpfer, K. L. (1991). How to get hard-to-reach parents involved in parenting programs. In U.S. Department of Health and Human Services (Ed.), *Parent training is prevention: Preventing alcohol and other drug problems among youth in the family* (DHHS Publication No. ADM 91-1715, pp. 87-95). Washington, DC: Government Printing Office.

Lochman, J. E., & Conduct Problems Prevention Research Group. (1995). Screening of child behavior problems for prevention programs at school entry. *Journal of Consulting and Clinical Psychology, 63,* 549-559.

Loeber, R., & Stouthamer-Loeber, M. (1986). Family factors as correlates and predictors of juvenile conduct problems and delinquency. In M. Tonry & N. Morris (Eds.), *Crime and justice* (Vol. 7, pp. 29-149). Chicago: University of Chicago Press.

McMahon, R. J. (1994). Diagnosis, assessment, and treatment of externalizing problems in children: The role of longitudinal data. *Journal of Consulting and Clinical Psychology, 62,* 901-917.

McMahon, R. J., & Estes, A. K. (in press). Conduct disorders. In E. J. Mash & L. G. Terdal (Eds.), *Behavioral assessment of childhood disorders* (3rd ed.). New York: Guilford.

McMahon, R. J., Forehand, R., Griest, D., & Wells, K. (1981). Who drops out of therapy during parent behavioral training? *Behavioral Counseling Quarterly, 1,* 79-85.

McMahon, R. J., & Wells, K. C. (1989). Conduct disorders. In E. J. Mash & R. A. Barkley (Eds.), *Treatment of childhood disorders* (pp. 73-132). New York: Guilford.

Miller, G. E., & Prinz, R. J. (1990). Enhancement of social learning family interventions for childhood conduct disorder. *Psychological Bulletin, 108,* 291-307.

Olweus, D. (1980). Familial and temperamental determinants of aggressive behavior in adolescent boys: A causal analysis. *Developmental Psychology, 16,* 644-660.

Orrell, J. K., Pinderhughes, E. E., & Valente, E. (1995, March). *Parent participation in intervention with children at risk for conduct disorder: Service provider influences.* Paper presented at the meeting of the Society for Research in Child Development, Indianapolis, IN.

Patterson, G. R. (1983). Stress: A change agent for family process. In N. Garmezy & M. Rutter (Eds.), *Stress, coping, and development in children* (pp. 235-262). New York: McGraw-Hill.

Patterson, G. R., Dishion, T. J., & Chamberlain, P. (1993). Outcomes and methodological issues relating to treatment of antisocial children. In T. R. Giles (Ed.), *Handbook of effective psychotherapy* (pp. 43-88). New York: Plenum.

Reid, J. B. (1993). Prevention of conduct disorder before and after school entry: Relating interventions to developmental findings. *Development and Psychopathology, 5,* 243-262.

Rothbaum, F., & Weisz, J. R. (1994). Parental caregiving and child externalizing behavior in nonclinical samples: A meta-analysis. *Psychological Bulletin, 116,* 55-74.

Rutter, M., & Giller, H. (1983). *Juvenile delinquency: Trends and perspectives.* New York: Penguin.

Sanders, M. R., & Markie-Dadds, C. (1992). Toward a technology of prevention of disruptive behaviour disorders: The role of behavioural family intervention. *Behaviour Change, 9,* 186-200.

Wahler, R. G. (1980). The insular mother: Her problems in parent-child treatment. *Journal of Applied Behavior Analysis, 13,* 207-219.

Wahler, R. G., & Dumas, J. E. (1984). Changing the observational coding styles of insular and noninsular mothers: A step toward maintenance of parent training effects. In R. F. Dangel & R. A. Polster (Eds.), *Parent training: Foundations of research and practice* (pp. 379-416). New York: Guilford.

Wasik, B. H., Bryant, D. M., & Lyons, C. M. (1990). *Home visiting procedures for helping families.* Newbury Park, CA: Sage.

Webster-Stratton, C. (1987). *The parents and children series.* Eugene, OR: Castalia.

Webster-Stratton, C. (1990). Stress: A potential disruptor of parent perceptions and family interactions. *Journal of Clinical Child Psychology, 19,* 302-312.

6

A Social-Cognitive Intervention
With Aggressive Children

PREVENTION EFFECTS AND
CONTEXTUAL IMPLEMENTATION ISSUES

JOHN E. LOCHMAN

KAREN C. WELLS

I n this chapter, we will explore the role that childhood aggressive behavior plays with negative adolescent outcomes. To interrupt this negative developmental trajectory, a social-cognitive intervention program and its conceptual basis are presented. The structure and effects of the Anger Coping Program and the current Coping Power Program are presented. Finally, we will examine contextual problems that impair implementation of these programs and discuss methods of enhancing the involvement of teachers, peers, and parents.

AUTHORS' NOTE: We acknowledge the support of Grant DA 08453 from the National Institute of Drug Abuse in the preparation of this chapter. Correspondence should be addressed to John E. Lochman, Box 2917, Department of Psychiatry, Duke University Medical Center, Durham, NC 27710.

AGGRESSIVE BEHAVIOR
AS A RISK MARKER

Unusually frequent or intense levels of aggressive behavior in children are a common cause for referral to mental health clinics and to special services in school. Children's aggressive behavior can create highly aversive effects on the people around them. Children's physical and verbal aggressive behavior can hurt others directly and can cause substantial disruptions in the children's school and home environments. When classrooms become significantly affected, the academic progress of classmates can also be reduced. Aggression is a notably stable behavior pattern—longitudinal research has found that aggressive behavior from childhood through early adulthood is, along with intellectual functioning, among the most stable psychological characteristics of children (Olweus, 1979). Thus, children's chronic high aggressive behavior patterns often do not disappear without intervention.

In recent years, children's aggressive behavior has emerged as a central focus in prevention research as well as in treatment services and treatment research. Childhood aggression has become conceptualized as a risk marker on the developmental trajectories leading to a variety of negative adolescent outcomes, such as conduct disorder, delinquency, and substance use (Hinshaw, Lahey, & Hart, 1993; Loeber, 1990). Aggressive children have been found to be at risk for subsequent delinquent and criminal behavior and for poor school adjustment and dropout (Kupersmidt & Coie, 1990; Stattin & Magnusson, 1989; Tremblay et al., 1992). Coie, Lochman, Terry, and Hyman (1992) found with an African American sample that 3rd-grade peer-rated aggression predicted self- and parent-reported externalizing disorder and teacher-rated school adjustment in middle school. In this study, a composite categorical measure of disorder was created by determining if two of the three sources of data (adolescent self-report of psychopathology, parent report of adolescents' externalizing behavior, and teacher report of poor school adjustment) indicated poor adjustment. Using this criterion, 18% of children who were neither aggressive nor rejected by their peer group in 3rd grade had poor adjustment in middle school, 40% of children who were aggressive but not rejected had poor adjustment, and 62% of children who were both aggressive and rejected had poor adjustment. Thus, being aggressive doubled a child's risk rate and being both aggressive and rejected by peers tripled a child's risk rate. A subsequent study has found that these aggressive-rejected children were at greater risk of continuing externalizing problems in 8th and 10th grades than were aggressive-only and rejected-only children (Coie, Terry, Lenox, Lochman, & Hyman, in press). Although these latter two groups of children had decreasing symptom patterns from 6th to 10th grade, the aggressive-rejected children had increasingly severe externalizing problems across the three time points.

Lochman and Wayland (1994) followed up a mixed-race sample of 114 adolescent boys 4 years after initial peer sociometric assessment when they were in elementary school. Boys' self-reports of delinquency indicated that boys identified by their elementary school peers as aggressive had significantly higher risk rates for crimes against persons than did nonaggressive boys. Boys' aggression status, however, did not predict their subsequent theft offenses, indicating that aggressive behavior is a better predictor of overt delinquency than covert delinquency. Interestingly, aggressive boys were also at significant risk for subsequent substance use. This finding supports prior research that found childhood antisocial behavior, rebelliousness, and anger to be predictive of adolescent substance use (Elliott, Huizinga, & Ageton, 1985; Kandel, 1982; Kellam & Brown, 1982; Kellam, Ensminger, & Simon, 1980; Swain, Oetting, Edwards, & Beauvais, 1989; Windle, 1990) and indicates that childhood aggression and anger are broadband risk markers for adolescent marijuana, alcohol, and drug use and delinquent activity involving interpersonal violence (Hawkins, Catalano, & Miller, 1992; Kumpfer, 1989).

Because childhood aggression has been demonstrated to be a relatively stable behavior pattern as well as a significant risk factor for subsequent conduct disorder and substance use difficulties, prevention efforts are warranted for elementary school children identified as aggressive and disruptive and who have difficulties with anger management (Gelfand, Ficola, & Zarbatany, 1986). Aggressive behavior in children (Dodge, 1991) and in adults (Averill, 1982) has been conceptualized as being due in part to an inability to regulate emotional responses to anger-inducing stimuli. Research has documented linkages between children's aggressive behavior and their emotional arousal in general (e.g., Cummings, Iannotti, & Zahn-Waxler, 1985) and their anger in particular (Fabes & Eisenberg, 1992; Klaczynski & Cummings, 1989; Underwood, Coie, & Herbsman, 1992). Interventions that target individuals who have been identified as high risk through early signs (e.g., anger and aggression) of later disorder are known as "indicated preventive interventions" (Institute of Medicine, 1994). The goal of preventive intervention is not only to reduce children's immediate levels of aggression but also to have distal outcomes of reducing the later incidence of disorder. To have these preventive effects, mediating factors that influence the risk marker and the later negative outcome are identified, and the preventive intervention is crafted to affect these malleable mediating factors. In our case, an anger arousal model has served as the conceptual basis for the Anger Coping Program, which is an indicated preventive intervention designed to reduce later substance use, delinquency, and conduct problems.

SOCIAL-COGNITIVE MODEL
OF ANGER AROUSAL

The social-cognitive model underlying the Anger Coping Program has been presented in greater detail elsewhere (Lochman, Dunn, & Klimes-Dougan, 1993; Lochman, Lampron, Gemmer, & Harris, 1987; Lochman & Lenhart, 1993; Lochman, Meyer, Rabiner, & White, 1991; Lochman, White, & Wayland, 1991) and will be reviewed briefly here. This social-cognitive model focuses on the cognitive distortions and cognitive deficiencies that have been found in research with aggressive children (Kendall, 1991; Kendall & Lochman, 1994) and is consistent with social-information-processing models of children's social competence (Crick & Dodge, 1994; Dodge, 1986).

Aggressive children have distortions in the initial appraisal stages of information processing. At the encoding stage, aggressive children attend to and remember hostile social cues (e.g., words, tone of voice, or facial expression) more than nonhostile social cues, have a recency bias in their memory of social cues, and attend to fewer cues before forming an interpretation of an event (Dodge & Newman, 1981; Dodge, Pettit, McClaskey, & Brown, 1986; Milich & Dodge, 1984). Even when verbal intelligence is controlled, highly aggressive boys have less accurate recall of social cues from videotaped vignettes than do nonaggressive boys (Lochman & Dodge, 1994). At the interpretation stage, aggressive children attribute more hostile intentions to peers and adults than do nonaggressive children, especially in ambiguous social situations (Dodge et al., 1986; Dodge, Price, Bachorowski, & Newman, 1990; Lochman & Dodge, 1994). These distortions in appraisal processes influence not only how aggressive children perceive others' behavior but also how they perceive their own behavior. In live dyadic competitive interactions with a peer, aggressive children rated their partners as being more aggressive than they were and rated themselves as being less aggressive than observers rated them (Lochman, 1987). In this study, children's ratings of self and others were compared to independent observers' ratings of the videotaped interactions. This pattern of results indicates that aggressive children attribute the relative responsibility for initial stages of verbal conflict to others, in contrast to nonaggressive children who have distorted perceptions in the opposite direction and who attribute more responsibility for the conflict to themselves than they objectively should.

In the next stages of information processing, aggressive children have characteristic deficiencies in their social problem-solving skills. At the response generation stage, highly aggressive children typically generate fewer solutions to social problems than do nonaggressive children (Lochman & Dodge, 1994). Although moderately aggressive children do not necessarily have this deficiency in quantitative response generation, they do have distinct patterns of the types of solutions they generate. Preadolescent aggressive children think of more direct action solutions and fewer verbal assertion solutions and tend to think of more physically aggressive solutions than do nonaggressive children (Asarnow & Callan, 1985; Dodge et al., 1986; Lochman & Lampron, 1986; Richard & Dodge, 1982). Aggressive adolescents generate fewer bargaining and compromise solutions and are less able to accurately perceive others' motives and to create solutions that integrate the needs of both self and other (Lochman, Wayland, & White, 1993). At the response decision stage, aggressive children choose aggressive responses because they believe their aggressive behavior will stop aversive behavior from others (Lochman & Dodge, 1994; Perry, Perry, & Rasmussen, 1986), and they believe that aggressive behavior will enhance self-esteem and will not be negatively evaluated by peers (Slaby & Guerra, 1988).

Other cognitive operations, schema, and appraisal processes that contribute to these distortions and deficiencies in information processing and ultimately to aggressive children's problematic behavior include their affect labeling, their automatic memory processes, and their social goals. Aggressive children experience higher levels of physiological arousal than nonaggressive children concurrent with their appraisal that they are in a provocative, frustrating social situation (Craven, 1995), and they are prone to mislabeling the affective arousal they experience. Aggressive children report that they experience more anger and less sadness and fear than do nonaggressive children (Garrison & Stolberg, 1983), and this tendency to minimize their self-awareness of emotions that make them feel vulnerable increases during adolescence (Lochman & Dodge, 1994). Thus, aggressive adolescent boys may be poorly prepared to cope with their affective reactions when they encounter situations that typically evoke fear or sadness in other people. Instead, their unanticipated arousal may detour and flood their social information processing in a preemptive manner.

Other research indicates that when aggressive children problem solve in conditions that promote automatic, preemptive memory operations, they generate less competent, more action-oriented solutions than when they think of solutions in a deliberate, slower manner (Lochman, Lampron, & Rabiner, 1989; Rabiner, Lenhart, & Lochman, 1990). When aggressive children retrieve strategy ideas from "memory bins" in a careful, evaluative manner, they can often generate surprisingly competent solutions to problems. When responding automatically, however, they quickly retrieve the most salient solution, which is at the top of the memory bin because of its frequent activation and use. Intervention can thus focus on making competent solutions that are lower in the memory bin more salient through repeated discussion and role plays about these other remembered solutions.

Children's social goals, which are conceptualized as cognitive schema or enduring patterns of cognitive beliefs (e.g., Lochman & Lenhart, in press), also have direct effects on problem solving. Aggressive adolescent boys have been found to place higher value on social goals for dominance and for revenge and lower value on affiliative goals than do nonaggressive adolescents (Lochman, Wayland, & White, 1993). This social goal pattern has been found to directly mediate the deficient problem-solving style of these boys and to be related to their substance use and delinquency difficulties.

ANGER COPING PROGRAM

The Anger Coping Program, which focuses on these cognitive distortions and deficiencies in aggressive children, has been hypothesized to have preventive effects on adolescent violence and substance use (Hawkins et al., 1992; Institute of Medicine, 1994; Larson, 1994). This school-based group intervention has been most frequently used with children in fourth through sixth grades, although it was originally developed for younger children in second and third grades (Lochman, Nelson, & Sims, 1981). We recommend that groups have four to six children and two coleaders. An optimal arrangement for coleaders has involved one leader, such as a school counselor, being from the school and the other coleader being a school psychologist or a psychologist, social worker, or psychiatrist from a local mental health center. Children are typically identified through teacher referrals of highly aggressive and disruptive children with anger management problems. We usually select children for the groups in the early fall, and groups meet for 18 weekly sessions through the remainder of the academic year. Group sessions last from 45 to 60 minutes and usually take place during the school day.

An extended outline of the Anger Coping Program indicates session objectives and activities (Lochman et al., 1987). The sessions address the basic structuring and purpose of the groups (Session 1), self-instruction training (Sessions 2 and 3), perspective taking (Sessions 4 and 5), awareness of physiological arousal (Session 6), goal setting (Session 7), and social problem solving (Sessions 8-18). In the first session, the Anger Coping Program introduces a behavior management system for in-group behavior and extends the system to out-of-group school behavior with the goal-setting component. Children receive points in the group for abiding by group rules and for positive participation, and they later earn additional points for meeting their behavior goal at school. This goal is mutually selected weekly by the group leader and the child and is monitored daily through teacher reports on goal-setting forms.

The self-instruction activities assist children in recognizing situations that typically provoke intense feelings and in using inhibitory self-instructions (e.g. "Stop! Think! What can I do?") to control automatic aggressive responses. Self-instruction training activities include tasks that range from screening out others' efforts to disrupt the child during a memory game to handling others' teasing behavior during a verbal taunting game.

Social perspective-taking tasks, using pictures of ambiguous social situations, promote children's discussions of the variety of intentions that peers and adults might have. Role playing is used to concretely illustrate how we can easily misjudge others' intentions during social interactions. Stress is placed on attending to nonhostile cues. To promote children's awareness of their physiological arousal when they become emotionally aroused, children discuss the arousal signs displayed by themselves and by videotaped peers. These arousal signs serve as cues to begin the problem-solving process. The social problem-solving portion of the program includes an initial discussion about a short set of problem-solving steps (e.g., problem identification, choices, and consequences) and repeated modeling and role playing of problem solving in action. In several sessions, children create and videotape a problem-solving scenario, which serves to increase the practice and internalization of the problem-solving process.

Anger Coping Outcomes

In an initial uncontrolled study of a 12-session version of the anger control program for second- and third-grade aggressive children, children had significant reductions in teacher-rated daily aggressive behavior and improvements in daily on-task behavior by the end of the 6-week treatment (Lochman et al., 1981). This led to four subsequent studies in which the effects of the Anger Coping Program were compared to those of alternative interventions or to untreated control conditions. Lochman, Burch, Curry, and Lampron (1984) found that 41 boys who received a 12-session version of the Anger Coping Program had significantly lower rates of disruptive-aggressive off-task classroom behavior according to independent observers, had significantly lower rates of parent-rated aggressive behavior, and tended to have higher levels of self-esteem following intervention in comparison to 35 boys in untreated and minimal intervention cells. In this study, anger-coping boys who also had a goal-setting component in their program tended to have stronger behavioral improvements than anger-coping boys who did not receive this component. Client characteristics that predicted better outcomes included having initially poorer problem-solving skills, having more anxiety and somatization symptoms, and being more disliked by the children's peer group (Lochman, Lampron, Burch, & Curry, 1985). In another study indicating the predictive role of peer rejection for aggressive children, Lochman, Coie, Underwood, and Terry (1993) found that a broader social relations program that included an anger-coping component had significant impact on teacher-rated and peer-rated behavior outcomes at a 1-year follow-up only with aggressive-rejected children and not with rejected-only children. In a follow-up quasi-experimental study, aggressive boys who received the 18-session version of the Anger Coping Program had stronger reductions in off-task classroom behavior than did the boys receiving the 12-session program (Lochman, 1985). These results suggest that the generalization of intervention effects can be augmented with a goal-setting component and with a longer intervention period.

Two subsequent studies have indicated that nonsocial self-instruction training (focusing on general impulsive behavior) and teacher consultation have not additionally enhanced intervention effects. Lochman and Curry (1986) found that the two forms of anger-coping programs produced similar improvements in independent-observer-rated on-task behavior, reductions in parents' ratings of boys' aggression, and increases in self-esteem. The inclusion of nonsocial self-instructional training, however, did not increase positive outcomes and actually produced weaker gains in disruptive-aggressive classroom behavior. Lochman, Lampron, Gemmer, Harris, and Wyckoff (1989) found that boys in anger-coping groups had significant reductions in disruptive-aggressive classroom behavior, significant improvements in perceived social competence, and trends for reductions in teacher-rated aggressive behavior in comparison to boys in an untreated control condition. A five-session teacher consultation component focusing on behavior management strategies and on improving children's problem-solving skills, however, did not improve outcomes. Intensive teacher consultations more narrowly focused on specific strategies for specific problems (e.g., Allen, Chinsky, Larcen, Lochman, & Selinger, 1976) may be necessary to produce additional effects beyond the basic anger-coping effects.

A long-term study of the preventive effects of the Anger Coping Program has found that, in comparison to boys with untreated aggression ($N = 52$), anger-coping boys ($N = 31$) followed up 3 years after intervention had significantly lower rates of marijuana, alcohol, and drug involvement (Lochman, 1992). These anger-coping boys also maintained their improvement in self-esteem and in social problem-solving skills; these maintained gains may have mediated these boys' delayed entry into substance use. On all these outcomes, the anger-coping boys were functioning at follow-up within the range of a nonaggressive comparison group ($N = 62$). A subset of anger-coping boys who had received a second-year booster intervention, consisting of six additional child sessions and five behavior management parent training sessions, maintained their reductions in passive off-task behavior. This latter finding, in the context of a lack of follow-up anger-coping effects on delinquent behavior, suggests that substantial longer-term maintenance and prevention effects may occur only if the Anger Coping Program is augmented with a longer intervention period across 2 school years and with a parent training component.

COPING POWER PROGRAM

The Coping Power Program (CPP) is being developed and evaluated by the authors on the basis of the prior findings (Lochman, 1992) that the Anger Coping Program had encouraging but limited preventive effects. In response to prior findings, the CPP extends the Anger Coping model by having a longer structured period of intervention (covering 15 months) and by including a direct focus on parent factors associated with the development and maintenance of children's aggressive behavior and of their subsequent negative adolescent outcomes.

Several programs of research have documented family-based risk factors that are associated with childhood aggression. This research, based on behavioral observation technologies used in the homes of aggressive children and their parents, shows certain parenting excesses and deficiencies associated with higher rates of child aggression. The most robust findings across studies conducted in several behavioral laboratories have shown that parents of aggressive children engage in excesses of aversive and harsh behaviors directed toward the child; excesses of poorly formulated and poorly delivered commands; frequent criticism; a higher rate of ineffective, corporal punishment; and a high rate of scolding, threatening, and nagging that is not backed up by effective, nonviolent punishment. Inconsistency in discipline has also been associated with child aggression (for reviews see Kazdin, 1995; Patterson, 1982; Wells, 1995).

Although these processes involving irritable, ineffective discipline are present in families of children with both overt (oppositional behavior, arguing, and physical aggression) and covert (stealing, lying, and truancy) forms of aggressive behavior, families with covertly aggressive children are further distinguished by a macroscopic parenting construct variously labeled supervision or monitoring (Patterson & Stouthamer-Loeber, 1984). This construct refers to failure on the part of parents of covertly aggressive children to monitor and track both the child's whereabouts and the child's performance of basic expectations.

Other macroscopic parenting constructs have also been associated with child aggression, including the ability of the parents to define and set house rules and to use effective problem-solving skills when confronted with new situations presented by the child (Patterson, 1982, 1984). Although both of these constructs show some empirical association with aggressive child behavior, the most robust predictors are irritable discipline and monitoring (Patterson & Bank, 1989). In addition, broader family context factors, such as parent personal distress, parent marital distress, and parent social insularity, have been associated with higher rates of aggression in children (Patterson, Reid, & Dishion, 1992).

The literature documenting the correlation, daily covariation, and direct functional relationship of parenting practices and child aggression is beyond the scope of this chapter (for reviews see Patterson, 1982; Wells, 1995). Although parenting practices are not the only predictors of child aggression, there is no doubt of their strong influence in the escalation and maintenance of these troubling behavior problems. For these reasons, the parent component in the CPP included direct attention to modifying these parenting excesses and deficits as part of the overall program for intervention for child aggression as a risk factor for later negative outcomes.

The CPP preventive intervention program is based on the hypothesis that reductions in childhood aggression (which is a risk marker for adolescent substance abuse) and changes in the mediating factors influencing both childhood aggression and adolescent substance use (e.g., children's problem-solving skills, parents' monitoring, and discipline skills) will result in lower adolescent substance use and substance abuse rates. The CPP identifies children as being at risk for substance use by selecting fourth- and fifth-grade children who are rated by teachers and parents as having problems with aggressive behavior. These "risk" children are randomly assigned to three conditions: (a) child-focused cognitive-behavioral intervention (CPP child component), (b) CPP child component plus parent-focused behavioral parent training (CPP parent component), and (c) untreated risk control groups. This design will permit us to determine the additive effect of parent training in combination with the child intervention. In addition, a nonaggressive group of children is matched to the risk groups on racial status, cognitive ability, and age, and this nonrisk control group will serve as a comparison group to examine whether the intervention conditions bring risk children into a range of substance use typical of nonrisk children. One hundred fifty-one boys were assigned to these four cells in Cohort 1 (identified in fourth and fifth grades in 1993 and 1994), and 90 more boys are being assigned in Cohort 2 (identified in fourth and fifth grades in 1994 and 1995). Sixty percent of the boys are African American, and the remainder are Caucasian. Only boys were selected for this study because longitudinal studies linking childhood aggression to adolescent substance use have most clearly demonstrated this link for boys (Lochman & Wayland, 1994). The CPP intervention conditions last from March of the risk-identification year through June of the following year (March 1994 to June 1995 for Cohort 1 and March 1995 to June 1996 for Cohort 2). Assessments are conducted before and after the intervention periods and at 1-year intervals during the follow-up outcome period, which is planned through the end of high school.

Coping Power Program Child Component

The CPP child component consists of 33 weekly group sessions over a 15-month period. Groups are co-led by CPP intervention staff and by a school counselor located at each school. Sessions occur during the school day at the children's school and last 45 to 60 minutes per session. The CPP child component groups are based on the anger-coping group sessions and include (a) additional emphasis on long-term goal setting; (b) awareness of feelings related to vulnerability; (c) more practice with self-instruction training and perspective taking; (d) application of social problem solving to specific situations involving friendship initiation, group entry, peer negotiation, sibling conflicts, school study skills, teacher conflict, and neighborhood problems; and (e) resistance to peer pressure. Sessions typically include a combination of activities, discussion, and role playing. We currently have a 79% attendance rate at CPP child component sessions; some of these non-attending children have moved to schools without groups.

The CPP child component also includes approximately one and a half brief one-to-one sessions per month between CPP staff and each intervention child. The goals of this contact are to (a) reinforce generalization of cognitive and behavioral gains to children's school and home behavior, (b) permit more extended problem solving about personal issues not easily dealt with within the group, and (c) enhance relationship development between target child and CPP staff. In addition, classroom observation and teacher consultation are provided for a subset of children who display improvement in group and one-to-one sessions but who continue to have significant classroom problems midway through the intervention period.

Coping Power Program Parent Component

In our current research investigation, we are examining the addition of a formal, intensive parent intervention component on enhancing the immediate outcome and the generalization effects of the school-based CPP child component described in the preceding section. The parent component begins at the same time as the child component in the spring of the first school year. Three introductory parent sessions occur over the spring and early summer.

These sessions focus on group cohesion building, review of summer programs and activities for children, planning logistics of group meetings in the fall, and assisting parents with school start-up. Then, parent intervention resumes in September and consists of a 15-session group format for a total of 18 meetings.

Parents meet in groups of four or five single parents or parent dyads with two coleaders. Assertive attempts are made to include mothers and fathers in parent groups, although in most cases only one parent (usually the mother) attends. For some sessions, the school counselor also joins the leaders in presenting material relevant to parent involvement in the school. Groups begin with weekly meetings that gradually fade over the course of the year to biweekly and then monthly sessions. Transportation is provided to meetings for parents who otherwise would not be able to attend and a supervised child waiting room is provided for parents who have no access to babysitters. Snacks and soft drinks are also provided at each group meeting.

The content of the CPP parent component is derived from social learning theory-based parent training programs developed and evaluated by prominent clinician-researchers in the field of child aggression (Forehand & McMahon, 1981; Patterson, Reid, Jones, & Conger, 1975) with adaptations for the special needs and requirements of this population. Over the course of the 15 sessions, parents learn skills for (a) identifying prosocial and disruptive behavioral targets in their children using specific operational terms, (b) rewarding appropriate child behaviors, (c) giving effective instructions and establishing age-appropriate rules and expectations for their children in the home, (d) applying effective consequences to negative child behavior, (e) managing child behavior outside the home, and (f) establishing ongoing family communication structures in the home (such as weekly family meetings).

In addition to these "standard" parent training skills, parents in this project also learn additional skills that support the social-cognitive and problem-solving skills that children learn in the CPP child component. These parent skills are introduced at the same time that the respective child skills are introduced so that parents and children can work together at home on what they are learning. For example, parents learn to set up homework support structures and to reinforce organizational skills around homework completion as children are learning organizational skills in the CPP child component. Parents also learn techniques for managing sibling conflict in the home as children are addressing peer and sibling conflict resolution skills in the group. Finally, parents learn to apply the problem-solving model to family problem solving so that child skills learned in the group will be prompted and reinforced in the family context. Some children (i.e., those who were brought with their parents due to lack of baby-sitting at home) attend the parent group on family problem solving after they have learned the problem-solving model in child group. These children and their parents role play the problem-solving skills in parent group, practicing these skills themselves and modeling for the other parents.

A final section of the CPP parent component includes two sessions on stress management for parents. Part of the rationale for this is to help parents learn to remain calm and in control during stressful or irritating disciplinary interactions with their children. We also emphasize, however, the importance of parents learning to "take care of themselves" for their own sake. Interestingly, anecdotal reports from the parents indicate that these sessions, in which we address their own personal needs and stresses and not just the parenting needs of their children, are a major "selling point" in the CPP parent component. When the parents are addressed as individuals and not just as parents, they seem to become more involved in the program and more motivated in their attendance and implementation of homework assignments.

IMPLEMENTATION ISSUES

The interpersonal contexts the child experiences have a substantial effect on the development and maintenance of the child's problem behaviors, on the implementation of intervention with the child, and ultimately on the child's ability to sustain behavioral improvement following the intervention period. Environmental changes in parent, teacher, and peer behavior may be necessary to begin the change process for many children. Promoting changes in how parents and teachers reinforce behavioral self-control and more constructive problem solving can reduce their noncontingent and excessive aversive discipline efforts and can increase their monitoring of appropriate and inappropriate behavior. These key aspects of behavior change programs for parents and teachers have been shown to decrease children's acting-out, aggressive behavior (e.g., Lochman, 1990), and they are key components of cognitive-behavioral intervention with these children. In addition to enhancing the strength and generalization of the intervention's immediate effects, an intervention focus on children's interpersonal contexts can also potentially produce more durable behavioral changes with less behavioral regression to preintervention levels.

When aggressive children successfully respond to a cognitive-behavioral intervention, they are still faced with the difficult task of how to maintain their behavioral improvements. Children who have had a history of chronic aggressive behavior typically exist in a series of interpersonal settings in which people have come to expect that these children will behave in noxious, antagonistic ways. Regardless of the degree to which these parents, siblings, teachers, and peers may have contributed to the initial development of the children's aggressive behavior, these significant-other people in aggressive children's lives come to develop expectations and beliefs about the children's aggressive behavior and hostile intentions. Once developed, these belief systems are self-maintaining. Teachers can begin to expect that an aggressive child is responsible for most classroom disruptions and can quickly and automatically blame the child for any ambiguously caused misdeeds. When unfairly blamed, the aggressive child responds with righteous anger and can quickly resort to aggressive response strategies. Thus, the change process for aggressive children is an unusually daunting one. The aggressive child's initial, often fragile efforts to respond in more competent ways to provocation may have to be maintained even though the other people around the child continue to have negative expectations and beliefs about the child.

The intervention task then includes a need to work with children's significant others to (a) maximize the strength and cross-setting generalization of behavioral improvement, and (b) maintain behavioral gains over time by continuing to reinforce competent behavior and by flexibly altering the negative expectations for the child when that is appropriate. The following sections discuss issues about effectively involving certain key figures in children's interpersonal context (e.g., teachers, classmates, and parents) in the implementation of an anger-coping or a coping power intervention. For ease of discussion, we will refer to both programs as coping power.

School Context Implementation Issues

In our most optimally functioning groups, school counselors, classroom teachers, and children's peers in the groups all actively work in their roles to reinforce children's problem-solving efforts. In practice, however, we find a great deal of variability from one school to another in their active support of and involvement in the program. When counselors are intensively involved in planning, coleading, and debriefing group sessions, we also typically find that they elicit greater principal support, more flexibility from teachers in scheduling group sessions, and more avid interest from teachers in the goal-setting process. When counselors are only passively and loosely involved as coleaders or when teachers are apathetic or have low expectations that this form of intervention would be effective, however, then goal-setting efforts often fail and there is more limited carryover of behavioral gains to classroom settings. Thus, it is important to review the expected roles for teachers and peers in the groups, to anticipate challenges and barriers to optimal involvement by teachers and peers, and to consider methods of enhancing the involvement of these individuals.

Teachers' Roles. In the usual course of CPP child component groups, teachers have two prominent functions. First, they provide ongoing information throughout the year about a child's behavioral difficulties. Because of the substantial amount of time in the classrooms with the children, teachers can be rich sources of information about factors that provoke specific children's aggressive and oppositional reactions and factors that promote these children's emotional regulation. In this context, group coleaders meet with teachers at the beginning of the group period and then periodically throughout the course of the group to identify an array of teacher-approved behavioral goals that are appropriate for CPP child component children in their classes. These goals are broadly related to anger-arousing problems that the children encounter and include aggression to peers, social skills with peers, oppositional and disruptive behavior in the classroom, and failure to complete various school tasks. During group sessions, we shape and reinforce children for generating behavioral goals for the goal-setting procedure that are included on the teachers' lists of goals to maximize the relevance of children's goals and the involvement of teachers in the goal-setting procedure.

Second, teachers have the role of monitoring children's goal completion on the weekly goal-setting forms. Typically, children have the responsibility to ask their teachers once per day to indicate on the form whether the children have met their goal or not for that day. Sometimes children's goals are monitored more often than daily, and this usually occurs when the target behavior occurs at a high rate throughout the day (hence requiring smaller units of time to assess reductions in the rate of behavior) or when children have distinct class periods with different teachers, such as in middle school. Children earn different numbers of points depending on the number of teacher signatures they receive for goal completion, and these points are added to the children's group points and can be redeemed for various rewards in the group meetings.

Challenges to Teachers' Involvement. The most overt indicator of low levels of teacher involvement is often evident in children's chronic failure to turn in signed weekly goal sheets. For our current implementation of the CPP with the first cohort, 50% of the goal sheets are not turned in each week. For the children who turn in goal sheets, they earn nearly two thirds of the possible number of points, indicating that when children turn in goal sheets they have usually completed their goals. Children do not turn in goal sheets for a variety of reasons, including issues related to the characteristics of the children themselves (e.g, impulsiveness, forgetfulness, disorganization, poor motivation, or inability to accomplish goal) and to obstacles that teachers experience.

Obstacles to adequate teacher involvement in the goal-setting procedure can occur because of teacher reactions to the goal-monitoring procedure itself or because of more general characteristics of the teachers. Common teacher concerns about the goal-setting procedures include their perception that a child's weekly goal is "too easy" and does not address the child's central problem, their reluctance to accurately indicate that a child met a daily goal (and hence will be reinforced) when the child has displayed other types of problem behaviors that day, and their perception that the child's request to have their daily goal sheet checked often disrupts the teachers' attention to educational tasks. The first two of these concerns can be addressed by careful explanations about the importance of "shaping" and of consistently enforced behavior-reinforcement contingencies with children with significant externalizing behavior problems by demonstrating to teachers that their general concerns are understood and can be added as comments on the goal sheets and by discussing with teachers how these children typically improve with gradual changes rather than with sharp "cures." The last concern is often a legitimate one and can best be resolved by careful problem solving with the teacher about the least intrusive and time-consuming way in which children can have their goal sheets reviewed.

Other, more general, teacher characteristics can also contribute to goal-setting failures. Teachers may be disinterested from the outset in working with the CPP child component program because they may place value only on academic work with their students, believing that any type of intervention may interfere with their teaching efforts. Alternatively, teachers may have strong beliefs or values that only certain types of intervention approaches are appropriate; other types of intervention may be perceived as culturally irrelevant or as excessively behavioristic, intrapsychic, or affective. Teacher noninvolvement may also be due to either feeling threatened or a sense of disillusioned hopelessness. Although the CPP child component is relatively nonintrusive in the classrooms, teachers may perceive through their periodic meetings with group leaders that they are being evaluated in some negative way. This perception of possible evaluation can lead teachers to feel threatened and to reduce contact with group leaders and target children. Other teachers feel hopeless that either this particular child will never change or their prior contacts with counselors, psychologists, and social workers have been ineffective in producing change in behaviorally disturbed children. In these cases, teachers have evolved strong, impervious schemas about the extreme stability of these children's behavior, and they do not expect that they or anyone else can facilitate meaningful improvements in these children's behavior.

Enhancing Teacher Involvement. Most of these obstacles to teacher involvement are related to teachers' lack of perceived ownership of the program. They are likely to be more actively engaged and cooperative with the program if they perceive that their role is important, valued, and at least partially under their control. When teachers perceive that they are being forced to participate in or work with a program, they can respond with active hostility or passive noninvolvement. We believe, then, that enhancing teachers' and counselors' perceived ownership of the CPP child component program is a key aspect of effective implementation. The four methods described in this section represent progressively more intense means of generating greater teacher involvement and perceived ownership of the program.

First, inclusion of school counselors as coleaders of the CPP child component groups is perhaps the most important mechanism in promoting teacher involvement and ownership. Counselors who assume roles as active and collaborative coleaders become advocates of the program with teachers and school administrators and are able to defuse teacher or principal concerns about intervention or assessment demands. Because the counselors are based in the schools, they can meet with teachers at times that are most convenient for teachers and they can quickly be available to consult and problem solve with teachers about difficulties with a child's goal attainment or with a child's escalating behavioral difficulties. Counselors often already have established working relationships with teachers, increasing the ease with which teachers can have open, trusting, and energized interactions with group coleaders.

Second, having either regularly scheduled or frequent ad hoc contacts between both group coleaders and the teachers also promotes teacher involvement. In addition to gathering basic information about children's behavior and goals in these contacts, coleaders can show they empathetically understand how aggressive children can cause frustration by interfering with teachers' other academic goals. The coleaders can also reframe teachers' attributions about the intentions of these difficult children, emphasizing how the children behave as they do because of information processing distortions and deficiencies, of their acquired schemas, of possible prior irregularities in parents' discipline and parenting practices, and of classmates' and teachers' rigid expectations about the children's hostility rather than necessarily because of innate "meanness" or deliberate efforts to frustrate and enrage the teacher. Coleaders can reinforce teachers for their positive expectations for eventual change and improvement by these aggressive children while promoting the realization that this change process is gradual and prone to periodic regressions.

Third, the group coleaders can orchestrate periodic "lab" exercises between teachers and their aggressive children. These meetings between child, coleaders, and teacher would be outside of the regular group time and class time. These meetings can be planned to coincide with relevant parts of the group program and would be teacher focused rather than problem focused. In a perspective-taking exercise, children can interview their teachers about their memories of their own favorite teachers, what they liked best and least about school when they were children, what their goals are when they are teaching in class, and when they have to handle a problem situation in class. In our CPP, we have compiled these interview responses into a newsletter distributed to the children and the teachers. The interview promoted greater tolerance by children and teachers of each other and allowed teachers to see these problematic children as engaged in a positive effort to understand some things about their teacher. Similarly, later in the year, children can interview teachers about how they try to solve difficult interpersonal problems and how they handle peer pressure. The group coleaders can coach the children, and occasionally the teachers, in how to carry out these communication exercises.

Fourth, we have found that it is useful midway through the intervention to assess whether children are responding well to the program, not responding at all, or are "slow responders." The slow responders are children who are displaying improvements during the group sessions but who are continuing to have some difficulties in the classroom. These children typically have some degree of motivation to change their behavior, but they need considerable external structuring to help them follow through with behavior change efforts. In the CPP, coleaders identified chronic classroom problems, such as noncompliance with the teacher, distractibility and highly active classroom behavior, and peer aggression, as problems on Strategy Forms for Slow-to-Respond Children. Coleaders then identified additional strategies to be tried, including placement in after-school tutoring programs, referral for Attention Deficit Hyperactivity Disorder evaluations, and teacher consultation. Teacher consultation started with one or two classroom observation sessions in which we attempted to identify causal factors stimulating children's problematic behaviors. Then we consulted with teachers to troubleshoot the teachers' existing behavior management system or to initiate new behavior management strategies. We found teachers to be generally appreciative of the extra interest and time taken with them, to usually be willing to try out alternate structuring and seating arrangements in class, and to be more intensely involved in the goal-monitoring process.

Peers' Roles. Because the CPP child component is a school-based group program, some of the children's schoolmates have roles as coparticipants in their groups. A group format is preferred for this type of intervention because it is a relatively efficient way to provide the service and because children's peers within the group can provide significant therapeutic functions. The peers in the group can provide models for positive problem-solving efforts, for use of self-instruction to inhibit aggression, and for competent social skills. Modeling research has indicated that individuals are most influenced by models who are similar to them in key ways such as age and life status (Bandura, 1985; Perry & Furukawa, 1986). Peers can typically have more substantial influence on how children can effectively try out new or refined social behaviors than can adult coleaders' directions. In addition, peers can provide highly valued social reinforcement for children's goal attainment and positive participation in the group. The presence of peers also permits the use of some activities, such as role playing and creation of videotaped problem-solving scenarios, that would be relatively difficult to implement in individual-focused interventions. These roles for peers in groups are identical to the functions of group members in clinic settings, but school-based groups have the added advantage of including peers from the child's natural environment at school. This enhances the understanding that peers have of the nature of children's social difficulties and the provocative situations they encounter and provides an opportunity for group members to reinforce each other for behavioral improvements during out-of-group time.

Challenges to Peers' Positive Involvement. A major disadvantage of working with aggressive children in groups is the negative reactive effect they can have on each other. These are children who are selected for the intervention because they emit angry, aggressive behavior to peers, and they are often noncompliant and challenging with adults. It is not surprising that these same behaviors often are emitted in the group. If a group member is heavily involved in challenging authority figures and is relatively well accepted by other group members, then this group member can stimulate oppositional power struggles between group members and group leaders. These power struggles can reduce all group members' group involvement and motivation for change. This is an example of a more general problem in which group members socially reinforce each other for aggressive, disruptive behavior in group sessions, contributing to the formation of a "deviant peer group." Developing friendships between children in some groups can be quite counterproductive for the overall aim of resolving aggressive behavior. Even when these negative peer effects are not produced in planful, proactive ways, groups can be easily affected by members' rapid emotional reactions and contagion. Reactive aggressive children have difficulty regulating their anger and arousal, causing their "hot" angry cognitions to interfere with their information processing. Within a group of aggressive children, it is not unusual to have a highly emotionally charged atmosphere at times, which can elicit bursts of aversive behavior.

Enhancing Peers' Positive Involvement. An overarching goal is then to create a positive peer climate in the group. To achieve this goal, certain structural and programmatic adaptations can be made. Structurally, group leaders can direct who sits next to whom, can strategically position themselves between volatile group members, can make transitions between activities easier with clearly stated expectations for children's behavior, and can use a firm voice tone and direct eye contact to give directions and feedback to children. Programmatic enhancements can include (a) inclusion of a positive feedback time at the end of each group session, with children giving compliments to each other about their positive participation and behavior in the group (defuses group tension and enhances friendships and self-esteem); (b) use of group contingencies that involve larger groups rewards, such as a pizza party, being contingent on the entire group earning a set total number of points for positive participation, abiding by group rules, and accomplishing the goals on the goal-setting forms (producing peer reinforcement for positive group behavior and goal attainment); (c) use of a "buddy" system in which a group member reminds another group member about his goal during the week and encourages him to get his goal sheet signed daily (produces peer cueing and peer reinforcement for goal attainment); (d) use of periodic one-to-one contacts between a group leader and a group member (provides for feedback about in-group social skills and enhances the relationship with the adult group leader); and (e) having the group work together to provide a constructive service to all of their classmates—for example, in the CPP when group members create a poster about drug refusal skills that can be placed in the school cafeteria or hallway (reinforces positive, prosocial peer climate). Other, more major structural changes that may be necessary if these strategies fail include (a) removing a chronically unmotivated and disruptive child from the group and instead use one-to-one meetings, (b) dividing the group into two smaller subgroups carefully constructed to avoid deviant peer coalitions, and (c) adding less problematic children to a group to promote more competent modeling of in-group problem-solving efforts and out-of-group friendships. The latter solution can produce iatrogenic effects with less problematic children and should be chosen cautiously. This set of enhancement activities and strategies can create a more positive, accepting peer climate within the immediate groups and can provide for greater generalization and maintenance of children's behavior changes.

Family Context Implementation Issues

Because our current project is an indicated prevention intervention project with an epidemiologically identified, high-risk population, several aspects of the design and implementation of the CPP parent component differentiate it from parent training programs described in the clinical literature. Because the population of parents and children is not a self-referred population, their motivation to be involved in an intensive and lengthy intervention is generally not as high at the beginning of the project as is true with a clinical (self-referred) population. For that reason, we have found that it is important to pay special attention to convenience and external motivational factors at the outset of the program.

To address these issues, CPP parent component group meetings are scheduled to occur as close to the community in which the families live as possible. Frequently, this has meant arranging with the school principal for meeting space in the school itself or with the local community recreation center director for meeting space in the center. In most cases, space has been made freely available to us, although occasionally the project has had to pay for space or for the school custodian's overtime to open and close the school after hours. Parents have told us that if they had to travel to our university-based offices they probably would not attend as regularly.

Having the CPP parent component groups take place in the schools also facilitates the attendance of the school counselors at some of the parent group sessions. Counselor attendance at parent groups is a notable advantage in facilitating understanding and cooperation between parents and the school, coordinating parent implementation at home of academic support programs (e.g., homework assignments given by the teacher), communicating with parents about programs at the school that may be useful to the child, and helping some parents overcome wariness of the school that may have developed over the years.

Another implementation issue in the CPP parent component is the use of coleaders for each group. The use of two leaders allows for a division of labor so that in any given group one leader takes primary responsibility for presenting the content of the parent training agenda for that meeting, and the second coleader observes the parents and responds to their reactions and questions. In addition, the use of coleaders allows for modeling of many of the parenting and interactional skills taught in the CPP parent component. One leader plays the part of parent and the other leader plays the part of child in these modeled scenarios. Modeling prepares the way for role playing by parents once they have a chance to observe the coleaders.

We have found it necessary to address the obstacles to attendance that exist for many parents. Because some of the parents in the project are single mothers with one or more children, living in insular community environments with limited resources, we have had to provide support services that make attendance possible. For example, intervention staff transport some mothers to the group before and after each meeting. Snacks and more substantial food are provided, especially when groups occur around the dinner hour. Intervention staff make themselves available throughout the day and into the evening hours to run groups at the most convenient time for the parents in each particular group. A supervised child waiting room is provided for parents who otherwise do not have access to baby-sitters in their own community. At times, the child supervision staff have conducted homework sessions so that parents' attendance at evening parent groups does not detract from the child's performance of homework. Finally, we provide a $10 stipend to parents at every group meeting to reimburse them for any other expenses that may be related to their attendance. Parents are at their discretion to use this money as they see fit. With these supportive efforts, we have accomplished a 49% attendance rate per session at group meetings across Cohort 1. This attendance rate compares very favorably to attendance rates for self-referred parents and children at clinic-based parent training programs (Prinz & Miller, 1994).

All of the factors described previously provide external support and motivation to parents to reinforce their early involvement in the CPP parent component. Our long-term goal, however, is to support parents in developing a sense of self-motivation and personal ownership of the parent program. We foster this development in a variety of ways. First, we use traditional methods of group cohesion building to assist the development of group identity and mutual parent support. Parents are encouraged to do a limited amount of personal sharing in the group, and group members are invited to assist other parents in problem solving concerning personal family issues. On other occasions, the group becomes a support network for families in those times of crisis that inevitably occur in any intervention program that spans 1.5 years. For example, a child in one of the intervention families was in a skating accident and incurred a significant head injury requiring months of hospitalization. The parent in that family understandably missed several group meetings. The other parents in the group sent cards and letters to the missing parent, some visited her in the hospital, and the group leaders also made hospital visits. When the parent returned to parent group, she was provided an opportunity to share with the group what she had been through, and group members were sympathetic and supportive listeners. Group leaders adapted some of the parenting techniques taught in the group to help this parent deal with new behavioral issues created by the brain injury suffered by her child. She later said that this group support had been very important to her and had made her even more committed to the CPP.

Another approach to enhancing parents' perceived ownership of the CPP parent component was the manner in which new skills were introduced and discussed. Whenever possible, parents were asked what they currently were using in any particular skill area. Presentations from the coleaders were framed as fine-tuning of parents' own ideas or as new possibilities to add to their current armamentarium of strategies. In addition, in any given skill area, parents were given several different techniques to choose from. For example, three different approaches to consequences for negative behavior were presented and parents selected the one they wished to implement at home. Active selection from among a variety of strategies allowed parents a sense of control over the overall plan put in place in their family.

One testimonial from an economically disadvantaged, insular mother at the end of the program gave some indication of the slow but ultimately successful process of instilling in the parents a sense of ownership of the program. In one of our final sessions, this mother gave an overview of her experience with the program. She said that at first she attended the group out of curiosity and to collect the $10 promised by project staff. She initially did not have much personal interest or motivation in attending the CPP parent component. After a few sessions, she stopped attending for awhile because she thought to herself, "Why do I need to go down there and have those people tell me how to raise my child?" After a few home visits by one of the coleaders, however, she decided to give it another try. She attended regularly after that, never missing another session. She said that she gradually developed trust in the staff and concluded that "maybe they do have some good ideas after all." By the end of the program, she reported that she felt she had done a good job and that she was proud of herself.

Challenges to Parent Intervention. Despite our efforts at aggressive outreach and engagement at the community level, some parents did not attend the CPP parent component meetings regularly or at all. At one point midway through Cohort 1, we conducted an informal telephone survey of these parents to assess the reasons for nonattendance, although we did not tabulate the results of this survey. At first, some of the parents were vague, but when they were read a list of possible reasons for nonattendance many became more open in their conversation with the staff member. The most frequent reason given for nonattendance was a chronic medical problem in themselves or a close family member. The next most frequent reason was scheduling conflicts and their own poor time management skills. Many of these parents said they would like to attend, and a few did begin attending when we included them in a more conveniently scheduled group. Others admitted that although the program sounded interesting and their children spoke to them of enjoying the child groups at school, they probably would never attend because they were simply too tired from working two (sometimes three) jobs and having little to no time for extra activities.

Some of these parents agreed to allow home visits in which CPP parent component skills were reviewed with them and the same handouts given to parents in the groups were provided. One parent, whose husband had cancer, happily welcomed the staff to her home and seemed pleased to receive the coleaders in this context. She attended the last CPP parent component group meeting even though she had not been to a group in months. Other parents did not accept the suggestion of home visits and said that they simply could not participate in the parent component under their present circumstances.

A third category of reasons for nonattendance had to do with psychosocial stresses that pulled parents away from a focus on parenting. Examples given in this category were impending divorce, abandonment by the husband, financial crises, and substance abuse in the parent or the spouse. One parent was homeless throughout the project but attended sporadically when she could be located and transported to group meetings. In many cases, our intervention staff provided some social support to these parents in need and referred many to appropriate social service agencies. Substance-abusing parents were referred to substance abuse treatment (but two said they had no intention of ceasing their use of substances). A strict contract was drawn up with one parent specifying that she must be sober when she attended parent group meetings. She agreed and adhered to this contract for all subsequent meetings.

Our telephone survey assessment of the reasons for nonattendance allowed us to problem solve with the parents some of the issues that were raised, and for a few parents our problem-solving efforts succeeded in increasing their attendance at groups or their acceptance of home visits. For other parents, the obstacles to their attendance were too overwhelming and we respected their right to refuse further intervention.

These extra efforts in the areas of social support and helping parents problem solve life difficulties outside of parenting are consistent with the work of Prinz and Miller (1994). These authors showed that an enhanced family treatment that included standard parent training and attention to other adult problems resulted in greater engagement and significantly lower drop-out rates compared to parent training alone.

Other challenges to the parent component arose in the areas of parent beliefs and value systems that were in conflict with the parent component skills presented. Some parents held the view that children should not be praised for behaviors that they should be expected to do automatically. Some of these parents had altered this view by the end of the program, but others held unshakably to it, still espousing the same point in the last meeting.

Another area of values conflict for some parents was in the arena of physical punishment. Some parents routinely used spanking and other physical (sometimes harsh) punishment as their main approach to discipline. Many of these parents had at one time tried time-out, felt that it was unsuccessful, and concluded that physical punishment was the only alternative. They expressed great skepticism at our presentation on the disadvantages of physical punishment and our statements that alternative (nonphysical) punishment techniques could be effective. We dealt with this by acknowledging their skepticism but asking them to listen to our alternatives and try one of them for 2 weeks. We then presented three alternative approaches to discipline. Most of the parents were curious enough to see if our strategies would work that they agreed to a 2-week contract, and many of these parents returned to the next group reporting surprise at their success with the new strategies. We found that these sessions on alternatives to physical punishment required the greatest clinical delicacy in not criticizing what parents currently were doing but challenging them to at least try some alternative approaches.

The issue of parents feeling criticized is inherent in the very concept of parent training. The fact that we are "training" parents implies to many of them that we have made a judgment of their parenting and found it to be lacking. Because of this implication, we did not use the label "parent training." Instead, we learned to refer to the program as a "child management skills" program for parents. In addition, throughout the program, intervention staff members were encouraged to maintain a very respectful stance toward parents. The usual strategy in group meetings was to ask parents what they currently were doing with regard to certain techniques and to build on any statement that was related to the concepts and techniques on the session agenda. Parents were never told that they must stop doing what they were doing and do it our way instead. Rather, they were challenged to think about whether their current strategies were working for them and to at least consider some of the alternatives that were presented. In some cases, we encouraged them to continue to be skeptical until they tried our suggestions to see if they worked for their family or not. In this way, parents retained the final decision-making authority in their own families. We believe that because each parent is the final arbiter of what will be done in his or her own household, any approach to parent training must find a way to allow parents to feel ownership of the final parenting plan. This is the challenge of parent training, and it requires innovative approaches not typically described in most treatment manuals.

IMPLICATIONS FOR
PREVENTIVE INTERVENTION
WITH EARLY ONSET RISK CHILDREN

The Anger Coping Program described in this chapter and other cognitive-behavioral, problem-solving interventions for aggressive or rejected children (e.g., Bierman, Miller, & Staub, 1987; Feindler, Ecton, Kingsley, & Dubey, 1986; Kazdin, Bass, Siegel, & Thomas, 1989; Kendall, Reber, McLeer, Epps, & Ronan, 1990; Larson, 1992; Vitaro & Tremblay, 1994) have produced significant intervention and prevention effects. To have maximal long-term impact with early onset chronically aggressive children, however, it is imperative that interventions do more than target children's transition into middle school and early adolescence as a time for intervention. Instead, children can be screened for risk at earlier ages, such as when they enter elementary school or preschool. Research has begun to document the stability and validity of high-risk screening in the early school years (e.g., Lochman & Conduct Problems Prevention Research Group, 1995). Once identified, these early onset, high-risk children can be offered comprehensive interventions that include indicated preventive interventions along with universal preventive interventions for their school environment, tutoring, and parent intervention and home visiting throughout the elementary school year (Conduct Problems Prevention Research Group, 1992; also see, Chapters 4 and 5, this volume). In the future, systems for preventive interventions for aggressive children may thus include comprehensive and long-lasting programs for early identified children and strategic, intensive programs for children identified later but prior to adolescence. In both cases, the preventive intervention will need to be carefully implemented within the children's relevant social contexts.

REFERENCES

Allen, G. J., Chinsky, J. M., Larcen, S. W., Lochman, J. E., & Selinger, H. V. (1976). *Community psychology and the schools: A behaviorally oriented multilevel preventive approach.* Hillsdale, NJ: Lawrence Erlbaum.

Asarnow, J. R., & Callan, J. W. (1985). Boys with peer adjustment problems: Social cognitive processes. *Journal of Consulting and Clinical Psychology, 53,* 80-87.

Averill, J. R. (1982). *Anger and aggression: An essay on emotion.* New York/Berlin: Springer-Verlag.

Bandura, A. (1985). Models of causality in social learning theory. In M. J. Mahoney & A. Freeman (Eds.), *Cognition and psychotherapy* (pp. 81-99). New York: Plenum.

Bierman, K. L., Miller, C. M., & Staub, S. (1987). Improving the social behavior and peer acceptance of rejected boys: Effects of social skills training with instructions and prohibitions. *Journal of Consulting and Clinical Psychology, 55,* 194-200.

Coie, J. D., Lochman, J. E., Terry, R., & Hyman, C. (1992). Predicting early adolescent disorder from childhood aggression and peer rejection. *Journal of Consulting and Clinical Psychology, 60,* 783-792.

Coie, J. D., Terry, R., Lenox, K., Lochman, J., & Hyman, C. (in press). Childhood peer rejection and aggression as predictors of stable patterns of adolescent disorder. *Development and Psychopathology.*

Conduct Problems Prevention Research Group. (1992). A developmental and clinical model for the prevention of conduct disorders: The FAST Track Program. *Development and Psychopathology, 4,* 509-527.

Craven, S. (1995). *Examination of the role of physiological and emotional arousal in reactive aggressive boys' hostile attributional biases in peer provocation situations.* Unpublished doctoral dissertation, Duke University, Durham, NC.

Crick, N. R., & Dodge, K. A. (1994). A review and reformulation of social information-processing mechanisms in childrens' social adjustment. *Psychological Bulletin, 115,* 74-101.

Cummings, E. M., Iannotti, R. V., & Zahn-Waxler, C. (1985). Influence of conflict between adults on the emotions and aggression of young children. *Developmental Psychology, 21,* 495-507.

Dodge, K. A. (1986). A social information processing model of social competence in children. In M. Perlmutter (Ed.), *Minnesota symposia on child psychology* (Vol. 18, pp. 75-127). Hillsdale, NJ: Lawrence Erlbaum.

Dodge, K. A. (1991). Emotion and social information processing. In J. Garber & K. A. Dodge (Eds.), *The development of emotion regulation and dysregulation* (pp. 159-181). New York: Cambridge University Press.

Dodge, K. A., & Newman, J. P. (1981). Biased decision making processes in aggressive boys. *Journal of Abnormal Psychology, 90,* 375-379.

Dodge, K. A., Pettit, G. S., McClaskey, C. L., & Brown, M. M. (1986). Social competence in children. *Monographs of the Society for Research in Child Development, 51,* (2, Serial No. 213).

Dodge, K. A., Price, J. M., Bachorowski, J., & Newman, J. P. (1990). Hostile attributional biases in severely aggressive adolescents. *Journal of Abnormal Psychology, 99,* 385-392.

Elliott, D. S., Huizinga, D., & Ageton, S. S. (1985). *Explaining delinquency and drug use.* Beverly Hills, CA: Sage.

Fabes, R. A., & Eisenberg, N. (1992). Young children's coping with interpersonal anger. *Child Development, 63,* 116-128.

Feindler, E. L., Ecton, R. B., Kingsley, D., & Dubey, D. R. (1986). Group anger-control training for institutionalized psychiatry male adolescents. *Behavior Therapy, 17,* 109-123.

Forehand, R., & McMahon, R. J. (1981). *Helping the noncompliant child: A clinician's guide to parent training.* New York: Guilford.

Garrison, S. T., & Stolberg, A. L. (1983). Modifications of anger in children by affective imagery training. *Journal of Abnormal Child Psychology, 11,* 115-130.

Gelfand, D. M., Ficola, T., & Zarbatany, L. (1986). Prevention of childhood behavior disorders. In B. A. Edelstein & L. Michelson (Eds.), *Handbook of prevention* (pp. 133-152). New York: Plenum.

Hawkins, J. D., Catalano, R. F., & Miller, J. Y. (1992). Risk and protective factors for alcohol and other drug problems in adolescence and early adulthood: Implications for substance abuse prevention. *Psychological Bulletin, 112,* 64-105.

Hinshaw, S. P., Lahey, B. B., & Hart, E. L. (1993). Issues of taxonomy and comorbidity in the development of conduct disorder. *Development and Psychopathology, 5,* 31-34.

Institute of Medicine. (1994). *Reducing risks for mental disorders: Frontiers for preventive intervention research.* Washington, DC: National Academy Press.

Kandel, D. B. (1982). Epidemiological and psycho-social perspectives in adolescent drug abuse. *Journal of the American Academy of Child Psychiatry, 21,* 328-347.

Kazdin, A. E. (1995). *Conduct disorders in childhood and adolescence* (2nd ed.). Thousand Oaks, CA: Sage.

Kazdin, A. E., Bass, D., Siegel, T., & Thomas, C. (1989). Cognitive-behavioral therapy and relationship therapy in the treatment of children referred for antisocial behavior. *Journal of Consulting and Clinical Psychology, 57,* 522-535.

Kellam, S., Ensminger, M., & Simon, M. B. (1980). Mental health in first grade and teenage drug, alcohol and cigarette use. *Drug and Alcohol Dependence, 5,* 273-304.

Kellam, S. G., & Brown, H. (1982). *Social adaptational and psychological antecedents of adolescent psychopathology ten years later.* Baltimore, MD: Johns Hopkins University Press.

Kendall, P. C. (1991). Guiding theory for therapy with children and adolescents. In P. C. Kendall (Ed.), *Child and adolescent therapy: Cognitive-behavioral procedures* (pp. 3-22). New York: Guilford.

Kendall, P. C., & Lochman, J. E. (1994). Cognitive-behavioral therapies. In M. Rutter, E. Taylor, & L. Hersov (Eds.), *Child and adolescent psychiatry: Modern approaches* (pp. 857-884). Oxford, UK: Blackwell Scientific.

Kendall, P. C., Reber, M., McLeer, S., Epps, J., & Ronan, K. R. (1990). Cognitive-behavioral treatment of conduct-disordered children. *Cognitive Therapy and Research, 14,* 279-297.

Klaczynski, P. A., & Cummings, E. M. (1989). Responding to anger in aggressive and nonaggressive boys: A research note. *Journal of Child Psychology and Psychiatry and Allied Disciplines, 30,* 309-314.

Kumpfer, K. L. (1989). Prevention of alcohol and drug abuse: A critical review of risk factor and prevention strategies. In D. Shaffer, I. Phillips, & N. Enzer (Eds.), *Prevention of mental disorders, alcohol and other drug use in children and adolescents* (pp. 309-371). Rockville, MD: Office for Substance Abuse Prevention.

Kupersmidt, J. B., & Coie, J. D. (1990). Preadolescent peer status, aggression, and school adjustment as predictors of externalizing problems in adolescence. *Child Development, 61,* 1350-1362.

Larson, J. D. (1992). Anger and aggression management techniques through the Think First curriculum. *Journal of Offender Rehabilitation, 18,* 101-117.

Larson, J. D. (1994). Violence prevention in the schools: A review of selected programs and procedures. *School Psychology Review, 23,* 151-163.

Lochman, J. E. (1985). Effects of different treatment lengths in cognitive-behavioral interventions with aggressive boys. *Child Psychiatry and Human Development, 16,* 45-56.

Lochman, J. E. (1987). Self and peer perceptions and attributional biases of aggressive and nonaggressive boys in dyadic interactions. *Journal of Consulting and Clinical Psychology, 55,* 404-410.

Lochman, J. E. (1990). Modification of childhood aggression. In M. Hersen, R. Eisler, & P. M. Miller (Eds.), *Progress in behavior modification* (Vol. 25, pp. 47-85). Newbury Park, CA: Sage.

Lochman, J. E. (1992). Cognitive-behavioral interventions with aggressive boys: Three-year follow-up and preventive effects. *Journal of Consulting and Clinical Psychology, 60,* 426-432.

Lochman, J. E., Burch, P. P., Curry, J. F., & Lampron, L. B. (1984). Treatment and generalization effects of cognitive-behavioral and goal setting interventions with aggressive boys. *Journal of Consulting and Clinical Psychology, 52,* 915-916.

Lochman, J. E., Coie, J. D., Underwood, M., & Terry, R. (1993). Effectiveness of a social relations intervention program for aggressive and nonaggressive rejected children. *Journal of Consulting and Clinical Psychology, 61,* 1053-1058.

Lochman, J. E., & Conduct Problems Prevention Research Group (1995). Screening of child behavior problems for prevention programs at school entry. *Journal of Consulting and Clinical Psychology, 63,* 549-559.

Lochman, J. E., & Curry, J. F. (1986). Effects of social problem-solving training and self-instruction training with aggressive boys. *Journal of Clinical Child Psychology, 15,* 159-164.

Lochman, J. E., & Dodge, K. A. (1994). Social-cognitive processes of severely violent, moderately aggressive and nonaggressive boys. *Journal of Consulting and Clinical Psychology, 62,* 366-374.

Lochman, J. E., Dunn, S. E., & Klimes-Dougan, B. (1993). An intervention and consultation model from a social cognitive perspective: A description of the Anger Coping Program. *School Psychology Review, 22,* 458-471.

Lochman, J. E., & Lampron, L. B. (1986). Situational social problem-solving skills and self esteem of aggressive and nonaggressive boys. *Journal of Abnormal Child Psychology, 14,* 605-617.

Lochman, J. E., Lampron, L. B., Burch, P. R., & Curry, J. E. (1985). Client characteristics associated with behavior change for treated and untreated boys. *Journal of Abnormal Child Psychology, 13,* 527-538.

Lochman, J. E., Lampron, L. B., Gemmer, T. C., & Harris, S. R. (1987). Anger coping intervention with aggressive children: A guide to implementation in school settings. In P. A. Keller & S. R. Heyman (Eds.), *Innovations in clinical practice: A source book* (Vol. 6, pp. 339-356). Sarasota, FL: Professional Resource Exchange.

Lochman, J. E., Lampron, L. B., Gemmer, T. C., Harris, R., & Wyckoff, G. M. (1989). Teacher consultation and cognitive-behavioral interventions with aggressive boys. *Psychology in the Schools, 26,* 179-188.

Lochman, J. E., Lampron, L. B., & Rabiner, D. (1989). Format and salience effects in the social problem-solving of aggressive and nonaggressive boys. *Journal of Clinical Child Psychology, 18,* 230-236.

Lochman, J. E., & Lenhart, L. A. (1993). Anger coping intervention for aggressive children: Conceptual models and outcome effects. *Clinical Psychology Review, 13,* 785-805.

Lochman, J. E., & Lenhart, L. A. (in press). Cognitive behavioral therapy of aggressive children: Effects of schemas. In H. P. J. Van Bilsen, P. C. Kendall, & J. H. Slavenburg (Eds.), *Cognitive-behavioral approaches for children and adolescents: Challenges for the next century.* New York: Plenum.

Lochman, J. E., Meyer, B. L., Rabiner, D. L., & White, J. J. (1991). Parameters influencing social problem-solving of aggressive children. In R. Prinz (Ed.), *Advances in behavioral assessment of children and families* (Vol. 5, pp. 31-63). London: Kingsley.

Lochman, J. E., Nelson, W. M., III, & Sims, J. P. (1981). A cognitive-behavioral program for use with aggressive children. *Journal of Clinical Child Psychology, 13,* 527-538.

Lochman, J. E., & Wayland, K. K. (1994). Aggression, social acceptance, and race as predictors of negative adolescent outcomes. *Journal of the American Academy of Child and Adolescent Psychiatry, 33,* 1026-1035.

Lochman, J. E., Wayland, K. K., & White, K. J. (1993). Social goals: Relationship to adolescent adjustment and to social problem-solving. *Journal of Abnormal Child Psychology, 21,* 135-151.

Lochman, J. E., White, K. J., & Wayland, K. K. (1991). Cognitive-behavioral assessment and treatment with aggressive children. In P. C. Kendall (Ed.), *Child and adolescent therapy: Cognitive-behavioral procedures* (pp. 25-65). New York: Guilford.

Loeber, R. (1990). Development and risk factors of juvenile antisocial behavior and delinquency. *Clinical Psychology Review, 10,* 1-42.

Milich, R. L., & Dodge, K. A. (1984). Social information processing in child psychiatric populations. *Journal of Abnormal Child Psychology, 12,* 471-490.

Olweus, D. (1979). Stability of aggressive behavior patterns in males: A review. *Psychological Bulletin, 86,* 852-875.

Patterson, G. R. (1982). *Coercive family process.* Eugene, OR: Castalia.

Patterson, G. R. (1984). Beyond technology: The next stage in developing an empirical base for parent training. In L. L'Abate (Ed.), *Handbook of family psychology and psychotherapy* (pp. 1344-1379). New York: Dow Jones-Irwin.

Patterson, G. R., & Bank, L. (1989). Some amplifying mechanisms for pathologic processes in families. In M. R. Gunnar & E. Thelen (Eds.), *Systems and development: The Minnesota symposia on child psychology* (Vol. 22, pp. 167-209). Hillsdale, NJ: Lawrence Erlbaum.

Patterson, G. R., Reid, J. B., & Dishion, T. J. (1992). *Antisocial boys.* Eugene, OR: Castalia.

Patterson, G. R., Reid, J. B., Jones, R. R., & Conger, R. E. (1975). *A social learning approach to family intervention. Vol. 1. Families with aggressive children.* Eugene, OR: Castalia.

Patterson, G. R., & Stouthamer-Loeber, M. (1984). The correlation of family management practices and delinquency. *Child Development, 55,* 1299-1307.

Perry, D. G., Perry, L. C., & Rasmussen, P. (1986). Cognitive social learning mediators of aggressive children. *Child Development, 57,* 700-711.

Perry, M. A., & Furukawa, M. J. (1986). Modeling methods. In F. H. Kanfer & A. P. Goldstein (Eds.), *Helping people change: A textbook of methods* (3rd ed., pp. 66-110). New York: Pergamon.

Prinz, R. J., & Miller, G. E. (1994). Family-based treatment for childhood antisocial behavior: Experimental influences on dropout and engagement. *Journal of Consulting and Clinical Psychology, 62,* 645-650.

Rabiner, D., Lenhart, L., & Lochman, J. E. (1990). Automatic versus reflective social problem-solving in popular, average, and rejected children. *Developmental Psychology, 26,* 1010-1016.

Richard, B. A., & Dodge, K. A. (1982). Social maladjustment and problem solving in school aged children. *Journal of Consulting and Clinical Psychology, 50,* 226-233.

Slaby, R. G., & Guerra, N. G. (1988). Cognitive mediators of aggression in adolescent offenders: An assessment. *Developmental Psychology, 24,* 580-588.

Stattin, H., & Magnusson, D. (1989). The role of early aggressive behavior in the frequency, seriousness, and types of later crime. *Journal of Consulting and Clinical Psychology, 57,* 710-718.

Swain, R. C., Oetting, E. R., Edwards, R. W., & Beauvais, F. (1989). Links from emotional distress to adolescent drug use: A path model. *Journal of Consulting and Clinical Psychology, 57,* 227-238.

Tremblay, R. E., Masses, B., Perron, D., Leblanc, M., Schwartzman, A. E., & Ledingham, J. E. (1992). Early disruptive behavior, poor school achievement, delinquent behavior, and delinquent personality: Longitudinal analyses. *Journal of Consulting and Clinical Psychology, 60,* 64-72.

Underwood, M. K., Coie, J. D., & Herbsman, C. R. (1992). Display rules for anger and aggression in school-age children. *Child Development, 63,* 366-380.

Vitaro, F., & Tremblay, R. E. (1994). Impact of a prevention program on aggressive children's friendships and social adjustment. *Journal of Abnormal Child Psychology, 22,* 457-475.

Wells, K. C. (1995). Parent management training. In G. P. Sholevar (Ed.), *Conduct disorders in children and adolescents: Assessment and intervention.* Washington, DC: American Psychiatric Association.

Windle, M. (1990). A longitudinal study of antisocial behavior in early adolescence as predictors of late adolescence substance use: Gender and ethnic group differences. *Journal of Abnormal Child Psychology, 99,* 86-92.

7

Improving Availability, Utilization, and Cost Efficacy of Parent Training Programs for Children With Disruptive Behavior Disorders

CHARLES E. CUNNINGHAM

The externalizing or Disruptive Behavior Disorders (DBD) (Attention-Deficit Hyperactivity Disorder [ADHD], Oppositional Defiant Disorder, and Conduct Disorder) (American Psychiatric Association, 1994) are among the most prevalent, persistent, and vexing of the early childhood problems referred to children's mental health centers. Although these disorders reflect the complex interplay of genetic factors, parental psychopathology, marital interactions, family functioning, peer relationships, educational experiences, and larger socioeconomic variables, parenting is almost universally consid-

AUTHOR'S NOTE: Preparation of this chapter was supported by a Senior Research Fellowship from the Ontario Mental Health Foundation. Evaluation of the COPE Program was supported by an award from the Health Innovation Fund of the Premier's Council on Health, Well Being and Social Justice. The author expresses appreciation for the helpful comments provided by Rebecca Bremner, Donna Bohaychuk, and H. I. J. van der Spuy. The COPE Program's leader manuals and videotapes are available by contacting Dr. Charles E. Cunningham, Department of Psychology, Chedoke-McMaster Hospitals, Hamilton, Ontario, Canada, L8N 3Z5.

ered to play a mediating role in their emergence, maintenance, or longer-term developmental course (Dishion, Patterson, Stoolmiller, & Skinner, 1991; Loeber & Dishion, 1983; Patterson, 1982; Shaw, Keenan, & Vondra, 1994). The severity of the difficulties encountered by children with DBD, the counterproductive response of many parents (Patterson, 1982), and links between parenting and longer-term adjustment disorders (Dishion et al., 1991; Loeber & Dishion, 1983) suggest that programs providing the skills parents need to improve relations with their child, promote prosocial behavior, and respond effectively to aggression should be an important component in more comprehensive prevention and intervention programs (Dumas, 1989; Kazdin, 1987; Webster-Stratton, 1991). Clinical trials confirm that parent training programs have proven to be a useful intervention for children with both ADHD (Anastopoulos, Shelton, DuPaul, & Guevremont, 1993; Dubey, O'Leary, & Kaufman, 1983; Freeman, Phillips, & Johnston, 1992; Pisterman et al., 1989) and conduct disorders (Bank, Marlowe, Reid, Patterson, & Weinrott, 1991; Eisenstadt, Eyberg, McNeil, Newcomb, & Funderburk, 1993; Forehand & McMahon, 1981; McNeil, Eyberg, Eisenstadt, Newcomb, & Funderburk, 1991; Patterson, Chamberlain, & Reid, 1982; Webster-Stratton, 1984). Most programs yield an increase in parental confidence and child management skills, a decrease in parental stress, and a reduction in conduct problems. Follow-up studies report that these gains are maintained over both short- (Anastopoulos et al., 1993; Dubey et al., 1983; Freeman et al., 1992; Patterson & Fleischman, 1979; Pisterman et al., 1989; Webster-Stratton, 1984) and longer-term follow-up intervals (McMahon, 1994).

LIMITATIONS OF
PARENT TRAINING PROGRAMS

Despite their promise, the efficacy of parent training programs is limited by several factors. First, DBD is among the most prevalent childhood psychiatric disorders (Offord et al., 1987) and one of the most frequent referrals to outpatient clinics. Indeed, the percentage of children with DBD needing help may be increasing (Achenbach & Howell, 1993). Utilization studies in both Canada (Boyle, 1991) and the United States (Tuma, 1989; Zahner, Pawelkiewicz, DeFrancesco, & Adnopoz, 1992), however, suggest that a significant percentage of children do not receive professional assistance. In the Ontario Child Health Study, for example, only about one in six of a sample of psychiatrically disturbed children received assistance from social service agencies (Offord et al., 1987).

The low utilization evident in most studies is the complex function of a variety of factors. First, access to mental health resources is increasingly limited by financial constraints (Boyle & Offord, 1988). Given a fixed budget for children's mental health services, the availability of parent training is restricted by locating programs in expensive clinic or hospital settings, devoting a disproportionate percentage of resources to comprehensive yet expensive pretreatment diagnostic assessments (Barkley, 1990), and a preference for individual training programs.

Second, little is known regarding the extent to which a population of families of children with DBD would use parent training programs (Webster-Stratton, 1991). Indeed, epidemiological studies suggest that a significant majority of parents of children with DBD do not feel that assistance is needed (Boyle, 1991) and are unlikely to participate in parent training programs.

Third, families of children who are at greatest risk are least likely to access parent training. Thus, younger, economically disadvantaged, socially isolated, or depressed parents of children with the most severe DBD are least likely to enroll in or complete intervention programs (Firestone & Witt, 1982; Kazdin, 1990; Kazdin, Mazurick, & Bass, 1993; Kazdin, Mazurick, & Siegel, 1994).

Fourth, hospital- or clinic-based parent training programs may present financial or logistical barriers that prevent potentially interested parents from participating. Work schedules that do not allow daytime attendance, extracurricular activities, difficulties arranging child care, travel time, or transportation costs may prevent parents from enrolling in or consistently attending parent training programs.

Fifth, the psychological or cultural implications of seeking professional mental health assistance may represent barriers to other families. Indeed, our own studies suggest that immigrants or families using English as a second language are less likely to use parent training programs offered at children's mental health centers (Cunningham, Bremner, & Boyle, 1995).

Finally, the design of parent training programs may inadvertently compromise outcome. For example, the didactic approach used to teach new child management skills in many parent training programs may inadvertently increase resistance (Patterson & Forgatch, 1985), reduce positive in-session participation, increase late arrivals, decrease homework completion, and compromise attendance (Cunningham, Davis, Bremner, Dunn, & Rzasa, 1993). Moreover, a parent training curriculum that does not allow parents to discuss other issues of personal concern may reduce overall effectiveness (Prinz & Miller, 1994).

REDESIGNING PARENT TRAINING PROGRAMS

Increasing Availability of Parent Training: Large-Group Courses

Given a programmatic goal that the limited funds available to our service should be shared equitably among parents in our community, we elected to develop and evaluate a model that would yield a substantial increase in the availability of parent training programs. In 1989, our service shifted from individual family (Cunningham, 1990) and small-group parent training models to large courses capable of enrolling from 25 to 35 participants (Cunningham, Bremner, & Boyle, 1995; Cunningham, Bremner, & Secord-Gilbert, 1993), a model we call the Community Parent Education (COPE) Program.

Redesigning Training Process

In many parent training programs, leaders introduce new skills by describing the strategy, discussing its merits, demonstrating its application to common child management problems, assigning homework projects, and suggesting solutions to problems in implementation. Because this approach may increase resistance (Cunningham, Davis, et al., 1993; Patterson & Forgatch, 1985), the COPE Program uses a coping modeling problem-solving approach (Cunningham, 1990; Cunningham, Bremner, & Boyle, 1995; Cunningham, Davis, et al., 1993) in which parents formulate a general set of child management strategies by discussing videotaped child management errors, considering the consequences of these mistakes, formulating alternative strategies, and discussing their merits. To enable large groups of parents to participate actively in the problem-solving discussions, modeling exercises, and role-playing activities that represent the critical skill-building components of our individual programs (Cunningham, 1990), much of the work of the course is accomplished in smaller (e.g., five members) sub-

TABLE 7.1   Basic Components of a Large-Group COPE Parenting Session

Large-group informal networking
Subgroups review homework successes
Subgroup leaders summarize homework reviews to larger group
Subgroups identify videotaped parenting errors
Subgroups discuss consequences of videotaped errors
Subgroup leaders summarize discussion to larger group
Subgroups formulate alternative child management strategies
Subgroups discuss advantages of proposed alternatives
Subgroup leaders summarize proposed alternatives to larger group
Leader models proposed solutions
Subgroups formulate detailed individual homework plans
Dyads role play strategies
Leader closes sessions

groups. Within these subgroups, parents review the successful application of new strategies during the preceding week's homework assignment, discuss solutions to videotaped child management errors, explore the application of new strategies to problems at home, rehearse new skills, and formulate homework goals. Each subgroup nominates a chair responsible for keeping members on task, encouraging participation, and summarizing the subgroup's discussions to the larger group. The course leader assigns problem-solving tasks to the subgroups, prompts each subgroup's leader to share their conclusions with the larger group, and integrates the suggestions of individual subgroups. The course leader then models the skills suggested by the group, prompts the larger group to solve problems encountered in the implementation of new strategies, helps the group resolve disagreements, and supports parents dealing with particularly challenging children (Cunningham, Bremner, et al., 1993). The basic structure of a COPE parenting session is summarized in Table 7.1.

Developing a Family and
Community Systems Focus

Because parenting is influenced by a complex set of personal, family systems, and community network variables (Miller & Prinz, 1990; Simons, Lorenz, Wu Chyi-In, & Conger, 1993; Webster-Stratton, 1994), the COPE

TABLE 7.2   Sample COPE Curriculum

Session 1. Information night and course introduction
Session 2. Attending and reward strategies
Session 3. When-then strategies
Session 4. Planned ignoring
Session 5. Point systems I
Session 6. Planning ahead
Session 7. Point systems II (response cost)
Session 8. Time-out I
Session 9. Time-out II
Session 10. Working with the school (home daily report cards)
Session 11. Problem-solving skills
Session 12. Selected problems I
Session 13. Selected problems II
Session 14. Closing session

Program devotes a portion of each session's activities to enhancing family functioning (Cunningham, 1990). The program's family systems goals include sharing child management responsibility, improving problem-solving skills, and enhancing supportive communication. Moreover, given the influence of extended family support on both parent-child interactions (Dumas, 1986) and response to parent training (Wahler, 1980), the COPE Program's large-group, neighborhood school-based model provides an opportunity to increase contacts among parents sharing similar problems and to encourage an exchange of information regarding potentially useful local resources.

Designing the Curriculum
of Parent Training Programs

As in many parent training programs (Barkley, 1987; Forehand & McMahon, 1981) the COPE Program's basic curriculum (Table 7.2) begins with skills for increasing prosocial behavior; moves to strategies for encouraging planning, problem solving, and self-regulation; develops responses to noncompliance and aggressive behavior; and concludes with solutions to outstanding problems. Consumer feedback in our own programs, however, suggests that some parents of very difficult to manage children are interested in more immediate solutions to aggressive behavior, a factor that may contribute to poor participation and early attrition. Interestingly, Eisenstadt et al. (1993) found that a program teaching control strategies first yielded better outcomes and more favorable consumer evaluations than a more traditional sequence beginning with positive strategies. The optimal curriculum sequence for different diagnostic subgroups merits further study.

Contacting Potential Participants

To use the case-carrying potential of large-group parenting courses, programs must contact a significantly larger percentage of the population than is typically referred to children's treatment centers (Boyle, 1991). Although schools represent a point of virtually universal contact with parents who might benefit from parent training programs, teachers and parents seldom agree on childhood difficulties (Szatmari, Boyle, & Offord, 1989). Moreover, parents are more likely to use mental health resources when they, as opposed to the child's teacher, feel the child needs assistance (Boyle, 1991). The COPE Program, therefore, contacts parents directly by advertising upcoming courses in school newsletters, placing posters on school parent information boards, and utilizing the local media's community service advertising opportunities.

Community physicians provide an alternative contact with families who might benefit from parent training. Within Ontario's universal first dollar health insurance plan, for example, at least half of the childhood population visits a physician within a 6-month period (Woodward et al., 1988). Moreover, 70% of those children perceived by their parents to have behavioral and emotional problems are seen by a physician at least once during that period. Because younger children are more likely to visit a physician than older children, using general practice, family medicine, or pediatric office visits to contact parents allows more preventive programs during the child's preschool years when parent training may be more effective (Dishion & Patterson, 1992). In addition, a number of the sociodemographic factors that signal risks for childhood psychopathology do not represent barriers to physician's office visits (Woodward et al., 1988). Although the COPE Program notifies community physicians of upcoming courses, child management concerns rarely manifest themselves in office settings (Sleator & Ullman, 1981) and may not be the focus of the consultation. The program, therefore, advertises directly to parents by placing posters in the waiting rooms of local physicians that announce COPE courses.

Capitalizing on Critical Windows

Although schools and physicians' offices provide a cost-effective, universal point of contact with potentially interested participants, most parents of children with psychiatric disorders do not feel that professional assistance is required (Boyle, 1991). In an effort to catch parents during critical windows when interest in parent training emerges and family schedules permit participation, the COPE Program advertises repeatedly and schedules courses during fall, winter, and spring terms of the school year.

A Community-Based Continuing Adult Educational Model of Parent Training

Parent training programs for children with DBD are often offered through children's mental health centers or hospitals in which enrollment requires professional referral, formal intake interviews, multidisciplinary assessments, and conferencing. Although comprehensive assessments represent an important component in the management of children with psychiatric disorders, several considerations led us to offer the COPE Program's courses as a community-based, continuing parent educational program that did not require clinic referral. First, given limited financial resources, the cost of clinic-based services restricts parent training to a small percentage of children at risk for or suffering from behavioral disorders (Boyle, 1991). In a publicly funded mental health system in which costs are shared by an entire community, it is questionable whether the benefits of an expensive service for small numbers of children justify the inequitable access that inevitably results.

Second, the intake and assessment capabilities of children's mental health centers often limit the number of families that are available at a point in time for referral to clinic-based parent training programs. Because families who have been assessed may be uninterested or unavailable at the time parent training is scheduled, clinic settings often fail to use the service delivery potential of large groups.

Third, although an effective parent training program might prevent minor child management problems from escalating into more serious difficulties, clinic referrals may not be triggered until problems reach relatively high severity thresholds. Readily available, large-group parenting courses, in contrast, encourage a more preventive approach to parent training. Indeed, enrollment in our trials suggests that a significant percentage of families choose to enroll in COPE programs before problems reach a level that would warrant formal diagnosis and referral.

Fourth, access to parent training programs should not be limited to families of children with identified psychiatric disorders (Boyle, 1991). A broader definition of the risks warranting referral to parent training might include limited parenting skill, parental conflict regarding child management strategies, economic disadvantage, single-parent status, or social isolation.

Fifth, Ontario utilization studies suggest that a significant percentage of the children receiving service in mental health centers do not evidence significant psychiatric disorders (Boyle, 1991). Thus, parents of children with less severe difficulties who might benefit from a community-based parent training program may be utilizing the more sophisticated clinic-based services needed by those with more severe disorders, families unable to benefit from parent training, or couples needing assistance with related marital difficulties (Boyle, 1991).

Sixth, the limited availability of mental health resources inevitably creates waiting lists that delay the entry of parents who might benefit from parent training programs. Because the perception of need varies as a function of other events in family life, the critical window when parents are interested in participating may be lost.

Finally, although it might be argued that a differential diagnosis is needed prior to enrollment, the day-to-day management problems faced by parents of children with different DBDs are very similar. Moreover, the general strategies introduced in programs for children with different DBDs are quite generic (Barkley, 1987; Cunningham, 1990; Cunningham, Bremner, et al., 1993; Forehand & McMahon, 1981; Webster-Stratton, 1991). Parents of children with different diagnoses may well find similar strategies useful in solving common child management problems. Indeed, 85% of a sample of 418 parents completing early versions of the COPE Program reported that the strategies introduced were helpful with the siblings of the referred child.

Reducing Barriers to Participation

To reduce logistical, cultural, and psychological barriers, COPE courses are scheduled at conveniently located neighborhood schools. To accommodate the schedules of a population in which a majority of parents are employed full-time, courses are conducted at times during morning, afternoon, and evening. Parents who are unable to secure or afford reliable child care can enroll their children in a social skills activity group conducted by volunteer co-op students from McMaster University.

Controlling the Costs of
Parent Training Programs

Given fixed funding, the availability of parent training varies as a function of its cost. The major expenses incurred in parent training programs include the costs of referral, assessment, personnel, and facilities. The broader societal costs of parent training include the travel, parking, and opportunity (e.g., lost income-earning time) expenses incurred by participants. A longer-term costing of parent training must consider the program's effects on subsequent utilization of more expensive clinic or residential programs, potential reductions in antisocial behavior (e.g., vandalism or theft), and subsequent decreases in police, court, and incarceration costs.

To maximize utilization and reduce overall service delivery costs, the COPE Program enrolls 25 to 35 participants per course. Second, because a model requiring the presence of a coleader increases program costs and reduces availability, COPE programs are conducted by an individual leader. Because costs vary with the professional background of the leader and the expense of training in this model, detailed leader training manuals (Cunningham, Bremner, & Secord, 1995), videotaped analogs, and an annual training program allow cost-effective dissemination of this approach to professionals with different backgrounds. Finally, cost-benefit analyses suggest that offering courses at decentralized settings across the community reduces the travel, parking, and opportunity costs incurred by participants in parent training programs (Cunningham, Bremner, & Secord, 1995).

Developing More Comprehensive Programs

With notable exceptions (McNeil et al., 1991), the effects of parent training programs do not consistently generalize to related problems at school. A number of studies suggest that the impact of parent training might be enhanced by combining programs that focus on different situations (e.g., home plus school), mediators (e.g., parents plus teachers), or target problems (prosocial behavior plus aggression) (Kazdin, Siegel, & Bass, 1992). To supplement COPE's impact, communities should develop cost-effective programs that are themselves capable of meeting the needs of large populations. These might include schoolwide social skills training programs (Hundert & Taylor, 1993), peer-mediated conflict resolution programs (Schrumph, Crawford, & Usadel, 1991), more comprehensive violence-prevention programs (Olweus, 1991), and extracurricular skill-building programs (Jones & Offord, 1989). Moreover, because COPE courses will not meet the needs of all parents, this program should be integrated into a more comprehensive range of child and family services.

Potential Benefits of Large-Group, Community-Based Courses

In addition to a substantial increase in availability and cost efficacy, large, community-based COPE courses have a number of advantages over individual or small-group interventions. First, informal interactions, subgroup exercises, and larger group discussions allow a valuable exchange of information regarding normal child behavior, common problems at different ages, and potentially useful child management strategies. Data from our own trials, for example, suggest that larger groups generate more potential solutions to child management problems than individual parenting programs (Cunningham, Bremner, & Secord, 1995). Moreover, a problem-based model in which parents explore a wider range of child management strategies emphasizes a flexible approach that may better meet the diverse temperamental and developmental needs of this population (Grusec & Goodnow, 1994). Alternatively, their consensus-building capabilities seem to allow larger groups to more effectively resolve disagreements precipitated by parents expressing extreme positions on issues, such as the use of corporal punishment.

Second, in the COPE Program parents practice a general approach to problem solving, use other parents as resources, and give one another supportive feedback. These activities provide an opportunity to strengthen the systemic skills needed by families of children with DBD (Eyberg & Robinson, 1982; Miller & Prinz, 1990; Webster-Stratton, 1994).

Third, social psychological research suggests that formulating solutions, devising supporting rationales, and setting personal goals in a group context should improve commitment and adherence to new strategies (Janis, 1983; Leary & Miller, 1986; Meichenbaum & Turk, 1987), enhance a sense of personal efficacy (Bandura, 1982), and reduce the resistance evident in more didactically oriented models (Patterson & Forgatch, 1985). To explore this, we randomly assigned residential parents to either a mastery modeling program in which leaders taught skills more didactically or a coping modeling condition in which participants formulated their own solutions to videotaped staff-resident errors (Cunningham, Davis, et al., 1993). Participants in the coping modeling condition, in which strategies were formulated by the group, attended significantly more training sessions than those in the mastery modeling condition, in which skills were taught more didactically. In addition, coping modeling participants arrived late to fewer sessions, completed significantly more homework assignments, interacted more positively during training sessions, reported a significantly higher sense of personal efficacy, and rated the program more favorably than those who were introduced to new skills more didactically.

Fourth, formal feedback suggests that large, neighborhood school-based COPE courses provide an important sense of membership in a group sharing common problems, provide a perspective regarding the severity of child management problems, and normalize the experience of parent training. Because parents of difficult children often find themselves isolated (Cunningham, Benness, & Siegel, 1988), informal interactions, discussions regarding local resources, car pooling, and the opportunity to collaborate in the solution of common problems encourage the supportive contacts that parents need to cope with the stress of managing a difficult child (Cochran & Brassard, 1979). Indeed, assisting other parents in the solution of problems may represent an important source of altruistic satisfaction to other participants (MacKenzie, 1990). Moreover, although COPE sessions focus on a relatively standard curriculum of child management skills, informal interactions, subgroup discussions, and issues raised by the larger group provide parents with a forum to discuss related concerns—an opportunity that appears to enhance the efficacy of parent training (Prinz & Miller, 1994).

Finally, larger groups appear less vulnerable than smaller groups to the potentially disruptive effects (MacKenzie, 1990) of the inevitable dropouts that occur in parent training. With notable exceptions (Eyberg & Matarazzo, 1980), small-group parent training programs appear to be a cost-effective alternative to individual interventions (Brightman, Baker, Clark, & Ambrose, 1982; Christensen, Johnson, Phillips, & Glasgow, 1980; Kovitz, 1976; Pevsner, 1982; Raue & Spence, 1985). To examine the effectiveness of this larger-group COPE model, we prospectively screened a community sample of 4-year-olds entering junior kindergarten programs, identified children more than 1.5 standard deviations above the mean on a measure of behavior problems at home (Barkley & Edlebrock, 1987), and randomly assigned a sample of 150 participants to a large, neighborhood school-based COPE course, an individual family clinic-based parent training program, or a waiting-list control group (Cunningham, Bremner, & Boyle, 1995). Preprogram, postprogram, and 6-month follow-up assessments suggest that, in comparison to clinic-based individual parent training programs, large-group, community-based services enhance utilization among socioeconomically disadvantaged families, families from minority backgrounds, and families with higher-risk children (Cunningham, Bremner, & Boyle, 1995). Larger groups yielded greater improvements in objectively measured problem-solving skills, greater reductions in reported child management problems, and improved maintenance at 6-month follow-up.

CONCLUSIONS

Large-group, community-based parent training programs represent a promising approach to increasing the availability, accessibility, and utilization of parent training programs for families of children with DBD. In addition to their cost efficacy, the breadth and complexity of the cognitive, behavioral, systemic, and social processes operating in large groups may enhance the outcome of more traditional parent training models. Although promising, the development of these programs must be guided by controlled trials regarding their costs and benefits. Finally, although this chapter has been restricted to a discussion of factors limiting the availability of parent training programs for children with DBD, utilization studies suggest that access to professional assistance is limited for children with other psychiatric disorders. A more general discussion of the design of services for children with psychiatric disorders is indicated.

REFERENCES

Achenbach, T. M., & Howell, C. T. (1993). Are American children's problems getting worse? A 13-year comparison. *Journal of the American Academy of Child and Adolescent Psychiatry, 32,* 1145-1153.
American Psychiatric Association. (1994). *Diagnostic and statistical manual of mental disorders* (4th ed.). Washington, DC: Author.

Anastopoulos, A. D., Shelton, T. L., DuPaul, G. J., & Guevremont, D. C. (1993). Parent training for Attention Deficit Hyperactivity Disorder: Its impact on child and parent functioning. *Journal of Abnormal Child Psychology, 21*, 581-596.

Bandura, A. (1982). Self-efficacy mechanism in human agency. *American Psychologist, 37*, 122-147.

Bank, L., Marlowe, H., Reid, J. B., Patterson, G. R., & Weinrott, M. R. (1991). A comparative evaluation of parent-training interventions for families of chronic delinquents. *Journal of Abnormal Child Psychology, 19*, 15-33.

Barkley, R. A. (1987). *Defiant children: A clinician's manual for parent training.* New York: Guilford.

Barkley, R. A. (1990). *Attention Deficit Hyperactivity Disorder: A handbook for diagnosis and treatment.* New York: Guilford.

Barkley, R. A., & Edlebrock, C. (1987). Assessing situational variation in children's problem behaviors: The Home and School Situations Questionnaires. In R. J. Prinz (Ed.), *Advances in behavioral assessment of children and families* (Vol. 3, pp. 157-176). Greenwich, CT: JAI.

Boyle, M. H. (1991). Children's mental health issues: Prevention and treatment. In L. C. Johnson & D. Barnhorst (Eds.), *Children, families and public policy in the 90's* (pp. 73-104). Toronto, Canada: Thompson Educational Publishing.

Boyle, M. H., & Offord, D. R. (1988). Prevalence of childhood disorder, perceived need for help, family dysfunction, and resource allocation for child welfare and children's mental health services in Ontario. *Canadian Journal of Behavioural Science, 20*, 374-388.

Brightman, R. P., Baker, B. L., Clark, D. B., & Ambrose, S. A. (1982). Effectiveness of alternative parent training formats. *Journal of Behavior Therapy and Experimental Psychiatry, 13*, 113-117.

Cochran, M., & Brassard, J. A. (1979). Child development and personal social networks. *Child Development, 50*, 601-615.

Christensen, A., Johnson, S. M., Phillips, O., & Glasgow, R. E. (1980). Cost effectiveness in behavioral family therapy. *Behavior Therapy, 11*, 208-225.

Cunningham, C. E. (1990). A family systems approach to parent training. In R. A. Barkley (Ed.), *Attention Deficit Hyperactivity Disorder: A handbook for diagnosis and treatment* (pp. 432-461). New York: Guilford.

Cunningham, C. E., Benness, B., & Siegel, L. S. (1988). Family functioning, time allocation, and parental depression in the families of normal and ADDH children. *Journal of Clinical Child Psychology, 17*, 169-177.

Cunningham, C. E., Bremner, R., & Boyle, M. (1995). Large group community-based parenting programs for families of preschoolers at risk for Disruptive Behaviour Disorders: Utilization, cost effectiveness, and outcome. *Journal of Child Psychology and Psychiatry, 36*, 1141-1159.

Cunningham, C. E., Bremner, R., & Secord, M. (1995). *COPE: The Community Parent Education Program: A school based family systems oriented workshop for parents of children with Disruptive Behaviour Disorders: Leaders manual.* Unpublished manuscript.

Cunningham, C. E., Bremner, R., & Secord-Gilbert, M. (1993). Increasing the availability, accessibility, and cost efficacy of services for families of ADHD children: A school-based systems-oriented parenting course. *Canadian Journal of School Psychology, 9*, 1-15.

Cunningham, C. E., Davis, J. R., Bremner, R., Dunn, K., & Rzasa, T. (1993). Coping modelling problem solving versus mastery modelling: Effects on adherence, in-session process, and skill acquisition in a residential parent training program. *Journal of Consulting and Clinical Psychology, 61,* 871-877.

Dishion, T. J., & Patterson, G. R. (1992). Age effects in parent training outcome. *Behavior Therapy, 23,* 719-729.

Dishion, T. J., Patterson, G. R., Stoolmiller, M., & Skinner, M. (1991). Family, school, and behavioral antecedents to early adolescent involvement with antisocial peers. *Developmental Psychology, 27,* 172-180.

Dubey, D. R., O'Leary, S., & Kaufman, K. F. (1983). Training parents of hyperactive children in child management: A comparative outcome study. *Journal of Abnormal Child Psychology, 11,* 229-246.

Dumas, J. (1986). Indirect influence of maternal social contacts on mother-child interactions: A setting event analysis. *Journal of Abnormal Child Psychology, 14,* 302-216.

Dumas, J. (1989). Treating antisocial behavior in children: Child approaches. *Clinical Psychology Review, 9,* 197-222.

Eisenstadt, T. H., Eyberg, S., McNeil, C. B., Newcomb, K., & Funderburk, B. (1993). Parent-child interaction therapy with behavior problem children: Relative effectiveness of two stages and overall treatment outcome. *Journal of Clinical Child Psychology, 22,* 42-51.

Eyberg, S., & Matarazzo, R. G. (1980). Training parents as therapists: A comparison between individual parent-child interaction training and parent group didactic training. *Journal of Clinical Psychology, 2,* 492-499.

Eyberg, S., & Robinson, E. A. (1982). Parent-child interaction training: Effects on family functioning. *Journal of Clinical Child Psychology, 11,* 130-137.

Firestone, P., & Witt, J. (1982). Characteristics of families completing and prematurely discontinuing a behavioral parent training program. *Journal of Pediatric Psychology, 7,* 209-221.

Forehand, R., & McMahon, R. J. (1981). *Helping the noncompliant child: A clinician's guide to parent training.* New York: Guilford.

Freeman, W., Phillips, J., & Johnston, C. (1992, June). *Treatment effects on hyperactive and aggressive behaviours in ADHD children.* Paper presented at the meeting of the Canadian Psychological Association, Quebec City.

Grusec, J. E., & Goodnow, J. (1994). Impact of parental discipline methods on the child's internalization of values: A reconceptualization of current point of view. *Developmental Psychology, 30,* 4-19.

Hundert, J., & Taylor, L. (1993). Classwide promotion of social competence in young students. *Exceptionality Education Canada, 3,* 79-101.

Janis, I. (1983). The role of social support in adherence to stressful decisions. *American Psychologist, 38,* 143-160.

Jones, M. G., & Offord, D. R. (1989). Reduction of antisocial behavior in poor children by non-school skill development. *Journal of Child Psychology and Psychiatry, 30,* 737-750.

Kazdin, A. (1987). Treatment of antisocial behavior in children: Current status and future directions. *Psychological Bulletin, 102,* 187-203.

Kazdin, A. (1990). Premature termination from treatment among children referred for antisocial behavior. *Journal of Child Psychology and Psychiatry, 31,* 414-425.

Kazdin, A. E., Mazurick, J. L., & Bass, D. (1993). Risk for attrition in treatment of antisocial children and families. *Journal of Clinical Child Psychology, 22,* 2-16.

Kazdin, A. E., Mazurick, J. L., & Siegel, T. C. (1994). Treatment outcome among children with externalizing disorder who terminate prematurely versus those who complete psychotherapy. *Journal of the American Academy of Child and Adolescent Psychiatry, 33,* 549-557.

Kazdin, A. E., Siegel, T. C., & Bass, D. (1992). Cognitive problem-solving skills training and parent management training in the treatment of antisocial behavior in children. *Journal of Consulting and Clinical Psychology, 60,* 733-747.

Kovitz, K. E. (1976). Comparing group and individual methods for training parents in child management techniques. In E. J. Mash, L. C. Handy, & L. A. Hamerlynck (Eds.), *Behavior modification approaches to parenting* (pp. 124-138). New York: Brunner/ Mazel.

Leary, M. R., & Miller, R. S. (1986). *Social psychology and dysfunctional behavior.* New York/Berlin: Springer-Verlag.

Loeber, R., & Dishion, T. (1983). Early predictors of male delinquency: A review. *Psychological Bulletin, 94,* 68-99.

MacKenzie, K. R. (1990). *Introduction to time limited group psychotherapy.* Washington, DC: American Psychiatric Association.

McMahon, R. J. (1994). Diagnosis, assessment, and treatment of externalizing problems in children: The role of longitudinal data. *Journal of Consulting and Clinical Psychology, 62,* 901-917.

McNeil, C. B., Eyberg, S. M., Eisenstadt, T. H., Newcomb, K., & Funderburk, B. (1991). Parent-child interaction therapy with behavior problem children: Generalization of treatment effects to the school setting. *Journal of Clinical Child Psychology, 55,* 169-182.

Meichenbaum, D., & Turk, D. C. (1987). *Facilitating treatment adherence: A practitioner's guidebook.* New York: Plenum.

Miller, G. E., & Prinz, R. J. (1990). Enhancement of social learning family interventions for childhood conduct disorder. *Psychological Bulletin, 108,* 291-307.

Offord, D. R., Boyle, M. H., Szatmari, P., Rae-Grant, N., Links, P. S., Cadman, D. T., Byles, J. A., Crawford, J. W., Munroe Blum, H., Byrne, C., Thomas, H., & Woodward, C. (1987). Ontario Child Health Study. II. Six month prevalence of disorder and rates of service utilization. *Archives of General Psychiatry, 44,* 832-836.

Olweus, D. (1991). Bully/victim problems among school children: Basic facts and effects of a school based intervention program. In D. J. Pepler & K. H. Rubin (Eds.), *The development and treatment of childhood aggression* (pp. 411-448). Hillsdale, NJ: Lawrence Erlbaum.

Patterson, G. R. (1982). *Coercive family process.* Eugene, OR: Castalia.

Patterson, G. R., Chamberlain, P., & Reid, J. B. (1982). A comparative evaluation of a parent-training program. *Behavior Therapy, 13,* 638-650.

Patterson, G. R., & Fleischman, M. J. (1979). Maintenance of treatment effects: Some considerations concerning family systems and follow-up data. *Behavior Therapy, 10,* 168-185.

Patterson, G. R., & Forgatch, M. S. (1985). Therapist behavior as a determinant for client noncompliance: A paradox for behavior modification. *Journal of Consulting and Clinical Psychology, 53,* 846-851.

Pevsner, R. (1982). Group parent training versus individual family therapy: An outcome study. *Journal of Behavior Therapy and Experimental Psychiatry, 13,* 119-122.

Pisterman, S., McGrath, P. J., Firestone, P., Goodman, J. T., Webster, I., & Mallory, R. (1989). Outcome of parent-mediated treatment of preschoolers with Attention Deficit Disorder with Hyperactivity. *Journal of Consulting and Clinical Psychology, 57,* 636-643.

Prinz, R. J., & Miller, G. E. (1994). Family-based treatment for childhood antisocial behavior: Experimental influences on dropout and engagement. *Journal of Consulting and Clinical Psychology, 62*, 645-650.

Raue, J., & Spence, S. H. (1985). Group versus individual applications of reciprocity training for parent-youth conflict. *Behaviour Research and Therapy, 2*, 177-186.

Schrumph, F., Crawford, D., & Usadel, H. C. (1991). *Peer mediation: Conflict resolution in schools.* Champaign, IL: Research Press.

Shaw, D. S., Keenan, K., & Vondra, J. I. (1994). Developmental precursors of externalizing behavior: Ages 1 to 3. *Developmental Psychology, 30*, 335-364.

Simons, R. L., Lorenz, F. O., Wu, C.-I., & Conger, R. D. (1993). Social network and marital support as mediators and moderators on the impact of stress and depression on parental behavior. *Developmental Psychology, 29*, 368-381.

Sleator, E. K., & Ullman, R. L. (1981). Can the physician diagnose hyperactivity in the office? *Pediatrics, 67*, 13-17.

Szatmari, P., Boyle, M., & Offord, D. R. (1989). ADDH and conduct disorder: Degree of diagnostic overlap and differences among correlates. *Journal of the American Academy of Child and Adolescent Psychiatry, 28*, 865-872.

Tuma, J. M. (1989). Mental health services for children: The state of the art. *American Psychologist, 44*, 188-199.

Wahler, R. G. (1980). The insular mother: Her problems in parent-child treatment. *Journal of Applied Behavior Analysis, 13*, 207-219.

Webster-Stratton, C. (1984). Randomized trial of two parent-training programs for families with conduct disordered children. *Journal of Consulting and Clinical Psychology, 52*, 666-678.

Webster-Stratton, C. (1991). Strategies for helping families of conduct disordered children. *Journal of Child Psychology and Psychiatry, 32*, 1047-1062.

Webster-Stratton, C. (1994). Advancing videotape parent training: A comparison study. *Journal of Consulting and Clinical Psychology, 62*, 583-593.

Woodward, C. A., Boyle, M. H., Offord, D. R., Cadman, D. T., Links, P. S., Munroe-Blum, H., Byrne, C., & Thomas, H. (1988). Ontario Child Health Study: Patterns of ambulatory medical care utilization and their correlates. *Pediatrics, 2*, 425-434.

Zahner, G. E. P., Pawelkiewicz, J., DeFrancesco, J. J., & Adnopoz, J. (1992). Children's mental health service needs and utilization patterns in an urban community: An epidemiological assessment. *Journal of the American Academy of Child and Adolescent Psychiatry, 31*, 951-960.

8

Parental Engagement in Interventions for Children at Risk for Conduct Disorder

RONALD J. PRINZ

GLORIA E. MILLER

THE CHALLENGE OF
PARENTAL ENGAGEMENT

Family-based intervention is an important, if not essential, part of a comprehensive treatment strategy for children at risk for conduct disorder (Kazdin, 1987; Miller & Prinz, 1990). The consistent relationships found between social interactions within the family and severe antisocial behaviors in childhood clearly emphasize the importance of parental involvement in intervention (Patterson, 1986; Vuchinich, Bank, & Patterson, 1992). The most promising family-based intervention approaches focus on improving interpersonal relations between children and adults, view parents as critical change agents in the modification of child behavior, and conceive intervention as a collaborative process that involves coaching, instruction, modeling, self-regulation, and practice (Kazdin, 1987; Miller & Prinz, 1990). Despite moderate success rates with childhood antisocial behavior, the greatest stumbling block for family interventions, such as parent management training, has been insufficient engagement of parents.

Family-based interventions for childhood conduct problems often experience a high rate of sporadic participation and premature dropout, with dropout rates as high as 50% to 60% (Armbruster & Kazdin, 1994; Firestone, Kelly, & Fike, 1980; Firestone & Witt, 1982; Forehand, Middlebrook, Rogers, & Steffe, 1983; Kazdin, 1990; McMahon, Forehand, Griest, & Wells, 1981). Unlike school-based interventions in which the children continually participate in programming, family-based approaches depend on the parent remaining in treatment. Parental dropout is extremely costly to service systems in terms of inefficient utilization, to youth whose trajectory to conduct disorder is not redirected, and to society when others are victimized by delinquency and aggression of youth who failed to receive full intervention. The problem is further compounded by the fact that dropout rates are not reported in family intervention studies or true dropout rates are camouflaged because potential dropout families were screened out before the formal intervention began (Forehand et al., 1983). Parental engagement and dropout have obvious implications for generalizability (or lack thereof), intervention effectiveness, and conceptual models of family functioning. Despite the critical importance of parental engagement relative to childhood antisocial behavior, only a small amount of empirical work has been conducted specifically on parental engagement and dropout (e.g., Kazdin, 1990; Prinz & Miller, 1994; Weisz, Weiss, & Langmeyer, 1987).

Premature dropout is not the only index of inadequate parental engagement. Behavioral signs of insufficient engagement also include sporadic attendance, missed and late appointments, last minute cancellations, skipped sessions without attempting to cancel, and failure to complete assigned homework (Carr, 1990; Firestone & Witt, 1982; Forehand et al., 1983; Gould, Shaffer, & Kaplan, 1985). Additional signs of limited involvement pertain to the quality of participation during intervention sessions, such as low level of interaction, frequent complaints and arguments, giving up on new skills at the first sign of failure, or refusing to practice or role play (Chamberlain & Baldwin, 1987).

CONCEPTUAL FRAMEWORK:
DOMAINS AFFECTING ENGAGEMENT

At least four domains presumably affect parental engagement: the therapeutic-intervention process, personal constructs, intervention characteristics, and situational demands and constraints (Miller & Prinz, 1990; Webster-Stratton & Hammond, 1990).

Interpersonal-Therapeutic Processes in Intervention

Recent work has strived to uncover the client-therapist interactions that occur during parent training. A pioneering study conducted by Chamberlain, Patterson, Reid, Kavanagh, and Forgatch (1984) focused on resistance in traditional parent training and found that one pattern of resistance, identified as the struggle and work-through pattern, was predictive of positive outcomes. For families exhibiting this pattern, in-session resistance peaked soon after parents were exposed to new skills and then steadily decreased over time, leading to better outcomes for youth with aggressive behavior. Families evidencing either no resistance or consistently high resistance did not fare as well in parent training.

Patterson and Forgatch (1985) found that certain behaviors by therapists, such as ones involving confrontation and teaching, can precipitate resistance in parents, whereas supportive therapist behaviors can mitigate resistance. Although there is a large body of literature describing the specific content of various parent training approaches, there is a dearth of studies focusing on actual therapeutic processes used by therapists (or other interventionists) or on what happens during specific attempts to change parents' behaviors, attitudes, and practices (Webster-Stratton & Herbert, 1993). It is assumed, however, that how the interventionist interacts with participating family members plays a crucial role in the engagement process. Independent of content or format, a family-based intervention relies heavily on the interpersonal relationship between the interventionist and the family. Style of interaction, communication skills, sensitivity, and overall interpersonal skillfulness of the interventionist undoubtedly influence engagement and intervention impact.

If parents feel criticized or misunderstood by the interventionist, there is undoubtedly a much greater risk of dropout. How interventionists handle the interpersonal dynamics of either group or individual family programs probably makes a much greater impact on intervention success or failure than the field has been able to document to date.

Personal Expectations, Attributions, and Beliefs

Personal constructs of a cognitive and perceptual nature play a key role in how parents feel, think, and motivate themselves to behave (Bandura, 1982, 1989). For example, tacit expectations, interpersonal attributions, and operative beliefs have been hypothesized to contribute to poor interpersonal relations (Dodge, 1991) and therapy outcome (Miller, 1985; Webster-Stratton & Herbert, 1993). This work has been extended to explain ineffective parenting and less than optimal parental participation and outcomes (Johnston, 1988). Through extensive qualitative analyses of session videotapes, Spitzer, Webster-Stratton, and Hollinsworth (1991) found that parents exhibit substantial cognitive, emotional, and social changes during participation in a group-delivered parent training program. This work clearly emphasizes the need to address personal constructs that can interfere with parents' motivation and ability to apply or adapt essential parenting skills.

Tacit Expectations

People who have unmet or competing tacit expectations about their role or about the purpose of particular actions are less likely to enroll or to fully participate in any type of activity (Szapocznik, Kurtines, Santisteban, & Rio, 1990). A growing body of literature supports the finding that personal expectations can sometimes interfere with help seeking, participation in mental health treatment, and adherence to medical regimens (Meichenbaum & Turk, 1987). Reduced compliance and limited behavioral outcomes have been strongly related to mismatched ideas between consumers and helping agents about the goals and expected roles and activities of treatment (Karoly, 1980; Miller, 1985).

Parent training presents many sources of potential misalignment between parents' and interventionists' expectations (Darling, 1991; Miller & Prinz, 1990). For example, parents vary with respect to expectations regarding the focus of intervention on reducing child misbehavior versus changing parenting behavior (Furey & Basili, 1988). Another potential area of divergence is the expectation that personal nonchild issues, such as marital problems or parental adjustment, will (or will not) be addressed during the intervention (Prinz & Miller, 1994). Moreover, parents and interventionists may have different ideas about expected levels of active involvement, including the need to role play and to carry out assigned activities at home.

Parents also can hold tacit expectations that conflict with the realities of intervention. For example, they may assume treatment will lead to only positive reactions and changes in child behavior and that such changes will be immediate and long-lasting. Finally, parents and helping agents may have vastly different opinions regarding the value and acceptability of different treatment approaches (Kalfus & Razzano, 1992; Miller & Kelly, 1992). Treatment acceptability is affected by cultural attitudes that reinforce the idea that families should stick together and not seek outside help when facing difficulties (Ivey, 1991; Prinz & Miller, 1991).

Attributions

A significant body of literature points to the importance of attending to personal attributions when working with families of aggressive youth. Attribution theory suggests that people make decisions and are motivated to act based on interpretations made in social situations about why people behave as they do and how behavior relates to outcomes in a situation (Weiner, 1986). It is likely that parents' dysfunctional attributions concerning their child's or the therapist's behavior may seriously jeopardize therapeutic progress (MacKinnon, Lamb, & Belsky, 1990). Causal attributions, especially during highly emotional, negative, or unexpected situations, can share at least three common properties regarding the locus, stability, and controllability of a behavior (Hudley, 1994). That is, parents may perceive their child's negative behavior as internally driven, enduring (i.e., genetics/low ability), and deliberate in nature versus externally driven, temporary (i.e., conditions of the environment), and accidental in nature. Indeed, "explanations" of negative child behavior that reflect these two orientations might include the following:

> He was born just like his father. He always has been like this and he will never change. It never fails, he looks for ways to torment me or to get even each night at dinner;

versus

> His behavior gets much worse when he is really stressed or worried. I probably will see a great change once his father and I get our divorce. He is not always aware of his anger, sometimes he doesn't even know he has hurt his sister.

Although the majority of research in this area has focused on attributions that perpetuate aggression between individual children and peers or between parents and children (Dodge, 1991), similar conclusions can be drawn regarding attributions between parents and therapists. That is, parents may make negative attributions about therapist behaviors or requests (e.g., "This therapist is never going to understand me or my child," or "This therapist is out to make me look bad"). Such faulty or incomplete attributions regarding either a child's or therapist's overtures may lead to increased aggression or possible rejection of further suggestions, which would ultimately interfere with parental engagement and participation (Hudley, 1994; Miller & Prinz, 1990).

Self-Efficacy Beliefs

Self-efficacy beliefs are personal attributions about the locus, durability, and controllability of one's behavior and living environment. Self-efficacy theory suggests that people are motivated to act because of the beliefs they form about what they can do and the likely outcomes of their actions (Bandura, 1982, 1993). Beliefs about self-efficacy are hypothesized to affect ability to consistently perform, meet competing demands, cope with stress, and exercise control of life events. Recent work has pointed to the critical influence of parental belief systems on child learning and development (Siegel, McGillicuddy-DeLisi, & Goodnow, 1992). This work also has strong implications for predicting parental responses to parent training. Parents' self-efficacy beliefs may be critical to the regulatory and problem solving necessary to successfully learn, use, and maintain effective parenting skills. Moreover, such beliefs can contribute to treatment engagement by determining the goals people work toward, the perseverance shown in the face of difficulties, as well as resilience to failure.

The influence of parents' belief systems on treatment engagement may be illustrated through the following examples. Parents with low self-efficacy beliefs come into treatment believing that "parenting" is an inherent or fixed ability with little hope of change. For them, parenting performance may be considered a reflection of "inherent intellect" or an endowed capability that a person does or does not possess. Parents with such belief systems are likely to feel threatened by failure or the thought of failure and also may view the need to put forth effort as a lack of ability. When encountering challenges or problems, they become flustered and erratic and tend to give up quickly. Thus, chances to expand parenting skills frequently are avoided to minimize the risk of appearing incompetent or incapable. These parents also tend to view the environment as dangerous, magnify the severity of perceived threats, and anticipate the futility of efforts to modify their life situation. Unfortunately, parents who feel little control over their environment tend to have lower overall aspirations for success and are less likely to affect personal change. Indeed, many will demonstrate classic signs of limited engagement, including in-session resistance and premature termination.

On the other hand, high-efficacy parents regard parenting as an acquirable skill that can be increased and changed over time. Such parents see child management errors as a natural part of parenting and are not easily rattled by challenges or failures. They tend to view mistakes as learning experiences rather than as personal failures. These parents will exert even greater effort after failure to master a challenge or new skill. Parents with high self-efficacy also believe they have the capability to cope with and to exercise control over environmental stresses. As a result, they are seen as resilient, persistent, and creative in figuring out ways to gain control and to set challenging personal goals. Indeed, such parents are likely to experience lower overall anxiety about parenting and to be highly engaged during sessions. Moreover, these parents would tend to "stick-with-it" even in the face of severe obstacles because challenges are viewed as an unavoidable part of learning.

Situational Demands and Constraints

Treatment initiation, subsequent participation, and behavioral outcomes are strongly affected by a multitude of situational demands and constraints. Poverty, unemployment, and other long-standing and acute financial and social stressors clearly have an adverse impact on personal well-being, parent-child relations, and parental engagement in treatment (Diamond, Bernal, & Flores-Ortiz, 1991; Dumas, 1984, 1986; Peterson, 1984; Zuravin, 1989). Moreover, poor interpersonal relations and marital distress or discord have deleterious effects on family therapy outcomes (Dadds, Schwartz, & Sanders, 1987; Eyberg, Boggs, & Rodriguez, 1992; McDonald & Jouriles, 1991; Sayger, Horne, & Glaser, 1993). Reduced treatment motivation and participation have also been linked to personal distress in the form of poor health, depression, and drug addiction (Miller & Prinz, 1990).

Although the independent presence of any of these pretreatment conditions clearly interferes with the building of a necessary therapeutic relationship, concomitant exposure to several of these conditions over a period of time (i.e., a year or more) is a serious impediment to long-term adjustment and treatment success (Blechman, 1991). In fact, Wahler (1980) has noted that multiply stressed families often feel isolated and receive limited social support. The patterns of "insularity" observed in these families consist of social contacts that are perceived as negative and coercive. When faced with extremely stressful living conditions and relationships, it is unlikely that families would receive the support or encouragement necessary to attend and participate meaningfully in treatment.

Moreover, the presence of ordinary daily hassles (e.g., car repairs or a sick family member) are exacerbated in families who already must contend with a multitude of environmental and personal stressors (DeFrain, 1989). Inflexible and demanding work schedules, a lack of child care coverage, and unreliable transportation pose substantial situational obstacles for families experiencing multiple sources of distress. Such issues compete for a family's resources, time, and energy and subsequently limit participation in and benefits from intervention. It is common for parents' attributions about missed appointments and reasons for premature dropout to center around these types of situational obstacles (Prinz & Miller, 1994).

Alternative competing demands also exist in financially secure families who are overcommitted to individual pursuits (e.g., volunteer work or church) and recreational activities (e.g., sports or clubs). Such competing demands take time away from family involvement and often lead to inflexible or infrequent scheduling of treatment sessions. Moreover, the disorganized and hectic routines that characterize some of these families make it difficult for them to practice new skills introduced in treatment.

Families living in stressful life conditions who experience many competing demands are likely to expend much of their energy trying to navigate the treacherous storms of their daily existence. Such constraints severely limit the effort and time required to learn and use new parenting skills. Thus, successful interventions with multiproblem families will depend on finding ways to help alleviate environmental conditions and constraints that obstruct engagement and impede progress.

Intervention Characteristics

Few experimental studies have been conducted to examine how variations in interventions affect parental engagement. It is likely, however, that specific features of interventions contribute to or magnify personal and situational conditions and limit engagement. Thus, careful consideration of intervention characteristics may be needed to capitalize on or overcome critical family attributes (Allgood & Bischoff, 1992).

One such determination is whether to administer parent training in groups or to one family at a time. Although group interventions provide parents with support and the opportunity to learn from the experience of others, the group format can impede participation and behavioral outcomes when a group includes families with widely different cognitive attributes, interpersonal skills, or values in regard to aggression, parenting, or discipline. In such cases, barriers occur when one set of parents dominates the group or intimidates others. Marital status and the severity and type of a child's presenting problems also can affect engagement during group intervention because participants do not get to focus immediately on priority concerns (e.g., how to keep the child from being expelled from school).

The scheduling of sessions and the setting where family interventions are conducted are two other intervention considerations that may significantly affect engagement. Family participation is most likely to falter when the timing of sessions (i.e., either too often or too infrequent) causes frustration or impatience and leads to decreased motivation for change. Such feelings can also occur when scheduled sessions interfere with important family obligations or routines. Lower participation also might be expected when more than one parent, or other relatives such as grandparents or stepparents, are required to attend all sessions (Williams & Houts, 1991). This is especially true when children are not included in treatment sessions. Hardships for families are compounded when interventions require extensive travel and are conducted in distant clinic settings rather than in neighborhood settings (e.g., school, church, or community center) or in the family's home (Dunst & Trivette, 1987).

Therapeutic techniques employed during treatment can also affect engagement. Specifically, a family's limited in-session participation may be due more to discomfort experienced during active role play or in vivo practice than to resistance about learning specific skills. Finally, the type and amount of assigned homework required outside of sessions can discourage parental participation, particularly if assignments are too complex or time intensive (Peterson, 1984).

STRATEGIES FOR
ADDRESSING ENGAGEMENT

Interpersonal-Therapeutic Processes

Although published studies on interventions for childhood antisocial behavior have generally tended to ignore issues pertaining to therapeutic process, there are a number of potentially useful considerations that have accrued from clinical application that could affect parental engagement. A first consideration is the quality of the initial contact with the parent. The therapist (or other interventionist) often is not the first staff member of a program to have contact with parents. Receptionists and other support personnel often account for the initial impressions a parent forms about the nature and receptivity of a program. Even if parents enter the program after less than optimal initial contact, negative impressions or misconceptions may linger and constrain the level of later engagement. Consequently, it is important to train frontline staff to be supportive, patient, and appropriately informed.

Interpersonal communication between interventionist and family members is obviously central to successful family-based interventions even though the outcome literature does not attend much to this issue. A useful heuristic for conceptualizing dyadic communication, which has been well articulated by Blechman and others (Blechman, 1990, 1991; Dumas, Blechman, & Prinz, 1992), emphasizes the role of information exchange as the foundation of effective communication. Quality information exchange is deemed essential for the more complex facets of communication involving behavior influence and problem solving. Accordingly, there are a number of communication guidelines that can enhance the effectiveness of interventionists: (a) thorough information exchange before any initiation of behavioral influence or problem solving; (b) avoidance of unsolicited advice giving (which is behavior influence without sufficient information exchange); (c) heavy use of facilitative listening—a key aspect of information exchange that includes pertinent questions and other supportive communications that demonstrate accurate listening and promote open responding; (d) clear and unambiguous communication; (e) use of encouragement and avoidance of criticism; (f) emphasis on sincerity and avoidance of sarcasm; (g) nonverbal behavior consistent with verbal behavior; (h) enthusiastic and nonjudgmental style; (i) consistent modeling of effective communication when interacting with families; and (j) avoidance of common errors such as cultural bias, inattention, inaccurate comprehension, or frequent interrupting.

All of these communication guidelines apply to parent training and family interventions in clinic as well as in prevention settings. Parents are often looking for answers from the interventionists, so it is easy to fall into the advice-giving trap. Instead, parent educators should look for ways of promoting the acquisition of principles and strategies rather than telling parents how they should handle each situation that arises with their child. Similarly, parent educators and therapists need to be acutely aware of how offhanded or potentially critical remarks can easily alienate parents. Interventionists have to work very hard to avoid communications that imply mother blaming (McCollum & Russell, 1992), cultural bias (Malgady, Rogler, & Costantino, 1990; Meyers, 1992), or condescension (Darling, 1991). Interventionists can still be resources for concepts and procedures (e.g., reinforcement procedures, teaching methods, or self-control strategies for parents), but the mode of delivery needs to actively solicit parents' involvement and decision making.

Personal Expectations, Attributions, and Beliefs

A major goal of treatment is not only to teach parenting skills but also to create a supportive environment that encourages communication of parental expectations, attributions, and self-beliefs that can impede effective use of these skills. Greater motivation and commitment may be obtained when treatment matches parents' expectancies, overcomes damaging attributions, and seeks to build a strong sense of parenting efficacy. Regardless of actual skill level, treatments that address such personal constructs will increase parental engagement and promote parents who are more persistent in the face of failure and who have more positive attitudes about parenting.

Acknowledge Initial Feelings

Parents typically enter therapy with many negative reactions, such as anger and frustration, self-blame, depression, and guilt. Parents often feel disconnected, isolated from, and stigmatized by other adults (i.e., neighbors, relatives, and teachers). As a result, they often block sincere attempts from others to give social support. By acknowledging and normalizing such feelings, the therapist creates an atmosphere of openness in which parents feel their concerns and ideas will be heard, understood, and accepted. Previous experiences with and personal feelings about seeking help are two other important issues that must be addressed in early sessions. Parents should be asked directly about negative and positive reactions toward prior therapy experiences to clarify differences between and to understand possible reactions to past versus present approaches. In addition, questions should focus on parents' present concerns and feelings about seeking help and on the reactions of close relatives and friends who often foster or maintain negative perceptions of therapy.

Clarify Expectations

An important goal of initial sessions is to set up a framework of openness that stresses the importance of parent input, participation, and joint collaboration. Such a collaborative approach must clearly specify the facilitative versus authoritative role of the therapist and the active versus passive role of the parents. Another often overlooked expectation is the fact that parents often anticipate discussions of personal as well as child concerns during sessions. Traditionally, such discussions have taken a backseat to educating parents on child management skills. When specific times are designated and encouraged for such discussions, however, parental engagement, participation, and child outcomes have strongly improved (Prinz & Miller, 1994).

Efforts must also focus on clarifying the overall goals of treatment. It is important to recognize that parents frequently seek help in the midst of a crisis or in response to specific instances of inappropriate child behavior. This is especially true when a family has been forced to seek treatment because of court, school, or social service agency recommendations. In such cases, parents often view the most important objective as reducing a particular negative child behavior to overcome the crisis (e.g., getting a child re-enrolled in school). Thus, the importance of focusing on and increasing prosocial alternatives as a first step in most parent training programs already conflicts with many families' initial expectations. In addition, parents often consider the final outcome of therapy as a change in their child's behavior rather than also considering ultimate success as changes in their own parenting style. Thus, an explanation is needed about why there is more focus on parents' management and communication skills rather than on child behavior.

Finally, parents must be given information about the rationale for specific requests and techniques. In particular, the theoretical principles behind specific procedures should be clearly presented so parents gain an appreciation of the logic and strength of selected procedures. Such open discussions will help identify parents' impressions of specific interventions and also can increase feelings of acceptability (Miller & Kelly, 1992).

Anticipate Frustrations and Setbacks

Parents often come into therapy expecting quick cures and with hopes that their child's problems will be easily solved. Therapists can help parents to modify potential negative reactions to treatment by anticipating such expectations. Orientation during initial sessions must help parents to recognize that changes (a) will require a substantial commitment on everyone's part and (b) will require long-term investments of time and energy to maintain desired results.

Parents should also be alerted to potential setbacks that can occur during therapy. One setback that can cause great disappointment if left undisclosed is the fact that initial increases in targeted problems might be expected when parents shift attention from negative to positive child behavior. Another perceived obstacle may occur if initial child problems (e.g., physical aggression) are replaced by other negative behaviors (e.g., theft). A third setback that occasions feelings of personal defeat, failure, and frustration is the likelihood that there will be periods of regression after periods of noted success. Parents must be encouraged to recognize and reframe such events as unique opportunities to experiment with newly acquired management skills rather than as personal shortcomings or therapeutic impediments. Advanced discussion and preparation increases the likelihood that clients face such events with increased confidence and success (Hoen-Saric et al., 1964; Spitzer et al., 1991). Advanced preparation also promotes the self-assurance and confident attitudes that are critical to effective coping strategies (Folkman & Lazarus, 1988).

Identify Attributions That Impede Progress

Frequent discussions should be held to illuminate potentially dysfunctional attributions that may impede therapeutic progress. Initially, it is important to ask parents about the causes of their child's misbehavior. Ongoing assessments are also needed to elicit parents' interpretations of therapists' actions. In this way, misperceptions and oversights can be discussed before they are translated into resistance or rejection of further assistance. Parents may need to learn formal strategies that help them to challenge deficient attributions and to more fully engage in reciprocal behaviors that support their and their child's attempts to change (Miller, 1994). Such strategies might include discussion to broaden acceptance of individual child characteristics.

Increase Parental Self-Efficacy
and Self-Control

People work best when they feel control and when they feel that what they do matters. Such feelings of control breed ownership, and ownership breeds commitment. In particular, parents need to have an influence on the decisions and procedures that affect their family. It is important to stress collaboration—working together as equals, parents should be fully involved in the development, planning, and evaluation of various interventions.

Although parents cannot always alter environmental factors, they can learn how to alter perceptions that tend to strengthen or diminish beliefs in their parenting capabilities. An old Chinese proverb is useful in this regard: "You cannot prevent the birds of worry and doom from flying over your head, but you can stop them from building a nest in your head." Thus, an important goal of treatment is to help parents begin to focus on what they can do to control their own reactions and environments. Several suggestions are offered: (a) integrate self-management and self-control strategies into the intervention protocol; (b) help parents come to terms with the demanding nature of parenting; (c) help parents accept their own parenting imperfections with the understanding that it is not possible to be an errorless parent; (d) encourage acceptance and respect for their child's particular character, with an emphasis on understanding their child's perspective; (e) stress the importance of positive parenting behaviors to parents as a way of "refueling" oneself when things have not been going well; (f) encourage parents to generalize acquired strategies to other children, places, or behaviors and to be proactive (Celiberti, Nangle, & Drabman, 1993); (g) anticipate what might happen when a parent temporarily lets down, and then problem solve in advance what can be done to prevent the undesirable outcome; and (h) model decision-making processes relative to child and family situations.

Highlight Progressive Mastery and Persistence

Most parents assess their capabilities in relation to the attainments of others. The people whom we compare ourselves to influence our ability judgments, affect our self-esteem, and determine how much satisfaction we get from our accomplishments (Bandura, 1993). It is important to de-emphasize competitive social comparisons and instead to highlight personal achievements and progressive mastery. In addition, parents must be taught to focus on their own achievements and progress rather than on remaining shortcomings or deficiencies. For example, if the parent competently completes 75% of an assignment, positive self-feedback would highlight the 75% progress already attained rather than the 25% unattempted. Therapist feedback must also highlight achievements and progress over time and should go beyond recognition of positive performance changes to include recognition of risk taking, ingenuity, and persistence in the face of failure.

Modifying Intervention Characteristics to Address Situational Demands and Constraints

It is likely that newly acquired parenting competencies and skills will be best used when treatment is designed to alleviate environmental obstacles and stressors and to build on family competencies.

Enhance Family Competencies

An important means of enhancing engagement is to design interventions that build on competencies that families already possess. People develop commitment to what they perceive they do well; thus, time must be taken to identify a family's perceived and actual strengths and capabilities (Dunst & Trivette, 1987). A second related goal of treatment is to consistently assess and look for ways to overcome obstacles that block or hinder the effective use of such competencies (Hawkins & Catalano, 1992). One means of accomplishing these goals is to use or build on already existing social support networks. In one successful enhancement effort, Wahler, Cantor, and Fleischman (1993) asked mothers to bring a close friend to treatment to strengthen social support networks. The success of such enhancement efforts depends on attitudes of mutual respect and collaboration that stress joint problem solving and cooperation.

Customize Program to Family

Another way to address parental engagement is to create a supportive environment that overcomes (rather than adds to) various competing stressors that can hinder a family's participation and derived benefits. Determinations must consider how well any intervention meshes with the family's lifestyle. The ideal is to design interventions that are not only culturally sensitive but that are also responsive to each family's values, needs, and routines (Szapocznik, Kurtines, Santisteban, & Rio, 1990). A first step in this direction is to clearly establish parenting values through questions such as "What is your family's number one priority?" or "What do you value or cherish most about your family?" Similarly, parental reservations and concerns associated with the use of newly learned skills in the home setting need to be routinely explored. For example, the use of reinforcement or time-out may not automatically fit into many families' value systems because such procedures are viewed as either too manipulative or not sufficiently punitive. Thus, education and discussion of specific benefits and drawbacks of particular parenting skills must precede skill building.

Ultimately, intervention success will depend on finding ways to provide support without forgetting that parents have many other competing responsibilities and demands. Efforts to customize plans must be in line with the cultural context, style, values, and home life of each family. Attempts to accommodate interventions more easily into daily routines might be achieved through procedural modifications and adjustments. For example, specific procedures (i.e., time-out) often are difficult to administer effectively because severe environmental constraints make the procedure much more difficult to administer (e.g., overcrowded living areas or limited space) (Baker, Landen, & Kashima, 1991). Thus, parents could be asked to suggest alternative strategies or adjustments that could be made to take such constraints into consideration (e.g., use an easily movable towel designated for a child to sit on during time-out). Another important strategy is to increase the ease with which newly learned skills and treatment sessions fit into daily family routines. Services could be offered during more flexible hours or in more convenient locations, such as the school or the home, to best accommodate working and single parents (Sperry, 1993) and to improve the likelihood of involving fathers and other caregivers in the family (Williams & Houts, 1991). In addition, transportation assistance in the form of car pooling, cab fare, or pick-up and child care coverage could be provided (Diamond et al., 1991). Further adaptations might focus on offering treatment formats that accommodate personal needs and styles. For example, parents could be given a choice of group versus individual family sessions. Other adaptations that might increase engagement and subsequent outcomes include occasional phone versus in-person contact or time-limited modifications of treatment that involve only one person (Szapocznik, Kurtines, Perez-Vidal, Hervis, & Foote, 1990).

Broaden Focus of Treatment

The focus of family-based interventions can be broadened by targeting a variety of life skills in the child (e.g., peer relations, academic remediation, and coping skills) and the parents (e.g., relaxation, marital communication, and vocational development) (Miller & Prinz, 1990). Several broadening and enhancement strategies have emerged, such as (a) adding marital components to reduce marital stress and discord (Dadds et al., 1987); (b) considering medication options, when relevant, for the child and in some cases for a parent (Stewart, Myers, Burket, & Lyles, 1990); (c) focusing on improving the child's cognitive-behavioral (Lochman, White, & Wayland, 1991) and peer-relationship (Bierman & Montminy, 1993) skills as an additional means of reducing aggressive behavior; and (d) combining interventions that target both parent and child behaviors (Villeneuve & LaRoche, 1993). For example, children could learn cognitive problem-solving procedures while parents are seen concurrently for structured parent training (Cousins & Weiss, 1993; Heinicke, 1990; Holden, Lavigne, & Cameron, 1990). This dual approach has begun to surface in clinical (e.g., Kazdin, Siegel, & Bass, 1992) and prevention trials (e.g., Conduct Problems Prevention Research Group, 1992). Alternatively, parents and children could both be coached in the acquisition of cognitive-behavioral strategies to overcome hostile attributions, biased processing of social cues, and aggressive responding. Finally, enhancement efforts have also been designed to overcome a family's initial resistance to entering treatment by recognizing that the treatment process begins with the first phone contact and by implementing concurrent techniques that focus solely on getting the family into treatment (Szapocznik & Kurtines, 1989).

Build Social Connections

Family interventions must go beyond the direct modification of parenting behavior to take into account the broader contextual factors that relate to child adjustment. Interventions must stress the interdependence of child, family, school, and community systems and the patterns of communication within and between these systems in treating severe childhood behavior disorders (Henggeler & Borduin, 1990). This will require work across multiple life settings (i.e., home, school, and peers) to coordinate links of support for the family and to encourage the use of available resources. Interagency cooperation will be essential especially in regards to building home, school, and community communication links (Evans, Okifuji, & Engler, 1993). Such approaches will not only require interagency outreach but will also require greater case management coordination, consistent monitoring (Henggeler & Borduin, 1990), and follow-up (Carlson & Sincavage, 1987). The Fast Track Program provides a concrete example of how to build home-school connections into the intervention plan in a prevention context (see Chapter 5, this volume).

CONCLUSION

Research on parental engagement in intervention, applied to childhood conduct disorder as well as other problems, is important but not without its share of major challenges. In a free society, people have a right to choose not to participate, even if it is to their own or possibly their children's detriment. Furthermore, the collection of attrition data, or even the expectation of attrition, is not always compatible with the aims of community programs or grant-funding agencies. Nonetheless, progress in the evolution of interventions for childhood conduct problems depends in part on researchers themselves staying engaged to meet the challenges associated with parental engagement and treatment attrition.

REFERENCES

Allgood, S. M., & Bischoff, R. J. (1992). Therapist interventions: Do they really influence client resistance? *American Journal of Family Therapy, 20,* 333-340.

Armbruster, P., & Kazdin, A. E. (1994). Attrition in child psychotherapy. In T. H. Ollendick & R. J. Prinz (Eds.), *Advances in clinical child psychology* (Vol. 16, pp. 81-108). New York: Plenum.

Baker, B. L., Landen, S. J., & Kashima, K. J. (1991). Effects of parent training on families of children with mental retardation: Increased burden or generalized benefit? *American Journal of Mental Retardation, 96,* 127-136.

Bandura, A. (1982). Self-efficacy mechanisms in human agency. *American Psychologist, 37,* 122-147.

Bandura, A. (1989). Regulations of cognitive processes through perceived self-efficacy. *Developmental Psychology, 25,* 729-735.

Bandura, A. (1993). Perceived self-efficacy in cognitive development and functioning. *Educational Psychologist, 28,* 117-148.

Bierman, K., & Montminy, H. P. (1993). Developmental issues in social-skills assessment and intervention with children and adolescents. *Behavior Modification, 17,* 229-254.

Blechman, E. A. (1990). A new look at emotions and the family: A model of effective family communication. In E. A. Blechman (Ed.), *Emotions and the family: For better or for worse* (pp. 201-223). Hillsdale, NJ: Lawrence Erlbaum.

Blechman, E. A. (1991). Effective communication: Enabling multiproblem families to change. In P. Cowan & M. Hetherington (Eds.), *Family transitions* (pp. 219-244). Hillsdale, NJ: Lawrence Erlbaum.

Carlson, C. I., & Sincavage, J. M. (1987). Family-oriented school psychology practice: Results of a national survey of NASP members. *School Psychology Review, 16,* 519-526.

Carr, A. (1990). Failure in family therapy: A catalogue of engagement mistakes. *Journal of Family Therapy, 12,* 371-386.

Celiberti, D. A., Nangle, D. W., & Drabman, R. S. (1993). A proactive approach to disruptive behavior in public settings. *Child and Family Behavior Therapy, 15,* 1-4.

Chamberlain, P., & Baldwin, D. V. (1987). Client resistance to parent training: Its therapeutic management. In T. R. Kratochwill (Ed.), *Advances in school psychology* (Vol. 6, pp. 131-171). New York: Plenum.

Chamberlain, P., Patterson, G., Reid, J., Kavanagh, K., & Forgatch, M. (1984). Observation of client resistance. *Behavior Therapy, 15,* 144-155.

Conduct Problems Prevention Research Group. (1992). A developmental and clinical model for the prevention of conduct disorder: The FAST Track Program. *Development and Psychopathology, 4,* 509-527.

Cousins, L. S., & Weiss, C. (1993). Parent training and social skills training for children with attention-deficit hyperactivity disorder: How can they be combined for greater effectiveness? *Canadian Journal of Psychiatry, 38,* 449-461.

Dadds, M. R., Schwartz, S., & Sanders, M. R. (1987). Marital discord and treatment outcome in behavioral treatment of child conduct disorders. *Journal of Consulting and Clinical Psychology, 55,* 396-403.

Darling, R. B. (1991). Parent-professional interaction: The roots of misunderstanding. In M. Seligman (Ed.), *The family with a handicapped child* (pp. 119-149). Boston: Allyn & Bacon.

DeFrain, J. (1989). The healthy family: Is it possible? In M. J. Fine (Ed.), *The second handbook on parent education: Contemporary perspectives* (pp. 53-74). San Diego, CA: Academic Press.

Diamond, G., Bernal, G., & Flores-Ortiz, Y. (1991). Engagement and recruitment for family therapy research in community settings. *Contemporary Family Therapy, 13,* 255-274.

Dodge, K. (1991). Emotion and social information processing. In J. Garber & K. Dodge (Eds.), *The development of emotion regulation and dysregulation* (pp. 159-181). New York: Cambridge University Press.

Dumas, J. E. (1984). Child, adult-interactional, and socioeconomic setting events as predictors of parent training outcome. *Education and Treatment of Children, 7,* 351-364.

Dumas, J. E. (1986). Indirect influence of maternal social contacts on mother-child interactions: A setting event analysis. *Journal of Abnormal Child Psychology, 14,* 205-216.

Dumas, J. E., Blechman, E. A., & Prinz, R. J. (1992). Helping families with aggressive children and adolescents change. In R. DeV. Peters, R. J. McMahon, & V. L. Quinsey (Eds.), *Aggression and violence throughout the lifespan* (pp. 126-154). Newbury Park, CA: Sage.

Dunst, C. J., & Trivette, C. M. (1987). Enabling and empowering families: Conceptual and intervention issues. *School Psychology Review, 16,* 443-456.

Evans, I. M., Okifuji, A., & Engler, L. (1993). Home-school communication in the treatment of childhood behavior problems. *Child and Family Behavior Therapy, 15,* 37-60.

Eyberg, S. M., Boggs, S. R., & Rodriguez, C. M. (1992). Relationships between maternal parenting stress and child disruptive behavior. *Child and Family Behavior Therapy, 14,* 1-10.

Firestone, P., Kelly, M. J., & Fike, S. (1980). Are fathers necessary in parent training groups? *Journal of Clinical Child Psychology, 9,* 44-47.

Firestone, P., & Witt, J. E. (1982). Characteristics of families completing and prematurely discontinuing a behavioral parent-training program. *Journal of Pediatric Psychology, 7,* 209-222.

Folkman, S., & Lazarus, R. S. (1988). Coping as a mediator of emotion. *Journal of Personality and Social Psychology, 54,* 466-475.

Forehand, R., Middlebrook, J., Rogers, T., & Steffe, M. (1983). Dropping out of parent training. *Behaviour Research and Therapy, 21,* 663-668.

Furey, W. M., & Basili, L. (1988). Predicting consumer satisfaction in parent training for noncompliant children. *Behavior Therapy, 19,* 555-564.

Gould, M. S., Shaffer, D., & Kaplan, D. (1985). The characteristics of dropouts from a child psychiatry clinic. *Journal of the American Academy of Child Psychiatry, 24,* 316-328.

Hawkins, J. D., & Catalano, R. F. (1992). *Communities that care: Action for drug abuse prevention.* San Francisco: Jossey-Bass.

Heinicke, C. M. (1990). Toward generic principles of treating parents and children: Integrating psychotherapy with the school-aged child and family intervention. *Journal of Consulting and Clinical Psychology, 58,* 713-719.

Henggeler, S. W., & Borduin, C. M. (1990). *Family therapy and beyond: A multisystemic approach to treating behavior problems of children and adolescents.* Pacific Grove, CA: Brooks/Cole.

Hoen-Saric, R., Frank, J. D., Imber, S. D., Nash, E. H., Stone, A. R., & Battle, C. C. (1964). Systematic preparation of patients for psychotherapy: Effects of therapy behavior and outcome. *Journal of Psychiatric Research, 2,* 267-281.

Holden, G. W., Lavigne, V. V., & Cameron, A. M. (1990). Probing the continuum of effectiveness in parent training: Characteristics of parents and preschoolers. *Journal of Clinical Child Psychology, 19,* 2-8.

Hudley, C. A. (1994). Perceptions of intentionality, feelings of anger, and reactive aggression. In M. J. Furlong & D. C. Smith (Eds.), *Anger, hostility and aggression: Assessment, prevention, and intervention strategies for youth* (pp. 83-116). Brandon, VT: Clinical Psychology Publishing.

Ivey, A. E. (1991). *Developmental strategies for helpers: Individual, family, and network interventions.* Pacific Grove, CA: Brooks/Cole.

Johnston, C. (1988). A behavioral-family systems approach to assessment: Maternal characteristics associated with externalizing behavior in children. In R. J. Prinz (Ed.), *Advances in behavioral assessment of children and families* (Vol. 4, pp. 161-187). Greenwich, CT: JAI.

Kalfus, G. R., & Razzano, K. M. (1992). Maternal acceptability of treatments for child withdrawal and aggression. *Child and Family Behavior Therapy, 14,* 11-22.

Karoly, P. (1980). Person variables in therapeutic change and development. In P. Karoly & J. J. Steffen (Eds.), *Improving the long-term effects of psychotherapy* (pp. 195-261). New York: Gardner.

Kazdin, A. E. (1987). Treatment of antisocial behavior in children: Current status and future directions. *Psychological Bulletin, 102,* 187-203.

Kazdin, A. E. (1990). Premature termination from treatment among children referred for antisocial behavior. *Journal of Child Psychology and Psychiatry, 31,* 415-425.

Kazdin, A. E., Siegel, T. C., & Bass, D. (1992). Cognitive problem-solving skills training and parent management training in the treatment of antisocial behavior in children. *Journal of Consulting and Clinical Psychology, 60,* 733-747.

Lochman, J. E., White, K. J., & Wayland, K. K. (1991). Cognitive behavioral assessment and treatment with aggressive children. In P. C. Kendall (Ed.), *Child and adolescent therapy: Cognitive-behavioral procedures* (pp. 25-65). New York: Guilford.

MacKinnon, C. E., Lamb, M. E., & Belsky, J. (1990). An affective-cognitive model of mother-child aggression. *Development and Psychopathology, 2,* 1-17.

Malgady, R. G., Rogler, L. H., & Costantino, G. (1990). Culturally sensitive psychotherapy for Puerto Rican children and adolescents: A program of treatment outcome research. *Journal of Consulting and Clinical Psychology, 58,* 704-712.

McCollum, E. E., & Russell, C. S. (1992). Mother-blaming in family therapy: An empirical investigation. *American Journal of Family Therapy, 20,* 71-76.

McDonald, R., & Jouriles, E. N. (1991). Marital aggression and child behavior problems: Research findings, mechanisms, and intervention strategies. *The Behavior Therapist, 14,* 189-190.

McMahon, R., Forehand, R., Griest, D., & Wells, K. (1981). Who drops out of therapy during parent behavioral training? *Behavioral Counseling Quarterly, 1,* 79-85.

Meichenbaum, D., & Turk, D. C. (1987). *Facilitating treatment adherence: A practitioner's guidebook.* New York: Plenum.

Meyers, C. (1992). Among children and their families: Consideration of cultural influences in assessment. Special issue: Cross-cultural perspectives in occupational therapy. *American Journal of Occupational Therapy, 46,* 737-744.

Miller, D. L., & Kelly, M. L. (1992). Treatment acceptability: The effects of parent gender, marital adjustment, and child behavior. *Child and Family Behavior Therapy, 14,* 11-24.

Miller, G. E. (1994). Enhancing family-based interventions for managing childhood anger and aggression. In M. J. Furlong & D. C. Smith (Eds.), *Anger, hostility and aggression: Assessment, prevention, and intervention strategies for youth* (pp. 83-116). Brandon, VT: Clinical Psychology Publishing.

Miller, G. E., & Prinz, R. J. (1990). The enhancement of social learning family interventions for childhood conduct disorder. *Psychological Bulletin, 108,* 291-307.

Miller, W. R. (1985). Motivation for treatment: A review with special emphasis on alcoholism. *Psychological Bulletin, 98,* 84-107.

Patterson, G. R. (1986). Performance models for antisocial boys. *American Psychologist, 41,* 432-444.

Patterson, G. R., & Forgatch, M. S. (1985). Therapist behavior as a determinant for client noncompliance: A paradox for the behavior modifier. *Journal of Consulting and Clinical Psychology, 53,* 846-851.

Peterson, P. (1984). Effects of moderator variables in reducing stress in mothers of children with handicaps. *Journal of Psychosomatic Research, 28,* 337-344.

Prinz, R. J., & Miller, G. E. (1991). Issues in understanding and treating childhood conduct problems in disadvantaged populations. *Journal of Clinical Child Psychology, 20,* 379-385.

Prinz, R. J., & Miller, G. E. (1994). Family-based treatment for childhood antisocial behavior: Experimental influences on dropout and engagement. *Journal of Consulting and Clinical Psychology, 62,* 645-650.

Sayger, T. V., Horne, A. M., & Glaser, B. A. (1993). Marital satisfaction and social learning family therapy for child conduct problems: Generalization of treatment effects. *Journal of Marital and Family Therapy, 19,* 393-402.

Siegel, I. E., McGillicuddy-DeLisi, P., & Goodnow, J. J. (1992). *Parental belief systems: The psychological consequences for children.* Hillsdale, NJ: Lawrence Erlbaum.

Sperry, L. (1993). Tailoring treatment with dual-career couples. *American Journal of Family Therapy, 21,* 51-59.

Spitzer, A., Webster-Stratton, C., & Hollinsworth, T. (1991). Coping with conduct-problem children: Parents gain knowledge and control. *Journal of Clinical Child Psychology, 20,* 413-427.

Stewart, J. T., Myers, W. C., Burket, R. C., & Lyles, W. B. (1990). A review of the pharmacotherapy of aggression in children and adolescents. *Journal of the American Academy of Child and Adolescent Psychiatry, 29,* 269-277.

Szapocznik, J., & Kurtines, W. (1989). *Breakthroughs in family treatment.* New York: Springer.

Szapocznik, J., Kurtines, W., Santisteban, D. A., & Rio, A. T. (1990). Interplay of advances between theory, research, and application in treatment interventions aimed at behavior problem children and adolescents. *Journal of Consulting and Clinical Psychology, 58,* 696-703.

Szapocznik, J., Kurtines, W. M., Perez-Vidal, A., Hervis, O. E., & Foote, F. H. (1990). One person family therapy. In R. A. Wells & V. J. Giannetti (Eds.), *Handbook of brief psychotherapies. Applied clinical psychology* (pp. 493-510). New York: Plenum.

Villeneuve, C., & LaRoche, C. (1993). The child's participation in family therapy: A review and a model. *Contemporary Family Therapy, 15,* 105-120.

Vuchinich, S., Bank, L., & Patterson, G. R. (1992). Parenting, peers, and the stability of antisocial behavior in preadolescent boys. *Developmental Psychology, 28,* 510-521.

Wahler, R. G. (1980). The insular mother: Her problems in parent-child treatment. *Journal of Applied Behavior Analysis, 13,* 207-219.

Wahler, R. G., Cantor, P. G., & Fleischman, J. (1993). The impact of synthesis teaching and parent training with mothers of conduct disordered children. *Journal of Abnormal Child Psychology, 21,* 425-437.

Webster-Stratton, C., & Hammond, M. (1990). Predictors of treatment outcome in parent training for families with conduct problem children. *Behavior Therapy, 21,* 319-337.

Webster-Stratton, C., & Herbert, M. (1993). What really happens in parent training? *Behavior Modification, 17,* 407-456.

Weiner, B. (1986). *An attributional theory of motivation and emotion.* New York: Springer-Verlag.

Weisz, J. R., Weiss, B., & Langmeyer, D. B. (1987). Giving up on child psychotherapy: Who drops out? *Journal of Consulting and Clinical Psychology, 55,* 916-918.

Williams, C. J., & Houts, A. C. (1991). Father involvement in parent training for oppositional child behavior: Progress or stagnation. *Child and Family Behavior Therapy, 13,* 29-52.

Zuravin, S. J. (1989). Severity of maternal depression and three types of mother-to-child aggression. *Journal of the American Academy of Child and Adolescent Psychiatry, 59,* 377-384.

9

Preventive Interventions
for High-Risk Youth

THE ADOLESCENT TRANSITIONS PROGRAM

THOMAS J. DISHION

DAVID W. ANDREWS

KATE KAVANAGH

LAWRENCE H. SOBERMAN

Problem behavior in children is not a disease that can be cured with one treatment; it is highly situational, ebbing and flowing as a function of context and development (Dishion, French, & Patterson, 1995). It is becoming increasingly clear that a dental model of prevention may be most helpful

AUTHORS' NOTE: This research was supported by Grants DA 05304 and DA 07031 from the National Institute of Drug Abuse, U.S. Public Health Service, to Thomas J. Dishion. Partial support for reporting the research was provided by Grant P50 MH46690 from the Prevention Research Branch, National Institute of Mental Health, U.S. Public Health Service, to Dr. John B. Reid. The authors thank Margaret McKean and Jan Mustoe along with the as a guiding metaphor for preventing child and adolescent problem behavior. Just as preventive interventions for tooth decay are needed throughout the life span, preventive interventions for problem behavior are needed throughout childhood (ages 0-18). As in a dental model, prevention is necessarily individualized and may consist of both treatment and prevention depending on the vulnerabilities and protective factors at each stage of development.

The Adolescent Transitions Program (ATP) is an evolving menu of intervention and assessment resources that was conceptualized under the dental model framework. The basic intervention components offer protective skills to parents and teens for problem behavior reduction and prevention in early adolescence across contexts. In this chapter, we describe the evolution of ATP in regard to its empirical foundation, intervention components (i.e., parent-focused and teen-focused programs), and outcome results. Our goal is to impart theory and practical intervention tools and suggest future directions and hypotheses regarding interventions directed at problem behavior in adolescence.

The rationale for developing preventive interventions for early adolescence is clear. There is a dramatic increase in problem behavior during this developmental period across all industrialized nations (Gottfredson & Hirschi, 1994). Although these behaviors are more prevalent and persistent in some teens than in others (Loeber & Dishion, 1983; Sampson & Laub, 1990), rates of problem behaviors are invariantly highest during an individual's adolescence (Britt, 1990; Greenberg, 1991; Hirschi & Gottfredson, 1983). In statistical terms, the display of some problems during adolescence is a normative event. It does not follow, however, that if left alone they will fade away. Although onset of delinquent behavior in middle adolescence has a reduced risk of recidivism compared with that in early onset (Moffitt, 1993; Patterson, 1992), these teens have an increased risk of young adult problems compared with those who do not commit delinquent offenses in adolescence (Stattin & Magnusson, 1991; West & Farrington, 1977). In addition, substance use in adolescence is a unique risk factor for the escalation to drug and alcohol problems in young adulthood (Robins & Przybeck, 1985) and

entire staff of the Adolescent Transitions Project for their contributions and for the effort and devotion. We also thank all the parents and teens who have participated in ATP and the administration, staff, and students of the Bethel and Springfield school districts for their enthusiastic participation. Reprints or more information about program implementation may be requested from Tom Dishion at the Oregon Social Learning Center, 207 East 5th Avenue, Suite 202, Eugene, OR 97401.

can undermine the achievement of academic, occupational, and relationship goals crucial to adaptation to adulthood (Yamaguchi & Kandel, 1985).

Knowledge of the individual characteristics, processes, and social conditions that underlie increases in adolescent problem behavior is a critical first step in prevention. Effective interventions for any problem behavior (e.g., drug use, delinquency, or risky sexual behavior) must clearly identify and target the underlying causes of problem behavior rather than focusing on the associated symptoms. Decades of research have identified antisocial behavior as an antecedent to emerging adolescent problems. Antisocial misbehavior is considered covert (e.g., lying and stealing) and overt (e.g., noncompliance and aggression). Although certainly children can be found that demonstrate only overt or covert patterns of antisocial behavior (Loeber & Schmaling, 1985), the two forms are highly correlated (Dishion et al., 1995; Patterson, Reid, & Dishion, 1992) and are equally prognostic of adolescent delinquency (Loeber & Dishion, 1983) and substance use (Smith & Fogg, 1979). Therefore, it seems reasonable to target young adolescent antisocial behaviors early to prevent the escalation of problem behavior in adolescence.

There is a substantial body of research that indicates that poor parenting practices exacerbate antisocial behavior in childhood and adolescence (Dishion et al., 1995). Patterson and colleagues (Patterson, 1982; Patterson et al., 1992) have proposed a stage model to explain how the emergence of antisocial behaviors in childhood can progress to more serious forms of problem behavior in adolescence. In this program of research, harsh coercive parenting has been associated with antisocial behavior and is correlated with academic problems, peer rejection, and depression. These secondary outcomes, coupled with poor parental monitoring, are related to a child's drift into deviant peer association (Dishion, Patterson, Stoolmiller, & Skinner, 1991) and the risk of experiencing a multitude of problem behaviors (Elliott, Huizinga, & Ageton, 1985). Association with a deviant peer group—not the early child or parent traits—best predicts early onset substance use (Dishion, Capaldi, Spracklen, & Li, 1995).

These developmental progressions in the nature and range of problem behaviors do not occur in a vacuum. Both the dependent (antisocial behavior) and independent variables (parenting and peer environments) are highly affected by community contexts (Patterson et al., 1992). For this reason, an ecological model may be most appropriate in understanding problem behaviors across development and in guiding prevention design (Dishion et al., 1995). Several research programs are currently promoting this ecological focus on maladaptive development (Kellam, 1990; Magnusson, 1988; Rutter, 1989). Bronfenbrenner (1979, 1986, 1989) provides a cogent and organized conceptual framework for considering the network of findings related to the etiology of antisocial behavior. The ecology of child development is conceptualized as a hierarchy of nested systems beginning with face-to-face interactions among people, continuing on to behavior settings in which relationships take place, and on to more macrocontextual influences that are usually referred to as cultural and community practices.

One implication of an ecological model is that for an intervention program to effectively reduce risk, it may be necessary to attend to the contextual factors that influence underlying causal processes (Biglan, in press). Clearly, a major field of influence on adolescent problem behavior is school (Kellam, 1990). Schools are a convenient meeting place and training ground for deviant peer groups (Dishion, Patterson, & Griesler, 1994). Communication between the school and parents is key to enabling parents' potential for monitoring, limit setting, and supporting academic progress (Reid, 1993). A vast majority of children within the United States attend school up to and through middle school. Preventive intervention programs need to consider schools as a "potential site for service delivery as well as serve as potential objects of intervention activity" (Trickett & Berman, 1989, p. 361). The work of Botvin and colleagues (Chapter 10, this volume; Botvin, Baker, Dusenbury, Tortu, & Botvin, 1990; Botvin, Schinke, & Orlandi, 1995), suggests the promise of social influence intervention strategies for the reduction of substance use. The Fast Track preventive intervention model is state of the art in identifying high-risk children within a school environment and in delivering interventions to the children, their parents, and peers (Conduct Problems Prevention Research Group, 1992).

An example of the promise of focusing on schools as an object of preventive interventions can be found in the important work of Gottfredson and colleagues (Gottfredson, Gottfredson, & Hybl, 1993). Interventions that target middle school policies and practices regarding problem behavior reduce the level of such behavior in the school. Moreover, interventions can target a school's strategy for communicating with parents. Heller and Fantuzzo (1993) found that specific, neutral, and regularly provided information to parents regarding attendance, homework, and class behavior can greatly enhance parents' ability to monitor and support their youngsters' school engagement.

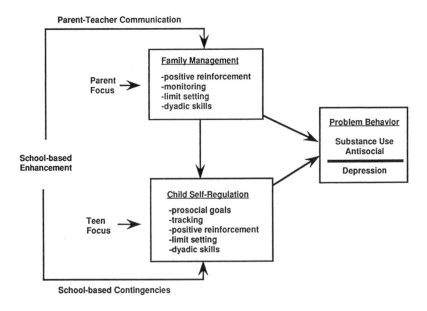

Figure 9.1. Overview of the Adolescent Transitions Program

We need to develop prevention strategies that integrate institutional change with individualized interventions—if both prove to be effective. This is the long-term goal of ATP (Dishion, Kavanagh, & Soberman, in press).

ADOLESCENT TRANSITIONS PROGRAM: GOALS AND INTERVENTIONS

ATP is intended to be an intervention for high-risk youths formulated on the basis of a social interactional model for the development of antisocial behavior in childhood and problem behavior in adolescence (Dishion & Kavanagh, in press; Patterson & Reid, 1984; Patterson et al., 1992). There are two basic intervention targets: the parents (parent focus) and the young adolescents (teen focus). Group interventions with the parents sought to improve parent family management skills; interventions with the youth aimed for development of self-regulation of problem behavior (see Figure 9.1). Each intervention program has an extensive curriculum for group leaders and participants as well as six 10-minute videotapes to exemplify the targeted skills and practices (Dishion et al., 1995). The two curricula are designed to parallel each other, and skill development exercises frequently include parent-child activities.

The specific goals of the parent-focused and teen-focused interventions as well as how a school-based implementation could enhance the effectiveness of the individualized intervention programs are shown in Figure 9.1. The effectiveness of the teen intervention, we hypothesize, would be improved by providing school-based contingencies for demonstrating skills emphasized in the curriculum. Similarly, regular communication to parents regarding their youths' behavior at school is expected to enhance the parents' ability to monitor and provide support for positive school behavior. Targeting school policies and practices (Gottfredson et al., 1993) would be expected to have an additional benefit in the overall reduction of problem behavior at the school level.

Parent Focus

The parent-focused curriculum is based on three key family management skills determined by 20 years of clinical and research investigations to be critical for healthy child adjustment: prosocial fostering, limit setting, and problem solving (Patterson, 1982). The 12 group sessions are strengthened by four individual meetings with each family to address issues arising from attempts to make family changes. The social learning parent training approach is a stepwise, skill-based approach to developing effective parenting skills. Groups optimally consist of eight families, ranging from 8 to 16 parents attending each session.

Teen Focus

The teen-focused intervention was modeled after descriptions of cognitive-behavioral primary intervention curricula described by Botvin and Wills (1985) and employs a social learning approach to behavior change—teaching at-risk adolescents to set realistic behavior change goals, develop appropriate small steps toward goal attainment, develop and provide peer support for prosocial and abstinent behavior, set limits, and learn problem-solving skills. Goal setting is the first step of the intervention program. The goal selected is negotiated with the parents and adolescents. As much as possible, all sessions are delivered to address the self-interest of the adolescents. Tokens are used in groups to encourage on-task behavior and engagement in home-work. Groups are of mixed gender and optimally consist of eight adolescents.

Peer Consultants

A key feature of the curricula is the use of parent and teen peer consul-tants who act as a bridge between the group leader and participants. Consul-tants have typically completed the program or have had experience strug-gling with and successfully negotiating the problem behaviors of early adolescence. The role of the consultants is to model appropriate parenting or self-regulation skills, to offer support for successes, and to suggest coping strategies for difficult situations.

Family Consultation Sessions

An integral part of the group prevention program is the blending of the individual family therapy model that serves as the basis of ATP. This is done through four family consultations for the purposes of tailoring skills to individual family needs and for family discussion of their progress. The sessions are placed at strategic points in the intervention (Figure 9.2). The first session occurs in the family's home and provides an opportunity for each member to individually identify the changes that he or she would like to make during the program. The other three sessions occur after the delivery of each of the three key family management components. These sessions allow for "fine tuning" skills and the discussion of family strengths and barriers in the implementation of these skills.

COMPONENT ANALYSIS OF ATP

Our first step in developing ATP was to do a component analysis (see Dishion & Andrews, 1995) in which 119 high-risk families were randomly assigned to one of the following four components: parent focus, teen focus, parent and teen focus, and self-directed materials only. In addition, 39 quasi-experimental control families were subsequently recruited but did not ex-perience the intervention. The initial 119 families and the 39 quasi-experi-mental control families were recruited by newspaper advertisements, school

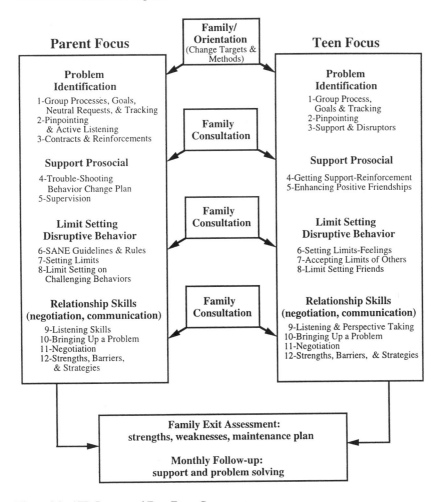

Figure 9.2. ATP: Parent- and Teen-Focus Components

postings, and counseling services. Over the telephone, parents were first interviewed about the presence of 10 areas of early adolescent risk. This brief interview is based on risk-factor research by Bry and colleagues (Bry, McKeon, & Pandina, 1982). Families in which parents reported four or more of these risk factors as current concerns were accepted in the intervention study. Informed consent specified the full range of assessments as well as the random assignment procedures for the experimental families ($n = 119$).

For the quasi-experimental control, solicitation was identical, but recruitment focused simply on the assessments. Referrals were provided to any family on request.

Study retention was high; 143 of the original 158 families participated in the evaluation study (90% retention). Dishion and Andrews (1995) report that the sample was primarily European American, low income, and statistically comparable across intervention conditions. The youths (equally distributed by gender) showed elevations (average T score 60 and above) on the teacher and parent Child Behavior Checklist (CBCL; Achenbach, 1992) across internalizing and externalizing scales. Teacher CBCL reports categorized 17% of the sample as "borderline clinical" or "clinical" for externalizing behaviors, and 13% were categorized as such for internalizing behaviors. Parents reported a higher incidence of these borderline clinical and clinical levels for the youths; 37% were classified as externalizing and 32% classified as internalizing.

The evaluation of an intervention strategy is a complex problem. A classic issue is to what extent are the different outcomes associated with an intervention component real differences or do they reflect an Assessment × Intervention interaction (Campbell & Stanley, 1963). In other words, to what extent does the intervention affect how people respond to the testing on which evaluations are based? Prevention programs in school settings that rely on youth reports of substance use eventually need to address the issue of whether the interventions changed how the youth responded to the survey but not their actual behavior.

There are two ways to handle this problem. The first is by design (e.g., the four-group Solomon design): pre- and postassessments are randomly assigned so that the effect of testing can be evaluated. The second is to collect a multiagent and multimethod assessment battery so that intervention effects can be examined across a variety of measures. We elected the latter strategy and included direct observations of family interaction in a problem-solving task, parent reports, teacher reports, youth reports, physiological measures of the youths' smoking, and consumer satisfaction ratings of the program. The four basic components of ATP were evaluated using the 158 families described previously. The detailed reports of this evaluation presented in Andrews, Soberman, and Dishion (1995) and Dishion and Andrews (1995) are summarized below. In addition, we will report findings on the analyses of the effectiveness of the intervention components on substance use after involvement with ATP. We begin our review of these evaluation studies by examining overall levels of parent and youth engagement.

Intervention Engagement

Consistent with our dental metaphor of prevention, it is important that parents and teens be actively engaged in the intervention. Andrews et al. (in press) report that basic engagement and knowledge acquisition for these families were positive. Group sessions were generally well attended. Parent group sessions had an average of seven families represented at each meeting. Parents attended an average of 69% of the sessions. Youth participation was also high. Teen group size averaged six youths per session. Youths attended an average of 71% of the sessions.

Parent and youth evaluations of the program were very positive: 64% of parents reported that the program was helpful. Interestingly, mothers (60%) reported liking the program considerably more than fathers (26%). Youths also reported satisfaction with the program. Fifty-three percent reported that it was generally helpful, 48% said it was helpful with parent interactions, and 41% reported it helped with peer interactions.

A structured assessment of curriculum knowledge for parents and youths was conducted after the ATP intervention. This assessment presented audio-taped problem scenarios to the parents and youths separately. Their solutions to these hypothetical scenarios were rated on social learning knowledge. An analysis of these data (Andrews et al., in press) revealed that those youth who were randomly assigned to the teen-focused intervention had higher scores on curriculum knowledge ($p < .05$). The trend was similar for parents involved in the parent-focused intervention but was statistically marginal ($p < .11$). Inspection of the means for each group revealed that, in general, all parents scored relatively high on the postassessment of knowledge, producing a "ceiling effect" and limiting variation between groups. This finding also suggests that knowledge of positive parenting principles was rather ubiquitous in this group.

Family Interaction Patterns

A more important measure of intervention effects is the actual manner in which parents and youths interact in the process of discussing and solving

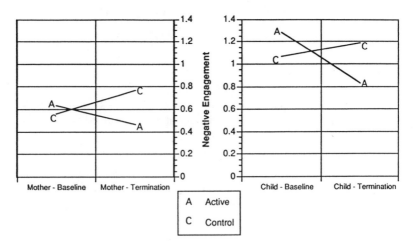

Figure 9.3. Short-Term Outcome on Child and Mother Negative Engagement in Family Interaction

real family problems. Consequently, participants were filmed in 25-minute problem-solving tasks and coded with a structured behavioral observation system for families, the Family Process Code (Dishion, Gardner, Patterson, Reid, & Thibodeaux, 1983). Four clusters are derived from this coding system: negative engagement, positive engagement, converse, and directives. Of greatest interest in our evaluations of the parent-focused and teen-focused interventions is the negative engagement score because this is an important index of family conflict that has been used in many studies of parent training outcome (see Patterson, 1982).

Dishion and Andrews (1995) examined the extent to which the mother's and child's rate per minute of negative engagement in the problem-solving task decreased as a function of the ATP intervention components. A multivariate analysis of covariance (MANCOVA) revealed that termination conflict varied as a function of which intervention component the family received. In short, both the child (Wilks's lambda = .96; $p < .10$) and the mother (Wilks's lambda = .91; $p < .01$) showed reductions as a function of the parent-focused and teen-focused interventions compared with the control groups (self-directed and quasi-experimental control). Figure 9.3 displays the mother and child negative engagement in those receiving the "active" intervention conditions compared with the control group; a post hoc analysis shows these comparisons to be highly significant. Note that the combined

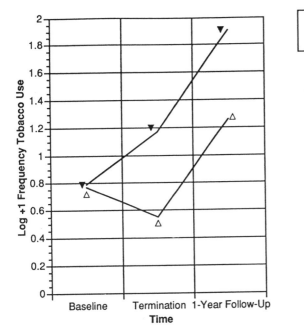

Figure 9.4. One-Year Outcome on Self-Reported Adolescent Tobacco Use as a Function of Peer Group Intervention

parent and teen intervention condition had the same level of effect on reductions in observed parent-child negative engagement as did either intervention condition alone. This finding did not support our hypothesis of a synergistic effect when working with both the youth and his or her parents.

Youth Problem Behaviors

When examining teacher ratings on the CBCL externalizing scale, we found that only the parent-focused intervention had a short-term effect ($p <$ .06) on problem behavior at school compared with the control group. Analyses of 1-year outcomes, however, revealed an unexpected finding. The teen-focused groups were actually getting worse on problem behavior at school compared with the control group ($p < .05$). The same trend was observed for the youths' report of smoking; those youths randomly assigned to the teen-focused conditions actually smoked more than those in the control group ($p < .05$). This is clearly observable by inspecting Figure 9.4. In contrast, there was a modest trend for the youths of families who received the parent-focused-only intervention to smoke less than those in the control group. This trend was not evident in the combined condition.

We have carefully examined the substance use patterns of the youths after their involvement with ATP. Three months after their termination assessment, families began a series of monthly telephone interviews regarding events in their family and the child's problem behavior. These interviews were administered monthly between the 3-months posttermination and the 1-year follow-up assessments (for a possible total of nine interviews). The telephone interview was administered to the parents and the child. They were asked if the youth had tried or used tobacco, marijuana, or alcohol over the past month. If either the parent or the child reported a yes, that was a positive sign of drug use for that month. The number of yes responses was aggregated over the 9-month period and analyzed by intervention condition, combining the self-directed and control conditions into one control group. These data are presented in boxplots in Figure 9.5. Boxplots provide the capability of visually inspecting the full range of the distribution of substance use for each intervention condition. This includes the maximum and minimum values (top and bottom lines), the mean (white line), the range of values falling between the 25th and 75th percentiles, and the confidence interval surrounding the estimate of the mean. Note that during this developmental period (12-15 years of age), tobacco use is the most prevalent substance use behavior.

Inspection of the boxplots of the tobacco, alcohol, and marijuana use across the three conditions shows a consistent trend by the youths in the parent-focused-only condition to show less substance use compared with the those in the control condition. There was also a trend for those youths randomly assigned to the teen-focused condition to show higher levels of substance use, consistent with the iatrogenic effect described previously. To test the hypothesis that substance use varied as a function of the intervention component, a MANCOVA was computed. In this analysis, a construct referred to as child deviance was formed, which consisted of the child's report of delinquent behavior and substance use at baseline as well as the teacher report of problem behaviors on the externalizing CBCL instrument. This construct served as the baseline covariate, controlling for baseline differences that could affect outcome across the interventions among the young adolescents. Note that the control condition showed the lowest level of child deviance at baseline.

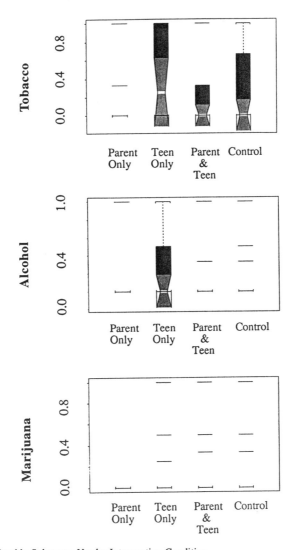

Figure 9.5. Monthly Substance Use by Intervention Condition

The multivariate effect for the intervention condition was statistically significant (Wilks's lambda = .84; $p < .05$). Univariate analyses for the omnibus condition effect on each of the substances indicated that the youths' tobacco use reliably varied as a function of intervention condition ($p < .01$). Planned comparisons revealed that the parent-focused-only condition (Wilks's lambda = .94; p = .11) had a statistically marginal but beneficial effect, whereas the teen-focused-only condition (Wilks's lambda = .91; $p < .05$) had a statistically reliable negative effect. The univariate analyses on individual substances indicated that there was a significant reduction in tobacco and marijuana use in the parent-focused-only condition compared with the control condition ($p < .05$). The iatrogenic effect for the teen-focused condition was confined primarily to tobacco use ($p < .05$). As reported in our previous analyses, there was no synergistic effect for combining the parent- and teen-focused intervention.

Summary of Component Analyses

Short-term analyses suggest that the parent-focused and teen-focused interventions work in harmony to benefit the youth and family in terms of reducing conflict and negative interactions. An analysis of longer-term outcomes across multiple indices, however, suggests that (a) parent focus is the optimal intervention strategy in terms of minimizing iatrogenic effects and producing positive outcomes, and (b) aggregating high-risk youths into homogeneous intervention groups can actually exacerbate substance use as well as their problem behavior at school. Teens experiencing the combined interventions showed neither an increase nor a decrease in problem behavior, suggesting that the two conditions were working against one another. These conclusions are reached whether assessments are based on teacher, parent, or youth report.

Concurrent with the component analysis, we developed a strategy for implementing ATP in the schools. At the onset of the study, we did not expect (of course) the iatrogenic effect of the teen-focused intervention. Thus, we compared the full version of ATP as implemented in a community setting with what was implemented in the school. We now discuss the school implementation strategy and a study conducted to determine its effectiveness over administering the program with a standard outpatient protocol.

SCHOOL-BASED IMPLEMENTATION

Implementing ATP in a school setting presented many new opportunities and challenges. Procedures used to enhance the effectiveness of ATP included (a) developing a cost-effective risk assessment, (b) recruiting high-risk families, (c) collaborating with school liaisons, (d) providing behavioral consultation, and (e) integrating high-risk students with low-risk students.

Risk Assessment

One of the key issues in prevention is allocating intervention resources where they are most needed. Building on an earlier program of research (Patterson et al., 1992), we selected the four middle schools that are located in neighborhoods with the highest rates of juvenile arrests within the study community. We selected teacher ratings to identify families within these middle schools for involvement in the school implementation study. Previous research consistently demonstrates that teachers are quite capable of accurately identifying youths most at risk for adolescent problem behavior (Dishion & Patterson, 1992; Loeber & Dishion, 1983; Loeber, Dishion, & Patterson, 1984; Walker & Severson, 1991). Building on this information, we developed an instrument that efficiently used teachers' expertise to screen youths for involvement in ATP. The risk factors model tested by Bry et al. (1982) was put into a format that could be used by teachers to rate a complete class. The Teacher Risk Screening Index (Soberman, 1994) is a 12-item checklist and includes a roster of all sixth-grade students to be evaluated. Teachers rated each student ("yes" or "no") for the presence of each of the risk factors. If boys displayed at least four of the risk factors, they were invited to participate in ATP. Because of the lower incidence of problem behavior in school, a cut score of two risk factors was used for girls.

Soberman (1994) extensively analyzed the psychometric properties of this instrument. The 12 items were clustered into six dimensions of behavior: internalizing (2 items), externalizing (3 items), substance use (2 items), deviant peer associations (2 items), academic deficiencies (2 items), and family stress (1 item). Eight-week retest stability was found to be quite high for these clusters, ranging from .71 for externalizing to .63 for internalizing ($N = 246$). The externalizing cluster showed the highest and most consistent predictive validity to multiple measures of problem behavior derived from the parents' and youths' reports.

Recruitment

We were aware that getting parents involved could be a major stumbling block. Hawkins and Lishner (1987) report that as few as 45% of parents take advantage of parent training programs offered to them. We attempted to counter this trend by designing a parent-driven system of recruitment. Letters were mailed home to the families of students who met risk status criteria. The letter was from the principal and written on the school's letterhead. The rationale for participation used neutral and nonstigmatizing language. Phrases such as "As you know, the teenage years involve changes and challenges to both parents and teens," "I am pleased that this program is available to families in our community and believe that it will help your child be more successful at home and in school," "Your family will benefit from this free program," "Because of limited resources, only some families can be offered ATP this year," and "Your family's full involvement in the 12-week program will help prevent substance abuse, problem behavior, and emotional turmoil in your teenage son or daughter" were used to encourage parents to volunteer. Our initial work with this strategy, using four middle schools in two consecutive school years (1991 and 1992), has been quite successful. We have successfully recruited up to 70% of the targeted parents using this strategy.

More than 50% of the families that eventually participated in the program volunteered within a week after receiving the letter. The remaining families were contacted by telephone. The program staff did not pressure parents to agree to participate but invited them to review the program in the comfort of their home. During the home visit, the program was described in detail, and the concerns of the parents and youths were addressed.

School Liaisons

Two consultants were drawn from the schools to be ATP liaisons and were used to facilitate the procedural details (e.g., allocating space, collecting information, and communicating with teachers) of the school-based implementation. We were also focused on maximizing the recruitment of school staff. The entire staff at each school was brought together and presented with the opportunity to be involved with ATP. From the volunteers, the principal selected those staff members considered the most suitable to work with parents and youths. The school liaisons provided a valuable link between the participants and the school. In addition to attending and participating in all the ATP groups, the consultants met with the students each week to check on skill development and practice. They also became advocates for the students, who typically have multiple school problems and limited support.

The school liaisons also attended the ATP meetings. In the parent groups, their responsibility was to provide weekly information on a "home-school card." Data were collected on each student's academic and social behavior, establishing an ongoing linkage between the parents and the school. In addition, the weekly card presented opportunities to report on positive behaviors.

The school liaisons attended teen-focused groups with the intention of providing school-based incentives for youths making progress on intervention goals. After involvement in the 12-week program, school liaisons organized and led interventions intended to integrate high-risk ATP youths with low-risk youths in the same school. Similar to the teen-focused groups in the component analysis reported earlier, older peer consultants were also used in the 12-week program.

Behavioral Consultants

Behavioral consultation to teachers for ATP youth was also provided when requested. The goal was to offer additional support and consultation to students and teachers for academic or social behavior in the classroom and other school settings (e.g., lunchroom, playground, and bus). First, they consulted with teachers and other school staff involved with the ATP students. Teachers and consultants developed behavior change plans ranging from improving classroom academic work or social behavior to teaching social skills. Because most of the teens participating in ATP were not identified as special education students, they were not ordinarily eligible for this level of support. ATP was implemented intensively in each middle school for a 3-month duration; we found that behavioral consultation services were requested for only three or four students.

Integrating High-Risk and Low-Risk Youths

After the first 12 weeks of the program, students in the teen groups were mixed with low-risk youth to create a video project that addressed topics related to substance use-abuse and other pressures facing middle school students and their families. Cooperative learning strategies were used to ensure that all the youths participated equally in the process. The groups met once or twice a week for a total of 1.5 hours per week to decide on topics, negotiate format, and produce the project. Each high-risk youth was paired with a low-risk student, and they worked together on assigned tasks. The school liaisons led the enhancement groups. Themes from the teen-focus curriculum were reinforced and used whenever possible. The specific goals of the peer enhancement component were as follows:

1. To produce a video project with an "antiproblem behavior" message related to the effects on physical and mental health, family, and peer pressure
2. To integrate the ATP high-risk youths into prosocial groups and activities
3. To reinforce skills taught during the first 12 skill-building sessions
4. To inform students of the risks of substance use and other problem behaviors

AN ANALYSIS OF
SCHOOL IMPLEMENTATION

Overview

To test the effectiveness of implementing ATP in the schools, we randomly assigned 63 families into two conditions: (a) community-based implementation, and (b) school-based implementation. All families in each condition received both the teen-focused and the parent-focused interventions. At the time the study was planned, we did not have information about the negative effects of aggregating high-risk children into teen-focused groups. We expected the school implementation of ATP to be more effective in reducing escalations in problem behavior compared with the community-based implementation. We used the same measures employed in the first component analysis described previously by Dishion and Andrews (1995).

School Receptivity

At a very basic level, we felt it was important to evaluate the school staffs' receptivity to the program. Informal feedback revealed that school personnel were very supportive and impressed by the effectiveness of the program. School consultants were particularly pleased with the behavioral consultant component as well as the improved home-school communication facilitated by the teen and parent consultants. They were less enthusiastic, however, about the weekly meetings with students following implementation of the basic ATP. Making the videotapes was considered time-consuming. On the other hand, student-produced videotapes were well received by fellow students. Although the school personnel were quite pleased with ATP in their schools, none of the four middle schools implemented a single feature of the program in the year after their participation despite our offers of free consultation and assistance. This finding is a chronic problem in prevention (Kelly, 1988) and underscores the need to attend to the contextual factors that influence the adoption of effective prevention programs (Biglan, in press).

Outcome

The hypothesis that the school-based implementation of ATP would be superior to the community-based implementation was not supported by a majority of the data. Although the rates of negative engagement were not statistically different from those of the active interventions in the ATP component analysis presented earlier (Dishion & Andrews, 1995), there was no reliable difference between the school- and community-based implementation. Similarly, there were no differences found between the two groups on termination teacher ratings or substance use in the period between termination and the 1-year follow-up. Only teacher ratings on the CBCL externalizing scale showed significantly less problem behavior in the school compared with the community implementation group at 1-year follow-up, $F(1, 56) = 3.99, p < .05$. Because the teachers providing the 1-year follow-up ratings were different from those with direct knowledge of the experimental condition, this may well be a valid intervention effect.

SUMMARY AND FUTURE DIRECTIONS

The basic components of ATP (parent focus and teen focus) were effective in engaging students and their parents and in improving parent-child relations. In addition, the parent-focus curriculum had a short-term effect on the incidence of aggressive and delinquent behaviors in young teens. Parent training and involvement in schools were once again supported as effective strategies for improving student behavior and in reducing the escalation of drug use during the year after program participation.

The teen-focused curriculum, although enhancing parent-child relations, did not influence problem behavior in short-term evaluations. Long-term outcome data highlight the need to look closely at any effort to bring high-risk youths into close proximity with one another. Youths participating in this condition, designed originally to teach skills that would lead to reductions in problem behavior, seemed to escalate in their problem behavior after experiencing the intervention. A closer inspection of these results is currently under way, as is the design of alternative school-based intervention strategies to bolster positive peer influences for high-risk youths.

The school implementation of ATP was superior to the community implementation only on teachers' ratings of problem behavior at school at 1-year follow-up. It is clear from the initial inspection of these data, reports from participating school personnel, and anecdotal evidence from project staff that there is a need to alter the school environment to (a) further increase parent involvement and home-school communication and (b) to develop more heterogeneous peer environments as a means of countering the effects of deviant peer groups. One difficulty with this evaluation study is the strong possibility of negative effects secondary to aggregating high-risk youths to deliver the teen-focused curriculum.

In conclusion, the data from the component analyses suggest that future work should concentrate on building on the parent training component of ATP. An ecological perspective strongly suggests that we should continue to deliver ATP in the school setting, and that interventions to increase clear and specific communication between the home and school could be strengthened. Our initial efforts suggest that parents of high-risk youths can be recruited successfully into interventions that offer parenting resources. In line with our dental metaphor, interventions in middle school need to be anticipatory. This simply means that an accepted part of the school experience is proactive problem identification as well as resources for problem remediation. Risk can be conceptualized as environmental risk, and "decay" in the environment is present in the form of school failure, deviant peers, and antisocial behavior. Detection of environmental decay at school and effective interventions are unimportant, however, if we cannot facilitate families' receptivity to this risk information or their access to interventions.

We suggest that one component of a preventive model should explicitly address parenting practices that complement school efforts to educate and prepare young people for adulthood. Stouthamer-Loeber, Loeber, Van Kammen, and Zhang (in press) published results indicating that only 40% of the parents of an early-starting delinquent sought professional help for their youngster by the time he or she had reached the eighth grade. We suspect that a fair number of these were court mandated. Moreover, there was no information on the quality of the support services provided to parents. It seems clear that a majority of the families in dire need of support and remedial intervention are not seeking help. Are the services not available? Do the families not know about them? Are families actively rejecting professional support? Given the empirical support for the impact of interventions that support parenting practices of antisocial behavior, answers to these questions are critical (Dishion & Patterson, 1992; Kazdin, 1987; Patterson, Dishion, & Chamberlain, 1993).

A Multiple Gating Approach

We propose a framework for recruitment, assessment, and service delivery that may facilitate reaching high-risk families and titrating intervention services to the families' needs. The first step is a cost-effective strategy for screening and allocating resources to families most in need of parenting support. A proactive preventive approach requires that the specific processes (e.g., deviant peers, school failure, and antisocial behavior) associated with escalating problem behavior be identified early and interrupted before they unfold. Over the past 10 years, we have investigated a systematic approach to early identification for prevention, which we refer to as multiple gating (Dishion & Patterson, 1992; Loeber & Dishion, 1987; Loeber et al., 1984). This approach has been integrated into the Systematic Screening for Behavior Disorders (SSBD; Walker & Severson, 1991) procedure that is standardized and currently used in school settings.

Second, we need to design interventions that maximize parent satisfaction and engagement (McMahon, Tiedemann, Forehand, & Griest, 1984). As indicated in this volume, promising studies of parental engagement are emerging (e.g., Prinz & Miller, Chapter 8, this volume). We know that the quality of therapists' interactions with parents of problem children can dramatically affect the dropout rate. Using a supportive, problem-solving strategy that addresses the concerns of the parents can lead to greater retention in parent training (Patterson, 1985; Patterson & Forgatch, 1987; Prinz & Miller, 1994). This seems to be a particularly salient issue for families with older children that are more likely to drop out of parent training interventions (Dishion & Patterson, 1992).

Progress on the problem of engagement has been most remarkable in clinical interventions for problem-drinking adults (Miller & Rollnick, 1991).

It is reasonable to say that the initial step in any intervention program for people identified as being high risk is enhancing their motivation to change. Miller and Rollnick (1991) found that a brief intervention—referred to as the drinker's check-up—could reduce problem drinking as much as could a 28-day inpatient program.

The drinker's check-up follows what has been called a FRAMES model: F stands for providing feedback to the client on the basis of objective assessments; R means that parents are encouraged to accept responsibility for those practices that are within their power to change and control; A stands for advice provided by the consultant on the basis of what is known to be effective interventions for high-risk children; M means that a menu of intervention options, rather than an intervention solution, is offered to clients, and the consultant and client together decide what is realistic and in the best interest of each family; E represents accurate empathy, a basic ingredient in all effective therapeutic interactions with clients (Rogers, 1957); and S refers to self-efficacy through support and realistic advice. The client walks away from the drinker's check-up feeling empowered about specific things to do to improve the outcome for the child and to continue the practices that are strengths for the family.

The process underlying this dramatic effect seems to be that a realistic appraisal of one's risk status in the company of a knowledgeable and supportive professional enhances one's motivation for change and for using those intervention resources that are most appropriate for that purpose.

We hypothesize that a parallel brief intervention, which we refer to as the family check-up, will enhance at-risk parents' motivation to change, resulting in greater use of parenting resources, briefer interventions, and reductions in substance use and problem behavior. If the request for intervention is from the parents rather than the "experts," we might assume greater engagement and feelings of ownership in the change process. To date, parental engagement has been informally embedded in strategies of individual family consultation, the use of consultants, letters of recruitment, and the offering of interventions in the school context. We now propose a more structured specific approach to parental engagement.

Figure 9.6 provides a schematic diagram of a proposed three-stage engagement strategy that integrates what has often been conceptualized as prevention and treatment interventions. Again, within a dental model, efforts to prevent and treat are integral. The multiple gating framework suggests three intervention stages.

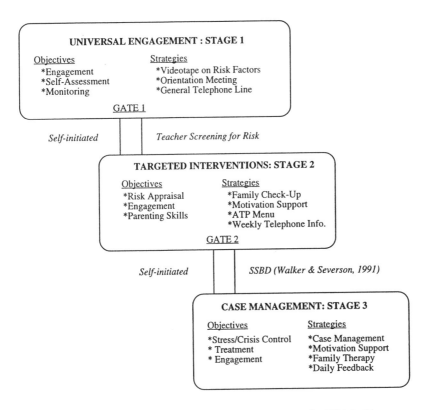

Figure 9.6. A Multiple Gating Approach to Prevention and Intervention With Problem Behavior in Middle School Adolescents

Universal Intervention: Stage 1. The first effort to intervene is embedded within a universal information-based intervention that all parents receive. We suggest that all parents routinely be provided with interesting and engaging materials that apprise them of normative problem behavior levels and of state-of-the-art knowledge regarding how parents can affect the adjustment of their child. These interventions can be motivational for parents of low-risk youths and serve as self-assessments for parents of high-risk youths. During their child's first year of middle school, parents may be presented with a videotape demonstrating key parenting skills related to promoting child cooperation in the home, reducing unsupervised time with peers, and promoting constructive problem solving and communication.

This could be accomplished in the context of an all-parent orientation meeting in the school. On the basis of a 20-minute videotape, parents can self-assess their child's level of problem behavior and their interest in getting more information regarding their family, child, or parenting practices. All schools need to have a parent resource room that contains validated information on parenting practices and that is staffed by professionals trained to work effectively with parents. Parents should have access to solid information on all of the aspects of family management, adolescent development, and other issues of interest.

Targeted Intervention: Stage 2. We suggest developing a procedure parallel to the drinker' check-up (Miller & Rollnick, 1991; Miller & Sovereign, 1989) for families, referred to as the family check-up (two 2-hour sessions). The first session should assess the child, parent, and family variables using multiagents and multimethods. Normative data are needed on those constructs of most concern: the child's problem behavior, parent-child interactions and communication processes, monitoring, and the child's peer network. Thus, a second session presents families with specific norms regarding the status of their child and family and supportive consultation regarding steps to take to improve their family life and their child's adjustment. This is a minimal intervention strategy that has a primary objective of enhancing the parents' appraisal of risk and supporting their interest in change. We hypothesize that such a minimal intervention would produce improvements for many families in the moderate range of risk.

Motivational interviewing is used to change risk appraisal and to support parents' commitment to change strategies. After families are provided with information in the family check-up, decisions will be made regarding the next step. Many families in an identified risk group will have strengths that outweigh weaknesses or risk factors. For these families, the family check-up will serve to support their existing efforts and provide them with a realistic appraisal of their future risk. Concerns regarding risk will be more salient in other families, and in this situation a family consultant might discuss an intervention menu in regard to each family's needs. The family consultant role is to support parents in making informed selections and to offer advice when requested.

In addition to making parenting resources available and individually tailored, we suggest that parents of high-risk students be supported in their efforts through a school monitoring service of their child. This service, akin to the home-school card, can easily provide a weekly telephone summary of attendance, behavior in class, and homework completion. Such telephone contacts can be greatly enhanced by voice-mail technology. To increase parents' use of family management skills and minimize punitive coercive discipline, we suggest that the home-school monitoring system be made available to parents contingent on their attending at least two parent training sessions; one prior to involvement and the second session 3 weeks after involvement to refine and clarify skills. These training sessions would focus on teaching parents how to provide incentives for positive school weeks and how to communicate with school staff about school problems.

Selected Intervention: Stage 3. The key component of Stage 3 is parent training using approaches described in several intervention protocols for parent training (Dishion & Patterson, 1992; Forehand & McMahon, 1981; Patterson, 1982) as well as those used by other behavioral, structural, and eclectic family therapists working with problematic adolescents (Bry, McGreene, Schutte, & Fishman, 1991; Henggeler, Melton, & Smith, 1992; Szapocznik & Kurtines, 1989).

On the basis of results of an adaptation of the SSBD (Walker & Severson, 1991), 10% of the families will be identified as in need of intensive intervention and support. The number of sessions and the goals of the family intervention will be negotiated with the parents. The optimal strategy is to work with the entire family. When that is not feasible, however, such as in the case of a reluctant parent figure, we suggest working with whomever is willing and relevant to addressing the best interests of the youth (Szapocznik et al., 1988).

The first step in our parent training model is to have parents target a primary area of concern. Our clinical experience and theoretical model direct us to have parents clearly specify their concerns and then initially track these targeted behaviors as they occur at home and at school. In consultation with parents, we then move to develop strategies to reinforce the prosocial opposite of the targeted behavior. For example, a "bad attitude" can lead to parents targeting "cooperating with requests to help around the house." Parents will also be taught to use daily information from the school to support and reinforce their middle school student's success. Parents will be encouraged, as a first step, to reinforce positive behavior at home and at school. The second step for many parents is to reduce the use of irritable, harsh reactions to misbehavior and to be more consistent in setting limits with their adolescent. Third, once parents are more effective in rewarding and limit setting, they can also be more effective in monitoring and supervising their youth's whereabouts, and especially unsupervised time with deviant peers. Communication skills are the foundation for a positive parent-child relationship and for negotiating solutions to conflict (Forgatch, 1989). In collaboration with parents, we will work through each of these issues as they are relevant to the parents' targeted concerns.

Supervision and support for intervention staff is an integral component of our prevention model. The integrity of the Stage 3 intervention level is ensured by close supervision and weekly case-review sessions. Family sessions should be either videotaped or audiotaped to continue the analysis of client engagement in the intervention process. The in-depth review is a problem-solving session, and the intervention team serves two functions: (a) providing support to the staff primarily responsible for the case and (b) brainstorming intervention strategies that would be effective in dealing with barriers to behavior change and consistent with our model of intervention. Finally, a culture of expertise and support emerges within the clinical group that is essential for working with high-risk families.

In summary, the success of prevention work on adolescent problem behaviors depends on the relevance to the developmental stage, context, and the ongoing engagement of parents and teens. We end this chapter as we began—with the use of the dental model as a guiding metaphor for these interventions. Problem behavior has stability across development and within context. Knowledge of early antisocial antecedents, long-term sequelae, and negative outcomes provide guidance in the preventive procedures necessary for young adolescents and their parents. We propose that regular check-ups provide a nonstigmatizing mechanism for assessing levels of decay and gathering the necessary resources across contexts to prevent further decay and eventual loss of these youths to our society.

References

Achenbach, T. M. (1992). New developments in multiaxial empirically based assessment of child and adolescent psychopathology. In J. C. Rosen & P. McReynolds (Eds.), *Advances in psychological assessment* (Vol. 8, pp. 75-102). New York: Plenum.

Andrews, D. W., Soberman, L. H., & Dishion, T. J. (1995). The Adolescent Transitions Program: A school-based program for high-risk teens and their parents. *Education and Treatment of Children, 18,* 478-484.

Biglan, A. (in press). *A contextual framework for changing cultural practices.* Reno, NV: Context Press.

Botvin, G. J., Baker, E., Dusenbury, L., Tortu, S., & Botvin, E. M. (1990). Preventing adolescent drug abuse through a multimodal cognitive-behavioral approach: Results of a 3-year study. *Journal of Consulting and Clinical Psychology, 58,* 437-446.

Botvin, G. J., Schinke, S. C., & Orlandi, M. A. (1995). School-based health promotion, substance abuse, and sexual behavior. *Applied and Preventive Psychology, 4,* 167-184.

Botvin, G. J., & Wills, T. A. (1985). *Personal and social skills training: Cognitive-behavioral approaches to substance abuse prevention. Prevention research: Deterring drug abuse among children and adolescents* (NIDA Research Monograph No. 63). Rockville, MD: National Institute on Drug Abuse.

Britt, C. (1990). *Crime, criminal careers, and social control.* Unpublished doctoral dissertation, University of Arizona, Tucson.

Bronfenbrenner, U. (1979). *The ecology of human development: Experiments by nature and by design.* Cambridge, MA: Harvard University Press.

Bronfenbrenner, U. (1986). Ecology of the family as a context for human development. *Developmental Psychology, 22,* 723-742.

Bronfenbrenner, U. (1989). Ecological systems theory. In R. Vasta (Ed.), *Annals of child development. Vol. 6. Six theories of child development: Revised formulations and current issues* (pp. 187-249). London: JAI.

Bry, B. H., McGreene, D., Schutte, C., & Fishman, C. A. (1991). *Targeted family intervention manual.* Unpublished technical report, Rutgers State University, Princeton, NJ.

Bry, B. H., McKeon, P., & Pandina, R. J. (1982). Extent of drug use as a function of number of risk factors. *Journal of Abnormal Psychology, 91,* 273-279.

Campbell, D. T., & Stanley, J. C. (1963). *Experimental and quasi-experimental designs for research.* Chicago: Rand McNally.

Conduct Problems Prevention Research Group (1992). A developmental and clinical model for the prevention of conduct disorder. The FAST Track Program. *Development and Psychopathology, 4,* 509-527.

Dishion, T. J., & Andrews, D. W. (1995). Preventing escalation in problem behaviors with high-risk young adolescents: Immediate and 1-year outcomes. *Journal of Consulting and Clinical Psychology, 63,* 538-548.

Dishion, T. J., Capaldi, D., Spracklen, K. M., & Li, F. (1995). Peer ecology of male adolescent drug use. *Development and Psychopathology, 7,* 803-824.

Dishion, T. J., French, D. C., & Patterson, G. R. (1995). The development and ecology of antisocial behavior. In D. Cicchetti & D. Cohen (Eds.), *Manual of developmental psychopathology* (pp. 421-471). New York: John Wiley.

Dishion, T. J., Gardner, K., Patterson, G. R., Reid, J. B., & Thibodeaux, S. (1983). *The Family Process Code: A multidimensional system for observing family interactions.* Unpublished technical manual. (Available from Oregon Social Learning Center, 207 E. 5th Street, Suite 202, Eugene, OR 97401)

Dishion, T. J., & Kavanagh, K. (in press). *Adolescent problem behavior: Theory and intervention.* New York: Guilford.

Dishion, T. J., Kavanagh, K., & Soberman, L. (in press). *Adolescent Transitions Program: Assessment and intervention sourcebook.* New York: Guilford.

Dishion, T. J., & Patterson, G. R. (1992). Age effects in parent training outcome. *Behavior Therapy, 23,* 719-729.

Dishion, T. J., Patterson, G. R., & Griesler, P. C. (1994). Peer adaptation in the development of antisocial behavior: A confluence model. In L. R. Huesmann (Ed.), *Aggressive behavior: Current perspectives* (pp. 61-95). New York: Plenum.

Dishion, T. J., Patterson, G. R., Stoolmiller, M., & Skinner, M. (1991). Family, school, and behavioral antecedents to early adolescent involvement with antisocial peers. *Developmental Psychology, 27,* 172-180.

Elliott, D. S., Huizinga, D., & Ageton, S. S. (1985). *Explaining delinquency and drug use.* Beverly Hills, CA: Sage.

Forehand, R., & McMahon, R. J. (1981). *Helping the noncompliant child: A clinician's guide to parent training.* New York: Guilford.

Forgatch, M. S. (1989). Patterns and outcome in family problem solving: The disrupting effect of negative emotion. *Journal of Marriage and Family, 51,* 115-124.

Gottfredson, D. C., Gottfredson, G. D., & Hybl, L. G. (1993). Managing adolescent behavior: A multiyear, multischool study. *American Educational Research Journal, 30,* 179-215.

Gottfredson, M. R., & Hirschi, T. (1994). A general theory of adolescent problem behavior: Problems and prospects. In R. D. Ketterlinus & M. E. Lamb (Eds.), *Adolescent problem behaviors* (pp. 41-56). Thousand Oaks, CA: Sage.

Greenberg, D. (1991). Modeling criminal careers. *Criminology, 29,* 17-46.

Hawkins, J. D., & Lishner, D. M. (1987). School and delinquency. In E. H. Johnson (Ed.), *Handbook on crime and delinquency prevention* (pp. 179-221). New York: Greenwood.

Heller, L. R., & Fantuzzo, J. W. (1993). Reciprocal peer tutoring and parent partnership: Does parent involvement make a difference? *School Psychology Review, 22,* 517-534.

Henggeler, S. W., Melton, G. B., & Smith, L. A. (1992). Family preservation using multisystemic treatment: An effective alternative to incarcerating serious juvenile offenders. *Journal of Consulting and Clinical Psychology, 60,* 953-961.

Hirschi, T., & Gottfredson, M. (1983). Age and the explanation of crime. *American Journal of Sociology, 89,* 552-584.

Kazdin, A. E. (1987). Treatment of antisocial behavior in children: Current status and future directions. *Psychological Bulletin, 102,* 187-203.

Kellam, S. G. (1990). Developmental epidemiological framework for family research on depression and aggression. In G. R. Patterson (Ed.), *Depression and aggression in family interaction* (pp. 11-48). Hillsdale, NJ: Lawrence Erlbaum.

Kelly, J. G. (1988). *A guide to conducting preventive research in the community: First steps.* New York: Hallworth.

Loeber, R., & Dishion, T. (1983). Early predictors of male delinquency: A review. *Psychological Bulletin, 94,* 68-99.

Loeber, R., & Dishion, T. J. (1987). Antisocial and delinquent youths: Methods for their early identification. In J. D. Burchard & S. N. Burchard (Eds.), *Prevention of delinquent behavior* (pp. 75-89). Newbury Park, CA: Sage.

Loeber, R., Dishion, T. J., & Patterson, G. R. (1984). Multiple gating: A multistage assessment procedure for identifying youths at risk for delinquency. *Journal of Research in Crime and Delinquency, 21,* 7-32.

Loeber, R., & Schmaling, K. B. (1985). The utility of differentiating between mixed and pure forms of antisocial child behavior. *Journal of Abnormal Child Psychology, 13,* 315-336.

Magnusson, D. (1988). Aggressiveness, hyperactivity, and autonomic activity/reactivity in the development of social maladjustment. In D. Magnusson (Ed.), *Paths through life: Individual development from an interactionary perspective: A longitudinal study* (Vol. 1, pp. 153-175). Hillsdale, NJ: Lawrence Erlbaum.

McMahon, R. J., Tiedemann, G. L., Forehand, R., & Griest, D. L. (1984). Parental satisfaction with parent training to modify child noncompliance. *Behavior Therapy, 15,* 295-303.

Miller, W. R., & Rollnick, S. (1991). *Motivational interviewing: Preparing people to change addictive behavior.* New York: Guilford.

Miller, W. R., & Sovereign, R. G. (1989). The checkup: A model for early intervention in addictive behaviors. In T. Loberg, W. R. Miller, P. E. Nathan, & G. A. Marlatt (Eds.), *Addictive behaviors: Prevention and early intervention* (pp. 219-231). The Netherlands: Sweta & Zeitlinger.

Moffitt, T. E. (1993). Adolescence-limited and life course persistent antisocial behavior: Developmental taxonomy. *Psychological Review, 100,* 674-701.

Patterson, G. R. (1982). *Coercive family process.* Eugene, OR: Castalia.

Patterson, G. R. (1985). Beyond technology: The next stage in the development of a parent training technology. In L. L'Abate (Ed.), *Handbook of family psychology and therapy* (Vol. 2, pp. 1344-1379). Homewood, IL: Dorsey.

Patterson, G. R. (1992). Developmental changes in antisocial behavior. In R. DeV. Peters, R. J. McMahon, & V. L. Quinsey (Eds.), *Aggression and violence throughout the lifespan* (pp. 52-82). Newbury Park, CA: Sage.

Patterson, G. R., Dishion, T. J., & Chamberlain, P. (1993). Outcomes and methodological issues relating to treatment of antisocial children. In T. R. Giles (Ed.), *Effective psychotherapy: A handbook of comparative research* (pp. 43-88). New York: Plenum.

Patterson, G. R., & Forgatch, M. S. (1987). *Parents and adolescents: I. Living together.* Eugene, OR: Castalia.

Patterson, G. R., & Reid, J. B. (1984). Social interactional processes within the family: The study of moment-by-moment family transactions in which human social development is embedded. *Journal of Applied Developmental Psychology, 5,* 237-262.

Patterson, G. R., Reid, J. B., & Dishion, T. J. (1992). *Antisocial boys.* Eugene, OR: Castalia.

Prinz, R. J., & Miller, G. E. (1994). Family-based treatment for childhood antisocial behavior: Experimental influences on dropout and engagement. *Journal of Consulting and Clinical Psychology, 62,* 645-650.

Reid, J. B. (1993). Prevention of conduct disorder before and after school entry: Relating interventions to developmental findings. *Development and Psychology, 5,* 243-262.

Robins, L. N., & Przybeck, T. R. (1985). Age of onset of drug use as a factor in drug and other disorders. In C. L. Jones & R. J. Battjes (Eds.), *Etiology of drug abuse: Implications for prevention* (NIDA Research Monograph No. 56, pp. 178-193). Rockville, MD: National Institute on Drug Abuse.

Rogers, C. R. (1957). The necessary and sufficient conditions of therapeutic personality change. *Journal of Consulting Psychology, 21,* 95-103.

Rutter, M. (1989). Pathways from childhood to adult life. *Journal of Child Psychology and Psychiatry, 30,* 23-51.

Sampson, R. J., & Laub, J. H. (1990). Crime and deviance over the life course: A salience of adult social bonds. *American Sociological Review, 55,* 609-627.

Smith, G. M., & Fogg, C. P. (1979). Psychological antecedents of teenage drug use. *Research in Community Mental Health, 1,* 87-102.

Soberman, L. (1994). *Psychometric validation of a brief teacher screening instrument.* Unpublished doctoral dissertation, University of Oregon, Eugene.

Stattin, H., & Magnusson, D. (1991). Stability and change in criminal behaviour up to age 30. *British Journal of Criminology, 31,* 327-346.

Stouthamer-Loeber, M., Loeber, R., Van Kammen, W., & Zhang, Q. (in press). Uninterrupted delinquent careers: The timing of parental help-seeking in juvenile court contact. *Studies on Crime and Crime Prevention.*

Szapocznik, J., & Kurtines, W. M. (1989). *Breakthroughs in family therapy with drug-abusing and problem youth.* New York: Springer.

Szapocznik, J., Perez-Vidal, A., Brickman, A. L., Foote, F. H., Santisteban, D., & Hervis, O. (1988). Engaging adolescent drug abusers and their families in treatment: A strategic structural systems approach. *Journal of Consulting and Clinical Psychology, 56,* 552-557.

Trickett, E. J., & Berman, D. (1989). Taking ecology seriously: A community development approach to individually based preventive interventions in the schools. In L. A. Bond & B. E. Compas (Eds.), *Primary prevention and promotion in the schools* (pp. 361-390). Newbury Park, CA: Sage.

Walker, H. M., & Severson, H. H. (1991). *Systematic screening for behavior disorders: Training manual.* Longmont, CO: Sopris West.

West, D. J., & Farrington, D. P. (1977). *The delinquent way of life.* New York: Crane, Russak.

Yamaguchi, K., & Kandel, D. B. (1985). On resolution of role incompatibility: A life event history analysis of family roles and marijuana use. *American Journal of Sociology, 90,* 1284-1325.

10

Substance Abuse Prevention
Through Life Skills Training

GILBERT J. BOTVIN

THE PROBLEM OF DRUG ABUSE

Drug abuse is a major public health problem in the United States and Canada. Cigarette smoking is a risk factor for heart disease, various cancers, and chronic obstructive lung disease and accounts for over 430,000 deaths per year in the United States (U.S. Public Health Service, 1989). Alcohol is not only related to chronic diseases such as cirrhosis of the liver but is also a major factor in auto fatalities and homicides. Beyond this, adolescent drug use predicts a number of other undesirable outcomes, such as reducing traditional educational accomplishments and job stability, increasing the likelihood of marrying and having children at younger ages, and increasing the likelihood of engaging in criminal behavior (Newcomb & Bentler, 1988).

The results of a national survey of high school seniors in the United States (Johnston, O'Malley, & Bachman, 1994) showed that 31% of the seniors had used illicit drugs in the past year and 42.9% had done so during their lifetime. For specific drugs, the annual prevalence rate for marijuana was 26% and the lifetime rate was 35.3%, the annual inhalant prevalence rate was 7% and the lifetime rate was 17.4%, the annual LSD prevalence rate was 6.8% and the lifetime rate was 10.3%, and the annual stimulant prevalence rate was 8.4% and the lifetime rate was 15.1%. The annual alcohol rate was 76% and the lifetime rate was 87%. Although annual rates for smoking were not provided, the lifetime rate was 61.9% and the 30-day rate was 29.9%.

Despite considerable public attention and the expenditure of well over a billion dollars in the past few years alone, little if any progress has been made toward reducing drug abuse. In fact, the problem appears to be getting worse. National survey data in the United States collected in 1993 and recently released (Johnston et al., 1994) show a sharp rise in marijuana use among 8th, 10th and 12th graders as well as an increase for all three grade levels in cigarette smoking and the use of stimulants, LSD, and inhalants. These increases reverse a decade-long decline in the use of marijuana and represent a new move upward for cigarette smoking, which had remained largely unchanged over the past 10 years, and LSD, which has been at relatively low levels since the end of the 1960s. One obvious concern is that these changes may herald the beginning of a new drug epidemic.

THE NEED FOR EFFECTIVE
PREVENTION APPROACHES

Attempts to develop effective treatment programs have been costly, difficult, and only moderately successful (Dusenbury, Khuri, & Millman, 1992). Not surprisingly, increased emphasis has gradually been placed on efforts to prevent the initiation and early stages of drug abuse. These efforts have targeted children and adolescents and have taken several forms, including public education campaigns, school-based approaches, and legislation restricting availability and use of drugs. The most commonly used prevention strategy involves the dissemination of information concerning the adverse health, social, and legal consequences of use (Botvin & Botvin, 1992). This approach is based on the implicit assumption that drug abuse is the result of a rational decision and that individuals who choose to use drugs do so because they are unaware of the dangers of drug use. When the problem of drug abuse is framed in this way, the apparent solution is to educate adolescents about the negative consequences of using drugs. It is assumed that once armed with the appropriate information, adolescents will make a rational and informed decision not to use drugs. Other approaches to drug abuse prevention include "alternative" programs, which attempt to provide adolescents with activities designed to serve as alternatives to drug use, or "affective education," which attempts to promote emotional development and feelings of self-esteem.

Reviews of the prevention research literature (e.g., Botvin & Botvin, 1992) and meta-analytic studies (e.g., Bangert-Drowns, 1988; Bruvold & Rundall, 1988; Tobler, 1986) have indicated that drug abuse prevention programs using these approaches are ineffective. Studies testing these approaches have not been able to produce reductions in drug use behavior. Clearly, given the importance and magnitude of the problem of drug abuse, it is essential that effective approaches be identified and tested. The most promising approaches, according to available evidence, are those that target the psychosocial factors implicated in the initiation of drug abuse (Bangert-Drowns, 1988; Botvin & Botvin, 1992; Bruvold & Rundall, 1988; Tobler, 1986). One such program, called Life Skills Training (LST), is the topic of this chapter. The background and rationale for the LST approach to drug abuse prevention is discussed, the intervention materials and methods are described, and the research studies testing its efficacy are summarized. Unlike many of the approaches discussed in this volume, this is a universal or primary prevention intervention that has been tested on several different populations of adolescents in school settings. Before describing the LST approach to drug abuse prevention, it is worth summarizing what is currently known regarding the causes of drug abuse and its developmental progression.

DRUG ABUSE ETIOLOGY

Causes and Developmental Progression

The development of effective prevention programs requires an understanding of the etiology of drug abuse with respect to the age of onset, developmental progression, etiologic determinants, and causal pathways. The initiation and early stages of drug abuse generally begin during the early adolescent years and progress in a well-defined sequence (Millman & Botvin, 1992). Drug use typically begins with the use of alcohol and tobacco and later progresses to the use of marijuana, and, for some, to the use of stimulants, opiates, hallucinogens, and other illicit substances (Kandel, 1978). Not surprisingly, this progression corresponds exactly to the prevalence and availability of these substances—with alcohol being the most prevalent form of drug use and the most widely available, followed by tobacco (cigarettes) and marijuana. Because alcohol, tobacco, and marijuana are among the first substances used, they have been referred to as "gateway" substances. Although the probability of using illicit drugs increases substantially with the use of each gateway substance, however, the use of one or more gateway substances does not necessarily lead to the use of other drugs or to increased drug involvement. In its early stages, drug use occurs infrequently and is limited to a single substance (usually cigarettes or alcohol) and to social situations. As drug involvement increases, use increases in both frequency and amount and progresses from a single substance to multiple substances— that is, to polydrug use.

Although experimental or occasional use does not lead invariably to destructive patterns of use, heavy use has a destructive effect on relationships, functioning, and psychosocial development (Newcomb & Bentler, 1988). Moreover, experimentation with drugs at younger ages (i.e., below 15 years of age) increases risk for problems with drugs later in life. Therefore, developing effective prevention programs targeting tobacco, alcohol, and marijuana use is important not only because of its potential for reducing the mortality and morbidity related to those drugs but also because preventing early use of gateway drugs can prevent or delay the use of other substances (Botvin, 1993).

Factors Promoting Drug Use

The initiation of drug use is the result of the complex combination of many diverse factors (Hawkins, Catalano, & Miller, 1992; Newcomb & Bentler, 1989). There is no single pathway or single variable that serves as a necessary and sufficient condition for the development of either drug use or drug abuse. Figure 10.1 presents a general domain model of the variables that etiology research indicates are among the most important factors leading to initial drug use and eventually to drug abuse. As is evident from this model, etiologic factors associated with drug use can be grouped into three broad categories or domains. The sociocultural domain consists of a collection of background variables found to be associated with drug use, such as demographic factors (age, gender, or social class), biological factors (temperament and sensation seeking), cultural factors (ethnic identity or acculturation), and environmental factors (availability of drugs, community resources, and neighborhood disorganization). The social domain includes school factors (school bonding, school size, and school climate), family factors (family management practices, communication, discipline, monitoring, parental at-

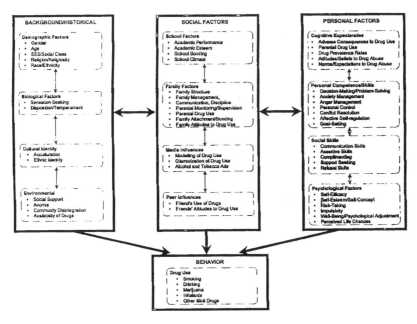

Figure 10.1. Integrated Domain Model of Drug Use Behavior

titudes toward drug use, and parental drug use), media influences promoting attitudes and norms conducive to drug use (TV, movies, rock videos, and tobacco and alcohol advertising), and peer influences (friends' drug use and prodrug attitudes). These factors serve to shape and interact with factors composing the personal domain, including the adolescent's cognitive expectancies (attitudes, beliefs, normative expectations, and knowledge about the adverse effects of drug abuse), general competencies (personal self-management skills and social skills), and a set of skills that are specific to resisting social influences to use drugs from the media and peers. In addition, susceptibility is affected by psychological factors, such as self-efficacy, self-esteem, sense of personal control, psychological adjustment, risk taking, impulsivity, and perceived life chances.

Theoretical Framework

Many theories have been advanced to explain drug abuse (see Lettieri, Sayers, & Pearson, 1980). The most prominent among these focus on social

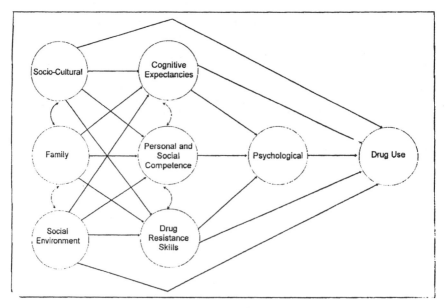

Figure 10.2. Hypothetical Model of Drug Use Initiation

learning (Bandura, 1977), problem behaviors (Jessor & Jessor, 1977), self-derogation (Kaplan, 1980), persuasive communications (McGuire, 1968), peer clusters (Oetting & Beauvais, 1987), and sensation seeking (Zuckerman, 1979).

Figure 10.2 presents a general (nomothetic) model of drug use initiation incorporating key aspects of these various theoretical perspectives. This model organizes the variable domains presented in Figure 10.1 into a causal framework in which these domains are conceptualized as superordinate constructs having specific relationships to one another. This model presents these constructs and their hypothesized interrelationships, representing a number of different possible pathways to drug use.

Several caveats are in order in considering the extent to which this model "explains" the etiology of drug abuse. First, it is important to note that the domain model presented in Figure 10.1 does not include an exhaustive list of all factors found to be associated with drug use (although it is reasonably comprehensive), nor does the model presented in Figure 10.2 specify all possible relationships (pathways) among these constructs. Second, the etiology of drug abuse involves a dynamic process that unfolds over many years. Models such as the one presented in Figure 10.2 are essentially snapshots of the etiology of drug abuse and do not adequately capture the developmental complexity of the process or its recursive nature with feedback loops and reciprocal relationships. For example, a combination of sociocultural, biological, interpersonal, and intrapersonal factors (including drug-related attitudes and normative beliefs) may increase risk for experimentation with tobacco or alcohol at an early age, which leads to affiliation with a more deviant peer group, which in turn reinforces prodrug attitudes and norms and leads not only to an increased frequency of drug use but also to increased risk for illicit drug use.

Like most models of human behavior, drug abuse is conceptualized from a person-environment interactionist perspective. Social influences to use drugs (along with the availability of drugs) interact with individual susceptibility. Some individuals may be influenced to use drugs by the media (TV shows and movies glamorizing drug use or suggesting that drug use is normal or socially acceptable as well as advertising efforts to promote the sale of alcohol and tobacco products), by family members who use drugs or convey prodrug attitudes, by friends and acquaintances who use drugs or hold attitudes and beliefs supportive of drug use, or by all three. Others may be propelled toward drug use or a drug-using peer group because of intrapersonal factors, such as low self-esteem, high anxiety or other dysphoric feelings, or the need for excitement. Because there are multiple pathways leading initially to drug use and later to drug abuse, a more useful way of conceptualizing drug abuse is from a risk factor perspective similar to that used in the epidemiology of chronic diseases such as cancer and heart disease. From this perspective, the presence of specific risk factors is less important than their accumulation. As more risk factors accumulate, so does the likelihood that an individual will become a drug user and eventually a drug abuser. Thus, the presence of multiple risk factors is associated with both initial drug use and the severity of drug involvement (Newcomb & Felix-Ortiz, 1992; Scheier & Newcomb, 1991).

Implications for Prevention

Although some of the variables associated with drug abuse (e.g., demographic or biological factors) are not amenable to intervention, many of the factors associated with drug abuse are potential intervention targets. Moreover, in view of what is known about the sequence and developmental progression of drug abuse as well as the importance of gateway drug use in terms of prevalence and mortality, preventive interventions should target tobacco, alcohol, and marijuana use. This not only offers the potential of reducing the mortality and morbidity associated with each of these substances but also offers the potential for interrupting the normal developmental progression from these substances to other forms of drug use and abuse.

Examination of the model contained in Figure 10.2 suggests several potential points of intervention to prevent drug abuse or reduce drug abuse risk. Interventions can be developed to target individual, family, and community determinants of drug use and abuse. Although it might be advisable to develop multiple interventions to maximize opportunities for preventing drug abuse or reducing drug abuse risk, most prevention research has centered on the development and testing of school-based interventions targeting individual-level risk factors. Based on this model, a preventive intervention is likely to effectively prevent drug abuse if it affects drug-related expectancies (knowledge, attitudes, and norms), drug-related resistance skills, and general competence (personal self-management skills and social skills). By modifying drug-related expectancies and resistance skills, adolescents are provided with the information and skills needed to promote the development of antidrug attitudes and norms as well as to resist peer and media pressure to use drugs. Promoting the development of effective self-management skills and social skills offers the potential to reduce intrapsychic motivations to use drugs and to reduce vulnerability to social influences to use drugs.

LIFE SKILLS TRAINING PROGRAM

Consistent with the theoretical framework discussed previously, the LST program was developed to affect drug-related expectancies, teach skills for resisting social influences to use drugs, and promote the development of general personal self-management skills and social skills. The LST prevention program can best be conceptualized as consisting of two general skills training components to enhance overall personal competence and a problem-specific component relating to drug abuse. The LST program consist of 15 class periods (roughly 45 minutes each). A summary of the intervention methods and materials is provided in the following sections as well as in Botvin and Tortu (1988).

Personal Self-Management Skills

The personal skills component of the LST program is designed to affect an array of self-management skills. To accomplish this, the personal skills component contains material to (a) foster the development of decision making and problem solving (e.g., identifying problem situations, defining goals, generating alternative solutions, and considering consequences); (b) teach skills for identifying, analyzing, interpreting, and resisting media influences; (c) provide students with self-control skills for coping with anxiety (e.g., relaxation training) and anger-frustration (inhibiting impulsive reactions, reframing, and using self-statements); and (d) provide students with the basic principles of personal behavior change and self-improvement (e.g., goal setting, self-monitoring, and self-reinforcement).

Social Skills

The social skills component is designed to have an impact on several important social skills and enhance general social competence. This social skills component contains material designed to help students overcome shyness and improve general interpersonal skills. This material emphasizes the teaching of (a) communication skills; (b) general social skills (e.g., initiating social interactions, conversational skills, complimenting); (c) skills related to boy-girl relationships; and (d) both verbal and nonverbal assertive skills.

Drug-Related Information and Skills

This component is designed to affect knowledge and attitudes concerning drug use, normative expectations, and skills for resisting drug use influences from the media and peers. The material contained in this component is similar to that contained in many psychosocial drug abuse prevention programs that focus on the teaching of social resistance skills. Included is material concerning (a) the short- and long-term consequences of drug use; (b) knowledge about the actual levels of drug use among both adults and adolescents to correct normative expectations about drug use; (c) information about the declining social acceptability of cigarette smoking and other drug use; (d) information and class exercises demonstrating the immediate physiological effects of cigarette smoking; (e) material concerning media pressures to smoke, drink, or use drugs; (f) information concerning the techniques used by cigarette and alcoholic beverage advertisers to promote the use of these drugs and skills for resisting them; and (g) techniques for resisting direct peer pressure to smoke, drink, or use drugs.

Booster Intervention

In addition to the initial (primary) year of intervention in Grade 7, the LST approach contains a 2-year booster intervention designed to be implemented in Grades 8 and 9. Designed to reinforce the material covered during the first year, the drug abuse booster curriculum consists of 10 sessions in Grade 8 and 5 sessions in Grade 9. The focus of the personal and social skills components is on the continued development of the general life skills that enable students to cope more effectively with the various pressures and problems confronting them as adolescents.

Intervention Materials

Curriculum materials have been developed to increase the standardization of implementing the LST program and increase its exportability. These materials consist of a teacher's manual and a student guide for each year of the program. The teacher's manual contains detailed lesson plans consisting of the appropriate content and activities for each intervention session as well as an overall unit goal and session objectives. The student guide contains reference material for each session, class exercises, and homework assignments to both prepare students for specific sessions and reinforce the skills and information already covered. The student guide also contains goal-setting principles, basic principles of self-directed behavior change, and material for a semester-long "self-improvement" project.

Intervention Methods

The LST program is taught using a variety of intervention methods, including the use of traditional didactic teaching methods, facilitation-group discussion, classroom demonstrations, and cognitive-behavioral skills training. Although lecturing and conventional didactic teaching methods are appropriate for some of the material taught in the LST program, most of the material can be more effectively taught by facilitating group discussion and skills training, with skills training clearly being the primary intervention method. Because a major emphasis of the LST program is on the teaching of general personal self-management skills, social skills, and skills for resisting social influences to use drugs, the central role of intervention providers is that of skills trainer or coach. The cognitive-behavioral skills taught in the LST program are taught using a combination of instruction, demonstration, behavioral rehearsal, feedback, social reinforcement (i.e., praise), and extended practice in the form of behavioral homework assignments.

Intervention Providers, Selection, and Training

The LST program has been successfully implemented by several different types of intervention providers. These have included health professionals from outside the school (Botvin, Eng, & Williams, 1980; Botvin, Schinke, Epstein, & Diaz, 1994), older peer leaders (Botvin, Baker, Botvin, Filazzola, & Millman, 1984; Botvin & Eng, 1982), and regular classroom teachers (Botvin, Baker, Dusenbury, Tortu, & Botvin, 1990; Botvin, Baker, Renick, Filazzola, & Botvin, 1984; Botvin, Renick, & Baker, 1983). Because prevention effects can be produced with classroom teachers as well as other types of providers and because teachers are readily available, the most natural and logical provider for a school-based prevention program is a regular classroom teacher. In addition to availability, teachers are a logical choice because they generally have more teaching experience and better classroom management skills than other potential intervention providers. Peer leaders (same-age or older students) can assist the teachers in implementing the curriculum and serve an important informal function as positive role models for the kinds of skills and behavior being taught in the curriculum. Selection of program providers should be based on their interest, experience, enthusiasm, and commitment to drug abuse prevention; the extent to which they will be a positive role model; and their willingness to attend the training workshop, implement the intervention carefully and completely according to the provider's guide, and complete the necessary process evaluation forms. To enhance the potential for delivering the prevention program carefully and completely according to the intervention protocol, care should be taken in recruiting providers to engender a spirit of collaboration.

Provider training generally consists of a 1- or 2-day training workshop. In one study (Botvin et al., 1990), provider training was made available to the teachers in one condition on videotape. The purpose of the training workshop is to familiarize intervention providers with the prevention program and its rationale, the results of prior studies, and to provide them with an opportunity to learn and practice the skills needed to successfully implement the prevention program (Tortu & Botvin, 1989). In an effort to improve implementation fidelity, the original provider training model used in previous studies testing the LST intervention has been modified to increase the knowledge, skills, and confidence that program providers need to effectively implement this type of prevention program. The length of the workshop has been increased from 1 day to 2 days, new material has been added concerning state-of-the-art prevention methods and evidence of their effectiveness, and more time has been allocated for practicing key intervention components. The current provider training workshop is less didactic, is more interactive, and emphasizes the use of well-established skills training techniques, such as instruction, demonstration, feedback, reinforcement, and practice. Training for peer leaders has involved an initial half-day workshop to provide them with a general orientation to the prevention program and their responsibilities as well as to provide them with the information and skills needed to implement the prevention program. Teachers meet with peer leaders prior to each session to provide them with session-specific preparation for the upcoming session and debrief them regarding the last session.

EVALUATION RESULTS

Over the past 15 years, a series of evaluation studies has been conducted to test the effectiveness of drug abuse prevention approaches based on the LST approach. These studies have been conducted in a logical sequence intended to facilitate the development of a prevention approach that is effective with different problem behaviors, when implemented by different types of providers, and with different populations. The focus of the early LST research was on cigarette smoking and involved predominantly white middle-class populations. Later research extended this work to other problem behaviors, including the use of alcohol, marijuana, and, most recently, illicit drugs other than marijuana. In addition, this research has increasingly focused on the utility of the LST approach when used with inner-city minority populations. Finally, this research has assessed the long-term durability of the LST prevention model, its impact on hypothesized mediating variables, implementation fidelity, and methods of improving implementation fidelity. These studies are briefly described, along with the key findings, in the following sections.

Smoking Prevention Pilot Research

Pilot research (Botvin et al., 1980) examined the short-term effectiveness of the LST approach to smoking prevention by focusing on the immediate negative consequences of cigarette smoking and cognitive-behavioral self-management skills. Participants were 281 students in the 8th, 9th, or 10th grades of two comparable suburban schools that were randomly assigned to either the experimental condition, in which students received the 10-session prevention program, or the comparison control condition. Results of this study indicated a 75% reduction in the number of new cigarette smokers at the initial posttest and a 67% reduction in new smoking at the 3-month follow-up.

Peer Leader Study

A second study (Botvin & Eng, 1982) tested the effectiveness of this prevention approach when implemented by older peer leaders (11th and 12th graders) with 7th graders ($N = 426$). To dramatize the immediate physical effects of cigarette smoking, a unit was added to the prevention program that employed biofeedback apparatus in class experiments. A methodological improvement introduced in this study to enhance the validity of smoking self-report data and to provide an objective measure of smoking status (saliva thiocyanate) involved the collection of saliva samples prior to the collection of self-report data in a variant of the procedure initially suggested by Evans and colleagues (Evans, Henderson, Hill, & Raines, 1979). Posttest results indicated that there were significantly fewer new smokers in the experimental group. These results were corroborated by the results of the saliva analysis that showed a significant increase in smoking for the students in the control group but no increase for students in the experimental group. In addition, there was a 58% reduction in new smoking at the initial posttest and a 56% reduction in regular (weekly) smoking at the 1-year follow-up. Significant treatment effects were also found on several hypothesized mediating variables, including smoking knowledge, psychosocial and advertising knowledge, social anxiety, and influenceability.

Teachers, Scheduling Format, and Boosters Effects

A third study (Botvin et al., 1983) was conducted to test the efficacy of this prevention approach when implemented by regular teachers, using two different implementation schedules, and including booster sessions. Seventh-grade students ($N = 902$) from seven suburban New York schools were randomly assigned to three conditions: a treatment condition that involved conducting the prevention program once a week for 15 weeks, a treatment condition that involved conducting the program several times a week for about 5 weeks, and a control condition. As in the previous study, saliva samples were collected to ensure high-quality self-report data.

Significant treatment effects were found at the initial posttest using the monthly measure of cigarette smoking. Comparison of the relative effectiveness of the integrated weekly intervention format and the intensive minicourse format indicated that both conditions were equally effective in preventing the onset of new (monthly) smoking. Significant intervention effects for monthly, weekly, and daily smoking were found at the 1-year follow-up. Conditions receiving additional booster sessions had half as many regular (weekly or daily) smokers as those not receiving booster sessions. Follow-up 1.5 years after the conclusion of the prevention program showed reduced smoking onset rates for the monthly, weekly, and daily smoking.

Preventing Alcohol Use

To assess the effectiveness of this intervention strategy for other forms of drug use, a pilot study was conducted with seventh graders from two comparable New York City public schools ($N = 239$) randomly assigned to experimental and control conditions (Botvin, Baker, Renick, et al., 1984). The intervention was modified to include material concerning the consequences of alcohol misuse and, when appropriate, skills were taught in relation to situations that might promote alcohol use. Although no effects were evident at the initial posttest, program effects emerged at the 6-month follow-up data collection. Significantly fewer (54%) experimental students reported drinking in the past month, 73% fewer reported heavy drinking, and 79% fewer reported getting drunk one or more times per month.

Preventing Alcohol and Marijuana Use

Subsequently, a larger study was conducted to replicate the results with alcohol, test the generalizability of the LST approach to marijuana use, and test the relative effectiveness of this type of prevention strategy when implemented by older (10th and 11th grade) peer leaders or regular classroom teachers. The study included 1,311 7th-grade students from 10 suburban New York junior high schools that were randomly assigned to (a) teacher-led prevention curriculum, (b) peer-led prevention curriculum, (c) teacher-led prevention curriculum and booster sessions, (d) peer-led prevention curriculum and booster sessions, and (e) control group. In the first year, both booster and nonbooster conditions were combined because booster sessions were not implemented until the second year of the study. Results of the first year (Botvin, Baker, Renick, et al., 1984) showed significant prevention effects for tobacco, alcohol, and marijuana use. Adolescents who participated in the LST program drank significantly less alcohol per drinking occasion and were drunk less often, with the students in the peer-led condition being superior to the students in both the teacher-led and control conditions. With respect to marijuana, not only were there fewer students reporting monthly and weekly marijuana use but the magnitude of these effects was quite substantial. The LST program reduced experimental marijuana use by 71% for students in the peer-led condition and reduced regular (weekly or daily) marijuana use by 83%. Effects were also evident on several cognitive, attitudinal, and personality variables in a direction consistent with decreased drug use risk.

The results of the 1-year follow-up (Botvin et al., 1990) provide further support for the effectiveness of the LST prevention approach. Depending on the measure used, there were 79% to 82% fewer smokers in the peer-led booster group and 69% to 78% fewer marijuana users, 44% to 50% fewer smokers in the high-fidelity teacher-led group, 47% fewer experimenters with marijuana, and 51% fewer drinkers.

Large-Scale Controlled
Randomized Prevention Trial

A large-scale randomized prevention trial involving students ($N = 5,954$) from 56 schools in New York State focused on the efficacy of the LST approach for preventing tobacco, alcohol, and marijuana use (Botvin et al.,

1990). The sample was approximately half (52%) male and predominantly (91%) white. With spring 1985 smoking rates used as a blocking variable, schools within each of three geographic regions of New York State were randomly assigned to E1 (prevention program with training and support by project staff), E2 (prevention program with no project staff involvement), and control conditions. Sample retention (based on all available students at the pretest) was 93% at the initial posttest (mid-7th grade), 81% at the 16-month follow-up (end of the 8th grade), 75% at the 28-month follow-up (end of the 9th grade), and 67% at the 40-month follow-up (end of the 10th grade). Retention rates were virtually identical across conditions.

Using both the individual and the school as the unit of analysis, prevention effects were found for drug use behavior as well as for several hypothesized mediating variables at the 28-month follow-up and the 40-month follow-up for students who received at least 60% of the intervention program. The results of the individual-level analysis at the 28-month follow-up showed significantly less smoking and marijuana use among the E1 and E2 groups and less problem drinking in the E2 group than among controls. Results of the school-level analysis at the 28-month follow-up revealed that both the E1 and E2 groups had significantly less cigarette smoking than controls. At the 40-month follow-up, there was significantly less marijuana use in the E1 group and less excessive drinking in both the E1 and E2 groups than among controls.

Long-Term Effectiveness

To determine the durability of drug abuse prevention in general and the LST approach in particular, a long-term follow-up study was conducted (Botvin, Baker, Dusenbury, Botvin, & Diaz, 1994). Students ($N = 3,597$) from 56 schools in New York State who participated in the drug abuse prevention trial described previously, which began in the fall of 1985 (when they were in the 7th grade), were located and data were collected by telephone or by mail or both at the end of the 12th grade. The average length of follow-up was 6 years after the initial baseline assessment. Follow-up results indicated that there were significantly fewer smokers, "heavy" drinkers, or marijuana users among students who received the LST prevention program during the 7th grade and had booster sessions during the 8th and 9th grades.

To assess the impact of the prevention program on more serious levels of drug involvement, treatment and control students were also compared in terms of polydrug use (defined in this study as the monthly or weekly use of multiple gateway substances). At the end of the 12th grade, there were 44% fewer LST students than controls who used all three gateway drugs (tobacco, alcohol, and marijuana) one or more times per month and 66% fewer LST students who reported using all three substances one or more times per week. Prevention effects were also found for 12 hypothesized mediating variables in the direction of decreased drug abuse risk. The strongest prevention effects were produced for the students who received the most complete implementation of the prevention program. Although prevention effects were produced regardless of whether providers were trained at a formal training workshop with periodic feedback and consultation from project staff or merely viewed a provider training videotape without feedback or support, the strongest effects were produced by the teachers who attended annual training workshops and received ongoing support. Prevention effects were found using both the individual and the school as the unit of analysis. Moreover, attrition rates were equivalent for treatment and control conditions as were pretest levels of drug use for the final analysis sample, which supports the conclusion that prevention effects were the result of the intervention and not the result of differential attrition or pretest nonequivalence.

Prevention of Illicit Drug Use

An underlying assumption of primary prevention efforts is that if they prevent or reduce the use of tobacco, alcohol, marijuana, or all three they will have a corresponding impact on the use of other substances further along the developmental progression. In other words, preventing gateway drug use will also translate into later reductions in the use of illicit drugs such as cocaine or heroin. Despite the fact that this rationale is commonly used to justify targeting gateway drug use, however, it has never been tested. This issue was addressed by analyzing data collected from an anonymous subsample of students involved in the long-term follow-up study described previously. Data were collected by mail from 454 individuals (mean age 18.86) who were contacted after the end of the 12th grade. The length of follow-up was 6.5 years from the initial baseline. The survey assessed the use of 13 illicit drug categories following those used by the University of Michigan's Monitoring the Future Study (e.g., Johnston et al., 1994). Significantly lower levels of drug involvement (relative to controls) were found for the LST students on two composite measures of illicit drug use as well as for specific illicit drug categories. There were lower levels of illicit drug use using the composite measure that assessed any illicit drug use and using the measure that assessed illicit drug use other than marijuana. By individual drug category, significantly lower levels of use were found for the E1 group for LSD-other psychedelics as well as for PCP use. Significantly lower levels of heroin use were found for both the E1 and E2 conditions. Finally, significant prevention effects were found for the use of inhalants for both LST groups.

Prevention With Minority Youth

A gap in the drug abuse-prevention field that has only recently begun to be addressed concerns the lack of high-quality research with minority populations. In developing preventive interventions for minority populations, two strategies have been followed. One strategy, based on the assumption that the etiology of drug abuse is different for different populations, involves the development of interventions designed to be population specific. The other strategy, based on the assumption that the etiology of drug abuse is more similar than different across populations, involves the development of interventions designed to be generalizable to a broad range of individuals from different populations.

Research with the LST program has followed the second course—making modifications where warranted to maximize generalizability, cultural sensitivity, relevance, and acceptability to varied populations. Although there are only limited data concerning the etiology of drug abuse among minority populations, existing evidence suggests that there is substantial overlap in the factors promoting and maintaining drug use-abuse among different racial-ethnic groups (Bettes, Dusenbury, Kerner, James-Ortiz, & Botvin, 1990; Botvin, Baker, et al., 1993; Botvin, Epstein, Schinke, & Diaz, 1994; Botvin, Goldberg, Botvin, & Dusenbury, 1993; Dusenbury, Kerner, et al., 1992; Epstein, Dusenbury, Botvin, & Diaz, 1994). A second reason for pursuing this course concerns the fact that most urban schools contain individuals from multiple racial-ethnic groups. Therefore, even if there were differences across populations warranting different interventions, it would be extremely difficult to implement separate interventions for different racial-ethnic groups for both logistical and political reasons. Thus, given the choice of two or more effective interventions, it would be important to give consideration to issues of feasibility as well as effectiveness.

Although some Asians have been included in the studies conducted with the LST program, the major racial-ethnic groups involved in the most recent research studies with minority populations include African American and Hispanic youth. As was the case with previous research with white, middle-class youth, the initial focus of this research was on cigarette smoking followed by a focus on other gateway substances. Research testing the generalizability of the LST prevention approach to inner-city, minority youth has progressed through the following sequence: (a) exploratory-qualitative research consisting of focus group testing and key informant interviews, (b) expert review of intervention methods and materials, (c) consumer-based review of intervention materials and methods, (d) small-scale pilot studies, and (e) large-scale randomized field trials. Modifications in intervention materials and methods were made, as necessary, throughout the process of development and testing. None of the modifications deriving from the etiologic literature concerning minority youth or the review process delineated previously involved changes to the underlying prevention strategy. Rather, these changes related to the reading level of intervention materials, the inclusion of appropriate graphics (e.g., illustrations or pictures of minority youth), language, role-play scenarios, and examples appropriate to the target population.

Prevention Research With Hispanic Youth. The first study testing the effectiveness of the LST approach with a minority population involved predominantly Hispanic youth (Botvin, Dusenbury, Baker, James-Ortiz, & Kerner, 1989). The study included 471 seventh graders (46% male) attending eight public schools in the New York metropolitan area. The sample consisted of predominantly lower-income Hispanic students (74%) as well as a small percentage of African American (11%) and white (4%) students. Schools were randomly assigned to conditions. Significant posttest differences between the experimental and the control group were found controlling for pretest smoking status, gender, social risk for becoming a smoker, and acculturation. Intervention effects were also found for knowledge concerning the immediate consequences of smoking, smoking prevalence, the social acceptability of smoking, decision making, normative expectations concerning adult smoking, and normative expectations concerning peer smoking.

Data from a large-scale randomized trial (Botvin et al., 1992) also demonstrated significant program effects when implemented with predominately Hispanic urban minority students. This study involved 3,501 students from 47 public and parochial schools in the greater New York City area. Intervention materials were modified (based on the results of our pilot study and input from consultants, teachers, and students) to increase their relevance to Hispanic youth as well as to ensure a high degree of cultural sensitivity. Schools were randomly assigned to experimental and control conditions. Using school means as the unit of analysis, significant reductions in cigarette smoking were found for the adolescents who received the LST program when compared to controls at the end of the 7th grade. Follow-up data demonstrated the continued presence of prevention effects through to the end of the 10th grade (Botvin, 1994).

Drug Abuse Prevention With African American Youth. Before testing the LST approach on African American youth, the intervention materials and methods were once again subjected to an extensive review to determine their cultural appropriateness for this population. Following this, a small-scale study was conducted with nine urban junior high schools in northern New Jersey (Botvin, Batson, et al., 1989). The pretest involved 608 seventh-grade students. Of these, 221 were in the treatment group and 387 in the control group. The sample was 87% African American, 10% Hispanic, 1% white, and 2% other. Schools were randomly assigned to treatment and control conditions within each of the three participating communities. Students in the treatment schools received the LST program, and students in the control schools received the smoking education curriculum normally provided by their school. Throughout the prevention program, classroom observation data and teacher feedback were collected.

A series of General Linear Model analyses were computed to assess the impact of this intervention approach on cigarette smoking. Pretest scores, age, grades, and social risk for smoking (the smoking status of friends) were used as covariates. Results indicated that there were significantly fewer posttest smokers in the treatment group than in the control group based on smoking status in the past month. Significant treatment effects were also found for knowledge of smoking consequences, normative expectations regarding adult smoking prevalence, and normative expectations regarding peer smoking prevalence.

A large-scale prevention trial involving predominantly African American youth from 46 inner-city schools in northern New Jersey provided additional empirical support for the effectiveness of this prevention approach with this population (Botvin & Cardwell, 1992). Schools were randomly assigned to treatment ($n = 21$) and control ($n = 25$) conditions after first blocking on schoolwide smoking rates. Students ($N = 2,512$) were pretested in the spring of 1990 while they were in the seventh grade, posttested in the early winter of 1991, and posttested again in the spring of 1991 at the end of the eighth grade. In the treatment condition, all eligible classes in participating schools received the LST intervention; in the control group, all classes received the health (smoking) education normally provided to its students. The final analysis sample was 97% minority and 3% white; of the total sample, 78% was African American, 13% was Hispanic, 1% was Native American, 1% was Asian, and 3% classified themselves as "other." Initial posttest results showed significantly less smoking for students in the treatment group who received the intervention in the seventh grade and booster sessions in the fall of the eighth grade when compared with students in both the nonbooster treatment group and the control group. At the final follow-up, students who received booster sessions and the original intervention had significantly lower rates of smoking than students in the control group.

Generic Versus Culturally Focused Approaches. A recently completed study tested the relative effectiveness of the LST approach, which had been previously found to be effective with a broad range of students, and a prevention approach specifically tailored to African American and Hispanic youth (Botvin, Schinke, et al., 1994). Both prevention approaches were similar in that they taught students a combination of generic "life skills" and skills specific to resisting offers to use drugs. The tailored or culturally focused approach, however, was designed to embed the skills training material in myths and legends derived from the African American and Hispanic cultures. Six junior high schools containing predominantly (95%) minority students were assigned to receive (a) the generic LST program, (b) the culturally focused prevention approach, or to serve as (c) an information-only control group. The sample was 48% African American, 37% Hispanic, 5% white, 3% Asian, and 8% other. Students were pretested and posttested during the seventh grade. Results indicated that students in both skills training prevention conditions had lower intentions to drink beer or wine relative to the students in the information-only controls, and the students in the LST condition had lower intentions to drink hard liquor and use illicit drugs. Both skills training conditions also affected several mediating variables in a direction consistent with nondrug use. These results show that both prevention approaches were equally effective, producing significant reductions in behavioral intentions to drink and use illicit drugs, and suggest that a generic drug abuse prevention approach with high generalizability may be as effective as one that is tailored to individual ethnic populations. These data, therefore, provide support for the hypothesis that a single drug abuse prevention strategy can be used effectively with multiethnic populations.

Follow-up data ($N = 456$) collected 2 years later at the end of the ninth grade found significant prevention effects for both prevention approaches (Botvin, Schinke, Epstein, Diaz, & Botvin, in press). Students in both skills training prevention conditions drank alcohol less often, became drunk less often, drank less alcohol per drinking occasion, and had lower intentions to use alcohol in the future relative to students in the controls. These data, however, also showed that the culturally focused intervention produced significantly stronger effects on these variables than the generic LST approach. The findings of the follow-up study are particularly interesting because, although they suggest that it may be possible to develop a preventive intervention that is effective for a relatively broad range of students, they indicate that tailoring interventions to specific populations can increase their effectiveness with inner-city minority populations.

SUMMARY, CONCLUSIONS, AND FUTURE DIRECTIONS

Drug abuse has been a major public health problem for several decades. Despite a general downward trend in the use of drugs by high school seniors over the past 10 years, recent data indicate that drug use is once again on the rise. The etiology of drug abuse is complex, involving multiple determinants and numerous developmental pathways. Evaluation studies have shown that widely used approaches to drug abuse prevention involving the dissemination of factual information about the adverse effects of drug use or drug pharmacology as well as approaches attempting to facilitate affective development or provide youth with alternatives to drug use are not effective. On the other hand, prevention approaches that target the social and psychological factors found to be associated with drug use and its initiation have produced significant reductions in drug use when social-resistance skills training approaches have been used either alone or in combination with personal and social skills training.

Studies testing the effectiveness of a drug abuse prevention approach that incorporates the teaching of social resistance skills and an array of general life skills have demonstrated prevention effects with respect to tobacco, alcohol, and marijuana use as well as on hypothesized mediating variables. The magnitude of reported effects of these approaches has typically been relatively large, with most studies demonstrating initial reductions (relative to controls) of 50% or more. These studies have generally produced reductions in both occasional (experimental) drug use as well as more serious levels of drug involvement. Research with the Life Skills Training approach includes studies testing its short-term effectiveness as well as its long-term durability, studies testing different delivery methods and the effectiveness of booster sessions, studies testing its effectiveness when conducted by different program providers, and studies testing its effectiveness with different populations. These studies have ranged from small-scale pilot studies involving two schools and a few hundred adolescents to large-scale, multisite, randomized field trials involving more than 50 schools and several thousand adolescents. Although considerable progress has been made in the past decade, further research is clearly needed. Additional research is under way to better understand the mechanism(s) through which this approach prevents drug use, to understand its effectiveness with different populations (particularly minority youth), and to determine its generalizability to other empirically and theoretically related behaviors such as violence.

REFERENCES

Bandura, A. (1977). *Social learning theory.* Englewood Cliffs, NJ: Prentice Hall.

Bangert-Drowns, R. L. (1988). The effects of school-based substance abuse education—A meta-analysis. *Journal of Drug Education, 18*, 243-265.

Bettes, B. A., Dusenbury, L., Kerner, J., James-Ortiz, S., & Botvin, G. J. (1990). Ethnicity and psychosocial factors in alcohol and tobacco use in adolescence. *Child Development, 61*, 557-565.

Botvin, G. J. (1993). *Reducing drug abuse and AIDS risk. Final report.* Submitted to NIDA (5 R01 DA06230), New York.

Botvin, G. J. (1994). *Smoking prevention among New York Hispanic youth: Results of a four-year evaluation study.* Unpublished manuscript.

Botvin, G. J., Baker, E., Botvin, E. M., Dusenbury, L., Cardwell, J., & Diaz, T. (1993). Factors promoting cigarette smoking among black youth: A causal modeling approach. *Addictive Behaviors, 18,* 397-405.

Botvin, G. J., Baker, E., Botvin, E. M., Filazzola, A. D., & Millman, R. B. (1984). Alcohol abuse prevention through the development of personal and social competence: A pilot study. *Journal of Studies on Alcohol, 45,* 550-552.

Botvin, G. J., Baker, E., Dusenbury, L. D., Botvin, E. M., & Diaz, T. (1994). *Long-term follow-up results of a randomized drug abuse prevention trial.* Unpublished manuscript.

Botvin, G. J., Baker, E., Dusenbury, L., Tortu, S., & Botvin, E. M. (1990). Preventing adolescent drug abuse through a multimodal cognitive-behavioral approach: Results of a three-year study. *Journal of Consulting and Clinical Psychology, 58,* 437-446.

Botvin, G. J., Baker, E., Renick, N., Filazzola, A. D., & Botvin, E. M. (1984). A cognitive-behavioral approach to substance abuse prevention. *Addictive Behaviors, 9,* 137-147.

Botvin, G. J., Batson, H., Witts-Vitale, S., Bess, V., Baker, E., & Dusenbury, L. (1989). A psychosocial approach to smoking prevention for urban black youth. *Public Health Reports, 104,* 573-582.

Botvin, G. J., & Botvin, E. M. (1992). Adolescent tobacco, alcohol, and drug abuse: Prevention strategies, empirical findings, and assessment issues. *Journal of Developmental and Behavioral Pediatrics, 13,* 290-301.

Botvin, G. J., & Cardwell, J. (1992). *Primary prevention (smoking) of cancer in Black populations* (Grant Contract No. N01-CN-6508. Final report to National Cancer Institute). Ithaca, NY: Cornell University Medical College.

Botvin, G. J., Dusenbury, L., Baker, E., James-Ortiz, S., Botvin, E. M., & Kerner, J. (1992). Smoking prevention among urban minority youth: Assessing effects on outcome and mediating variables. *Health Psychology, 11,* 290-299.

Botvin, G. J., Dusenbury, L., Baker, E., James-Ortiz, S., & Kerner, J. (1989). A skills training approach to smoking prevention among Hispanic youth. *Journal of Behavioral Medicine, 12,* 279-296.

Botvin, G. J., & Eng, A. (1982). The efficacy of a multicomponent approach to the prevention of cigarette smoking. *Preventive Medicine, 11,* 199-211.

Botvin, G. J., Eng, A., & Williams, C. L. (1980). Preventing the onset of cigarette smoking through life skills training. *Preventive Medicine, 9,* 135-143.

Botvin, G. J., Epstein, J. A., Schinke, S. P., & Diaz, T. (1994). Correlates and predictors of smoking among inner city youth. *Developmental and Behavioral Pediatrics, 15,* 67-73.

Botvin, G. J., Goldberg, C. J., Botvin, E. M., & Dusenbury, L. (1993). Smoking behavior of adolescents exposed to cigarette advertising. *Public Health Reports, 108,* 217-224.

Botvin, G. J., Renick, N., & Baker, E. (1983). The effects of scheduling format and booster sessions on a broad-spectrum psychosocial approach to smoking prevention. *Journal of Behavioral Medicine, 6,* 359-379.

Botvin, G. J., Schinke, S. P., Epstein, J. A., & Diaz, T. (1994). The effectiveness of culturally-focused & generic skills training approaches to alcohol and drug abuse prevention among minority youth. *Psychology of Addictive Behaviors, 8,* 116-127.

Botvin, G. J., Schinke, S. P., Epstein, J. A., Diaz, T., & Botvin, E. M. (in press). Effectiveness of culturally focused and generic skills training approaches to alcohol and drug abuse prevention among minority adolescents: Two-year follow-up results. *Psychology of Addictive Behaviors.*

Botvin, G. J., & Tortu, S. (1988). Peer relationships, social competence, and substance abuse prevention: Implications for the family. *Journal of Chemical Dependency Treatment, 1,* 245-273.

Bruvold, W. H., & Rundall, T. G. (1988). A meta-analysis and theoretical review of school based tobacco and alcohol intervention programs. *Psychology and Health, 2,* 53-78.

Dusenbury, L., Kerner, J. F., Baker, E., Botvin, G. J., James-Ortiz, S., & Zauber, A. (1992). Predictors of smoking prevalence among New York Latino youth. *American Journal of Public Health, 82,* 55-58.

Dusenbury, L., Khuri, E., & Millman, R. B. (1992). Adolescent substance abuse: A socio-developmental perspective. In J. H. Lowinson, P. Ruiz, R. B. Millman, & J. G. Langrod (Eds.), *Substance abuse: A comprehensive textbook* (2nd ed., pp. 842-927). Baltimore, MD: Williams & Williams.

Epstein, J. A., Dusenbury, L., Botvin, G. J., & Diaz, T. (1994). Acculturation, beliefs about AIDS and AIDS education among New York City Latino parents. *Hispanic Journal of Behavioral Sciences, 16,* 342-354.

Evans, R. I., Henderson, A. H., Hill, P. C., & Raines, B. E. (1979). Smoking in children and adolescents: Psychosocial determinants and prevention strategies. In U.S. Public Health Service (Ed.), *Smoking and health: A report of the Surgeon General.* Washington, DC: U.S. Department of Health, Education and Welfare.

Hawkins, J. D., Catalano, R. F., & Miller, J. Y. (1992). Risk and protective factors for alcohol and other drug problems in adolescence and early adulthood: Implications for substance abuse prevention. *Psychological Bulletin, 112,* 64-105.

Jessor, R., & Jessor, S. L. (1977). *Problem behavior and psychosocial development: A longitudinal study of youth.* New York: Academic Press.

Johnston, L. D., O'Malley, P. M., & Bachman, J. G. (1994). *National survey results on drug use from the Monitoring the Future Study, 1975-1993. Volume I. Secondary School Students.* Rockville, MD: U.S. Department of Health and Human Services.

Kandel, D. B. (1978). Convergences in prospective longitudinal surveys of drug use in normal populations. In D. B. Kandel (Ed.), *Longitudinal research on drug use: Empirical findings and methodological issues* (pp. 3-38). Washington, DC: Hemisphere.

Kaplan, H. B. (1980). *Deviant behavior in defense of self.* New York: Academic Press.

Lettieri, D. J., Sayers, M., & Pearson, H. W. (1980). *Theories on drug abuse: Selected contemporary perspectives.* Washington, DC: Government Printing Office.

McGuire, W. J. (1968). The nature of attitudes and attitude change. In G. Lindzey & E. Aronson (Eds.), *Handbook of social psychology* (pp. 136-314). Reading, MA: Addison-Wesley.

Millman, R. B., & Botvin, G. J. (1992). Substance use, abuse, and dependence. In M. Levine, N. B. Carey, A. C. Crocker, & R. T. Gross (Eds.), *Developmental-behavioral pediatrics* (2nd ed., pp. 451-467). New York: W. B. Saunders.

Newcomb, M. D., & Bentler, P. M. (1988). *Consequences of adolescent drug use: Impact on the lives of young adults.* Newbury Park, CA: Sage.

Newcomb, M. D., & Bentler, P. M. (1989). Substance use and abuse among children and teenagers. *American Psychologist, 44,* 242-248.

Newcomb, M. D., & Felix-Ortiz, M. (1992). Multiple protective and risk factors for drug use and abuse: Cross-sectional and prospective findings. *Journal of Consulting and Clinical Psychology, 63,* 280-296.

Oetting, E. R., & Beauvais, F. (1987). Peer cluster theory, socialization characterization, and adolescent drug use: A path analysis. *Journal of Consulting and Clinical Psychology, 34,* 205-213.

Scheier, L. M., & Newcomb, M. D. (1991, Spring). Psychosocial predictors of drug use initiation and escalation: An expansion of the multiple risk factors hypothesis using longitudinal data. *Contemporary Drug Problems,* 31-73.

Tobler, N. (1986). Meta-analysis of 143 adolescent drug prevention programs: Quantitative outcome results of program participants compared to a control or comparison group. *Journal of Drug Issues, 16,* 537-567.

Tortu, S., & Botvin, G. J. (1989). School-based smoking prevention: The teacher training process. *Preventive Medicine, 18,* 280-289.

U.S. Public Health Service. (1989). *Reducing the health consequences of smoking: A report of the surgeon general* (DHHS Publication No. CDC 89-8411). Washington, DC: Government Printing Office.

Zuckerman, M. (1979). *Sensation seeking: Beyond the optimal level of arousal.* Hillsdale, NJ: Lawrence Erlbaum.

11

The Strengthening Families Program
for the Prevention of
Delinquency and Drug Use

KAROL L. KUMPFER

VIRGINIA MOLGAARD

RICHARD SPOTH

Providing the support that families need to raise well-adjusted children is becoming increasingly important because of escalating rates of juvenile crime, drug abuse, and child abuse. One type of family support currently gaining in popularity is structured interventions for high-risk families, such as parent training and family skills training. According to the prevention classification scheme of universal, selective, and indicated prevention interventions (Gordon, 1987; Mrazek & Haggerty, 1994), the family interventions addressed in this chapter would primarily be classified as "selective" interventions. Selective prevention interventions target high-risk individuals or subgroups as opposed to "universal" prevention interventions, which target all members of an eligible population, or "indicated" prevention interventions, which target individuals manifesting precursors that identify them individually as being of high risk for the future development of a disorder.

241

This chapter describes the theoretical underpinnings, development, implementation, and results of evaluations of the Strengthening Families Program (SFP)—a family-focused prevention intervention for high-risk families from special populations. This program has two versions: (a) one for elementary school children and their families and (b) another for middle school or junior high school students and their families. The SFP is a comprehensive family-focused curriculum that includes three components: parent training, children's skills training, and family skills training. A number of evaluation and demonstration projects have evaluated the effectiveness of SFP for several populations at risk for substance abuse and delinquency. These have included children of substance abusers, children at risk for outplacement due to child abuse and neglect, and low-income rural and urban parents of different ethnic groups (i.e., African American, Asian, Pacific Islander, Latino or Mexican American, and French Canadian). New English language versions of SFP are being developed for Australian and Canadian families; versions for Spanish- or French-speaking families are also under development. This chapter discusses the results of the original SFP evaluation project, several replications with minority families, and a current National Institute of Mental Health-funded clinical trial in 19 Iowa counties. It concludes with suggestions for improving the implementation of family skills training programs in general.

THEORETICAL UNDERPINNINGS:
FAMILY RISK AND PROTECTIVE FACTORS

To be maximally effective, family-focused prevention programs must modify the relevant precursors of the youth problems they target whether that be drug abuse, delinquency, other mental disorders, or teenage pregnancy. The original SFP development (funded by the National Institute on Drug Abuse [NIDA] between 1981 and 1985) and subsequent cultural modifications have each been preceded by reviews of research and local data collection on family risk and protective factors. Possible precursors derived from literature searches were compared to existing local data. In the original Utah study, data on local drug-abusing families were available from a national, multisite study of drug-abusing parents and children (Sowder & Burt, 1978a, 1978b). The data on risk and protective factors were then reconciled with guiding theoretical models. The original model was the

Values-Attitudes-Stressors-Coping Skills and Resources Model (Kumpfer & DeMarsh, 1985). More recent theoretical models that have guided program development include the Resiliency Model (Richardson, Neiger, Jensen, & Kumpfer, 1990), which is a dynamic individual process model, and the empirically tested Social Ecology Model of Adolescent Substance Use (Kumpfer & Turner, 1990-1991). This latter model of primary environmental precursors of drug use suggests that perceived family climate or ecology is influential in the youth's perceptions of school climate. In addition, a positive family climate significantly affects self-esteem and school bonding. These are, in turn, related to prosocial peer association and reduced alcohol or drug use.

The following list of family risk factors for adolescent substance abuse includes recent additions from research with multiethnic families (Kumpfer & Alvarado, 1995). Similar empirically based risk factors have been employed to refine the theoretical models guiding the implementation of the SFP in specific populations. Criteria for rating family program comprehensiveness were derived from this listing for a national search for the most effective parenting and family programs conducted for the Office of Juvenile Justice and Delinquency Prevention (Kumpfer, 1993, 1994a). The list is useful in helping agencies to select the best family program for their target population.

Poor socialization practices, modeling of antisocial values and behaviors (Kandel & Andrews, 1987), failure to promote positive moral development (Damon, 1988), and neglect in teaching life, social, and academic skills to the child

Poor supervision of the child, including failure to monitor the child's activities (Loeber & Stouthamer-Loeber, 1986) and sibling violence (Steinmetz & Straus, 1974), and too few adults to care for the number of children

Poor discipline skills, including lax, inconsistent, or harsh discipline (Baumrind, 1985); parental conflict over child-rearing practices (Vicary & Lerner, 1986), failure to set clear rules and consequences for misbehavior (Kandel & Andrews, 1987), and developmentally unrealistic parental expectations (Kumpfer & DeMarsh, 1986)

Poor quality of parent-child relationships, including rejection of the child by the parents or of the parents by the child (Brook, Brook, Gordon, Whiteman, & Cohen, 1990), low parental attachment (Baumrind, 1985), cold and unsupportive maternal behavior (Shedler & Block, 1990), lack of involvement and time together (Kumpfer & DeMarsh, 1986), and maladaptive parent-child interactions (Kumpfer & Turner, 1990-1991)

Excessive family conflict, marital discord, and domestic violence associated with increased verbal, physical, or sexual abuse of the child (Kumpfer & Bayes, 1995; Kumpfer & DeMarsh, 1986); poor conflict resolution or anger management skills (Sowder & Burt, 1978a, 1978b); coercive family processes (Patterson, 1982; Patterson, Reid, & Dishion, 1992); and youth antisocial or aggressive behavior leading to illicit drug use and delinquency

Family chaos and stress associated with poor family management skills or life skills resulting in fewer consistent family rituals (Wolin, Bennett, & Noonan, 1979) and inappropriate role modeling and socialization (Patterson, DeBaryshe, & Ramsey, 1989)

Poor parental mental health, including depression, causing negative views of the child's behaviors, parent hostility to the child, and harsh discipline (Conger & Rueter, in press)

Family social isolation and lack of community support resources (Wahler, Leske, & Rogers, 1979)

Differential family acculturation and role reversal or loss of parental control over adolescents by parents who are less acculturated than their children (Delgado, 1990; Szapocznik, Santisteban, Rio, Perez-Vidal, & Kurtines, 1985)

Parental and sibling drug use, including role modeling (Brook et al., 1990), and lack of alcohol and drug family norms and rules (Hawkins, Arthur, & Catalano, 1994)

Rutter (1993) recommends that the field try to move beyond a focus on family risk factors to a more complete understanding of underlying family process mechanisms. This list of risk factors includes a number of static factors that are indicators of complex, long-term reciprocal parent-child processes. For instance, parental substance abuse is highly correlated with many other indicators of poor child environment—poverty, crime, family chaos and disorganization, family conflict, isolation, as well as child abuse and sexual abuse (Kumpfer & Bayes, 1995). The high incidence of maternal comorbidity of mental disorders and substance abuse also increases the level of clinical dysfunction in parent-child transactional processes (Hans, 1995; Kumpfer, 1996; Kumpfer & Bluth, in press). Studying transactional or dynamic interactions between a person (parent or child) and his or her environment, including other persons in that environment, presents many difficulties; thus, researchers are only beginning to address dynamic family processes. Coie and associates (1993) have suggested that studies of family prevention interventions could be used to better understand these complex family process mechanisms by examining variations in person-environment causal mechanisms and evaluating the impact on youth.

PROMISING MODELS FOR
FAMILY PREVENTION INTERVENTIONS

A search for model parenting and family programs was conducted (Kumpfer, 1994a) using multiple criteria derived from the prior list of family risk factors. After rating more than 500 family programs on program content and evaluation results, the primary conclusion of the Office of Juvenile Justice and Delinquency Prevention national search was that there is no single best family intervention program. There are many different types of parenting and family approaches that are effective in reducing specifically targeted risk factors. Many family programs, however, fail to have long-term impact on ultimate outcomes, such as delinquency and drug use in special high-risk populations, because they do not seek to address or alter the large number of risk factors affecting these children. The study articulated several principles for best practices in family programs. These included selecting programs that are (a) comprehensive, (b) family focused, (c) long term, (d) of sufficient dosage to affect risk or protective factors, (e) tailored to target populations' needs and cultural traditions, (f) developmentally appropriate, (g) beginning as early in the family life cycle as possible, and (h) delivered by well-trained, effective trainers.

In general, interventions engaging both parents and children appear to be more effective than those that involve only children or parents. Current reviews of early childhood programs support this conclusion (Mitchell, Weiss, & Schultz, in press). In recent years, there has been a shift from focusing therapeutic activities primarily on the child to improving parents' parenting skills and to recognizing the importance of changing the total family system. Recently developed family-focused skills training programs are more comprehensive and include structured parent training, children's social skills training, and family relationship enhancement or family skills training as well as a number of family support services (i.e., case management, home visiting, food, transportation, supportive counseling, and crisis intervention). A few examples of structured family-focused interventions used within family support programs include the SFP (Kumpfer, 1981; Kumpfer, DeMarsh, & Child, 1989), the Nurturing Program (Bavolek &

Comstock, 1983), Families and Schools Together (McDonald, Billingham, Dibble, Rice, & Coe-Braddish, 1991), and the Family Effectiveness Program (Szapocznik et al., 1985). These and other model family programs have been reviewed (see Kumpfer, 1994a).

Some researchers are employing these broad-based family skills programs as part of comprehensive intervention strategies targeting important domains of influence on problems beyond the family. The Fast Track Program described in this volume (see Chapters 4 and 5, this volume) is one example of such an approach.

THE STRENGTHENING FAMILIES PROGRAM
FOR ELEMENTARY-AGED HIGH-RISK CHILDREN

This section discusses the development and evaluation of the original SFP for elementary school-aged (6- to 12-year-old) children of substance abusers and modifications to the program for African American families in Alabama and Detroit as well as adaptations for multiethnic families in three counties in Utah.

Original SFP Research Design and Subjects

The program in the original NIDA-funded research was designed to reduce vulnerability to drug abuse in 6- to 12-year-old children of methadone maintenance patients and substance-abusing outpatients from community mental health centers. Employing an experimental dismantling design, families were randomly assigned to (a) a 14-session SFP parent training program based on Patterson's (1975, 1976) parent training model, (b) a combination of the parent training program and a children's skills training program based primarily on Spivack and Shure's (1979) social skills training, or (c) a three-part combination of the prior two programs plus a family skills training program based on Forehand and McMahon's (1981) intervention described in their book, *Helping the Noncompliant Child* and Bernard Guerney's 1977 Family Relationship Enhancement Program. The sample of 208 families consisted of 71 experimental intervention families, 47 no-treatment families matched with the treatment families on eight demographic characteristics, and 90 general population comparison families.

Program Format and Incentives

Parents in Group 1 attended only the 1-hour parent training sessions. Both parents and children in Group 2 attended separate classes for the first hour, and then those in Group 3 worked together in family sessions in the second hour. The Group 3 intervention format involved providing parent and child with training in their respective skills or roles and then bringing them together to practice those skills with each other. To increase recruitment and retention, a number of incentives were developed by the various sites implementing the program. These included snacks, transportation, rewards for attendance and homework completion (e.g., drawing tickets or vouchers for sporting, cultural, educational, and social family activities, movies, dinners, or groceries), rewards for program completion (vouchers for clothing, household items, and children's Christmas gifts), a nursery for child care of younger siblings, and recreation for older adolescents.

Program Content

The parent training program sessions in the original SFP included training relevant to group building, teaching parents to increase wanted behaviors in children by increasing attention and reinforcements, behavioral goal statements, differential attention, chore charts and spinners (pie charts with sections representing rewards mutually decided on), communication training, alcohol and drug education, problem solving, compliance requests, principles of limit setting (time-out, punishment, and overcorrection), limit-setting practice, generalization and maintenance, and development and implementation of behavior programs for their children.

The children's skills training program included training directed toward communication of group rules; understanding feelings; social skills of attending, communicating, and ignoring; increasing good behavior; problem solving; communication rules and practice; resisting peer pressure; questions and discussion about alcohol and drugs; compliance with parental rules; understanding and handling emotions; sharing feelings and dealing with criticism; handling anger; and resources for help and review.

The family skills training program sessions provided additional information and a time for the families to practice (with trainer support and feedback) their skills in the Child's Game (Forehand & McMahon, 1981), a structured play therapy session with parents trained to interact with their children in a nonpunitive, noncontrolling, and positive way. Research and observation have shown that dysfunctional, antisocial, and drug-abusing parents are very limited in their ability to attend to their children's emotional and social cues and to respond appropriately (Hans, 1995). Hence, the four sessions of Child's Game focused on training parents in therapeutic parent-child play. The next four sessions of family meetings trained parents and children to improve family communication. The last four sessions of Parents' Game focused on role plays during which the parents practiced different types of requests and commands with their own children.

Results

An extensive instrument battery of parent, child, and therapist report measures was employed to assess improvements of hypothesized risk and protective factor outcomes. The major standardized tests included in the testing battery were the Child Behavior Checklist (CBCL; Achenbach & Edelbrock, 1988), the Parent Attitude Scale (Cowen, 1968), and the Moos Family Environment Scale (FES; Moos, 1974). Analysis of the baseline data indicated that children of substance abusers in treatment had significantly more behavioral, academic, social, and emotional problems compared with the matched comparison group children of nonsubstance abusers and the children in the general population sample (Kumpfer & DeMarsh, 1985).

Outcome results suggested that the combined intervention, formerly called the Family Skills Training Program (Kumpfer, 1981) and now called the SFP (Kumpfer, DeMarsh, & Child, 1989), that includes all three components was the most powerful. SFP improved the child's risk status in three theoretically indicated and intervention-targeted areas: (a) children's problem behaviors, emotional status, and prosocial skills; (b) parent's parenting skills; and (c) family environment and family functioning (improved family communication, clarity of family rules, nonconflictual sibling relationships, and decreased family conflict and social isolation). In general, the pattern of results suggested that each program component was effective in reducing risk factors that were the most directly targeted by that particular component. For example, the parent training curriculum significantly improved parenting skills and parenting self-efficacy, the children's skills program improved children's prosocial skills, and the family program improved family relationships and environment. Reductions were demonstrated in use of tobacco and alcohol among older children and expectations to use alcohol and tobacco among nonusing children. Parents also reduced their drug use and improved in parenting efficacy (DeMarsh & Kumpfer, 1986).

RESEARCH METHODS AND SUMMARY
OF OUTCOMES OF SFP STUDIES
WITH SPECIAL POPULATIONS

Because of the previous promising research results, the SFP program has been replicated with Center for Substance Abuse (CSAP) funding in eight agencies with high-risk ethnic population families: African American low-income mothers in rural Alabama; inner-city African American drug abusers in Detroit; low-income Hispanic families in housing projects in Denver; Asian, Pacific Islander, and Latino families in three counties (four agencies) in Utah; and Asian and Pacific Islander families in Hawaii. The program has been translated into French and is being evaluated in Montreal with high-risk French Canadian families and in Ontario (and Australia) with English-speaking Canadian families with funding by the Canadian government. The results of the Alabama, Detroit, and Utah studies with multiethnic and rural populations replicated the general positive findings of the original NIDA research results. These results are summarized below. The final results for the Strengthening Hispanic Families Program in Denver and Strengthening Hawaii's Families Program in Hawaii should be available soon. The preliminary results support the prior positive results with other special populations.

Rural African American Families

The SFP program was modified to be culturally appropriate for African American families by African American social workers at the Cahaba Mental Health Center in Selma, Alabama (Kumpfer, Platt, & Hoke, 1989). African American single parents with a drug problem (all female) were recruited from mental health center clients, housing projects, special education classes, and informal contacts with African American community leaders, including ministers. Over 3 years, 62 families participated and 51 families (82%) completed at least 12 of the 14 SFP sessions. A quasi-experimental pretest, posttest and 1-year follow-up design was employed. Experimental groups consisted of a comparison group of 27 families with a low-drug-use parent and an experimental group of 24 families with a high-drug-use parent. Because posttest data were missing on either the parent or the child in 2 of the high-drug-use families, the data analysis was conducted on a total of 49 families.

Improvements were measured in hypothesized variables operationalized by scales on standardized instruments (primarily the CBCL and FES) included in a 409-item parent interview. A children's interview was also conducted. Pre- and posttest comparisons of the two experimental groups revealed significant reductions in FES family conflict in the high-drug-use families and increased organization in the low-drug-use families (Kumpfer, 1990, 1991). One unexpected benefit of the family program was that even without being in substance abuse treatment, the high-drug-use mothers significantly reduced their substance use as measured by a composite index of 30-day alcohol and drug quantity and frequency of use.

Intake data revealed that the children of the high-drug-using parents had significantly more behavioral and emotional problems than the children of the low-drug-use parents. By the end of the program, the children of the high-drug-use parents were rated as significantly improved on both the internalizing (depression, obsessive-compulsive, somatic complaints, social withdrawal, and schizoid) and externalizing (aggression, delinquency, and hyperactivity) broadband scales and all of the narrow-band scales of the CBCL (except the uncommunicative scale). Children of low-drug-use parents improved only on the clinical scales for which they manifest relatively higher scores on the intake pretest—namely obsessive-compulsive behavior, aggression, and delinquency. These results suggested that the SFP is effective in reducing maternal reports of children's problem behaviors when the child shows problems in the clinical or subclinical diagnostic range on the intake measures before the program begins.

Because this study used a quasi-experimental design without a randomly assigned, no-treatment control group, it is impossible to determine if these positive effects can be attributed to SFP participation. For example, regression to the mean could partially account for the results. In addition, these results are consistent with a pattern of positive findings from a number of studies conducted with varying types of populations—as is illustrated by the studies in the following section. As will be discussed, a larger scale, true experimental controlled study of SFP is currently being conducted in Iowa.

Because some researchers have suggested that parent training may not be effective with low-education parents, the results for the low-education parents (operationalized as no high school diploma or equivalent degree) were compared to those of higher-education parents. It was encouraging to find that SFP was equally effective in improving the parenting style and children's behaviors in families with less educated parents.

African American Inner-City Drug-Abusing Parents

The African American parent version of the SFP developed for the state of Alabama was modified for use in the 12-session Safe Haven Program (Kumpfer, Bridges, & Williams, 1993) of the Harbor Light Salvation Army and the Detroit City Health Department. Program contents, client demographics on the 88 participating families in the first 16 months, and reasons for the successful implementation of the program are reported by Aktan (1995). Parents in substance abuse treatment at a male and a female treatment center volunteered for the program. The program's popularity resulted in a waiting list for inclusion of 25 to 50 families at any one time. In the first three cohorts, 66% ($N = 58$) of families met criteria of completing 10 of the 12 SFP sessions. Less than half of the families in the first cohort met completion criteria, but with increased staff experience the completion rate rose to 80% and remained at least at that level for 4 years. The data analysis included 56 families because of missing data on one parent and one child posttest. The same nonequivalent comparison, repeated measures, quasi-experimental design with a high-drug-use group of 27 families and a low-drug-use group of 29 families, and the same instruments that were employed in the Alabama study were used with this sample.

The results (discussed in more detail in Aktan, Kumpfer, & Turner, in press) suggest that SFP had a significant positive impact on the participating children and the parents. Results on the FES showed significantly increased family cohesion in the total sample and decreased family conflict in the low-drug-use sample. The families reported spending more time together, increasing parent and child activities, and increasing the amount of time that the parent and child spent together.

Both groups of parents reported significantly decreased alcohol and drug use and family illegal drug use. The high-drug-using parents significantly reduced their depression and increased perceived parent efficacy. The combined sample of both groups showed significant reductions in all four of these variables. According to CBCL parental reports, the children of high-drug-using parents significantly reduced all their externalizing problem behaviors (aggression, hyperactivity, and delinquency) and all internalizing problem behaviors (depression, lack of communication, obsessive compulsive tendencies, social withdrawal, and schizoid tendencies), except somatic complaints, to the more normal levels found in the children of low drug users on the pretest. The children of the low-drug-using parents were reported to reduce their school problems. Parents in both groups reported increased school bonding and the amount of time children spent on homework. No significant unintended negative effects were reported. These parent reports matched the therapists' reports on behavioral improvements in the participating families. Whether these gains are retained will be the focus of the follow-up analysis in the third year of this research.

Utah Community Youth Activity
Project (CYAP) SFP Research

The Utah State Division of Substance Abuse was funded by CSAP to implement a quasi-experimental pretest, posttest, and 3-month follow-up study comparing the effectiveness of the 14-session SFP with an 11-session SFP variant (Communities Empowering Parents Program), which does not include the family skills training component. The study was implemented in three counties in Utah through eight agencies forming a partnership including two agencies serving primarily ethnic families—the Asian Association of Utah and Centro de la Familia de Utah. A total of 421 parents and 703 high-risk youth aged 6 to 13 were recruited through schools, community advertisements, and agency services clients to attend one of the two programs. Adult participants were 59% mothers, 33% fathers, and 8% guardians. About half (49%) were single-parent families and 66% were low income. Most (69%) were ethnic families composed of 26% Asian, 20% Pacific Islander, 18% Latino, and 5% Native American youth. The program materials for both programs and instrument battery were translated into Spanish, Vietnamese, Tongan, Korean, and Chinese for this project.

Attendance and completion of the program was very high, averaging 85% across the three county sites; unfortunately, because of lack of payment only

203 parents and 448 youth completed the posttest. On the pretest, 57% of the youth had behavioral and emotional problems as measured by the CBCL. The analysis of the SFP pre- and posttest change scores suggested significant improvements in the FES scales for family conflict and cohesion, parenting behaviors, and improvements in all the children's CBCL subscales for behavioral and emotional status. Although positive results were found for the comparison program, they were less impressive (Harrison, Proskauer, & Kumpfer, 1995).

A 5-year follow-up study of the participants in this three-county Utah CYAP/SFP study (Harrison et al., 1995) included 87 families confidentially interviewed by a research psychiatrist from Harvard University who was not involved in the program implementation. The results provide suggestive evidence of long-term positive impact on the subsample families and the children. A majority of the families were currently using the skills they were taught years earlier. For instance, 97% were "catching their children being good," 99% believed they were giving clear directions, 95% used reasonable consequences, 84% improved their problem solving with children, 94% enjoyed each other more, and 85% scheduled family play time regularly. Family meetings were still being used by 68% of the families at least once per month and 37% conducted them weekly. The parents reported lasting improvements in family problems (78%), stress-conflict levels (75%), amount of family fun (62%), family talking together more (67%), and showing positive feelings (65%). Although the use of family skills taught did decrease with time, major improvements were maintained even over the 5-year period.

Summary

The results from these SFP replications should be interpreted with caution because they are based on quasi-experimental studies. The repeated replications of a similar pattern of positive findings concerning improvements in targeted outcomes as indicated by standardized measures is noteworthy. It is also important that this family intervention does more than just improve parenting skills—it also decreases children's risk factors for substance abuse, such as family environment, school bonding, depression, and delinquency (Kumpfer & Turner, 1990-1991). Because of these positive results, NIDA has chosen the Strengthening Families Program as one of three model substance abuse prevention programs for dissemination through their Technology Transfer Package on Prevention. This package includes a videotape of the Strengthening Hispanic Families Program implemented by the Denver Area Youth Services agency and a monograph describing the Strengthening Families Program with a guide for implementation (Kumpfer, Williams, & Baxley, 1996).

OVERVIEW OF THE IOWA
STRENGTHENING FAMILIES PROGRAM (ISFP)
FOR PRE- AND EARLY TEENS

Based on preliminary, but promising, program results from these SFP studies, a group of researchers at the Center for Family Research in Rural Mental Health at Iowa State University selected the SFP for a clinical research trial targeting middle school-aged youth and their families in 19 economically disadvantaged counties in rural Iowa. To accommodate universal implementation to all sixth-grade families in selected schools, the number of sessions was reduced from 14 to 7. The same basic SFP content was incorporated and the same format was used entailing concurrent parent and youth groups followed by a family session. The content was modified to be age appropriate, match local culture, and include more resiliency-enhancing skills training.

Because of an emerging literature stressing the importance of parents supporting the development of resiliency in high-risk children (Garmezy, 1985; Kumpfer, 1994b; Rutter, 1987; Werner, 1986), combined with consideration of the risks in the targeted general population, the guiding theoretical framework for the new ISFP was modified to incorporate more emphasis on the resiliency model of Kumpfer (1994a, 1996) and Richardson et al. (1990). This modified model includes greater focus on protective processes in families associated with seven basic resiliency characteristics in youth (optimism, empathy, insight, intellectual competence, self-esteem, direction or purpose in life, and determination-perseverance) and seven associated coping or life skills (emotional management skills, interpersonal social skills, reflective skills, academic and job skills, ability to restore self-esteem, planning skills, and life skills and problem-solving ability). Additional theoretical guidance for the ISFP modification was derived from the empirically tested Social Ecology Model of Adolescent Substance Use (Kumpfer &

Turner, 1990-1991). This guidance was supplemented by local data on youth and family risk and protective factors obtained through the Iowa Youth and Families Project (Conger et al., 1992), a multi-informant, multimethod longitudinal study of young adolescents and their families.

To evaluate the appropriateness of activities tentatively selected on the basis of the previously described theoretical and empirical considerations, focus groups were conducted with sixth graders after they had engaged in planned ISFP exercises. Subsequently, two groups of Iowa families were selected to attend seven sessions that presented all program activities. Trainer recommendations and feedback from these families were used for further curriculum revisions.

ISFP Content

Following program modifications, the content of the youth sessions focused on strengthening prosocial goals for the future, dealing with stress and strong emotions, empathizing with and showing appreciation for parents and elders, increasing motivation for responsible behaviors, and building skills to deal with peer pressure. Parent sessions included discussions of parents' potential positive influence on pre- and young teens, understanding developmental characteristics of youth this age, providing nurturance and support, dealing effectively with children in everyday interactions, setting appropriate limits, following through with reasonable and respectful consequences, as well as sharing beliefs and expectations regarding alcohol and drug use. During the family sessions, parents and youth practiced listening and communicating with respect, identifying family strengths and family values, and using family meetings to teach responsibility, solve problems, and plan fun family activities. Youth, parent, and family sessions made use of discussions, skill-building activities, viewing videotapes that model positive behavior, and "games" designed to strengthen positive interactions between family members.

Videotapes of all parent sessions were made to standardize program delivery and improve parent learning by visually demonstrating skillful parent-child interactions. The use of videotapes had the additional benefit of reducing the need for one of two workshop leaders-instructors. The videotapes included didactic presentation and numerous vignettes of typical family situations and interactions (both positive and negative). Videotapes were also used for youth Sessions 5 and 6 to assist in skills training for resisting peer pressure. Two of the family sessions also made use of instructional videotapes demonstrating how to institutionalize positive family change and maintain ISFP program benefits by holding regular family meetings. The leaders facilitated discussions and group activities during breaks between videotape segments.

SFP Evaluation Procedures

Following feasibility studies and content revisions, a clinical trial including long-term follow-up evaluations (1- and 2-year follow-ups in addition to pre- and posttests) was undertaken in 19 counties in rural Iowa. To avoid contamination problems resulting from the frequent interaction of families in small rural communities, school was the unit of assignment and schools were selected on the basis of high percentages of families participating in a free or reduced-price school lunch program. The true experimental design included random assignment of 33 schools to three conditions: (a) ISFP; (b) Preparing for the Drug-Free Years (Hawkins, Catalano, & Miller, 1992), a five-session youth and family program explained in more detail in Chapter 13 in this volume by Spoth and Redmond; or (c) a minimal-contact control condition. Families in the control condition received four Cooperative Extension Service (CES) leaflets, which gave information on developmental changes of preteens and teens in physical, emotional, cognitive, and relational domains.

Outcome evaluations will entail the use of multi-informant, multimethod measurement procedures at pretest, posttest, 1-year, and 2-year follow-up data-collection points (Spoth, Molgaard, Conger, & Kumpfer, 1992). The assessment includes in-home videotapes of families in structured family interaction tasks as well as in-home interviews, including standardized measures such as the Youth Self Report (Achenbach, 1991), the Revised Behavior Problem Checklist (Quay & Peterson, 1987), and Symptom Checklist (SCL-90-R; Derogatis, 1991).

A total of 161 families, including 114 families who had completed an in-home pretest assessment, participated in 21 ISFP groups at 11 different schools. The group sizes ranged from 3 to 15 families with an average group size of 8 families composed of an average of 12 adults and 8 youths. Both single parents and two-parent families participated. In more than half of the two-parent families, both parents attended at least some of the sessions. Eighty-five percent of the families completed five of the first six sessions. Of the 161 parents who attended at least one of the sessions, 38% were fathers and 62% were mothers.

Recruitment Procedures

Recruitment of families for parenting and family programs can be difficult if not carefully planned, and engagement of families is not considered a major part of the program activities (Kumpfer, 1991; Spoth & Redmond, 1993a; Szapocznik et al., 1988; also see Prinz & Miller, Chapter 8, this volume; Spoth & Redmond, Chapter 13, this volume). Recruitment for ISFP followed procedures developed after extensive experience in recruiting local families for studies at the Center for Family Research in Rural Mental Health at Iowa State University. After receiving a letter of endorsement from their school principal, program flyers, and announcements in the school, each eligible family was sent an introductory letter followed by a phone call inviting them to participate in the research project. Families with sixth graders, including those who did not volunteer for the research and did not complete the pretest, were invited to attend the ISFP held in the local school. All families were called by a local parent to encourage their involvement. Parents and youth were also encouraged to participate by advertising incentives that included free grocery certificates for parents, given at two of the sessions, and coupons for free video rentals and food for the youth. In addition, the youth were told that they would receive a "graduation" gift of $25 if they and their parent(s) attended at least five of the first six sessions. These intensive recruitment procedures led to 49% of the eligible families participating in the ISFP program.

Group Leader Recruitment and Training

Three group leaders—two youth group leaders and one parent group leader—were required for each of the 21 ISFP groups. The leaders, as well as local arrangers, were recruited through the CES, schools, community leaders, and newspaper advertisements. CES staff played an important role in the ISFP implementation by contacting schools and procuring names for recruitment, identifying and interviewing potential facilitators and local arrangers, and participating in the design and training of group leaders. Known in rural communities as a trusted and impartial source of family information, resources, and support, the CES helped to provide access to local community leaders and rural families. Program developers plan to disseminate the ISFP through the CES in Iowa and throughout the country pending results from the project.

Fifty-five leaders were selected following a skills-based screening and interview process. They were trained via an initial 1-day session and a subsequent 2-day session approximately 1 month prior to program implementation by Drs. Kumpfer and Molgaard and other CES and ISFP project staff. Training procedures were modeled after the original SFP training format developed by Dr. Kumpfer. Teams of group leaders were trained to lead the ISFP sessions using the three structured workshop leaders' guides (parent, child, and family), videotapes, handouts, and transparencies.

During the 1-day introductory training session, project staff reviewed the program rationale, goals, and objectives and presented the first program session. Because each group required three leaders, teams also had the opportunity to become acquainted with their coleaders. In the second 2-day training 2 months later, each team prepared and presented a segment of the program with other training participants and staff role playing family members. This innovative aspect of the training allowed staff to assess strengths and weaknesses in teams, provide feedback and role modeling to improve delivery, quicken enhancement of skill levels of groups leaders, and increase the level of fun and involvement of all participants. Workshop facilitators were also trained to identify and make appropriate referrals for the few families who might demonstrate special problems, whether they occurred during the session or during follow-up phone contacts after the program. The local arrangers also received training concerning arrangements for local child care, providing food for snacks, and gaining access to buildings.

Fidelity of program delivery was randomly monitored by trained research staff who used detailed fidelity checklists to guide observations and ratings at two sessions of each youth and parent group concerning adherence to the standardized content and the quality of leader delivery. The pretest-posttest data analysis is ongoing. Initial analysis of the pretest-posttest data shows significant changes and improvements in the parent's and children's behaviors, knowledge, and skills.

PRACTICAL SUGGESTIONS
FOR IMPLEMENTATION OF
FAMILY-FOCUSED INTERVENTIONS

Local or Ethnic Cultural Sensitivity

The use of focus and pilot groups has proven very helpful in adapting the SFP so that it is sensitive to local ethnic cultures. Their success, however, hinges on the recruitment of group members that are representative of the targeted local population. Participating individuals can help plan program adaptations that will meet local needs; they can also help clarify when and where to hold the program, effective incentives, and what groups and agencies might be appropriate for marketing and program or implementation purposes. Professionals who are specialists in local cultural relevance have been employed to improve cultural sensitivity in program development, implementation, evaluation methods, and interpretation of results. For example, Detroit and Hawaii SFP programs contracted with volunteer cultural specialists who participated in ongoing cultural task forces, program reviews, site visits, and periodic cultural-appropriateness assessment reports. As another example, the Iowa application of the SFP involved a feasibility study in which two groups of families from a community similar to the targeted communities attended the total ISFP and offered invaluable suggestions to improve content and format.

Recruitment and Retention of Families

Effective recruitment of families, especially families at risk, is a challenging task in family-focused prevention programming. An important first step in recruitment is linking with other community family-serving agencies to enlist their support and assistance. Schools, local churches, drug treatment agencies, housing authorities, mental health centers, youth and social service agencies, the CES, and tribal councils are examples of appropriate groups that have been significant supporters of SFP and other family interventions. In the authors' experience, efforts expended in collaboration efforts with local leaders (including informal ethnic leaders) have greatly enhanced the ability to reach and attract appropriate hard-to-reach families (Kumpfer, 1991).

Several studies with Iowan parents concerning factors influencing participation in family-focused prevention programs have clearly indicated that time demands and schedule conflicts are primary reasons for declining to participate in multiple-session programs (Spoth, Ball, Klose, & Redmond, in press; Spoth & Redmond, 1993a, 1993b; Spoth, Redmond, Hockaday, & Shin, in press). Parents are often reluctant to leave their children one additional evening during a busy week. This issue may be addressed by using family interventions, such as the SFP, that involve youth as well as parents and also provide child care or structured groups for younger children.

One essential aspect of all SFP implementations is offering incentives that make program attendance attractive to both youth and their parents. Basic material supports to needy families provide a message that the staff really care about them. Incentives, such as free coupons for food or video rentals and a monetary gift at the conclusion of the program, may need to be limited in a locally sponsored program. Even a small local grant or the enlistment of support from local businesses, however, might provide incentives to help make the program appealing to prospective participants. Arranging to have the local police department, service clubs, or churches sponsor families is another way SFP sites have increased their ability to provide incentives.

In the program marketing phase, it is important to let families know about all incentives (e.g., free meals or snacks, child care, transportation, graduation gifts, parties, family outings, clothing and food banks, and support with referrals for legal, medical, housing, and financial aid). Flyers and posters distributed at the school, church, or other local agencies to parents and youth can help to increase local awareness. Articles in the local newspaper or school paper can help as well. Perhaps the most important recruitment tool is personal contacts from friends or neighbors. One strategy for maximizing positive peer pressure for parents is to identify a few natural leaders from among the targeted parent group, meet with them, enlist their support, and ask each of them to bring three or four families to the program, possibly offering an incentive for their assistance. School administration and teachers of prospective youth participants can help by "talking up" the program and encouraging attendance.

Retention is also an important issue; perhaps the most effective way to enhance retention is to have an interesting program that meets families' needs and involves them in relevant, meaningful activities. One idea for helping parents and youth feel committed to the program is to involve them in the practical aspects of the program, such as bringing snacks and helping with attendance or room setup. In the Iowa SFP application, small groups of families signed up during the first session to bring snacks for the whole group on a specific evening. In addition, most of the activities in the family session were designed to encourage personal interaction between a group leader and an individual family as well as among small groups of families. These types of activities can help a family less well connected in the group develop a sense of belonging to the group and, as a result, increase the likelihood that they will enjoy coming to subsequent sessions. Perhaps the most crucial part of retention is a positive relationship with the group leaders—for youth as well as for parents (Harrison et al., 1995). An essential part of facilitator training concerns techniques for being supportive and personable with participants. Finally, when a family misses a session, it is helpful for the facilitator, as well as class members, to call family members and indicate that they were missed, talk about the session content, and encourage them to attend the next session, offering assistance with transportation or other needs if possible.

Practical Considerations About
Program Site, Location, and Group Size

The group size and location of the program site are important factors to consider when implementing a family prevention program such as the SFP. Because the SFP involves both youth and parents in each session, it requires at least two rooms with one large enough to hold the number of people in the family sessions. Among the most convenient sites in urban settings have been family support centers in housing projects. These were used, for example, in the Denver Hispanic SFP site and other cooperative family interventions involving housing authorities. In these cases, parent and youth have only to walk to another unit in their building. Other convenient locations include free or low-cost facilities such as community centers, local churches, and schools. In the case of the geographically dispersed families in Iowa, the use of local schools allowed minimizing the average travel distance. One advantage of holding the program in schools is increasing school personnel involvement and increasing parent-school communication (see the discussions in Chapters 4 and 5, this volume).

Crucial to practical logistics in a clinical trial such as that in Iowa was the use of "local arrangers" personnel. These were generally parents trained and paid to help with duties such as securing and monitoring child care, making arrangements for building access, helping secure equipment, and providing snacks for child care and for the first and last program sessions (participating families provided snacks for other sessions). The degree of responsibility and motivation of these personnel made a big difference in how smoothly the program ran at the various sites.

Program developers originally projected that optimal group size would be 8 to 12 families. Experience in the ISFP project, however, suggests that groups with as few as 5 families (12-15 individuals) and as large as 14 families (46 individuals) can be effective (see Chapter 7, this volume). Needless to say, a group as large as 14 families needs to have unusually effective and well-organized facilitators. The smaller groups provided a more intimate, supportive atmosphere in which personal relationships between parents and youth and their group leaders flourished. In rural areas, one location had only 2 or 3 families and had to be combined with another area, thus adding to the required distance for travel to the sessions.

Selection and Training of Facilitators

As discussed in the section titled Recruitment and Retention of Families, appropriate advertising for leaders and solicitation of referrals (e.g., through the CES and schools) is crucial. Also, experience from numerous SFP projects has confirmed that it is advantageous to conduct the training in two separate sessions. After an introductory training, facilitators have a chance to study materials and prepare to present session activities in the second 2-day training session. It is helpful to have facilitators interact with and present activities with the same team members with whom they will teach. Training should include provision of background information on program goals and objectives as well as prior research results to help prospective leaders clearly understand why improving family dynamics can reduce later drug use, delinquency, and other negative youth outcomes.

Training in group process issues, including how to work with participants who are uninvolved, disruptive, or domineering, is also important. Information and individual coaching on presentation style are helpful. Facilitators also need to be trained on how to address parents or youth for whom a referral for additional help is indicated. Another important aspect of training is teaching facilitators how to handle program logistics, such as room setup, snacks, and activity details.

SUMMARY

Intensive, structured family interventions hold promise for the reduction of delinquency and drug use in high-risk populations. This chapter has discussed the development, implementation, and evaluation of the Strengthening Families Program, a family-focused prevention program for special, at-risk populations, particularly for drug-involved families. This program has been modified for many different cultural groups. Practical suggestions for improving implementation and program success in reducing drug use and delinquency were discussed.

REFERENCES

Achenbach, T. M. (1991). *Manual for the Youth Self Report and 1991 Profile.* Burlington: University of Vermont, Department of Psychiatry.

Achenbach, T. M., & Edelbrock, C. (1988). *Child Behavior Checklist (CBCL).* Burlington: University of Vermont, Center for Children, Youth, & Families.

Aktan, G. (1995). Organizational framework of a substance use prevention program. *International Journal of the Addictions, 30,* 185-201.

Aktan, G., Kumpfer, K. L., & Turner, C. (in press). The Safe Haven program: Effectiveness of a family skills training program for substance abuse prevention with inner city African American families. *International Journal of the Addictions.*

Baumrind, D. (1985). Familial antecedents of adolescent drug use: A developmental perspective. In C. L. Jones & R. J. Battjes (Eds.), *Etiology of drug abuse: Implications for prevention* (NIDA Research Monograph No. 56, DHHS Publication No. ADM 85-1335). Washington, DC: Government Printing Office.

Bavolek, S. J., & Comstock, C. M. (1983). *The nurturing program: A validated approach to reducing functional family interactions* (Final report, Grant No. 1R01MH34862). Rockville, MD: National Institute of Mental Health.

Brook, J. S., Brook, D. W., Gordon, A. S., Whiteman, M., & Cohen, P. (1990). The psychological etiology of adolescent drug use: A family interactional approach. *Genetic, Social, and General Monographs, 116* (Whole No. 2).

Coie, J. D., Watt, N. F., West, S. G., Hawkins, J. D., Asarnow, J. R., Markman, H. J., Ramey, S. L., Shure, M. B., & Long, B. (1993). The science of prevention: A conceptual framework and some directions for a national research program. *American Psychologist, 48,* 1013-1022.

Conger, R. D., Conger, K. J., Elder, G. H., Jr., Lorenz, F. O., Simons, R. L., & Whitbeck, L. B. (1992). A family process model of economic hardship and adjustment of early adolescent boys. *Child Development, 63,* 526-541.

Conger, R. D., & Rueter, M. A. (in press). Siblings, parents, and peers: A longitudinal study of social influences in adolescent risk for alcohol use and abuse. In G. Brody (Ed.), *Sibling relationships: Their causes and consequences.* Norwood, NJ: Ablex.

Cowen, E. L. (1968). *Parent Attitude Test (PAT).* Rochester, NY: University of Rochester, Department of Psychology.

Damon, W. (1988). *The moral child: Nurturing children's natural moral growth.* New York: Free Press.

Delgado, M. (1990). Hispanic adolescents and substance abuse: Implications for research treatment and prevention. In A. R. Stiffman & L. E. Davis (Eds.), *Ethnic issues in adolescent mental health* (pp. 303-320). Newbury Park, CA: Sage.

DeMarsh, J. P., & Kumpfer, K. L. (1986). Family-oriented interventions for the prevention of chemical dependency in children and adolescents. In S. Griswold-Ezekoye, K. L. Kumpfer, & W. Bukoski (Eds.), *Childhood and chemical abuse: Prevention and intervention* (pp. 117-152). New York: Haworth.

Derogatis, L. R. (1991). *SCL 90-R.* Riderwood, MD: Clinical Psychometric Research.

Forehand, R. L., & McMahon, R. J. (1981). *Helping the noncompliant child: A clinician's guide to parent training.* New York: Guilford.

Garmezy, N. (1985). Stress resistant children: The search for protective factors. In J. Stevenson (Ed.), *Recent research in developmental psychopathology. Journal of Child Psychology and Psychiatry, Book Supplement No. 4* (pp. 213-233). Elmsford, NY: Pergamon.

Gordon, R. (1987). An operational classification of disease prevention. In J. A. Steinberg & M. M. Silverman (Eds.), *Preventing mental disorders* (pp. 20-26). Rockville, MD: U.S. Department of Health and Human Services.

Guerney, B. G., Jr. (1977). *Relationship Enhancement Skills Training Program for therapy, problem prevention and enrichment.* San Francisco: Jossey-Bass.

Hans, S. (1995). Diagnosis in etiologic and epidemiologic studies. In C. Jones & M. De La Rosa (Eds.), *NIDA Technical Review: Methodological issues: Etiology and consequences of drug abuse among women.* Silver Spring, MD: National Institute of Drug Abuse.

Harrison, S., Proskauer, S., & Kumpfer, K. L. (1995). *Final evaluation report on Utah CSAP/CYAP project.* Manuscript submitted for publication. Salt Lake City: University of Utah, Social Research Institute.

Hawkins, J. D., Arthur, M. W., & Catalano, R. F. (1994). Preventing substance abuse. *Crime and Justice, 8*(24), 197-281.

Hawkins, J. D., Catalano, R. F., Jr., & Miller, J. Y. (1992). Parent training. In C. A. Maher & J. E. Zins (Eds.), *Communities that care* (pp. 84-100). San Francisco: Jossey-Bass.

Kandel, D. B., & Andrews, K. (1987). Processes of adolescent socialization by parents and peers. *International Journal of the Addictions, 22,* 319-342.

Kumpfer, K. L. (1981). *The family skills training program manuals.* (Available from Utah State Division of Alcoholism and Drugs, 150 West North Temple, Salt Lake City, UT 84112)

Kumpfer, K. L. (1990, March). *Services and programs for children and families.* Paper presented at the National Forum of the Future of Children and Families: Workshop on Children and Parental Illicit Drug Use, National Academy of Sciences, Washington, DC.

Kumpfer, K. L. (1991). *Safe Haven African American parenting project: Final evaluation report.* Manuscript submitted for publication. Salt Lake City: University of Utah, Health Behavior Laboratory, Department of Health Education.

Kumpfer, K. L. (1993, June). *Safe Haven African American parenting project: Second year evaluation report.* Manuscript submitted for publication. Salt Lake City: University of Utah, Health Behavior Laboratory, Department of Health Education.

Kumpfer, K. L. (1994a). *Strengthening America's families: Promising parenting and family strategies for delinquency prevention: User's guide* (Office of Juvenile Justice and

Delinquency Prevention, U.S. Department of Justice Grant No. 87-JS-CX-K495). Silver Spring, MD: Aspen Systems.

Kumpfer, K. L. (1994b, December). *Predictive validity of resilience for positive life adaptations.* Paper presented at National Institute of Drug Abuse (NIDA) Resiliency Symposium, Washington, DC.

Kumpfer, K. L. (1996). Factors and processes contributing to resilience: The resiliency framework. In M. Glantz, J. Johnson, & L. Huffman (Eds.), *Resiliency and development: Positive life adaptations.* New York: Plenum.

Kumpfer, K. L., & Alvarado, R. (1995). Strengthening families to prevent drug use in multiethnic youth. In G. Botvin, S. Schinke, & M. Orlandi (Eds.), *Drug abuse prevention with multiethnic youth* (pp. 255-294). Thousand Oaks, CA: Sage.

Kumpfer, K. L., & Bayes, J. (1995). Child abuse and drugs. In J. H. Jaffe (Ed.), *The encyclopedia of drugs and alcohol* (Vol. 1, pp. 217-222). New York: Simon & Schuster.

Kumpfer, K. L., & Bluth, B. (in press). Parent/child transactional processes predictive of substance abuse resilience or vulnerability. In J. L. Johnson & D. K. MetCaff (Eds.), *Chronicity of substance abuse.* Orlando, FL: Harcourt Brace.

Kumpfer, K. L., Bridges, S., & Williams, K. (1993, October). *The Safe Haven Program: Strengthening African-American families.* Manuscript submitted for publication. Salt Lake City: University of Utah, Department of Health Education.

Kumpfer, K. L., & DeMarsh, J. (1985, Fall). Genetic and family environmental influences on children of drug abusers. *Journal of Children in Contemporary Society, 3/4,* 117-151.

Kumpfer, K. L., & DeMarsh, J. P. (1986). Family environmental and genetic influences on children's future chemical dependency. In S. Griswold-Ezekoye, K. L. Kumpfer, & W. Bukoski (Eds.), *Childhood and chemical abuse: Prevention and intervention* (pp. 49-91). New York: Haworth.

Kumpfer, K. L., DeMarsh, J. P., & Child, W. (1989). *Strengthening Families Program: Children's skills training curriculum manual, parent training manual, children's skill training manual, and family skills training manual.* Manuscript submitted for publication. Salt Lake City: University of Utah, Social Research Institute, Graduate School of Social Work.

Kumpfer, K. L., Platt, P., & Hoke, D. (1989). *The Strengthening African-American Families Program.* Salt Lake City: University of Utah, Department of Health Education.

Kumpfer, K. L., & Turner, C. W. (1990-1991). The social ecology model of adolescent substance abuse: Implications for prevention. *International Journal of the Addictions, 25,* 435-463.

Kumpfer, K. L., Williams, M. K., & Baxley, G. (1996). *Selective prevention for children of substance abusing parents: The Strengthening Families Program.* Silver Springs, MD: National Institute on Drug Abuse, Technology Transfer Program.

Loeber, R., & Stouthamer-Loeber, M. (1986). Family factors as correlates and predictors of juvenile conduct problems and delinquency. In N. Morris & M. Tonry (Eds.), *Crime and justice: An annual review of research* (pp. 29-149). Chicago: University of Chicago Press.

McDonald, L., Billingham, S., Dibble, N., Rice, C., & Coe-Braddish, D. (1991). F.A.S.T.: An innovative substance abuse prevention program. *Social Work in Education, 13,* 118-128.

Mitchell, A., Weiss, H., & Schultz, T. (in press). *Evaluating education reform: Early childhood education. A review of research on early education, family support and parent education, and collaboration.* Manuscript submitted for publication.

Moos, R. H. (1974). *Family Environment Scale.* Palo Alto, CA: Consulting Psychologist Press.

Mrazek, P. J., & Haggerty, R. J. (1994). *Reducing risks for mental disorders: Frontiers for preventive intervention research.* Washington, DC: National Academy Press.

Patterson, G. R. (1975). *Families: Applications of social learning to family life (Rev. ed.).* Champaign, IL: Research Press.

Patterson, G. R. (1976). *Living with children: New methods for parents and teachers.* Champaign, IL: Research Press.

Patterson, G. R. (1982). *Coercive family process.* Eugene, OR: Castalia.

Patterson, G. R., DeBaryshe, B. D., & Ramsey, E. (1989). A developmental perspective on antisocial behavior. *American Psychologist, 44,* 329-335.

Patterson, G. R., Reid, J. B., & Dishion, T. J. (1992). *Antisocial boys.* Eugene, OR: Castalia.

Quay, H. C., & Peterson, D. R. (1987). *The Revised Behavior Problem Checklist.* Coral Gables, FL: University of Miami.

Richardson, G. E., Neiger, B. L., Jensen, S., & Kumpfer, K. L. (1990). The resiliency model. *Health Education, 21,* 33-39.

Rutter, M. (1987). Psychosocial resilience and protective mechanisms. *American Journal of Orthopsychiatry, 57,* 316-331.

Rutter, M. (1993). Resilience: Some conceptual considerations. *Journal of Adolescent Health, 14,* 626-631.

Shedler, J., & Block, J. (1990). Adolescent drug use and psychological health: A longitudinal inquiry. *American Psychologist, 45,* 612-630.

Sowder, B., & Burt, M. (1978a). *Children of addicts and non-addicts: A comparative investigation in five urban sites* (report to NIDA). Bethesda, MD: Gurt Associates.

Sowder, B., & Burt, M. (1978b). *Children of addicts: A population in need of coordinated comprehensive mental health services.* Paper presented at the American Association of Psychiatric Services for Children, Atlanta, GA.

Spivack, G., & Shure, M. (1979). Interpersonal cognitive problem solving and primary prevention: Programming for preschool and kindergarten children. *Journal of Clinical Child Psychology, 8,* 89-94.

Spoth, R., Ball, A. B., Klose, A., & Redmond, C. (in press). Illustration of a market segmentation technique using family-focused prevention program preference data. *Health Education Research.*

Spoth, R., Molgaard, V., Conger, R. D., & Kumpfer, K. L. (1992). *Rural youth at risk: Extension-based prevention efficacy.* Unpublished grant proposal.

Spoth, R., & Redmond, C. (1993a). Study of participation barriers in family-focused prevention: Research issues and preliminary results. *International Quarterly of Community Health Education, 13,* 365-388.

Spoth, R., & Redmond, C. (1993b). Identifying program preferences through conjoint analysis: Illustrative results from a parent sample. *American Journal of Health Promotion, 8,* 124-133.

Spoth, R., Redmond, C., Hockaday, C., & Shin, C. (in press). *Barriers to participation in family-focused preventive interventions and research projects: A replication and extension.* Manuscript submitted for publication.

Steinmetz, S. K., & Straus, M. H. (1974). *Violence in the family.* New York: Dodd, Mead.

Szapocznik, J., Perez-Vidal, A., Brickman, A., Foote, F. H., Santisteban, D., Hervis, O., & Kurtines, W. H. (1988). Engaging adolescent drug abusers and their families into treatment: A strategic structural systems approach. *Journal of Consulting and Clinical Psychology, 56,* 552-557.

Szapocznik, J., Santisteban, D., Rio, A., Perez-Vidal, A., & Kurtines, W. M. (1985). Family effectiveness training (FET) for Hispanic families: Strategic structural systems intervention for the prevention of drug abuse. In H. P. Lefley & P. B. Pedersen (Eds.), *Cross cultural training for mental professionals* (pp. 245-264). Springfield, IL: Charles C Thomas.

Vicary, J., & Lerner, J. (1986). Parental attributes and adolescent drug use. *Journal of Adolescence, 9,* 115-122.

Wahler, R., Leske, G., & Rogers, E. (1979). The insular family: A deviance support system for oppositional children. In L. S. Hamerlynck (Ed.), *Behavioral systems for the developmentally disabled. 1: School and family environments* (pp. 102-107). New York: Brunner/Mazel.

Werner, E. E. (1986). Resilient offspring of alcoholics: A longitudinal study from birth to age 18. *Journal of Studies on Alcohol, 47,* 34-40.

Wolin, S. J., Bennett, L. A., & Noonan, D. L. (1979). Family rituals and the recurrence of alcoholism over generations. *American Journal of Psychiatry, 136,* 589-593.

12

From Childhood Physical Aggression to Adolescent Maladjustment

THE MONTREAL PREVENTION EXPERIMENT

RICHARD E. TREMBLAY

LOUISE C. MÂSSE

LINDA PAGANI

FRANK VITARO

Physical aggression has been identified as one of the best predictors of later deviant behavior. Farrington (1991, 1994) has shown that aggressive boys between 8 and 10 years of age living in a low socioeconomic status (SES) environment of London were, by age 32, more likely to have been

AUTHORS' NOTE: Correspondence should be addressed to R. E. Tremblay, Research Unit on Children's Psycho-Social Maladjustment, University of Montreal, 750, Gouin Blvd. East, Montreal, Quebec, Canada, H2C 1A6. This study was supported by the following agencies: National Welfare Grants Program of the Canadian Ministry of Health and Welfare, Conseil Québecois de la Recherche Sociale, Fonds FCAR, Social Sciences and Humanities Research convicted, be chronic offenders, be unemployed, and have reported drunk driving. Stattin and Magnusson (1989) obtained similar results with a sample of girls and boys from central Sweden who were assessed at ages 10 and 13 and then followed up to age 26 for registered lawbreaking. Most longitudinal studies of aggression suggest that it is a highly stable behavior from both an ontogenetic perspective (Cairns, Cairns, Neckerman, Ferguson, & Gariépy, 1989; Cummings, Iannotti, & Zahn-Waxler, 1989; Olweus, 1979) and an intergenerational perspective (Huesmann, Eron, Lefkowitz, & Walder, 1984; Lahey et al., 1988; Lahey, Russo, Walker, & Piacentini, 1989; Robins, West, & Herjanic, 1975).

Surprisingly, few studies have linked preschool aggressive behavior to later deviant behavior. The studies cited previously either began data collection after 7 years of age or limited the data collection to the preschool years. If aggressive behavior is stable during individual development and if aggression is reproduced from one generation to the next, one would expect that aggressive preadolescents would have been aggressive preschoolers. These links have implications for both theory and prevention.

From a theoretical perspective, we need to understand what factors are involved in the development of an aggressive lifestyle. Family characteristics, peer relations, school failure, and individual characteristics (such as temperament, IQ, and hormones) have all been associated with aggressive behavior (Reiss & Roth, 1993). Most of these studies, however, focused on the correlates of aggressive behavior long after it had become an entrenched sociobehavioral pattern. By studying aggression from preschool onward, a clearer picture of the factors involved at the start of an aggressive way of life should be provided.

From a perspective of crime prevention, interventions with antisocial adolescents and adults have been far from effective (Gottfredson & Hirschi, 1990; Lipsey & Wilson, 1993). Eron (1990) has suggested that aggressive antisocial behavior crystallizes at approximately 8 years of age. If this is the

Council of Canada, Conseil de la Santé et des Services Sociaux Régional du Montréal Métropolitain, Fondation Cité des Prairies, and Centre d'Accueil le Mainbourg. Lucie Bertrand coordinated the intervention program. Rita Béland, Michel Bouillon, Raymond Labelle, Hélène O'Reilly, and Danièle Reclus-Prince implemented the intervention. Pierre Charlebois, Claude Gagnon, Serge Larivée, and Marc LeBlanc participated in the planning and implementation of parts of this study. Lucille David and Hélène Beauchesne coordinated the data collection. Lyse Desmarais-Gervais, Hélène Boileau, Muriel Rorive, and Maria Rosa created the data bank and helped with the statistical analyses. Minh T. Trinh provided the documentation.

case, one would expect that effective interventions aiming to deflect aggressive boys from a delinquent career would need to be implemented before the aggressive boys reach the age of "crystallization." The Institute of Medicine's Committee on Prevention of Mental Disorders (Mrazek & Haggerty, 1994) has identified eight preschool and early elementary school randomized prevention experiments that have demonstrated an impact on children's behavior problems (Hawkins et al., 1992; Ramey, Bryant, Campbell, Sparling, & Wasik, 1990; Rotheram, 1982; Shure & Spivack, 1980; Strayhorn & Weidman, 1991; Tremblay et al., 1992; Schweinhart, Barnes, & Weikart, 1993). Three of these studies (Hawkins et al., 1992; Tremblay et al., 1992; and Schweinhart, Barnes, & Weikart, 1993) have indicated a long-term reduction of delinquent behavior as well (see Tremblay & Craig, 1995).

This chapter describes one of these experiments—a longitudinal-experimental study aiming both to understand the development of aggressive kindergarten boys and to test the effectiveness of a bimodal intervention strategy. The experimental intervention was implemented from a pragmatic perspective (Schwartz, Flamant, & Lellouch, 1980). That is, the objective was to attenuate aggressive behavior and thus prevent delinquency involvement. Two modes of intervention (i.e., parent training and child training) were directed at variables that have been postulated to be causes of delinquency (i.e., poor parenting and aggressive behavior). Thus, if a change in these behaviors would lead to less delinquency involvement, then the hypothesis that such variables are causally linked to delinquency involvement would be supported.

The main focus of the chapter is the prevention experiment. We examine whether the intervention had an impact on aggression and later delinquent behavior. The longitudinal aspect of the experiment reported herein and some results from an associated epidemiological study will be presented to provide a context for the intervention and its results.

PHYSICAL AGGRESSION IN KINDERGARTEN

Aggression among peers is probably more frequent during the preschool years than at any other time in the life cycle. Restoin et al. (1985) have reported data showing that physical aggression among peers increases from age 6 to 24 months of age, whereas other studies have reported that agonistic behavior among peers becomes less frequent from 2 to 7 years of age (Dawe,

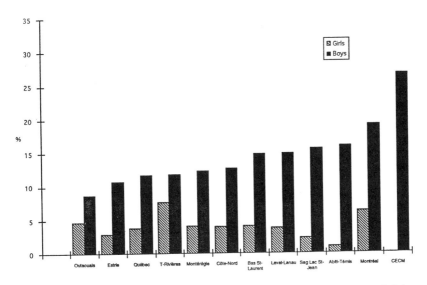

Figure 12.1. Percentage of Physically Aggressive Kindergarten Boys and Girls by Administrative Regions in Quebec ($N = 4,359$)

1934; Green, 1933; Hartup, 1974; Holmberg, 1980; Strayer, Moss, Trudel, & Jacques, 1986; Strayer & Trudel, 1984). This observed reduction, mainly in terms of diminished physically aggressive interactions (Strayer et al., 1986), may be considered part of the socialization process. Most children learn, during the first 5 years of life, that physical aggression is generally not the most effective way to satisfy one's needs. By the time children enter kindergarten, they should have learned to inhibit physically aggressive behavior and use alternative assertive and prosocial strategies to achieve their goals (Cairns, 1986; Dodge, Bates, & Pettit, 1990; Gouze, 1987; Hartup, 1974; Rubin & Clark, 1983). Thus, the kindergarten children who still frequently resort to physical aggression are often perceived as deviant by adults and tend to be rejected by their peers (Behar & Stringfield, 1974; Rubin & Clark, 1983; Vitaro, Tremblay, Gagnon, & Boivin, 1992).

Figure 12.1 shows results from an epidemiologic study of physically aggressive behavior using a stratified random sample of 4,359 kindergarten boys and girls from 11 administrative regions of the province of Quebec. Children were categorized as high on physical aggression when their teacher-rated physical aggression score (fights, kicks, bites, hits, and bullies) was

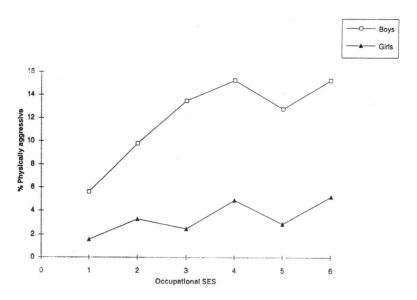

Figure 12.2. Percentage of Physically Aggressive Kindergarten Boys and Girls by Parents'
Occupational Socioeconomic Level

at least 2 standard deviations above the mean for the whole sample (i.e.,
above the 90th percentile) using the Social Behavior Questionnaire (SBQ;
Tremblay et al., 1991a). Overall, 13.9% of the boys and 4.4% of the girls
were classified in the high physical aggression group. As such, boys were
3.5 times (odds ratio) more at risk of being among the physically aggressive
group than girls. It can also be seen from Figure 12.1 that boys from a large
urban area (Montreal) were at highest risk. This could be partly because
Montreal has the largest concentration of poverty. The first column on the
right in Figure 12.1 shows the percentage of physically aggressive boys in
kindergarten classes of the 53 schools with the lowest socioeconomic rating
from the same Montreal school board (CECM, Montreal Catholic School
Board). It can be seen that the risk is even more elevated for these boys.

Figure 12.2 shows the association between physical aggression and parents' socioeconomic level based on the parent with the highest occupational
SES (Blishen, Carroll, & Moore, 1987). For both girls and boys, a trend
indicated that lower SES levels (1 = highest, 6 = lowest) were associated
with an increased risk of being rated as physically aggressive (i.e., the risk
of children from Category 6 is 2.9 times the risk of children from Cate-

TABLE 12.1 Differences Between Physically Aggressive and Nonphysically Aggressive Kindergarten Children on Teachers' and Mothers' Behavior Ratings

Behavior	Boys			Girls		
	Aggressive (N = 311)	Not Aggressive (N = 1,934)	t	Aggressive (N = 93)	Not Aggressive (N = 2,020)	t
Hyperactivity						
Teachers'	2.7	1.0	22.2***	2.2	0.5	11.1***
Mothers'	2.4	1.7	8.2***	2.1	1.5	3.7***
Inattention						
Teachers'	3.9	2.0	13.1***	3.4	1.4	7.7***
Mothers'	3.6	2.6	6.8***	3.1	2.1	4.3***
Opposition						
Teachers'	5.8	1.2	33.2***	5.9	0.8	22.2***
Mothers'	4.4	3.2	9.6***	4.0	2.9	4.1***
Anxiety						
Teachers'	2.8	2.3	3.0**	2.8	2.0	3.1**
Mothers'	4.1	3.9	1.4	4.1	3.7	1.2
Prosociality						
Teachers'	4.4	6.5	−8.4***	6.0	8.2	−5.3***
Mothers'	10.5	11.1	2.7**	10.9	12.2	−2.6**

$**p < .01; ***p < .001.$

gory 1). There was, however, a clear interaction between gender and SES. This interaction showed that girls in Level 3 appeared to be at lower risk than their same-sex peers in Level 2, whereas for boys, there was a linear increase from Levels 1 to 4 with a much steeper gradient.

Children who were not living with both their biological mother and father were found to be at increased risk of being in the physically aggressive group. Girls not living with both biological parents were 2.8 times more at risk of being in the physically aggressive group than girls living with both biological parents (7% vs. 3%), whereas boys not living with their biological parents were 2.1 times more at risk (21% vs. 11%).

The differences in teacher- and mother-rated behavioral characteristics between the kindergarten children rated high on physical aggression and the others are reported in Table 12.1. The physically aggressive children were rated (by both teachers and mothers) as more hyperactive, more inattentive, more oppositional, and less prosocial. The aggressive children also tended to be rated as more anxious by teachers and mothers, but the differences were significant only for teacher ratings. The convergence in behavior ratings by teachers and mothers indicates that teacher-rated physically aggressive kindergarten children are also perceived by their mothers as having serious behavioral problems.

Clearly, kindergarten boys from poor urban areas who are living in families with high adversity are more at risk of being among the most physically aggressive but also are the most hyperactive, inattentive, anxious, and the least prosocial. With the Montreal longitudinal-experimental study and the Jyvaskyla longitudinal study (Finland), we have shown that disruptive boys are at highest risk of frequent delinquent behaviors in preadolescence and criminal behavior in adulthood (Haapasalo & Tremblay, 1994; Pulkkinen & Tremblay, 1992; Tremblay, Pihl, Vitaro, & Dobkin, 1994). The negative outcomes in adolescence, however, are not limited to criminal behavior. Table 12.2 presents the nine kindergarten behavioral patterns created by Pulkkinen and Tremblay (1992) using cluster analysis. This analysis revealed three distinct groups of frequent fighters in kindergarten: (a) the "uncontrolled"—frequent fighters who were prosocial but hyperactive, inattentive, and anxious; (b) the "bullies"—frequent fighters who were hyperactive and inattentive but not prosocial and not anxious; and (c) the "multiproblem" kindergarten boys—frequent fighters who were also hyperactive, inattentive, and anxious but not prosocial. Table 12.2 shows the percentage of boys from each cluster who reported adjustment problems by 12 or 14 years of age. A logistic regression analysis compared the outcome of the "normal" group (i.e., boys who were not fighters, not hyperactive, not inattentive, not anxious, but who were prosocial) to the outcome of the other groups. It can be seen that the uncontrolled, the bullies, and the multiproblem groups (three groups who were frequent fighters in kindergarten) were at highest risk of school failure, poor health, having been drunk by age 12, and having had sexual intercourse by age 14. The uncontrolled and the multiproblem kindergarten boys were also more at risk of having been hospitalized by age 14 for an accident while driving (bicycle, car, etc.). The bullies and the multiproblem boys were more at risk of having started to take drugs by age 14. Note that the "anxious" kindergarten boys (i.e., those who were highly anxious but were not fighters, not hyperactive, not inattentive, and not prosocial) were as well adjusted in early adolescence as the normals. The adjustment problems of the "nervous," the "inattentive," and the "passive"

TABLE 12.2 Percentage of Adolescents With Different Adjustment Problems for Nine Groups With Different Behavioral Patterns in Kindergarten

	Group								
	Normal	Anxious	Nervous	Inattentive	Passive	Uncontrolled	Bully	Multiproblem	Miscellaneous
Not in age-appropriate regular classroom at age 14	24.6	31.9	52.7***	68.1***	56.9***	66.7***	55.0***	85.5***	33.3
Not in good health at age 14	14.1	24.3	18.2	21.2	19.3	31.4**	36.8**	36.5***	28.6*
Hospitalized for a driving accident before age 14	8.4	13.9	14.3	15.8	22.1**	22.0**	5.3	19.6*	21.4**
Drunk before age 12	16.6	17.6	20.4	45.9	25.2	29.4*	38.6**	27.9**	27.0
Had drugs before age 14	12.9	13.7	9.5	17.5	13.1	14.7	31.8**	27.9**	16.2
Had sexual intercourse before age 14	21.2	18.9	22.3	30.8	31.1	36.7*	52.6***	52.0***	44.6***

NOTE: Normal group: low aggression, anxiety, inattention, hyperactivity, and high prosociality; anxious group: high anxiety, low prosociality, aggression, inattention, and hyperactivity; nervous group: high anxiety, inattention, prosociality, low aggression, and hyperactivity; inattentive group: high inattention, hyperactivity, prosociality, and low anxiety; passive group: low aggression, anxiety, inattention, hyperactivity, and prosociality; uncontrolled group: high aggression, anxiety, inattention, hyperactivity, and prosociality; bully group: high aggression, inattention, hyperactivity, low prosociality, and anxiety; multiproblem group: high aggression, anxiety, inattention, hyperactivity, and low prosociality; miscellaneous group: high aggression, hyperactivity, prosociality, low anxiety, and inattention.

*p < .05; **p < .01; ***p < .001 (comparing each group with the normal group).

275

boys showed a tendency of not being in an age-appropriate regular classroom by age 14.

THE PREVENTION EXPERIMENT DESIGN

The prevention experiment was planned in the early 1980s when parent training (e.g., Patterson, 1982) and child social skills training (e.g., Camp, Blom, Hebert, & Van Doorminck, 1977) were proposed as alternative approaches to the treatment of aggressive prepubertal children and early adolescents. Both of these approaches to intervention were integrated into the program with the hope that simultaneous modification of child and parent behavior would have a greater impact than modifying either alone. The treatment plan also included fantasy play stimulation (Singer & Singer, 1981), television education (Singer, Singer, & Zuckerman, 1981), and teacher support. Unfortunately, not enough resources were available to implement the first two aspects of the treatment plan with the whole sample nor to fully implement the teacher support strategy.

The intervention was originally planned to start in the fall after the end of the kindergarten year when the boys' mean age would be 6 years and they would normally be entering first grade. It was also anticipated to last 2 full school years. Because funding was made available later than planned, the intervention started a year later when the boys' were, on average, 7 years of age (i.e., entering second grade). As planned, the intervention lasted 2 school years and ended when the boys were, on average, 9 years of age.

The longitudinal-experimental study began, in fact, in the spring of 1984 when each kindergarten teacher from the 53 Montreal schools with the lowest SES index (Crespo, 1977) was asked to assess each of their male students. The SBQ (Tremblay et al., 1991a) was completed by 87% of the teachers for a total of 1,161 boys. To maintain a culturally homogeneous (white, French speaking) sample, only boys with Canadian-born, French-speaking parents were kept in the sample. To ensure that the sample would be from families of low socioeconomic background, children of parents with more than 14 years of schooling were excluded. As such, families in which one parent would have completed postsecondary technical training (3 years of training after high school) were eliminated. This procedure reduced the sample to 904 subjects. Boys who were rated above the 70th percentile on the disruptive scale of the SBQ were randomly allocated to one of three different groups:

a treatment group that was offered the experimental intervention, a control group that was assessed regularly but did not receive the experimental intervention, and an attention-control group that was offered an intensive observational study of family and school interactions (Lavigueur, Saucier, & Tremblay, 1995; Lavigueur, Tremblay, & Saucier, 1993, 1995) and did not receive the experimental intervention. A total of 166 families (68.3%) that met the criteria described previously agreed to participate: 43 in the treatment group, 41 in the control group, and 82 in the attention-placebo group. The number of subjects in the attention-control group was greater than the number of subjects in the other two groups because of the resources required and available for the treatment and observational study.[1]

The groups were compared on kindergarten teacher SBQ ratings to examine whether the consent requirement had operated differently among the three conditions. A post hoc comparison of the consenters among the three groups showed no significant differences in kindergarten teacher ratings of disruptive behavior, fighting, oppositional behavior, hyperactivity, and prosocial behavior. A significant difference for inattentiveness found that the treatment group was between the attention-control group (which was highest) and the control group (which was lowest) on this scale. The control group appeared significantly less anxious as well. It should be noted, however, that in no case did the treatment group differ significantly from the other two (see Tremblay et al., 1991b, for further elaboration).

Similar analyses were conducted for family characteristics; there were no significant differences in number of children per home, family configuration, years of education for mothers and fathers, and age of parents at birth of their first child. The SES of the treatment group mothers, based on last occupation, was significantly lower than that of the two comparison groups, but no significant differences were observed for paternal SES. There was also a significant difference in the ages of the parents at birth of their son. Mothers in the attention-control group were younger than those in the control group, whereas fathers in the attention-control group were younger than those in the treated group (see Tremblay et al., 1991b).

The 166 participating disruptive boys were also compared to the 605 boys who were rated below the 70th percentile of the disruptive scale. Table 12.3 shows that the disruptive boys were significantly more physically aggressive, oppositional, hyperactive, inattentive, and anxious. They were also less prosocial and living in more adverse family conditions.

TABLE 12.3 Differences in Kindergarten Teacher Ratings (Means) for
Disruptive Boys in the Experiment and Nondisruptive Boys

	Disruptive (N = 166)	Nondisruptive (N = 605)	t	Two-Tailed Probability
Fighting	3.55	0.51	24.65	p < .001
Opposition	5.64	1.09	26.24	p < .001
Hyperactivity	2.87	0.78	20.24	p < .001
Inattentiveness	2.16	1.06	9.51	p < .001
Anxiety	2.91	2.16	3.54	p < .001
Prosociality	6.65	8.52	4.41	p < .001

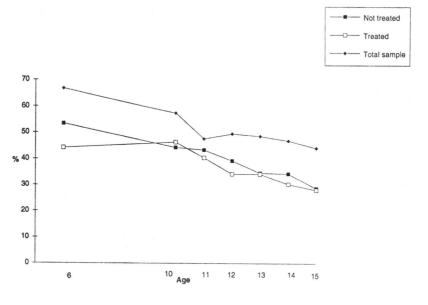

Figure 12.3. Percentage of Boys From 6 to 15 Years of Age in an Intact Family

Figure 12.3 shows the evolution of family status (boys living with their
two biological parents vs. others) for the whole sample, the treated, and
the untreated from ages 6 to 15. It can be seen that the number of boys living with their two biological parents decreases over time, but a much
smaller proportion of the disruptive boys participating in the experiment as
treated or untreated subjects were living with their two biological parents.

TABLE 12.4 Differences Between Families of Disruptive Boys in the
Experiment and Nondisruptive Boys (Means)

	Disruptive (N = 166)	Nondisruptive (N = 605)	t	Two-Tailed Probability
Age at birth of target son				
Mother	24.09	25.41	−3.31	$p < 0.001$
Father	27.01	28.56	−2.87	$p < 0.005$
Years in school				
Mother	10.02	9.95	0.36	$p > 0.05$
Father	9.70	9.71	−0.05	$p > 0.05$
Occupational SES				
Mother	35.10	36.58	−1.45	$p > 0.05$
Father	38.84	37.11	−1.34	$p > 0.05$
Family adversity index	0.40	0.32	3.63	$p < 0.001$

As can be seen from Table 12.4, the parents of the disruptive boys were also younger than the parents of nondisruptive boys. The Family Adversity Index (Tremblay et al., 1991a) is based on four variables: parents' schooling, parents' age at birth of child, parents' occupational SES, and family status. On the basis of these four indicators, the disruptive boys tended to live in families with a significantly higher level of adversity compared to the nondisruptive boys (Table 12.4).

TREATMENT PROGRAM

Parent Training Component

This component was based on a model developed at the Oregon Social Learning Center (Patterson, 1982; Patterson, Reid, Jones, & Conger, 1975). In brief, the procedure involved (a) giving parents a reading program, (b) training parents to monitor their children's behavior, (c) training parents to give positive reinforcement for prosocial behavior, (d) training parents to punish effectively without being abusive, (e) training parents to manage family crises, and (f) helping parents to generalize what they have learned. This component was complemented by having the professional who worked with a family meet with the boy's teacher to discuss his adjustment and means of helping him. Teachers, however, were generally not able to spend much time discussing teaching strategies for one child, and resources to implement a structured teacher training program (e.g., Hawkins et al., 1992) were not available; as a result, meetings between teachers and professionals were fewer than planned. We learned from this that teacher support should be offered for the whole class.

Work with parents and teachers was carried out by two university-trained child care workers, one psychologist, and one social worker all working full-time. The professionals were trained for 10 months before the start of the program and received regular supervision for the duration of the experiment. Each of these professionals had a caseload of 12 families. The team was coordinated by a fifth professional who worked on the project part-time. Work with the parents was planned to last for 2 school years with one session every 2 or 3 weeks. The professionals, however, were free to decide that a given family needed more or fewer sessions at any given time. The maximum number of sessions given to any family was 46 and the mean number of sessions over the 2 years was 17.4, including families that refused to continue.

Social Skills Training Component

This component was implemented in the schools in which one or two disruptive boys were included in groups of three to five peers who were identified by teachers as highly prosocial. The training was offered during lunchtime by the same group of professionals who conducted the parent training. To create a team approach, different professionals were responsible for the parent and child training with each family. The two professionals responsible for a given family met regularly to discuss treatment strategy. The multidisciplinary team of professionals also met weekly to study a few cases. This helped maintain a consistent treatment approach. For the social skills training component of our intervention, two types of training were given to the disruptive boys within a small group of prosocial peers in school. During the first year, a prosocial skills program was devised based on other programs (Cartledge & Milburn, 1980; Michelson, Sugai, Wood, & Kazdin, 1983; Schneider & Byrne, 1987). Nine sessions were given on themes such as "How to make contact," "How to help," "How to ask 'why?'," and "How to invite someone in a group." Coaching, peer modeling, role playing, and reinforcement contingencies were used during these sessions. The program was aimed at self-control during the second year. Using material from previous studies (Camp et al., 1977; Goldstein, Sprafkin, Gershaw, & Klein,

1980; Kettlewell & Kausch, 1983; Meichenbaum, 1977), 10 sessions were developed on themes such as "Look and listen," "Following rules," "What to do when I am angry," "What to do when they do not want me to play with them," and "How to react to teasing." Coaching, peer modeling, self-instructions, behavioral rehearsal, and reinforcement contingencies were also used during these sessions. The details of each session were documented by the professionals and implemented uniformly across groups (Bertrand, 1988).

FOLLOW-UP ASSESSMENTS

The total sample of boys assessed in kindergarten was assessed annually from age 10—1 year after the end of the intervention. At the time of the writing of this chapter, data were available up to age 15. Data were obtained from teachers, parents, peers, self-reports, and official records.

Class Placement

This variable was used as a global measure of school performance. Boys were considered to not be performing at the expected level if they were not in an age-appropriate regular classroom (AARC). A traditional measure of school performance (i.e., academic grades) was not appropriate given that a large proportion of the sample had repeated at least one class or had been placed in special classes or schools.

Teacher and Mother Ratings

Ratings were obtained with the Social Behavior Questionnaire that had been used for the original assessments in kindergarten. This questionnaire yielded main factor scores for disruptive behavior, anxiety, inattentiveness, and prosocial behavior. In addition, the disruptive factor was subdivided into fighting, oppositional behavior, and hyperactivity (Tremblay et al., 1991a).

Subject and Peer Assessments

These were obtained with the Pupil Evaluation Inventory (PEI; Pekarik, Prinz, Liebert, Weintraub, & Neale, 1976). The PEI contains 34 short behavior descriptors. Each child in the class of at least one of our subjects was asked to identify four children in the class who were best described by each of the descriptors. Children responded to the PEI in a group format. The PEI yields three factors: disruptive behavior[2]—composed of 20 items (e.g., those who cannot sit still, those who start a fight over nothing, and those who are rude to the teacher), withdrawal—composed of 9 items (e.g., those who are too shy to make friends easily, those whose feelings are easily hurt, and those who are unhappy or sad), and likability—composed of 5 items (e.g., those who are liked by everyone, those who help others, and those who are especially nice). Because each rater can nominate himself or herself for each item, the instrument provides both a self-rating and a peer rating for each scale. A question was added to the original questionnaire (those who are my best friends) to identify mutual friends (i.e., two children who name each other as best friend) and unilateral friends (i.e., a child chosen as best friend who did not reciprocate) in the classroom.

Boys' Reports of Family, School, and Social Experiences

Self-reports were obtained annually, in the spring, by having the boys answer a questionnaire at school. The questionnaire focused on a wide range of topics, including the following:

1. Juvenile delinquency—the boys responded to a self-report questionnaire addressing their involvement in antisocial behavior from age 10 to age 15 (Tremblay et al., 1994). Questions were asked about (a) theft (kept objects worth $10 or more, stole something from a store, stole $100 or more, entered without paying admission, stole money from home, stole something worth $10, stole something worth between $10 and $100, stole a bicycle, bought a stolen article, broke down a door to take something, or whether the boy had been in an unauthorized place); (b) alcohol and drug use (consumed alcohol, has been drunk, or consumed marijuana); and (c) vandalism (destroyed instruments at school, intentionally destroyed other's property, intentionally broke parts of school property, purposely broke something belonging to a family member, intentionally destroyed part of an automobile, and set fire). At age 10, the boys were asked to report if they had ever misbehaved in the specified ways. From age 11, they were asked whether they had engaged in such behaviors in the past 12 months. The response format for each question was never, once or twice, often, or very often. The mean internal consistency alpha between ages 11 and 15 was .91 (range .87 to .93).

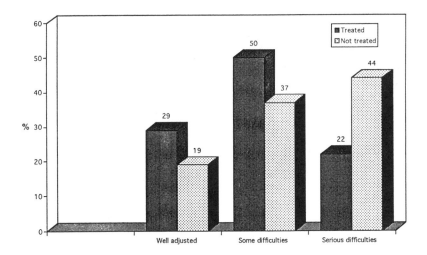

Figure 12.4. Percentage of Treated and Untreated Boys in Different School Adjustment Groups at Ages 11 and 12 (From Tremblay et al., 1992)

2. Gang membership—membership in a gang was assessed by asking the following question from ages 10 to 15: In the past 12 months, have you been a member of a gang that breaks the law? (yes-no).
3. Age at onset of sexual intercourse—this variable was assessed with the following question from ages 13 to 15: At what age did you have your first experience of sexual intercourse?
4. Motivation toward school—academic interest was assessed with the following question from ages 10 to 15: Do you like school? (scored on a Likert-type scale: like a lot, like, don't like, or don't like at all).

RESULTS

Impact on Elementary School Adjustment

Figure 12.4 represents a summary of the impact of the intervention on school adjustment at ages 11 and 12, when the boys normally should have been in their last 2 years of elementary school. The School Adjustment Index is a composite score of teacher and peer ratings of disruptive behavior and class placement (i.e., being in an AARC; see Tremblay et al., 1992). Boys classified as well adjusted were in an AARC and were rated below the 70th percentile on the teacher and peer scales of disruptive behavior. Boys classified in serious difficulty were not in an AARC and were rated as disruptive (above the 70th percentile) by teacher or peers. Boys classified as having some difficulties were either not in an AARC or were rated as disruptive. It can be seen that treated boys were significantly less likely to be classified as having serious difficulties compared to untreated boys (24% vs. 44%) and were more likely to be rated as being well adjusted or having only some difficulties, X^2 (1, 158) = 5.29, $p < .05$.

Statistically significant differences between the treated and untreated groups were also observed for quality of friends and self-reported delinquency. At ages 10 and 12, the treated boys had mutual friends who were rated as less disruptive by their classroom peers compared to the ratings received by the mutual friends of the control boys (see Vitaro & Tremblay, 1994). By 12 years of age, fewer treated boys reported having ever been involved in trespassing, stealing bicycles, and stealing other goods (McCord, Tremblay, Vitaro, & Desmarais-Gervais, 1994; see Tremblay et al., 1992).

Thus, results from class placement, teacher assessments, peer assessments, and self-reports indicate that the early intervention with disruptive kindergarten boys had a positive impact 3 years after the end of treatment when the boys were 12 years of age and should have been completing their final year of elementary school.

IMPACT ON ADJUSTMENT
DURING EARLY ADOLESCENCE

Early adolescence remains a time of important social and biological changes (Brooks-Gunn & Reiter, 1990; Keating, 1990). The boys are entering high school, and they are at the peak of their physical maturation. It was hoped that the intervention would maintain its effects, but we acknowledged that early adolescence is a period when the majority of adolescents exhibit some form of experimentation that can be labeled delinquent behavior. High school is also an important intellectual challenge for these boys from families in which most parents did not go beyond the 10th grade.

Gang Membership

Being part of a gang involved in lawbreaking would put these boys at higher risk of becoming heavily engaged in delinquency. Figure 12.5 shows

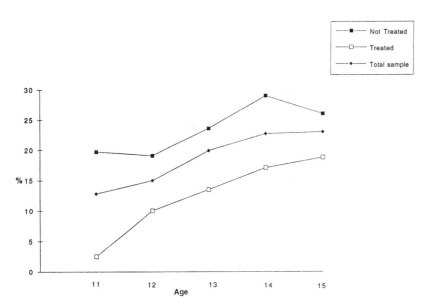

Figure 12.5. Percentage of Boys Between 11 and 15 Years Old Who Reported Being Gang Members

that the participation in deviant gangs, for the total sample of boys assessed in kindergarten (middle line), increased from 12.8% at age 11 to 23.0% at age 15. Only 2.5% of the treated boys reported being gang members at age 11 compared to 19.7% for the untreated boys. That difference was slightly reduced at age 12, but the comparison of the repeated measures (ages 11, 13, and 15) for the two groups (PRO CATMOD, SAS) indicated statistically significant differences, X^2 (1, 131) = 6.74, $p < .01$. Thus, the treated boys were less at risk of being involved in deviant gangs during the period when boys are at increased risk for this type of involvement.

Substance Abuse

Experimentation involving early alcohol and drug use is one of the important challenges youth must face. Substance abuse is associated with both delinquency and mental health problems (e.g., Elliott, Huizinga, & Menard, 1989). Figures 12.6 and 12.7 show the percentages of boys, from 11 to 15 years of age, who reported having been drunk or having taken drugs in the past 12 months. It can be seen that the percentage of boys from the

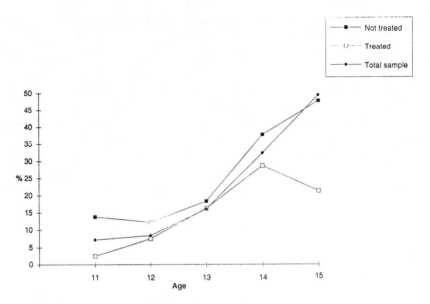

Figure 12.6. Percentage of Boys Between 11 and 15 Years Old Who Reported Having Been Drunk in the Past 12 Months

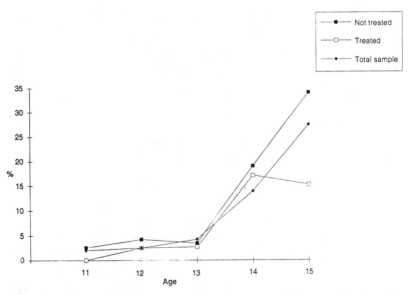

Figure 12.7. Percentage of Boys Between 11 and 15 Years Old Who Reported Having Taken Drugs During the Past 12 Months

total sample who reported having been drunk in the past 12 months increases linearly from age 12 (8.4%) to age 15 (47.6%). The treated and untreated boys follow that pattern up to age 14, but significantly fewer treated boys than untreated boys reported drinking to the point of being drunk at 15 years of age, X^2 (1, 132) = 6.57, $p < .02$. Similar results were obtained for drugs. The linear increase, however, began 1 year later (age 13), at a lower level (4.3% of the total sample), and reached 27.4% at age 15. At this particular age, significantly fewer treated boys reported having taken drugs compared to the untreated boys, X^2 (1, 133) = 4.25, $p < .05$.

Self-Reported Delinquency

Boys' annual reports on frequency of delinquent acts (stealing, vandalism, and substance use) indicate that the treated boys were significantly less involved in delinquency than the untreated boys from age 10 (1 year after the end of treatment) to age 15 (6 years after the end of treatment) (see Tremblay, Kurtz, Mâsse, Vitaro, & Pihl, 1995).

Subjects' Police Arrests

Being arrested by the police is not always the best indicator of delinquent behavior. Youth are not arrested for all their delinquent acts, and some are arrested although they have not committed any transgressions. The probability of being arrested, however, is generally associated with the frequency and severity of delinquent behavior (see Hindelang, Hirschi, & Weiss, 1981). Figure 12.8 presents the percentage of boys from ages 11 to 15 who reported having been arrested over a period of 12 months. No important differences were found between the treated and untreated groups from ages 11 to 13. Between ages 13 and 15, however, the differences between the treated and untreated boys increase systematically. The untreated boys tended to report more police arrests than the treated boys, PRO CATMOD X^2 (1, 129) = 3.35, $p = .07$.

Friends' Police Arrests

It was observed previously that, between 10 and 12 years of age, the treated boys had mutual friends who were less disruptive compared to the untreated boys. If the treatment had a lasting impact on quality of friends, one would expect that treated boys would show a lesser tendency of having

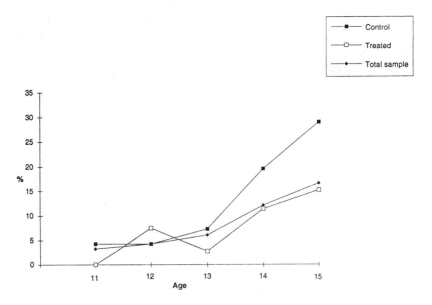

Figure 12.8. Percentage of Boys Between 11 and 15 Years Old Who Reported Having Been Arrested During the Past 12 Months

friends who get in trouble with the police. Gang membership described previously indicated that this was the case. Figure 12.9 shows that treated boys from ages 11 to 15 showed a lower frequency of having friends being arrested by the police than untreated boys. The between-group differences were not statistically significant from ages 11 to 13, but they were found to be significant from ages 13 to 15, PRO CATMOD X^2 (1, 124) = 4.41, $p <$ .05.

By comparing Figures 12.8 and 12.9, it can be observed that more boys report police arrests of friends than of themselves. This could be explained by the fact that most boys have more than one friend; thus, there are more friends to be arrested. The curvilinear trend of Figure 12.9, however, is surprising. The difference between friends' arrests and self-arrest is largest at 11 years of age. At least three explanations are plausible. First, at younger ages some boys may tend to exaggerate their friends' deviancy. Second, at age 11 the boys may be associating with older boys who are more likely to be arrested by the police, as can be seen by the self-report data of Figure 12.8. Finally, the "friend" definition at younger ages may be larger (nonmutual) than that at older ages (mutual).

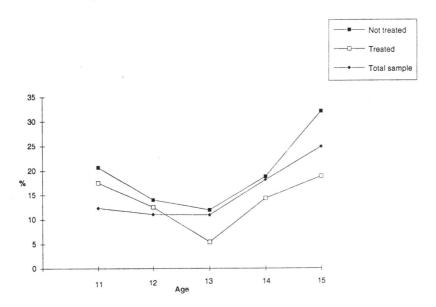

Figure 12.9. Percentage of Boys Between 11 and 15 Years Old Who Reported That Their Best Friends Were Arrested

Sexual Intercourse

Early initiation of sexual intercourse can be an indication of some form of adjustment problems (Hayes, 1987). Figure 12.10 shows that, from ages 13 to 15, more of the disruptive kindergarten boys compared to the total sample tended to report having had sexual intercourse. No significant differences, however, were observed between the treated and untreated boys.

School Motivation and Class Placement

As reported previously, the treated boys appeared to be better adjusted at the end of elementary school compared to the untreated boys. It was expected that this would be reflected in the boys' motivation for school and class placement in high school. Figure 12.11 shows that, from ages 10 to 15, the percentage of boys who reported liking school decreased linearly. The untreated group consistently had the smallest proportion of boys who reported liking school. The differences in proportions between the treated and untreated groups, however, was not found to be statistically significant. Class

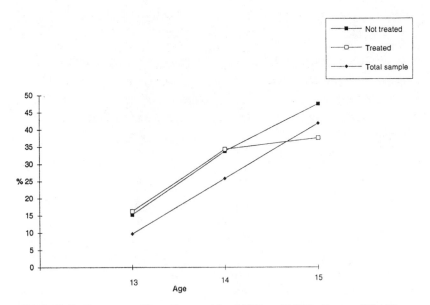

Figure 12.10. Percentage of Boys Between 13 and 15 Years Old Who Reported That They Had Sexual Intercourse

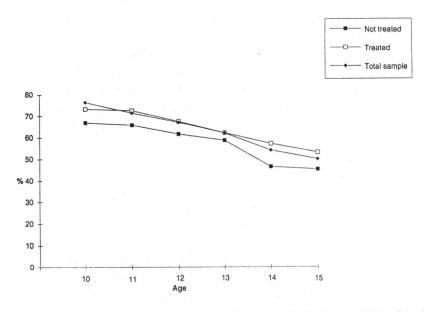

Figure 12.11. Percentage of Boys Between 10 and 15 Years Old Who Reported Liking School

placement at age 15 also revealed the absence of a significant difference between the treated and untreated groups. By that age, only 45.2% of the total sample were still in an AARC (33.3% treated and 32.2% untreated). These results suggest that the impact of the treatment on school achievement and school motivation, although statistically significant during the course of elementary school, may have been insufficient to help the treated boys overcome the new challenges of high school (see Tremblay et al., 1995). The current treatment, however, did not directly target school achievement or school motivation.

CONCLUSION

The Montreal longitudinal-experimental study represents an attempt to study both the development of boys' aggressive behavior and the effect of an early bimodal intensive intervention to prevent juvenile delinquency. The study has shown that (a) aggressive kindergarten boys have specific individual and family characteristics, (b) they are at high risk for delinquency and other adjustment problems during early adolescence, and (c) an intensive intervention during the first years of elementary school can have a positive impact on global adjustment during the latter part of the elementary school years and on delinquent behavior up to age 15.

The study demonstrates the usefulness of nesting a prevention experiment within the context of a repeated measures longitudinal study to better understand both the development of adjustment problems and the developmental impact of an intervention (Farrington, 1992; Tonry et al., 1991). From a strictly developmental perspective, results showed that the differences in adjustment problems between the disruptive kindergarten boys (represented by the untreated group in the figures) and the total sample varied over time and variables. For example, the difference in school placement had an inverted U shape—it increased from first grade to entry into high school and decreased thereafter (see Tremblay et al., 1995); the difference in gang membership and delinquency was present by age 11 and remained relatively stable up to age 15; and the difference in police arrests appeared only at age 14. From a treatment effect perspective, it was clear that the treatment appeared to show its most significant impact (i.e., the differences between the treated and untreated groups) when the differences between the disruptive kindergarten boys (represented by the untreated group) and the total sample were largest. For example, the largest difference between the treated and untreated groups for police arrests was at age 15 when the largest difference was observed between the total sample and the untreated group. When there were no differences between the total sample and the group of disruptive kindergarten boys, it would have been surprising to observe a difference between the treated and untreated group. Thus, to identify treatment effects, assessments must be made on the appropriate variable at the appropriate point in time. This rule could explain inconsistencies in results among treatment experiments that do not assess the same outcome at the same developmental period.

The treatment effects observed in this prevention experiment are encouraging. They show that an intensive intervention with disruptive boys during early elementary school can have a significant impact on different dimensions of their development over many years. The impact, however, is probably far from what is needed to bring most of these boys to a level of social adjustment that will enable them to be happy and productive members of the community. The follow-up of these boys in adulthood will enable us to confirm or disconfirm this prediction. For the moment, two courses of action appear necessary to increase the impact of these interventions.

First, because it is unlikely that any intervention at one point in time, however intensive, will have a lifelong impact, booster sessions should be offered at strategic points in the development of such boys (e.g., during the transition to high school). These booster sessions should obviously be targeted at age-specific developmental challenges (e.g., alcohol and gangs between ages 10 and 12 and drugs and sexual intercourse between ages 12 and 14). Parents may also benefit from booster workshops during their children's developmental transitions. Special emphasis can be placed on child-rearing issues that are particular to the developmental period their children are experiencing.

Second, because chronic physical aggression had been clearly in place by the kindergarten years for many of these boys, we need to offer interventions much earlier in that developmental process. Although the High/Scope Perry Preschool Study was not aimed at children with behavior problems, it showed that an intervention between ages 3 and 5 with poor children and their families had a long-term impact on antisocial behavior and other forms of social maladjustment (Schweinhart, Barnes, & Weikart, 1993). The Carolina Early Intervention Program (Ramey, Bryant, Campbell, Sparling, & Wasik, 1988), the Houston Parent-Child Development Center (Johnson,

1990), and the Syracuse University Family Development Research Program (Lally, Mangione, & Honig, 1988) all had similar long-term effects. From the perspective of a cumulative risk model (Barker, 1992; Coie et al., 1993; Tremblay & Craig, 1995; Yoshikawa, 1994), which proposes that the cumulation of multiple risk factors in early childhood can lead to a large variety of physical and mental health problems throughout the life span, it can be hypothesized that the earlier and the more comprehensive the intervention, the greater will be the impact over the life span.

It logically follows that interventions involving at-risk young girls and their mates before, during, and after pregnancy should be the most cost-effective form of preventive intervention. Unfortunately, most preventive and corrective efforts to prevent aggressive and antisocial behavior, including the present study, have been aimed at males clearly because they are more overtly disruptive to society. A true preventive approach, based on our present knowledge of human development, should result in more attention to girls with adjustment problems. Perhaps because they are less of an open threat to society than the antisocial male, they get less attention, including services (Offord, Bolye, & Racine, 1991). Nevertheless, if they mate with antisocial males or do not receive adequate support, they are at high risk of becoming the parents of the next generation of antisocial boys (Lahey et al., 1988, 1989; Quinton & Rutter, 1988; Robins et al., 1975; Serbin, Peters, McAffer, & Shwartzman, 1991).

We need to convince ourselves, policymakers, and the public at large that control of violent impulses is learned in the first 2 or 3 years of life. If self-control is not learned by age 3, the child is propelled into a feedback loop in which peer, teacher, and parent rejection justifies more and more aggressive reactions. Mothers are the main care providers during this critical period. In most cases, they provide the care needed to learn self-control and prosocial interactions. In many cases, they act as a buffer between the child and an inadequate father. When a mother has a history of behavior problems, however, she is unlikely to have a mate who will act as a buffer for the child. This child (male or female) is then unlikely to learn self-control and prosocial skills. Because females are more often the educators of very young children and because they appear to be more receptive to support, putting our limited resources into helping young girls who have adjustment problems would probably be more cost effective in the long run than putting most of our resources into trying to treat aggressive males.

NOTES

1. Two hundred forty-nine subjects were reported to have met the criteria of Tremblay et al. (1991b). Recent verification of the demographic information obtained from the families revealed that 6 of these subjects had one parent (four fathers and two mothers) with 15 years or more of schooling. (These subjects were not included in the analyses reported here.)

2. This factor was originally labeled "aggression," but it contains only two purely physical aggression items. The content is similar to that of the disruptive factor of the SBQ.

REFERENCES

Barker, D. J. P. (1992). *Fetal and infant origins of adult disease.* London: British Medical Association.

Behar, L. B., & Stringfield, S. (1974). A behavior rating scale for the preschool child. *Developmental Psychology, 10,* 601-610.

Bertrand, L. (1988). *Projet pilote de prévention du développement des comportements antisociaux chez des garçons agressifs à la maternelle: Guides d'intervention.* Montréal, Canada: Université de Montréal, Groupe de recherche inter-universitaire sur la prévention de l'inadaptation psychosociale.

Blishen, B. R., Carroll, W. K., & Moore, C. (1987). The 1981 socioeconomic index for occupations in Canada. *Canadian Review of Sociology and Anthropology, 24,* 465-488.

Brooks-Gunn, J., & Reiter, E. O. (1990). The role of pubertal processes. In S. S. Feldman & G. R. Elliott (Eds.), *At the threshold: The developing adolescent* (pp. 16-53). Cambridge, MA: Harvard University Press.

Cairns, R. B. (1986). An evolutionary and developmental perspective on aggressive patterns. In C. Zahn-Waxler, E. M. Cummings, & R. Iannotti (Eds.), *Altruism and aggression: Biological and social origins* (pp. 55-87). New York: Cambridge University Press.

Cairns, R. B., Cairns, B. D., Neckerman, H. J., Ferguson, L. L., & Gariépy, J. L. (1989). Growth and aggression: 1. Childhood to early adolescence. *Developmental Psychology, 25,* 320-330.

Camp, B. W., Blom, G. E., Hebert, F., & Van Doorminck, W. J. (1977). Think Aloud: A program for developing self-control in young aggressive boys. *Journal of Abnormal Child Psychology, 5,* 157-169.

Cartledge, G., & Milburn, J. F. (1980). *Teaching social skills to children. Innovative approaches.* New York: Pergamon.

Coie, J. D., Watt, N. F., West, S. G., Hawkins, J. D., Asarnow, J. R., Markman, H. J., Ramey, S. L., Shure, M. B., & Long, B. (1993). The science of prevention: A conceptual framework and some directions for a national research program. *American Psychologist, 48,* 1013-1022.

Crespo, M. (1977). *Un instrument pour le choix des écoles élémentaires dans le cadre de l'opération renouveau Montréal.* Montréal, Canada: Commission des Écoles catholiques de Montréal.

Cummings, E. M., Iannotti, R. J., & Zahn-Waxler, C. (1989). Aggression between peers in early childhood: Individual continuity and developmental change. *Child Development, 60,* 887-895.

Dawe, H. C. (1934). An analysis of 200 quarrels of preschool children. *Child Development, 5,* 139-157.

Dodge, K. A., Bates, J. F., & Pettit, G. S. (1990). Mechanisms in the cycle of violence. *Science, 250,* 1678-1683.

Elliott, S., Huizinga, D., & Menard, S. (1989). *Multiple problem youth.* New York/Berlin: Springer-Verlag.

Eron, L. D. (1990). Understanding aggression. *Bulletin of the International Society for Research on Aggression, 12,* 5-9.

Farrington, D. P. (1991). Childhood aggression and adult violence: Early precursors and life outcomes. In D. J. Pepler & K. H. Rubin (Eds.), *Development and treatment of childhood aggression* (pp. 5-29). Hillsdale, NJ: Lawrence Erlbaum.

Farrington, D. P. (1992). The need for longitudinal-experimental research on offending and antisocial behavior. In J. McCord & R. E. Tremblay (Eds.), *Preventing antisocial behavior: Interventions from birth through adolescence* (pp. 353-376). New York: Guilford.

Farrington, D. P. (1994). Childhood, adolescent, and adult features of violent males. In L. R. Huesmann (Ed.), *Aggressive behavior: Current perspectives* (pp. 215-240). New York: Plenum.

Goldstein, A. P., Sprafkin, R. P., Gershaw, N. J., & Klein, P. (1980). The adolescent: Social skills training through structured learning. In G. Cartledge & J. F. Milburn (Eds.), *Teaching social skills to children: Innovative approaches* (pp. 249-277). New York: Pergamon.

Gottfredson, M. R., & Hirschi, T. (1990). *A general theory of crime.* Stanford, CA: Stanford University Press.

Gouze, K. R. (1987). Attention and social problem solving as correlates of aggression in preschool males. *Journal of Abnormal Child Psychology, 15,* 181-197.

Green, E. H. (1933). Friendships and quarrels among preschool children. *Child Development, 4,* 237-252.

Haapasalo, J., & Tremblay, R. E. (1994). Physically aggressive boys from age 6 to 12: Family background, parenting behavior, and prediction of delinquency. *Journal of Consulting and Clinical Psychology, 62,* 1044-1052.

Hartup, W. W. (1974). Aggression in childhood. *American Psychologist, 29,* 336-341.

Hawkins, J. D., Catalano, R. F., Morrison, D. M., O'Donnell, J., Abbott, R. D., & Day, L. E. (1992). The Seattle Social Development Project: Effects of the first four years on protective factors and problem behaviors. In J. McCord & R. E. Tremblay (Eds.), *Preventing antisocial behavior: Intervention from birth through adolescence* (pp. 162-195). New York: Guilford.

Hayes, C. D. (1987). *Risking the future: Adolescent sexuality, pregnancy and child bearing.* Washington, DC: National Academy Press.

Hindelang, M. J., Hirschi, T., & Weis, J. G. (1981). *Measuring delinquency.* Beverly Hills, CA: Sage.

Holmberg, M. C. (1980). The development of social interchange patterns from 12 to 42 months. *Child Development, 51,* 448-456.

Huesmann, L. R., Eron, L. D., Lefkowitz, M. M., & Walder, L. O. (1984). Stability of aggression over time and generations. *Developmental Psychology, 20,* 1120-1134.

Johnson, D. L. (1990). The Houston Parent-Child Development Center Project: Dissemination of a viable program for enhancing at-risk families. In R. P. Lorion (Ed.), *Protecting the children: Strategies for optimizing emotional and behavioral development* (pp. 89-108). London: Haworth.

Keating, D. P. (1990). Adolescent thinking. In S. S. Feldman & G. R. Elliott (Eds.), *At the threshold: The developing adolescent* (pp. 54-89). Cambridge, MA: Harvard University Press.

Kettlewell, P. W., & Kausch, D. F. (1983). The generalization of the effects of a cognitive behavioral treatment program for aggressive children. *Journal of Abnormal Child Psychology, 11,* 101-114.

Lahey, B. B., Hartdargen, S. E., Frick, P. J., McBurnett, K., Connor, R., & Hynd, G. W. (1988). Conduct disorder: Parsing the confounded relation to parental divorce and antisocial personality. *Journal of Abnormal Psychology, 97,* 334-337.

Lahey, B. B., Russo, M. F., Walker, J. L., & Piacentini, J. C. (1989). Personality characteristics of the mothers of children with disruptive behavior disorders. *Journal of Consulting and Clinical Psychology, 57,* 512-515.

Lally, J. R., Mangione, P. L., & Honig, A. S. (1988). The Syracuse University Family Development Research Program: Long-range impact of an early intervention with low-income children and their families. In D. R. Powell (Ed.), *Parent education as early childhood intervention: Emerging directions in theory, research, and practice* (pp. 79-104). Norwood, NJ: Ablex.

Lavigueur, S., Saucier, J. F., & Tremblay, R. E. (1995). Supporting fathers and supported mothers in families with disruptive boys: Who are they? *Journal of Child Psychology and Psychiatry, 36,* 1003-1018.

Lavigueur, S., Tremblay, R. E., & Saucier, J. F. (1993). Can spouse support be accurately and reliably rated? A generalizability study of families with disruptive boys. *Journal of Child Psychology and Psychiatry, 34,* 689-714.

Lavigueur, S., Tremblay, R. E., & Saucier, J. F. (1995). Interactional processes in families with disruptive boys: Patterns of direct and indirect influence. *Journal of Abnormal Child Psychology, 23,* 359-377.

Lipsey, M. W., & Wilson, D. B. (1993). The efficacy of psychological, educational, and behavioral treatment: Confirmation from meta-analysis. *American Psychologist, 48,* 1181-1209.

McCord, J., Tremblay, R. E., Vitaro, F., & Desmarais-Gervais, L. (1994). Boys' disruptive behavior, school adjustment, and delinquency: The Montreal prevention experiment. *International Journal of Behavioral Development, 17,* 739-752.

Meichenbaum, D. (1977). *Cognitive-behavior modification: An integrative approach.* New York: Plenum.

Michelson, L., Sugai, D., Wood, R., & Kazdin, A. E. (1983). *Social skills assessment and training with children.* New York: Plenum.

Mrazek, P. J., & Haggerty, R. J. (Eds.). (1994). *Reducing risks for mental disorders: Frontiers for preventive intervention research.* Washington, DC: National Academy Press.

Offord, D., Boyle, M. C., & Racine, Y. A. (1991). The epidemiology of antisocial behavior in childhood and adolescence. In D. Pepler & K. Rubin (Eds.), *The development and treatment of aggression* (pp. 31-54). Hillsdale, NJ: Lawrence Erlbaum.

Olweus, D. (1979). Stability of aggressive reaction patterns in males: A review. *Psychological Bulletin, 85,* 852-875.

Patterson, G. R. (1982). *Coercive family process.* Eugene, OR: Castalia.

Patterson, G. R., Reid, J. B., Jones, R. R., & Conger, R. R. (1975). *A social learning approach to family intervention: Families with aggressive children* (Vol. 1). Eugene, OR: Castalia.

Pekarik, E. G., Prinz, R. J., Liebert, D. E., Weintraub, S., & Neale, J. N. (1976). The Pupil Evaluation Inventory. *Journal of Abnormal Child Psychology, 4,* 83-97.

Pulkkinen, L., & Tremblay, R. E. (1992). Patterns of boys' social adjustment in two cultures and at different ages: A longitudinal perspective. *International Journal of Behavioural Development, 15,* 527-553.

Quinton, D., & Rutter, M. (1988). *Parenting breakdown: The making and breaking of intergenerational links.* Aldershot, UK: Avebury.

Ramey, C. T., Bryant, D. M., Campbell, F. A., Sparling, J. J., & Wasik, B. H. (1988). Early intervention for high-risk children: The Carolina Early Intervention Program. In R. H. Price, E. L. Cowen, R. P. Lorion, & J. Ramos-McKay (Eds.), *14 ounces of prevention* (pp. 32-52). Washington, DC: American Psychological Association.

Ramey, C. T., Bryant, D. M., Campbell, F. A., Sparling, J. J., & Wasik, B. H. (1990). Early intervention for high-risk children: The Carolina Early Intervention Program. *Prevention in Human Services, 7,* 33-57.

Reiss, A. J., & Roth, J. A. (Eds.). (1993). *Understanding and preventing violence.* Washington, DC: National Academy Press.

Restoin, A., Montagner, H., Rodriguez, D., Girardot, J. J., Laurent, D., Kontar, F., Ullmann, V., Casagrande, C., & Talpain, B. (1985). Chronologie des comportements de communication et profils de comportement chez le jeune enfant. In R. E. Tremblay, M. A. Provost, & F. F. Strayer (Eds.), *Ethologie et développement de l'enfant* (pp. 93-130). Paris: Editions Stock/Laurence Pernoud.

Robins, L. N., West, P. A., & Herjanic, B. L. (1975). Arrest and delinquency in two generations: A study of black urban families and their children. *Journal of Child Psychology and Psychiatry and Allied Disciplines, 16,* 125-140.

Rotheram, M. J. (1982). Social skills training with underachievers, disruptive, and exceptional children. *Psychology in the Schools, 19,* 532-539.

Rubin, K. H., & Clark, M. L. (1983). Preschool teachers' ratings of behavioral problems: Observational, sociometric and social cognitive correlates. *Journal of Abnormal Child Psychology, 11,* 273-286.

Schneider, B. H., & Byrne, B. M. (1987). Individualizing social skills training for behavior-disordered children. *Journal of Consulting and Clinical Psychology, 55,* 444-445.

Schwartz, D., Flamant, R., & Lellouch, J. (1980). *Clinical trials.* New York: Academic Press.

Schweinhart, L. L., Barnes, H. V., & Weikart, D. P. (1993). *Significant benefits. The High/Scope Perry School Study through age 27.* Ypsilanti, MI: High/Scope Press.

Serbin, L. A., Peters, P. L., McAffer, V. J., & Shwartzman, A. E. (1991). Childhood aggression and withdrawal as predictors of adolescent pregnancy, early parenthood, and environmental risk for the next generation. *Canadian Journal of Behavioural Science, 23,* 318-331.

Shure, M. B., & Spivack, G. (1980). Interpersonal problem solving as a mediator of behavioral adjustment in preschool and kindergarten children. *Journal of Applied Developmental Psychology, 1,* 29-44.

Singer, D., Singer, J. L., & Zuckerman, D. M. (1981). *Getting the most out of TV.* Santa Monica, CA: Goodyear.

Singer, J. L., & Singer, D. G. (1981). *Television, imagination and aggression: A study of preschoolers' play.* Hillsdale, NJ: Lawrence Erlbaum.

Stattin, H., & Magnusson, D. (1989). The role of early aggressive behavior in the frequency, seriousness and types of later crime. *Journal of Consulting and Clinical Psychology, 57,* 710-718.

Strayer, F. F., Moss, E. S., Trudel, M., & Jacques, M. (1986). Activités agonistiques durant les années préscolaires. In J. LeCamus & J. Cosnier (Eds.), *Ethology and psychology* (pp. 67-76). Toulouse, France: Privat, I.E.C.

Strayer, F. F., & Trudel, M. (1984). Developmental changes in the nature and function of social dominance among young children. *Ethology and Sociobiology, 5,* 279-295.

Strayhorn, J. M., & Weidman, C. (1991). Follow-up one year after parent-child interaction training: Effects on behavior of preschool children. *Journal of the American Academy of Child and Adolescent Psychiatry, 30,* 138-143.

Tonry, M., Ohlin, L. E., Farrington, D. P., Adams, K., Earls, F., Rowe, D. C., Sampson, R. J., & Tremblay, R. E. (1991). *Human development and criminal behavior: New ways of advancing knowledge.* New York/Berlin: Springer-Verlag.

Tremblay, R. E., & Craig, W. (1995). Developmental crime prevention. In M. Tonry & D. P. Farrington (Eds.), *Building a safer society: Strategic approaches to crime* (Vol. 19, pp. 151-236). Chicago: University of Chicago Press.

Tremblay, R. E., Kurtz, L., Mâsse, L. C., Vitaro, F., & Pihl, R. O. (1995). A bimodal preventive intervention for disruptive kindergarten boys: Its impact through mid-adolescence. *Journal of Consulting and Clinical Psychology, 63,* 560-568.

Tremblay, R. E., Loeber, R., Gagnon, C., Charlebois, P., Larivée, S., & LeBlanc, M. (1991a). Disruptive boys with stable and unstable high fighting behavior patterns during junior elementary school. *Journal of Abnormal Child Psychology, 19,* 285-300.

Tremblay, R. E., McCord, J., Boileau, H., Charlebois, P., Gagnon, C., LeBlanc, M., & Larivée, S. (1991b). Can disruptive boys be helped to become competent? *Psychiatry, 54,* 148-161.

Tremblay, R. E., Pihl, R. O., Vitaro, F., & Dobkin, P. L. (1994). Predicting early onset of male antisocial behavior from preschool behavior: A test of two personality theories. *Archives of General Psychiatry, 51,* 732-738.

Tremblay, R. E., Vitaro, F., Bertrand, L., LeBlanc, M., Beauchesne, H., Boileau, H., & David, H. (1992). Parent and child training to prevent early onset of delinquency: The Montreal longitudinal-experimental study. In J. McCord & R. E. Tremblay (Eds.), *Preventing antisocial behavior: Interventions from birth through adolescence* (pp. 117-138). New York: Guilford.

Vitaro, F., & Tremblay, R. E. (1994). Impact of a prevention program on aggressive-disruptive children's friendships and social adjustment. *Journal of Abnormal Child Psychology, 22,* 457-475.

Vitaro, F., Tremblay, R. E., Gagnon, C., & Boivin, M. (1992). Peer rejection from kindergarten to grade 2: Outcomes, correlates, and prediction. *Merrill-Palmer Quarterly, 38,* 382-400.

Weikart, D. P., & Schweinhart, L. J. (1992). High/Scope preschool program outcomes. In J. McCord & R. E. Tremblay (Eds.), *Preventing antisocial behavior: Interventions from birth to adolescence* (pp. 67-86). New York: Guilford.

Yoshikawa, H. (1994). Prevention as cumulative protection: Effects of early family support and education on chronic delinquency and its risks. *Psychological Bulletin, 115,* 28-54.

13

Illustrating a Framework for Rural Prevention Research

PROJECT FAMILY STUDIES OF RURAL FAMILY PARTICIPATION AND OUTCOMES

RICHARD SPOTH

CLEVE REDMOND

A recent report on the prevention of mental disorders by the Institute of Medicine ([IOM], 1994) provides a framework for preventive intervention research that can be productively applied to rural populations. The "preventive intervention research cycle" presented by the IOM (pp. 359-414) articulates five phases of research. In summary form, these phases are

AUTHORS' NOTE: Work on this chapter was supported by Research Grant MH 49217-01A1 from the National Institute of Mental Health and by Research Grant DA 070 29-01A1 from the National Institute on Drug Abuse. The authors gratefully acknowledge comments and editorial assistance from Karol Kumpfer, Thomas Ward, and Jeffrey H. Kahn.

(a) identifying the problem and determining its distribution in the target population; (b) reviewing relevant etiological data on risk and protective factors; (c) conducting pilot, confirmatory, and replication studies of the intervention; (d) conducting large-scale field studies of the intervention's effectiveness; and (e) facilitating large-scale intervention implementation. The research cycle progresses through iterations of these phases, with research at a particular phase informing subsequent work specific to both earlier and later phases (see Muehrer, Moscicki, & Koretz, 1993). This chapter addresses key rural prevention research needs and illustrative responses to those needs within the IOM conceptual framework.

The IOM (1994) report presenting the preventive intervention research cycle discusses several intervention research needs important to the investigation of universal prevention programs for rural families. One relevant need stressed in the IOM report concerns the dearth of controlled studies of universal interventions or those designed for all people in an eligible population (see Gordon, 1983). Although universal interventions seeking to enhance family skills have been widely disseminated, there have been virtually no controlled studies examining their effects in terms of either specific risk reduction or the prevention of mental disorders (IOM, 1994; see also U.S. Department of Justice, 1992; Wiese, 1992; Yoshikawa, 1994). This chapter presents findings from a project that incorporates large-scale, controlled studies of theory-based, universal family skills programs offered to rural populations.

A second research need underscored in the IOM (1994) report concerns factors influencing variations in intervention participation among special populations. A key activity during the intervention research phases of the cycle is securing cooperation from appropriate participants. During these phases, it is useful to uncover values, goals, and motives associated with the intervention in the local population. Also, careful tracking of variations in participant responses to recruitment and retention strategies is of great importance (IOM, 1994). This chapter will illustrate several consumer research studies and a prospective investigation of participation predictors designed to evaluate factors associated with variations in rural population response to recruitment activities.

Another important activity during the intervention research phases of the cycle is the evaluation of target population characteristics that can influence the efficacy of intervention strategies designed to alter risk and protective factors. Variations in response to preventive intervention strategies can be expected among groups differing in characteristics such as educational level, rural versus urban composition, and other factors (IOM, 1994). Moreover, the IOM report emphasizes the need for researchers to be sensitive to characteristics of special populations, particularly cultural diversity. This chapter incorporates a discussion of the need for the study of variations in responses to prevention efforts in the targeted rural populations; it also presents models illustrating the examination of a range of factors influencing varying rural family outcomes.

The application of the preventive intervention research cycle to rural populations described in this chapter will follow the same sequence as the phases presented in the IOM's (1994) conceptual framework. Consistent with the problem identification and knowledge-base review phases of the preventive intervention research cycle, this chapter begins with a review of the need for prevention research targeting rural families (Phase 1) and a brief summary of family-related etiological factors, including recent rural family research conducted at our Center (Phase 2). An overview of project procedures and rural implementation strategies is then given (Phases 3 and 4). Finally, the chapter will illustrate studies used during Phases 3 and 4 to examine rural family characteristics influencing response to project recruitment strategies and to the project interventions.

The conceptual framework for preventive intervention research with rural families illustrated in this chapter is an initial step in articulating key research tasks, problems, and solutions in prevention research specifically targeting rural populations. This field of prevention research is very much in its formative stages. One indication of this formative stage of development is the almost complete absence of references on prevention of rural mental health problems in the *Rural Health Research Compendium* (National Rural Health Association, 1989). Key research issues of relevance to each phase of mental disorder prevention research in rural populations are just beginning to be addressed. A technical review sponsored by the National Institute of Mental Health has outlined a broad range of theoretical, methodological, and practical issues concerning rural prevention-relevant epidemiology, etiology, intervention evaluation, and service delivery (Spoth, 1994). This work, however, has only recently begun. Thus, this chapter focuses on a potentially helpful conceptual framework that can be considered a preliminary step toward future analyses of critical issues specific to each phase of prevention research.

THE NEED FOR PREVENTION
RESEARCH WITH RURAL FAMILIES

Comparisons of rural and urban populations suggest that there are disproportionately greater numbers of groups at risk for health problems in rural areas, such as families living in poverty (Human & Wassem, 1991; Wagenfeld, Murray, Mohatt, & DeBruyn, 1994). Moreover, worsening rural economic conditions have exacerbated the risks in these vulnerable groups (Murray & Keller, 1991; National Mental Health Association, 1988). In particular, economic stress in rural families has led to increased risk for emotional distress among parents and strains in family relations (Conger & Elder, 1994). Indeed, several studies over the past decade have indicated an increase in a range of mental health problems among farm families, among which depression has been most noteworthy (e.g., Beeson & Johnson, 1987; Wagenfeld et al., 1994).

The increasing prevalence of mental health problems among rural youth is of central importance to rural prevention efforts. Research documents a trend toward higher rates of conduct problems, substance use, and other adjustment difficulties among rural youth (Conger & Elder, 1994). Studies conducted in the rural Midwest provide some good examples. An investigation of 17,360 7th- through 12th-grade Minnesota youth (Blum, McKay, & Resnick, 1989) indicates that the incidence of antisocial acts of rural 7th to 9th graders is comparable to that found nationally. Other researchers have also documented problematic trends in antisocial behavior among rural youth and have suggested that economic stress among rural families contributes to these problems (Conger et al., 1992; Conger & Elder, 1994; Conger, Elder, Lorenz, Simons, & Whitbeck, 1991; Lempers, Clark-Lempers, & Simons, 1989).

Substance use among rural youth is another significant problem. Rates of rural substance use have often been found to match or exceed national levels and levels of use by urban youth (Johnston, O'Malley, & Bachman, 1989, 1994; Sarvela, Newcomb, & Duncan, 1988; Wagenfeld et al., 1994). For example, the Monitoring the Future Study (Johnston et al., 1994) confirms that nonurban (non-Standard Metropolitan Statistical Area [SMSA]) middle and high school students have prevalence rates of alcohol use similar to those of urban middle and high school students. To illustrate this point, the most recent Monitoring the Future survey has shown that the past-month prevalence rate of alcohol use is very similar when comparing eighth graders from non-SMSA areas with those from large SMSA areas (25.1% vs. 24.7%, respectively).

The project highlighted in this chapter, Project Family, targets youth in Iowa. Alcohol is the most commonly used substance by Iowa youth. Data from a comprehensive, triennial substance use survey of Iowa youth (Iowa Department of Education, 1994) show that alcohol use rates are higher than the national average, as indicated by the most recent national household survey (U.S. Department of Health and Human Services, 1994) as well as by the Monitoring the Future Study (Johnston et al., 1994). These data are also consistent with a trend reported by the U.S. General Accounting Office (1990) indicating a more rapid increase in rural-state substance abuse compared with urban-state substance abuse across several age groups, from roughly two thirds the level of urban abuse in the early 1980s to comparable levels by the end of the decade.

At the same time rural youth and their families are showing increasing levels of mental health and substance-related risk factors and problems, there seem to be increasing barriers to the delivery of effective preventive services. Although it has been over 18 years since the President's Commission on Mental Health Task Panel on Rural Mental Health concluded that many of the then-existing approaches to service delivery were inappropriate for rural areas, limited progress has been made in addressing these issues since then (Murray & Keller, 1991). Instead, deficiencies in the availability, accessibility, and acceptability of mental health services for rural families have become increasingly evident (Human & Wassem, 1991; Hunter & Windle, 1991; Murray & Keller, 1991; National Mental Health Association, 1988).

Given the prevalence of mental health problems among rural youth and families, the dearth of research on rural preventive interventions is particularly striking (see Wagenfeld et al., 1994). For example, a review of the *Rural Health Research Compendium* (National Rural Health Association, 1989) revealed that only 2 of 621 citations concerned prevention of mental disorders in rural populations. Furthermore, a conceptual framework to guide the development of a rural prevention services research agenda, carefully addressing the diversity of rural populations, has yet to be developed. The reports of the IOM (1994) and National Institute of Mental Health (Coie et al., 1993) on preventive intervention research could be productively applied toward this end.

FAMILY-RELATED ETIOLOGICAL
MODELS AND RURAL APPLICATIONS

The IOM (1994) report on preventive intervention research underscores the importance of the knowledge base on which intervention research is built. Central to the task of reviewing the extant knowledge base is an examination of predisposing biopsychosocial risk factors as well as personal and environmental protective factors. The empirical and theoretical bases for the Project Family work discussed below are consistent with this point of emphasis in the IOM model as well as with the results of studies suggesting that preventive interventions are crucial for diminishing family risk behaviors in those families experiencing significant stress (Conger & Elder, 1994; McCubbin, Needle, & Wilson, 1985; Patterson, 1986).

There are several risk factors for adolescent problem behaviors, particularly conduct problems and substance use, that are related to family processes and can be addressed through family-focused preventive interventions. Researchers have long noted that a variety of adolescent problem behaviors, including delinquency and drug use, frequently coexist (Elliott, Huizinga, & Ageton, 1982; Jessor & Jessor, 1978). The coexistence of conduct problems and substance use, and their frequent linkage through a general pattern of problem behaviors, suggests common etiological factors that have been supported by research (Caspi, Elder, & Bem, 1987; IOM, 1994; Kazdin, 1987). Risk factors shared by conduct problems and substance use problems are particularly evident in the case of family-related risks. Parental antisocial behavior predicts not only adolescent antisocial behavior but also adolescent drug use (Loeber & Dishion, 1983). Moreover, parenting practices seem to account for a large portion of the variance in both antisocial behavior and substance use in adolescent males (Patterson, 1986; Patterson, Dishion, & Bank, 1984).

The work of Patterson and colleagues (e.g., Patterson, 1986; Patterson, DeBaryshe, & Ramsey, 1989; Patterson et al., 1984) that has been directed toward the clarification of family-related risk factors for adolescent maladjustment and antisocial behaviors is especially relevant to a discussion of the etiological knowledge base for preventive, family-focused interventions in economically stressed rural areas. Risk factors cited by Patterson and colleagues include poor, noncontingent parental use of reinforcers and discipline, ineffective parental monitoring, and early conduct problems that set the stage for rejection by normal peers, academic failure, and commitment to a deviant peer group. In the models developed by Patterson and colleagues, family stressors and disadvantaged socioeconomic status disrupt family management practices and can increase the probability of antisocial or aggressive behavior. Complementing this research, extensive etiological studies of adolescent substance use support a number of key family-related risk factors (Hawkins, Catalano, & Miller, 1992; Kumpfer & Alvarado, 1995), including poor and inconsistent family management practices and related family conflict (see Kumpfer, Molgaard, & Spoth, Chapter 11, this volume).

Studies conducted in the rural Midwest are consistent with other data on family-related risk factors in suggesting the need to address the family's role in the prevention of rural adolescent drug and conduct problems. An ongoing study with rural Iowa families (Conger et al., 1992; Conger & Elder, 1994) was designed to evaluate a family process model linking economic stress to problematic and prosocial adolescent adjustment. In this model, objective economic stress (e.g., family per capita income) is related to parents' perceptions of increased economic pressure. This, in turn, is linked to increased parental depression and demoralization, leading to greater marital discord and disruptions in skillful parenting. Finally, this disrupted parenting is posited as having an adverse influence on adolescent adjustment. Latent-variable structural equation analyses of data from 215 rural families support the model, specifically indicating that economic stress-related disruptions in family functioning negatively affect adolescent adjustment primarily through deleterious effects on effective child-rearing behavior.

Just as disrupted parenting in rural families has adverse effects on child functioning, effective parenting can play a positive role (IOM, 1994). For example, data from the panel study of rural families described previously (Conger, Rueter, & Conger, in press) was used to test a theoretical model of parent and older sibling effects on early adolescent drinking behaviors that included moderating effects of parenting quality on the impact of older sibling drinking on adolescent alcohol use. Results from the study suggested that parenting quality had a protective effect. That is, it functioned as a moderator of older sibling drinking, reducing its deleterious effects on younger sibling alcohol use. Data from Project Family also suggest that rural parents play an important protective role in their children's lives, as discussed in the following section.

OVERVIEW OF PROJECT GOALS
AND RURAL IMPLEMENTATION STRATEGIES

The primary goal of Project Family is to evaluate the short- and long-term effects of universal parenting and family skills programs and to examine factors differentially influencing outcomes. The key outcomes evaluated include parenting skills, child life skills, and child substance use and conduct problems. A secondary goal of Project Family is to examine factors influencing participation in prevention programs among rural families.

To accomplish the primary goal, controlled studies of family-focused preventive interventions designed to delay the onset of adolescent substance use and reduce adolescent problem behaviors have been conducted among several hundred Iowa families. The project employs multi-informant, multimethod measurement procedures to evaluate the short- and long-term outcomes of two theory-based universal interventions addressing family-related risk and protective factors: Preparing for the Drug (Free) Years (PDFY; Hawkins, Catalano, & Kent, 1991) and the Iowa Strengthening Families Program for Pre- and Early Adolescents (ISFP; Molgaard & Kumpfer, 1993; also see Chapter 11, this volume).

At the time of this writing, the project is in transition between pilot phase studies and the implementation of a large-scale intervention trial. The pilot phase entailed several participation factor studies (summarized below) and a preliminary, controlled study of the PDFY with a sample of 209 rural families with sixth and seventh graders randomly assigned to intervention and wait-list control conditions. The PDFY is a skills training program based on the social development model (Hawkins et al., 1992). Its primary objective is to enhance protective family bonding and reduce family-related risk factors for adolescent substance abuse. Parent skills building is directed toward providing children with opportunities for positive family involvement as well as teaching children skills for positive involvement and rewarding them accordingly.

The PDFY is a five-session, multimedia program with an average session length of 2 hours. One of the five sessions requires that children attend and incorporates instruction on peer resistance skills. The other four sessions are solely for parents and include instruction on (a) identifying risk factors for adolescent substance abuse; (b) enhancing parent-child bonding; (c) developing effective child management practices, including clear guidelines about expected behaviors, monitoring compliance with guidelines, and providing appropriate, contingent consequences; (d) appropriately managing family conflict; (e) enhancing positive child involvement in day-to-day family tasks; and (f) utilizing family meetings as a vehicle for improving child management and positive child involvement. During the PDFY pilot phase implementation, trained observers monitored the fidelity of intervention implementation, focusing on group leader coverage of program content. Although there was some variability in content coverage by group leaders, fidelity observations showed all key program concepts were covered by all group leaders.

The clinical trial phase of the project entails a controlled study of both the PDFY and the ISFP. It began with a baseline survey of all eligible families with fifth graders in targeted schools that were receiving federal assistance for school lunches (i.e., those schools having higher concentrations of lower-income families). This survey took place before families were invited to participate in the clinical trial and thus enabled prospective study of factors influencing families' decisions to participate. Following this baseline survey, participating schools were randomly assigned to one of three conditions: the PDFY intervention, the ISFP intervention, or a control condition receiving reading materials on developmental changes in adolescents.

The ISFP is a seven-session program focusing on reducing risk factors for adolescent substance abuse and building protective factors in children, parents, and families. The format of the program is identical to that of a previously developed program designed for families with younger children (The Strengthening Families Program; Kumpfer, DeMarsh, & Child, 1988), with youth and parents in separate sessions for the first hour followed by a joint family session. Videotapes presenting skills concepts and vignettes modeling skillful parenting were developed to ensure standardized delivery of program content. ISFP implementation fidelity was also evaluated. A detailed description of the format and content of the ISFP is provided in Chapter 11.

EVALUATION OF RURAL FAMILY CHARACTERISTICS INFLUENCING PARTICIPATION AND OUTCOMES

A variety of methods have been employed in Project Family to evaluate factors influencing intervention participation and outcomes. Emphasis has been placed on the application of various multivariate approaches to the examination of individual difference and contextual factors influencing both participation and intervention outcomes. In the case of participation, a number of consumer research methods and the prospective study of participation factors have been applied. In the case of program outcome studies, theory-based models, which include intervention attendance and implementation effects, have been developed in addition to standard intervention-control comparisons. The following two sections will summarize (a) the rationale for examining individual difference and contextual factors in intervention participation and outcomes, (b) the general strategies for the study of functional relationships among variables associated with variations in participation and outcomes, as well as (c) illustrative methods and studies.

Factors Influencing Intervention Participation

In general, recruitment and retention in preventive intervention and prevention research projects have been highly problematic (Spoth & Molgaard, 1993; Spoth & Redmond, 1994). For example, recruitment rates for child health and behavior prevention trials have often been in the 20% to 25% range (Coie et al., 1993), posing a major threat to the generalizability of findings. Preventive intervention recruitment has proven to be particularly problematic when (a) at-risk or geographically dispersed rural populations are targeted, (b) the intervention incorporates an evaluation component, and (c) professionals offering the program are not familiar with the intervention needs and preferences of the targeted population (Spoth & Redmond, 1994b).

There are numerous barriers to effective intervention recruitment and retention, in general, and to intervention implementation with an evaluation component in particular. Typical barriers include time requirements (Spoth, 1990; Spoth & Redmond, 1993b; Spoth, Redmond, Hockaday, & Shin, in press) and unappealing intervention content (Spoth & Redmond, 1994; Wilson, 1990). In intervention evaluation studies, concern about being the subject of research can be a formidable barrier to participation (Spoth & Redmond, 1993b; Spoth et al., in press). Of course, these barriers vary by intervention and population type. In rural areas such as Iowa, barriers, such as travel distance required and time demands on parents in dual-career households, can compound one other (Spoth & Redmond, 1993b).

The need to address barriers has been cited in several areas of the literature ranging from family-focused prevention, to worksite health promotion, to community medical screening programs (Spoth & Molgaard, 1993). This need is part of a larger theme sounded in the literature on program evaluation over the past two decades: How can the demands of interventions and intervention research be reconciled with the practical needs of intervention consumers? (See Green, 1979.) One way to address this issue is to systematically incorporate the theory-based study of consumer participation factors in intervention studies. For example, the trade-offs often present in consumer decision making can be investigated (e.g., increased consumer willingness to drive some distance if there are fewer intervention sessions).

Systematic, consumer-oriented research is especially needed in family-focused intervention research. In addition to low recruitment rates that threaten external validity, low retention in these interventions can pose a threat to the validity of conclusions about the degree to which observed outcomes can be attributed to the intervention. Although the reporting of retention rates in family intervention studies is rare, available literature suggests that retention rates are wide ranging (15%-85%), with rates frequently in the 45% to 65% range (e.g., DeMarsh & Kumpfer, 1986; Firestone & Witt, 1982; Spoth & Redmond, 1994). Unfortunately, much of the prior conceptual and empirical work on factors influencing preventive intervention participation has focused on individuals rather than families. For example, value-expectancy formulations that explain decisions to engage in preventive health behaviors, such as the Health Belief Model (Janz & Becker, 1984), do not directly address issues related to multiple decision makers, family decision-making roles, and stage in the family life cycle (see Spoth & Redmond, 1993b).

The following sections briefly describe five approaches to the study of factors influencing rural family participation in Project Family. A summary of the methods and illustrative results are given for each of the five approaches.

Conjoint Analysis and Computer Simulation of Intervention Preferences. Conjoint analysis is a method of consumer preference study that is based on data collection strategies designed to approximate "real life" consumer choices (Johnson, 1974). Although there has been extensive application of conjoint analysis by consumer researchers, it has only recently been recommended for application to the study of health education and prevention programs (Spoth, 1989, 1990, 1991a, 1991b, 1992; Spoth, Redmond, & Ball, 1993).

When faced with choices about products of importance to them, consumers typically consider the value of preferred features of available products and try to select the product with the optimal combination of features. Unlike alternative approaches to the study of product preferences in which respondents are asked to rate their preference for an individual product feature, conjoint techniques require respondents to make a choice between product profiles, each of which includes two or more product features. When respondents provide preference information on a series of such choices, conjoint analytic techniques can be used to determine the relative importance of categories of product features (e.g., prevention program duration vs. meeting length) as well as the relative preference for individual features (e.g., program durations of 5 vs. 10 weeks).

Because it typically is impractical for respondents to rank a set of product profiles that contain all possible combinations of product features, consumer researchers have shown that results derived from a properly selected, comparatively small subset of program profiles (composed of subsets of product features) will closely approximate results derived from data collected using a full set of product profiles. Pairs of product profiles can be purposively selected through application of computer programs designed to collect and analyze conjoint data (e.g., Adoptive Conjoint Analysis; see Johnson, 1987). Computer-guided interviews by such software can greatly reduce respondent fatigue by presenting choice profiles tailored to the individual respondent in a manner designed to provide maximum information for preference estimation (cf. Spoth & Redmond, 1993a; Spoth, Redmond, & Ball, 1993; Wittink & Walsh, 1988). Most often, dummy variable regression techniques are employed to disaggregate preference data from conjoint interviews to estimate respondent preferences for individual product features. Conjoint preference data can subsequently be used to simulate a specific marketplace, estimating the distribution of consumer choices among a group of competing products. It can also be used for purposes of distinguishing among groups of consumers with similar product preferences (see next section, on Cluster Analysis and Target Population Segmentation). Conjoint analysis was used for each of these purposes in Project Family.

Project Family conjoint data were collected from 202 randomly selected parents of young adolescents enrolled in school districts eligible for a federally supported school lunch program (Spoth & Redmond, 1993a). Data were collected via computer-assisted telephone interviews (using Ci2 and ACA software) of approximately 20 minutes in length. Assessment items concerned parents' preferences for 39 family-focused prevention program features within 11 feature categories. Available research was used to guide selection of program features; in addition, preferences of likely importance to the targeted rural population were incorporated (e.g., driving distance and meeting location). Other data collected from parents concerned basic sociodemographic information and prevention-relevant health beliefs.

Results from this study indicated that meeting time, facilitator background, program duration, research base, and meeting location were the most important categories of features to respondents. The individual features within these categories that were most often preferred were weekday-evening meetings, child development specialists as facilitators, a 5-week program, an extensive research base, and meetings held in a school, respectively. The preference scores of the individual features within each feature category and the percentage of respondents for whom each category was important are presented in Table 13.1. The preference scores are roughly equivalent to standardized regression coefficients and represent the relative contribution a given feature would make to the overall preference for a prevention program having that feature. Negative values indicate comparatively undesirable features.

Subsequent to the conjoint preference analyses, preference data were used to conduct market simulations. These simulations were based on program profiles designed to represent four family-focused prevention programs available in the study's geographic area. A 5-week, research-based program facilitated by parents, meeting weeknights, and focusing on involving children in family activities was most preferred (see Spoth & Redmond, 1993a).

Cluster Analysis and Target Population Segmentation. Market segmentation techniques have proven useful in the development of effective product or service promotional strategies as well as in the creation of more satisfactory products and services (Boyd & Walker, 1990). The basis for segmentation is simple and straightforward for many consumer products. In the case of complex services such as prevention programs, however, many potentially important product features exist, and the relative importance of these features to prospective consumers is unclear. One approach to this problem is the employment of multivariate techniques such as conjoint analysis and cluster analysis for market segmentation purposes (Spoth, Ball, Klose, & Redmond, in press). In this context, cluster analysis can be used to identify segments of the population that have similar attitudes or preferences regarding preventive interventions. The identification of such population segments provides information supplementing

TABLE 13.1 Feature Preference Scores and Percentage of Respondents for
Whom Feature Categories Were Most Important (N = 202)

Feature Category (% for whom category is most important)	Preference Score	
	Mean	Standard Error
Meeting time (15.6)		
Meets on weekday evenings	.59	.03
Meets on weekends	−.13	.04
Meets on weekdays (daytime)	−.55	.05
Meeting location (9.9)		
Meets at school	.34	.03
Meets at church	.22	.03
Meets at homes of parents in the program	−.06	.04
Meets at the extension service	−.06	.03
Meets at place of work	−.58	.04
Facilitator background (14.4)		
Taught by child development specialists	.33	.04
Taught by experts in drug prevention	.28	.04
Taught by parents	−.36	.04
Taught by school teachers	−.36	.05
Program duration (13.9)		
Program lasts 5 weeks	.38	.04
Program lasts 10 weeks	.08	.03
Program lasts 1 week	−.11	.05
Program lasts 15 weeks	−.47	.05
Research base (11.6)		
Program is based on extensive research	.59	.04
Program is not based on research	−.64	.04
Distance to meetings (6.4)		
Travel 5 miles to meetings	.40	.03
Travel 10 miles to meetings	.00	.03
Travel 20 miles to meetings	−.49	.04
Program focus (7.4)		
Teaches family communication	.30	.04
Teaches child family involvement	.07	.04
Teaches family conflict management	−.11	.04
Teaches child behavior management	−.17	.04
Teaches children how to say no to drugs	−.23	.05
Program format (6.9)		
Meets every other week, self-help homework	.35	.04
Meets once each week, self-help homework	.12	.04
Meets only once, self-help homework	−.05	.03
Self-help homework, no program meetings	−.53	.04

TABLE 13.1 Continued

	Preference Score	
Feature Category (% for whom category is most important)	Mean	Standard Error
Meeting length (3.0)		
Meetings last 1 hour	.25	.03
Meetings last 2 hours	.16	.03
Meetings last 3 hours	−.50	.04
Endorsements (6.9)		
Endorsed by parents	.20	.05
Endorsed by teachers	−.08	.04
Endorsed by school administrators	−.20	.05
Support type (4.0)		
Uses support group of other parents	.16	.04
Participants may call in with questions	−.04	.04
Parenting specialists will call parents	−.20	.04

SOURCE: Adapted from Spoth, R., & Redmond, C. (1993a). Identifying program preferences through conjoint analysis: Illustrative results from a parent sample. *American Journal of Health Promotion, 8*(2), Table 3. Reprinted with permission.

program outcome data; it can be used to tailor promotions of prevention programs to highlight features that are desirable to targeted groups or segments of families.

In Project Family, cluster analysis was applied to conjoint-analytic preference data regarding family-focused preventive interventions (see the preceding section for a summary of the data-collection procedures). The purpose of this analysis was to identify subgroups of rural parents with similar preferences for specific family-focused intervention program features. Results of the analysis identified three clusters, or segments, of respondents with similar program feature preferences (Spoth, Ball, et al., in press). The first of these clusters was characterized by lower preferred levels of effort and limited concern with specific types of program content. Parents in this cluster preferred shorter program meetings and program durations; they also had little preference regarding program content, with a family communication focus only slightly more preferred than other program foci. Parents in the second cluster had a strong preference for a program focusing on drug abuse prevention and were predisposed toward longer programs (10 weeks in duration) with longer and more frequent meetings. The third cluster was characterized by a clear preference for a family communication program focus and was moderate with respect to preferred levels of effort (preferred frequent meetings but of shorter duration than those preferred by parents in the second cluster).

Comparative Study of Recruitment Strategies. Previous preventive intervention research efforts have often yielded poor subject recruitment rates (Spoth & Redmond, 1994). As noted in the introduction to this section, typical recruitment rates reported in the literature are problematically low. In addition, recruitment for Project Family was particularly challenging due to the need to recruit both parents and children, the generally demanding schedules of the targeted rural families, and the time requirements imposed by the multi-informant, multimethod assessment procedures used. In an effort to collect pilot phase data that could guide the refinement of recruitment strategies for the clinical trial phase, two variants of a recruitment protocol were tested. The development of the two recruitment strategies was consistent with (a) research on health belief factors influencing decisions to take preventive actions (see Spoth & Redmond, 1993b, 1994, in press) and (b) strategies successfully employed in earlier research projects at the Center. Results from the two strategies were compared and used to guide procedures in the clinical trial.

The first of the two recruitment strategies employed a two-stage project recruitment in which prospective participants were initially recruited into the pilot study pretest only. Following the pretest, participating families were asked to be involved in the remainder of the project (intervention or wait list control group and posttesting). In the second recruitment strategy, potential participant families were asked to commit to the entire project prior to pretesting. Potential participants in both conditions were mailed information concerning all phases of the project prior to initial telephone recruitment contacts. (See Spoth & Redmond, 1994, for a detailed description of the Project Family pilot recruitment procedures.)

Overall, both recruitment strategies employed were effective, yielding higher recruitment and retention rates than typically reported in the relevant literature. Nearly 57% of all families recruited for the project participated in the pretest, and 84.1% of all pretested families remained in the project through posttesting. Although both recruitment strategies yielded comparatively high participation rates, there were differences in levels of participation in the various project activities. The two-stage recruitment strategy yielded significantly higher rates of recruitment into the pretest than did the single-stage recruitment strategy (61.3% vs. 49.6% of contacted families). Attrition was also higher among two-stage recruitment families than among single-stage recruitment families, however, and there was no significant difference in the percentage of contacted families completing the posttest (46.7% vs. 44.4%, respectively). There were high program attendance rates for intervention families in both recruitment groups—86.4% of the families were represented at one or more sessions and 76.7% attended over half.

Although results of the Project Family recruitment study indicated that both strategies can yield comparatively high recruitment rates in a rural Midwestern population, the differences in families' initial recruitment and attrition rates suggest different applications for the two strategies. The two-stage strategy, with its higher recruitment rate into pretesting, would be the preferred method in intervention studies in which baseline population data were important. Applications in which population data were less important, however, could benefit from the reduced cost of the single-stage recruitment strategy. Under this strategy, fewer potentially expensive pretest assessments would be conducted with families that will fail to complete the study.

Retrospective Study of Refusal Reasons. There is a growing body of literature that calls for more research concerning health belief effects on participation in family-focused interventions, particularly the effects of perceived barriers to preventive actions (e.g., DeMarsh & Kumpfer, 1986; Frazer, Hawkins, & Howard, 1988; Spoth, Redmond, Yoo, & Dodge, 1993). There has been very limited attention to these issues among rural families (Spoth & Conroy, 1993). A Project Family study was designed to help address this issue and to provide information regarding differences between participants in the project and those who were unsuccessfully recruited (Spoth & Redmond, 1993b). Following completion of recruitment for the pilot-phase intervention evaluation study, a short, one-page questionnaire was mailed to families who were recruited but declined to participate in the pilot study. This questionnaire contained basic socio-demographic items (age, sex, family composition, education, and income) and a list of possible reasons for their decision not to participate. Refusal reasons listed on the questionnaire were selected on the basis of relevant literature and reasons given by families to project telephone recruiters at the time of participation refusal. Given recent research highlighting increasing time demands on rural families related to the numbers of rural women seeking employment outside of the home (e.g., Conger et al., 1991; McLoyd, 1989), the authors were particularly interested in time-related refusal reasons.

Questionnaires were mailed to the 167 families who refused participation in the Project Family pilot intervention study. Questionnaires were returned by 97 (58.8%) of these families. Results concerning refusal reasons indicated that time constraints and concerns about privacy, particularly the videotaped family interaction tasks (part of the project multimethod, multi-informant measurement procedures), were the most frequently cited reasons for non-participation. Interestingly, concerns about videotaping were rarely reported to telephone recruiters at the time of project refusal. There were no statistically significant sociodemographic differences found when pilot study participants were compared to project nonparticipants, suggesting that the recruited group was representative. Evidence, however, was found of refusal reason variations associated with some sociodemographic characteristics. For example, respondents with lower levels of education were more likely to report concerns with videotaping than were more educated respondents. A replication and extension of this study with a separate sample of 459 families refusing participation in the clinical trial phase has supported the primary findings from the earlier investigation. It also found that gender-specific family member influences were important. For example, the replication study showed that fathers generally had less motivation to participate than mothers, but that mothers were less likely to be strongly influenced by spousal disinclination to participate than were fathers (Spoth, Redmond, Hockaday, & Shin, in press).

Prospective Study of Participation Factors. Although the retrospective investigation of reasons for participation refusal or acceptance provides useful information and sociodemographic data from such studies can be helpful in assessing sample representativeness, this type of study suffers from methodological limitations. For example, attitude and belief factors can be susceptible to program-related shifts in attitudes and cognitive dissonance effects (e.g., Stromberg et al., 1974). Thus, a prospective study of a wide range of participation-relevant factors was designed for the clinical trial phase of Project Family. Data for the primary component of this study were collected via a telephone survey of all families eligible for participation in the clinical trial. This survey was conducted several months prior to recruitment for the clinical trial. Of the eligible families with working telephone numbers, 1,192 completed the telephone survey (a response rate of 89.9%; 4.4% of those contacted refused to be interviewed). Data collected in these interviews included family sociodemographic information, attitudes concerning family-focused interventions, child problem behaviors, history of prevention-related activities, parenting resource use, and key health belief variables related to the family-focused preventive interventions under study in the clinical trial (perceived child susceptibility to a range of teen problems, perceived severity of teen problems, perceived parental efficacy to prevent teen problems, perceived benefits of family-focused intervention programs, barriers to program participation, and inclination to enroll in a family-focused intervention).

Descriptive analyses of data collected indicated that parents in the sample felt that their preadolescent children were at relatively low risk of problems as teenagers. Parents also expressed generally high levels of efficacy associated with helping their children avoid problems as teenagers. There was an inverse relationship of perceived teen problem severity and perceived child susceptibility to problems. That is, the teen problems that were generally given relatively high severity ratings (such as drug or alcohol use) were also generally given low perceived child susceptibility ratings (see Spoth & Conroy, 1993).

In addition to descriptive analyses of health beliefs, structural equation modeling was conducted to examine the effects of family context factors and health beliefs on parents' inclination to enroll in a family-focused intervention (Spoth & Redmond, 1995). Two of the family context factors considered were found to be particularly important predictors of health beliefs: past parenting resource use and level of child problem behaviors. Past parenting resource use exhibited statistically significant effects on perceived program benefits and barriers to participation as well as on inclination to enroll in a parenting program. A significant positive effect of child problem behavior level on perceived child susceptibility to teen problem behaviors was observed, whereas a significant negative effect was observed on perceived severity of teen problem behaviors. The latter finding suggests that parents with children who frequently exhibit problem behaviors tend to view potential future problems with less concern than do parents with no such experience. As expected, perceived teen problem severity exhibited a positive effect on perceived program benefits; perceived program benefits and barriers to participation exhibited significant effects (positive and negative, respectively) on inclination to enroll in a parenting program.

STUDY OF CONTEXTUAL AND
INDIVIDUAL DIFFERENCE FACTORS
IN INTERVENTION OUTCOMES

The current strategy for analysis of expected intervention outcomes in Project Family involves distinct methodological and substantive points of emphasis. Methodologically, the project has taken two avenues of approach to the study of expected outcomes. First, standard, intervention-control comparisons have been conducted. Second, to better understand processes producing outcomes of interest, the project has conducted tests of theory-based models of family-related contextual and individual difference factors that incorporate intervention parameter variables (e.g., program attendance level, program implementation behaviors, and session implementation fidelity).

Standard statistical models employed in the experimental assessment of intervention-control differences (e.g., analysis of covariance [ANCOVA]) assume a constant, additive intervention effect for each subject in each condition. This type of outcome evaluation has been described as a "black box" approach (e.g., Chen & Rossi, 1983; Finney & Moos, 1989) because it reveals little about how outcomes of interest were produced and the roles played by contextual and individual difference factors. More specifically, the so-called black box approach fails to clarify (a) factors that interact with or otherwise intervene in the effects of the intervention on the outcomes of interest and (b) factors independently contributing to outcomes in addition to the intervention.

Conventional black box analyses of intervention outcomes can be supplemented by approaches that identify and explicitly model theory-based variables influencing proximal and distal intervention outcomes. In the case of parenting skills interventions, relevant model variables include a variety of parent and family characteristics. This approach is consistent with recommendations by evaluation theorists (e.g., Chen & Rossi, 1983, 1987) that randomized, controlled experiments be employed in conjunction with a priori knowledge and theory to build explanatory models of processes influencing intervention outcomes.

Project Family employs models evaluating a range of relationships among contextual or individual difference factors contributing to outcomes: cumulative, direct (or main) effects, mediating effects, and moderating (or interaction) effects (see Baron & Kenny, 1986, for a clarification of the distinction between moderating and mediating effects). It is particularly instructive to evaluate the relative strength of intervention attendance level, implementation, and fidelity effects vis-à-vis theory-based contextual (e.g., socioeconomic status) and individual difference factors (e.g., self-efficacy). This type of evaluation can facilitate a better understanding of factors that have cumulative direct effects on specific intervention-targeted outcomes in specific populations. In addition, it is useful to examine theory-based mediating and moderating effects of variables influencing those targeted intervention outcomes, as illustrated by the Project Family studies summarized in the following paragraphs.

Substantively, the models tested through Project Family emphasize protective family processes. Protective factors have frequently been articulated as those that (a) offset the effects of exposure to risk factors (Hawkins et al., 1992; Kumpfer & Alvarado, 1995; Masten, Best, & Garmezy, 1991; Rutter, 1990) or (b) reduce the likelihood of an initial occurrence of a risk factor (Coie et al., 1993; Rutter, 1990). As noted in its report on risk reduction for mental disorders, the IOM (1994) states that the quality of parent-child interactions is a major protective factor common to many disorders, including substance- and conduct-related ones. Parenting-related characteristics of a child's family environment, including effective child management behaviors and positive affect in parent-child interactions, can serve as protective factors (Benard, 1991; Coie et al., 1993; Conger et al., in press; Gest, Neemann, Hubbard, Masten, & Tellegen, 1993; IOM, 1994; Rutter, 1990).

Project Family studies described in this chapter sampled rural families with fifth, sixth, and seventh graders. Enhancing protective factors in the family environment can be particularly important as children enter the early adolescence, middle school years; the increased importance of peers as a socialization force and the transition from elementary to middle school environments can increase child exposure to a variety of risk factors (Catalano & Hawkins, in press; Eccles et al., 1993). Moreover, early adolescents in rural families experiencing economic stress are more likely to be exposed to family-related risks (e.g., poor family management practices) than rural families without economic stress (Conger et al., 1992); the families in this study were selected from an economically stressed rural area.

Initial Project Family outcome analyses have shown positive intervention effects on both parent-child interactional and child outcomes such as alcohol-refusal skills (Spoth, Yoo, Kahn, & Redmond, in press; see also Spoth & Redmond, in press; Spoth, Redmond, Huck, & Shin, 1995). Two of the initial outcome studies can be used to illustrate a combination of conventional intervention-control comparisons and the modeling approaches described previously (Spoth, Redmond, Haggerty, & Ward, 1995; Spoth, Redmond, Hockaday, & Yoo, 1995). In the first of these two studies, pre- and posttest data were assessed to determine intervention effects and to examine protective parenting outcomes associated with empirically based individual difference or aptitude variables. First, ANCOVAs were used to demonstrate intervention effects on (a) intervention-targeted parenting behaviors and (b) more general, intervention-relevant child management behaviors. The latter measure incorporated both self-report and observer ratings. Second, regression analyses were used to examine a model of hypothesized effects of (a) two individual difference-aptitude variables (readiness for parenting change and parent self-efficacy) on the intervention-targeted parenting behavior measure, (b) the number of program sessions attended on the targeted parenting measure, and (c) the targeted parenting behavior measure on the general child management measure (Spoth, Redmond, Haggerty et al., 1995).

ANCOVAs showed significant intervention-control differences on both outcome measures for both mothers and fathers. In addition, all but one of the hypothesized model effects were found to be statistically significant at the .05 level for both mothers and fathers. Also, as planned, direct effects of the two individual difference variables on the general child management measure were examined. These direct effects were not supported when the effect of the intervention-targeted parenting measure was included in the analysis, suggesting that the individual difference variable effects on general child management were indirect, via the intervention-targeted parenting behaviors, consistent with the hypothesized model. Finally, findings showed a significant interaction of intervention attendance level and intervention-targeted parenting at pretest for fathers. That is, the observed effects of intervention attendance level on intervention-targeted parenting behaviors at posttest varied with fathers' pretest levels of that measure, showing relatively greater effects among fathers having lower pretest levels of intervention-targeted parenting.

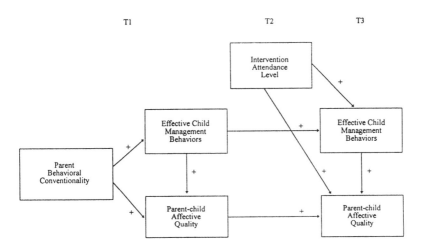

Figure 13.1. A Protective Parenting Process Model Incorporating Intervention Attendance Effects

A second illustration is a model suggested by family interactional theory (Brook, Brook, Gordon, Whiteman, & Cohen, 1990) and the social development model (Hawkins et al., 1992) focusing on the effects of skills training, attendance level, and parent conventionality on effective child management behaviors and parent-child affective quality (Spoth & Redmond, in press). This model is outlined in Figure 13.1. Covariance structure analyses have revealed (a) a strong overall model fit for mothers and fathers and (b) support for all hypothesized effects in both mother and father models, with the exception of this intervention attendance effect on fathers' affective quality with their child. Supplemental regression analyses also showed a mediating effect of child management behaviors on the relationship between parent behavioral conventionality with parent-child affective quality.

CONCLUDING COMMENTS

As reviewed in the first section of this chapter, available epidemiologic evidence can be construed as sounding a call for greater attention to research on preventive interventions targeting rural populations. This chapter illustrates a conceptual framework within which rural preventive intervention research needs can be addressed. Close examination of a variety of substantive and methodological issues would also help in addressing these needs.

From a substantive perspective, the epidemiological research with rural populations suggests both the population problems or disorders to be targeted by preventive interventions and the risk and protective factors linked to those problems. In addition, epidemiological work with varying types of populations underscores common risk and protective factors relevant in rural prevention, such as the protective effects of parenting quality (see IOM, 1994, p. 185). Although substantively relevant epidemiological and etiological research has guided the development and testing of Project Family interventions (see IOM, 1994, pp. 360-323), this type of preventive intervention research would clearly benefit from further refinement of the epidemiological knowledge base. First of all, measures that relate directly to clinical categories of rural population disorder need to be applied (see Wagenfeld et al., 1994). In addition, much of the etiological research guiding the Project Family interventions derives from studies with samples outside of the rural Midwest; the degree to which they generalize to rural Midwestern populations needs to be clarified. Consistent with the concept of a research cycle within which intervention studies can serve to refine previously developed etiological models, Project Family will provide useful data to address this generalizability issue. Finally, although the guiding etiological models for Project Family suggest modifiable family-related factors important to child adjustment outcomes, they do not specify indicated intervention strategies; the refinement of these change strategies will be informed by the research currently under way in Project Family.

From the perspective of intervention evaluation methodology, Project Family addresses a number of issues cited in the literature and important in the study of rural populations (IOM, 1994; U.S. Department of Justice, 1992; Wiese, 1992). These are addressed through true experimental, longitudinal designs; adequate sample sizes to achieve requisite statistical power; multi-informant, multimethod measurement procedures; and implementation fidelity checks (Spoth, Redmond, Haggerty et al., 1995; Yoo & Spoth, 1993). In addition to these particular methodological considerations, this chapter argues that there is a strong indication for methodologies that address mechanisms of change as well as contextual or individual difference factors influencing both rural population participation in interventions and the outcomes of those interventions. Current findings from Project Family support an important role for individual difference and family context factors. Thus, the methodological position adopted in this chapter is of primary importance: It is essential to evaluate functional relationships among contextual or individual difference factors influencing variations in outcomes even when studying theory-based, standardized interventions. The understanding of variations in outcomes among individuals within treatment groups is key in the development of maximally effective interventions; it is hoped that the results of Project Family studies will provide guidance for future prevention efforts among rural populations.

In conclusion, preventive interventions entail dynamic changes in immensely complex, "multivariate" social interactions (see Shoham-Salomon & Hannah, 1991). Characteristics of local rural populations influence these complex processes. This calls for methodologies that address complex, dynamic, intervention-related change and local variations in change processes within a programmatic research framework. At a minimum, such an approach requires examination of rural preventive interventions that extend beyond the standard evaluation of treatment-control comparisons using statistical methods such as the modeling approaches proposed in this chapter. Like the rural traveler in Frost's poem, however, researchers have "miles to go" before they can rest assured that the combination of substantive and methodological issues in rural prevention research have been adequately addressed. As noted in the beginning of this chapter, the Project Family studies illustrated in this chapter constitute an initial attempt to address key research needs in rural family-focused prevention within the prevention research cycle framework.

REFERENCES

Baron, R., & Kenny, D. (1986). The moderator-mediator variable distinction in social psychological research: Conceptual, strategic, and statistical considerations. *Journal of Personality and Social Psychology, 51,* 1173-1182.

Beeson, P., & Johnson, D. R. (1987). *A panel study of change in rural mental health status: Effects of rural crisis, 1981-1986.* Lincoln: Nebraska Department of Public Institutions.

Benard, B. (1991). *Fostering resiliency in kids: Protective factors in the family, school, and community.* Portland, OR: Northwest Regional Educational Library.

Blum, R. W., McKay, C., & Resnick, M. D. (1989). *The state of adolescent health in Minnesota.* (Grant No. MCH273460). Washington, DC: Federal Division of Maternal & Child Health.

Boyd, H. W., & Walker, O. C. (1990). *Marketing management.* Homewood, IL: Irwin.

Brook, J. S., Brook, D. W., Gordon, A. S., Whiteman, A. S., & Cohen, P. (1990). The psychosocial etiology of adolescent drug use: A family interactional approach. *Genetic, Social, and General Psychology Monographs, 116,* 111-267.

Caspi, A., Elder, G. H., & Bem, D. J. (1987). Moving against the world: Life course patterns of explosive children. *Developmental Psychology, 23,* 305-313.

Catalano, R. F., & Hawkins, J. D. (in press). The social development model: A theory of antisocial behavior. In J. D. Hawkins (Ed.), *Some current theories of delinquency and crime.* New York/Berlin: Springer-Verlag.

Chen, H. T., & Rossi, P. H. (1983). Evaluating with sense: The theory-driven approach. *Evaluation Research, 7,* 283-302.

Chen, H. T., & Rossi, P. H. (1987). The theory-driven approach to validity. *Evaluation and Program Planning, 10,* 95-103.

Coie, J. D., Watt, N. F., West, S. G., Hawkins, J. D., Asarnow, J. R., Markman, H. J., Ramey, S. L., Shure, M. B., & Long, B. (1993). The science of prevention: A conceptual framework and some directions for a national research program. *American Psychologist, 48,* 1013-1022.

Conger, R. D., Conger, K. J., Elder, G. H., Lorenz, F. O., Simons, R. L., & Whitbeck, L. B. (1992). A family process model of economic hardship and adjustment of early adolescent boys. *Child Development, 63,* 526-541.

Conger, R. D., & Elder, G. H. (1994). *Families in troubled times: Adapting to change in rural America.* Hillsdale, NJ: Aldine.

Conger, R. D., Elder, G. H., Lorenz, F. O., Simons, R. L., & Whitbeck, L. B. (1991, April). A family process model of economic hardship influences on adolescent adjustment. In R. Conger, G. Elder, & V. McLoyd (Chairs), *Impact of life stressors on adult relationships and adolescent adjustment.* Symposium conducted at the meeting of the Society for Research in Child Development, Seattle, WA.

Conger, R. D., Rueter, M. A., & Conger, K. J. (in press). The family context of adolescent vulnerability and resilience to alcohol use and abuse. *Sociological Studies of Children.*

DeMarsh, J., & Kumpfer, K. (1986). Family-oriented interventions for the prevention of chemical dependency in children and adolescents. *Prevention, 18,* 117-151.

Eccles, J. S., Midgley, C., Wigfield, A., Buchanan, C. M., Reuman, D., Flanagan, C., & MacIver, D. (1993). Development during adolescence: The impact of stage environment fit on young adolescents' experiences in schools and in families. *American Psychologist, 48,* 90-101.

Elliott, D. S., Huizinga, D., & Ageton, S. S. (1982). *Explaining delinquency and drug use* (Report No. 21). Boulder, CO: Behavioral Research Institute.

Finney, J. W., & Moos, R. H. (1989). Theory and method in treatment evaluation. *Evaluation and Program Planning, 12,* 307-316.

Firestone, P., & Witt, J. E. (1982). Characteristics of families completing and prematurely discontinuing a behavioral parent training program. *Journal of Pediatric Psychology, 7,* 209-222.

Frazer, M. W., Hawkins, J. D., & Howard, M. O. (1988). Parent training for delinquency prevention. *Child and Youth Services, 11,* 93-125.

Gest, S. D., Neemann, J., Hubbard, J. J., Masten, A. S., & Tellegen, A. (1993). Parenting quality, adversity, and conduct problems in adolescence: Testing process-oriented models of resilience. *Development and Psychopathology, 5,* 663-682.

Gordon, R. (1983). An operational classification of disease prevention. *Public Health Reports, 98,* 107-109.

Green, L. W. (1979). How to evaluate health promotion. *Hospitals, 53,* 106-108.

Hawkins, J. D., Catalano, R. F., & Kent, L. A. (1991). Combining broadcast media and parent education to prevent teenage drug abuse. In L. Donohew, H. E. Sypher, & W. J. Bukoski (Eds.), *Persuasive communication and drug abuse prevention* (pp. 283-294). Hillsdale, NJ: Lawrence Erlbaum.

Hawkins, J. D., Catalano, R. F., & Miller, J. Y. (1992). Risk and protective factors for alcohol and other drug problems in adolescence and early adulthood: Implications for substance abuse prevention. *Psychological Bulletin, 112,* 64-105.

Human, J., & Wassem, C. (1991). Rural mental health in America. *American Psychologist, 46,* 232-239.

Hunter, M., & Windle, C. (1991). NIMH support of rural mental health. *American Psychologist, 46,* 240-243.

Institute of Medicine. (1994). *Reducing risks for mental disorders: Frontiers for preventive intervention research.* Washington, DC: National Academy Press.

Iowa Department of Education. (1994). *1993-94 Iowa study of alcohol and drug attitudes and behaviors among youth.* Des Moines, IA: Author.

Janz, N. K., & Becker, M. H. (1984). The health belief model: A decade later. *Health Education Quarterly, 11,* 1-47.

Jessor, R., & Jessor, S. L. (1978). Theory testing in longitudinal research on marijuana use. In D. Kandel (Ed.), *Longitudinal research on drug use* (pp. 41-72). Washington, DC: Hemisphere.

Johnson, R. M. (1974). Trade-off analysis of consumer values. *Journal of Marketing Research, 11,* 121-127.

Johnson, R. M. (1987). Adaptive conjoint analysis. In R. M. Johnson & I. D. Ketchum (Eds.), *Proceedings of the Sawtooth Software Conference on perceptual mapping, conjoint analysis, and computer interviewing.* (pp. 253-266). Sun Valley, ID: Sawtooth Software.

Johnston, L. D., O'Malley, P. M., & Bachman, J. G. (1989). *Drug use, drinking, and smoking: National survey results from high school, college, and young adult populations, 1975-1988.* Ann Arbor: University of Michigan, Institute for Social Research for the U.S. Department of Health and Human Services, Alcohol, Drug Abuse, and Mental Health Administration, National Institute on Drug Abuse.

Johnston, L. D., O'Malley, P. M., & Bachman, J. G. (1994). *National survey results on drug use from the Monitoring the Future Study, 1975-1993* (Vol. 1). Rockville, MD: National Institute on Drug Abuse.

Kazdin, A. E. (1987). Treatment of antisocial behavior in children: Current status and future directions. *Psychological Bulletin, 102,* 187-203.

Kumpfer, K. L., & Alvarado, R. (1995). Strengthening families to prevent drug use in multiethnic youth. In G. Botvin, E. Schinke, & M. Orlandi (Eds.), *Drug abuse prevention with multiethnic youth* (pp. 255-294). Thousand Oaks, CA: Sage.

Kumpfer, K. L., DeMarsh, J., & Child, W. P. (1988). *Strengthening Families training manuals.* Salt Lake City: University of Utah, Social Research Institute.

Lempers, J. D., Clark-Lempers, D., & Simons, R. L. (1989). Economic hardship, parenting, and distress in adolescence. *Child Development, 60,* 25-39.

Loeber, R. T., & Dishion, T. (1983). Early predictors of male delinquency: A review. *Psychological Bulletin, 93,* 68-99.

Masten, A. S., Best, K. M., & Garmezy, N. (1991). Resilience and development: Contributions from the study of children who overcome diversity. *Development and Psychopathology, 2,* 425-444.

McCubbiṇ, H. I., Needle, R. H., & Wilson, M. (1985). Adolescent health risk behaviors: Family stress and adolescent coping as critical factors. *Family Relations, 34,* 51-62.

McLoyd, V. C. (1989). Socialization and development in a changing economy: The effects of paternal job and income loss on children. *American Psychologist, 44,* 293-302.

Molgaard, V., & Kumpfer, K. L. (1993). *The Iowa Strengthening Families Program for Pre- and Early Adolescents.* Ames: Iowa State University, Social & Behavioral Research Center for Rural Health.

Muehrer, P., Moscicki, E., & Koretz, D. (1993). Prevention as psychosocial intervention research. *NIMH Psychotherapy and Rehabilitation Research Bulletin, 1,* 9-16.

Murray, J. D., & Keller, P. A. (1991). Psychology and rural America: Current status and future directions. *American Psychologist, 46,* 220-231.

National Mental Health Association. (1988). *Report of the National Action Commission on the mental health of rural Americans.* Washington, DC: Author.

National Rural Health Association. (1989). *Rural health research compendium.* Kansas City, MO: Office of Rural Health Policy.

Patterson, G. R. (1986). Performance models for antisocial boys. *American Psychologist, 41,* 432-444.

Patterson, G. R., DeBaryshe, B. D., & Ramsey, E. (1989). A developmental perspective on antisocial behavior. *American Psychologist, 44,* 329-335.

Patterson, G. R., Dishion, T. J., & Bank, L. (1984). Family interaction: A process model of deviancy training. *Aggressive Behavior, 10,* 253-267.

Rutter, M. (1990). Psychosocial resilience and protective mechanisms. In J. Rolf, A. S. Masten, & D. Cicchetti (Eds.), *Risk and protective factors in the development of psychopathology* (pp. 181-214). New York: Cambridge University Press.

Sarvela, P. D., Newcomb, P. R., & Duncan, D. F. (1988). Drinking and driving among rural youth. *Health Education Research, 3,* 197-201.

Shoham-Salomon, V., & Hannah, M. T. (1991). Client-treatment interaction in the study of differential change process. *Journal of Consulting and Clinical Psychology, 59,* 217-225.

Spoth, R. (1989). Applying conjoint analysis of consumer preferences to the development of utility-responsive health promotion programs. *Health Education Research, 4,* 439-449.

Spoth, R. (1990). Multi-attribute analysis of benefit managers' preferences for smoking cessation programs. *Health Values: Health Behavior, Education & Promotion, 14,* 3-15.

Spoth, R. (1991a). Formative research in smoking cessation program attributes preferred by smokers. *American Journal of Health Promotion, 5,* 346-354.

Spoth, R. (1991b). Smoking cessation program preferences associated with stage of quitting. *Addictive Behaviors, 16,* 427-440.

Spoth, R. (1992). Simulating smokers' acceptance of modifications in a cessation program. *Public Health Reports, 107,* 81-92.

Spoth, R. (1995). *From problem identification to intervention efficiency study: Issues in rural mental disorder prevention research.* Manuscript submitted for publication.

Spoth, R., Ball, A. B., Klose, A., & Redmond, C. (in press). Illustration of a market segmentation technique using family-focused prevention program preference data. *Health Education Research.*

Spoth, R., & Conroy, S. (1993). Survey of prevention-relevant beliefs and efforts to enhance parenting skills among rural parents. *Journal of Rural Health, 9,* 227-239.

Spoth, R., & Molgaard, V. (1993). Consumer-focused data collection in prevention program evaluation: Rationale and illustrations. *Evaluation and the Health Professions, 16*, 278-294.

Spoth, R., & Redmond, C. (1993a). Identifying program preferences through conjoint analysis: Illustrative results from a parent sample. *American Journal of Health Promotion, 8*(2), 124-133.

Spoth, R., & Redmond, C. (1993b). Study of participation barriers in family-focused prevention: Research issues and preliminary results. *International Journal of Community Health Education, 13*, 365-388.

Spoth, R., & Redmond, C. (1994). Effective recruitment of parents into family-focused prevention research: A comparison of two strategies. *Psychology and Health: An International Journal, 9*, 353-370.

Spoth, R., & Redmond, C. (1995). Parent motivation to enroll in family skills programs: A model of contextual and health belief predictors. *Journal of Family Psychology, 9*(3), 294-310.

Spoth, R., & Redmond, C. (in press). A theory-based parent competency model incorporating intervention attendance effects. *Family Relations*.

Spoth, R., Redmond, C., & Ball, A. B. (1993). Stages of quitting and motivational factors relevant to smoking cessation. *Psychology of Addictive Behaviors, 7*, 29-42.

Spoth, R., Redmond, C., Haggerty, K., & Ward, T. (1995). A controlled parenting skills outcome study examining individual difference and attendance effects. *Journal of Marriage and the Family, 57*, 449-464.

Spoth, R., Redmond, C., Hockaday, C., & Shin, C. (in press). Barriers to participation in family-focused skills, preventive interventions and their evaluations: A replication and extension. *Family Relations*.

Spoth, R., Redmond, C., Hockaday, C., & Yoo, S. (1995). *Protective etiological processes in adolescent alcohol abstinence: Intervention, parent, peer, and child factors*. Manuscript submitted for publication.

Spoth, R., Redmond, C., Huck, S., & Shin, S. (1995). *Protective factors and school-related problem behaviors among young adolescents: Mastery-esteem, peer, and parent intervention implementation effects*. Manuscript submitted for publication.

Spoth, R., Redmond, C., Yoo, S., & Dodge, K. (1993). Sociodemographic factors and parent beliefs relevant to the prevention of adolescent behavior problems. *Family Perspective, 27*, 285-303.

Spoth, R., Yoo, S., Kahn, J. H., & Redmond, C. (in press). A model of the effects of protective parent and peer factors on early adolescent alcohol refusal skills. *Journal of Primary Prevention*.

Stromberg, J., David, J., Glasnow, I., Jaksic, Z., Kesic, B., Preburg, Z., Ray, D., Steinberger, C., & Vuletic, S. (1974). Predicting participation in a screening examination for ischaemic heart disease risk factors—Experience from the Zagres Preliminary Study. *Social Science and Medicine, 8*, 275-286.

U.S. Department of Health and Human Services. (1994). *Preliminary estimates from the 1993 National Household Survey on Drug Abuse* (Advance Report No. 7). Washington, DC: Government Printing Office.

U.S. Department of Justice, Office of Juvenile and Delinquency Prevention. (1992). *Strengthening America's families: Promising parenting and family strategies for delinquency prevention*. Washington, DC: Author.

U.S. General Accounting Office. (1990). *Rural drug abuse: Prevalence, relation to crime, and programs*. Washington, DC: Author.

Wagenfeld, M. O., Murray, J. D., Mohatt, D. F., & DeBruyn, J. C. (1994). *Mental health and rural America.* Washington, DC: U.S. Department of Health and Human Services, Office of Rural Health Policy.

Wiese, M. R. (1992). A critical review of parent training research. *Psychology in the Schools, 29,* 229-236.

Wilson, M. G. (1990). Factors associated with, issues related to, and suggestions for increasing participation in workplace health promotion programs. *Health Values, 14,* 29-36.

Wittink, D. R., & Walsh, J. W. (1988). *Conjoint analysis: Its reliability, validity, and usefulness.* Sawtooth Software Conference on Perceptual Mapping, Conjoint Analysis, and Computer Interviewing. Sun Valley, ID: Sawtooth Software.

Yoo, S., & Spoth, R. (1993). An alternative method for sample size determination in substance misuse prevention research. *International Journal of the Addictions, 28,* 1085-1094.

Yoshikawa, H. (1994). Prevention as a cumulative protection: Effects of early family support and education on chronic delinquency and its risks. *Psychological Bulletin, 115,* 1-26.

14

The State of Prevention
and Early Intervention

DAVID R. OFFORD

The overriding characteristic of children's emotional and behavioral problems is their heavy burden of suffering. When *DSM-III* criteria (American Psychiatric Association, 1980) were employed, the prevalence rates of
one or more psychiatric disorders in five community samples varied between
17.6% and 22.0% (Costello, 1989). The age ranges of the children and
adolescents included in these surveys also varied, with two studies including
children as young as 4 years old (Bird et al., 1988; Offord et al., 1987) and
one including adolescents as old as 20 years old (Velez, Johnson, & Cohen,
1989). Sources of the variability of the prevalence rates in these surveys
include the characteristics of the target sample, the sampling method, number
and types of disorders included, case definition, and assessment procedures
(Offord & Fleming, in press). Despite the variations in the prevalence rates
of psychiatric disorder in these community samples, it has been estimated
that at the very least 12% of children and adolescents have clinically
important emotional and behavioral disorders, and at least half of them are
deemed severely disordered or handicapped by their mental illness (Institute
of Medicine, 1989).

With regard to comorbidity, children with mental health problems not only suffer from troublesome symptoms and behaviors but also frequently exhibit difficulty in social relationships with their peers, parents, and teachers and in performing satisfactorily in school (Offord, Boyle, Fleming, Munroe Blum, & Rae-Grant, 1989; Sanford, Offord, Boyle, Peace, & Racine, 1992). Furthermore, the onset of these childhood difficulties often results in a lifetime of serious psychosocial problems. For example, children with antisocial behavior or conduct disorder are at increased risk for alcohol and drug use (Boyle et al., 1992). It has been found that a significant proportion of serious antisocial behavior in adulthood begins as conduct disorder in childhood and early adolescence (Patterson, DeBaryshe, & Ramsey, 1989), and almost half of all clinically identified antisocial youngsters become antisocial adults (Robins, 1966, 1970).

Finally, the costs of child mental health problems are extensive. They include health-related costs; non-health-related costs—for example, in the educational, child welfare, and juvenile justice systems; and indirect costs— primarily those related to lost lifetime earnings due to associated disabilities (Institute of Medicine, 1989).

Thus, children's emotional and behavioral problems rate extremely high on the three dimensions of burden of suffering: frequency of the disorder or condition, short-term and long-term morbidity, and costs in both fiscal and human terms.

CLINICAL ENTERPRISE

Attempts to lower this burden of suffering have relied to a large extent on child mental health and other clinical services that see identified children (and their families) one at a time. There are several limitations to this approach (Offord, 1987; Offord et al., 1987). First, in usual circumstances, by the time emotionally disturbed children (and their families) are assessed and treatment is initiated, they have suffered a good deal. The disturbance has usually been under way for a period of time resulting in distress and reduced life quality. Second, the evidence is consistent that existing treatment facilities service a minority of children who are disturbed, and those who are seen in such facilities are not necessarily the ones most in need of treatment. For example, in the Ontario Child Health Study, a large community study of emotional and behavioral problems in children 4 to 16 years of age, among the predictors of receiving specialized mental health or social services in the past 6 months, the presence of one or more psychiatric disorders ranked fourth in the size of its independent predictor effect (John, Offord, Boyle, & Racine, 1995). Low income, high education of the mother, and poor school performance all ranked ahead of it in strength of prediction.

It is difficult to provide equal access to services for children in different living circumstances. For example, children and families who live at a relatively long distance from services and who have to rely on public transportation are less likely to make use of these services. Furthermore, because services are available usually during daytime hours only, they are more readily accessible to parents who can take time off from work without too much difficulty. Third, the success in treating these conditions after they are under way is limited. This is especially so for aggressive or antisocial children (Kazdin, 1993). Finally, and perhaps the most telling limitation of all, is that the scope and magnitude of children's mental health problems are so great that it is unlikely that assessing and treating disturbed children and their families one at a time can ever result in large reductions in the burden of suffering attributable to these conditions (Offord & Fleming, in press).

CASE FOR PREVENTION

Because specialized clinical services can never make a meaningful dent in the burden of suffering from children's emotional and behavioral problems, programs that can prevent these problems before they are full blown and programs that focus on groups of children instead of dealing with children one at a time are needed (Offord, 1987). This combination of prevention and a population approach is the most promising strategy for making meaningful reductions in the burden of suffering from these conditions.

STRENGTHS OF PREVENTION PROJECTS

This volume illustrates many of the strengths of current prevention initiatives. They will be covered under the general headings of design, intervention, evaluation, and replication.

Design

Strength. The Canadian Task Force on the Periodic Health Examination (1979) has developed a classification of study designs to rank the strength of scientific evidence supporting the effectiveness of interventions. From weakest to strongest, it includes opinions of respected authorities, comparisons between times and places with or without intervention, well-designed cohort or case-control analytic studies, well-designed controlled trials without randomization, and well-designed randomized controlled trials. Much of the evidence supporting the effectiveness of prevention and treatment programs in the child mental health field is of the weakest kind scientifically—namely, opinions of respected authorities. It is impressive that there are several prevention studies in this volume that are using the strongest design to evaluate their effectiveness (i.e., a randomized controlled trial). Examples include the Fast Track Program (see the discussions in Chapters 4 and 5, this volume), the Montreal Prevention Experiment (see Chapter 12, this volume), the Comprehensive Child Development Program (described in Chapter 3, this volume), the Life Skills Training approach to prevent substance abuse (discussed in Chapter 10, this volume), and the evaluations of two prevention programs in rural populations, Preparing for the Drug (Free) Years and the Iowa Strengthening Families Programs for Pre- and Early Adolescents (described in Chapter 13, this volume).

Guiding Model. The presence of a model indicating the developmental pathways of children leading to the onset of psychopathology is an important prerequisite for intervention efforts. Such a model can identify potential causal risk factors that assume importance at various ages, and thus the justification of the different elements of the intervention program is made clear. For example, the Fast Track Program, by specifying a fairly detailed model of the development of early onset antisocial behavior, is able to use this to guide the choices of the elements of its intervention program (see Chapter 1, this volume). Thus, it becomes possible to lay out in diagrammatic fashion the identified causal risk factors, the interventions aimed at the particular risk factors, the proximal results of importance, and finally the more distal outcome variables.

Interventions

Compliance. One can argue that it is important to demonstrate in the first instance that an intervention does more good than harm in ideal circumstances in which, for example, compliance is not an issue. This is termed the *efficacy of an intervention* (Tugwell, Bennett, Sackett, & Haynes, 1985). In the real world, however, one is concerned about effectiveness— that is, does an intervention do more good than harm under routine conditions in which, of course, compliance becomes an issue. This volume includes examples of work aimed at determining what factors are likely to increase the rates of compliance of parents with intervention efforts (see the discussions in Chapters 7, 8, and 13). Knowledge in this area is necessary if the field is to move from efficacious interventions to effective interventions.

Multiple Elements Included and Described. Although this volume includes examples of single interventions to prevent antisocial behavior (see Chapter 7, this volume), many programs include multiple interventions. Fast Track, for example, is composed of seven integrated components— namely, parent training, home visiting, parent-child relationship enhancement, academic tutoring, a universal prevention curriculum used by teachers, a social skill training group program for targeted high-risk children, and a peer-pairing program (described in Chapter 4, this volume). Given the multiple causal risk factors involved in producing antisocial behavior in children, prevention programs with more than one intervention element will have the greatest chance of success.

In most instances in this volume, the individual elements of an intervention program are described in detail. Examples include the parent programs (e.g., Chapters 5 and 7, this volume) and social skill training for children and youth (e.g., Chapters 4 and 11, this volume). These detailed descriptions not only make it possible to monitor program integrity but also allow others to use these interventions in their own settings.

Evaluation

Independent Outcomes. Outcomes that are measured by the reports of different informants (e.g., parents and teachers) are open to all kinds of potential biases and are not likely to agree with each other (Offord & Fleming, in press). This volume provides examples of the measurement of outcomes that are based on observational data. For example, Spoth and Redmond (Chapter 13, this volume) measure parenting outcomes of their intervention, such as intervention-relevant child management behaviors, not only by self-reports but also by observer ratings.

Long-Term Follow-Up. It is one thing to be able to show changes in short-term proximal measures and quite another to ascertain whether a prevention program early on has long-term beneficial effects. A prerequisite in determining the latter, of course, is the availability of follow-up data. The Montreal Prevention Experiment is an impressive example in which, in a randomized controlled trial initiated in kindergarten, the sample has been currently followed into early adolescence (Chapter 12, this volume). The plan for a 20-year follow-up of children involved in the Better Beginnings, Better Futures Project (Chapter 2, this volume) will, if successful, provide more useful data than those obtained in the short term.

Replication

It is important to replicate interventions in different populations that have been shown to be effective in one population. The work of Botvin and colleagues (see Chapter 10, this volume) provides a wonderful example of this endeavor. Their program to prevent substance abuse was first tested and found to be effective in a predominantly white population and then subsequently tested in predominantly Hispanic and African American populations.

ISSUES

As the previous section has illustrated, there have been important advances in the study of prevention and early intervention of childhood emotional and behavioral problems. There are, however, many remaining issues that need to be addressed, several of which are covered in this section.

Developmental Epidemiology

The more knowledge that is available about the developmental pathways leading to childhood psychopathology, the more rational and precise intervention efforts can be. Two issues concerning risk factors are especially important. The first centers on the distinction among correlate, concomitant or consequence, invariant risk factor, variable risk factor, marker, and causal risk factor (Kraemer et al., 1995). A correlate is associated with an outcome, a concomitant or consequence does not precede the outcome, whereas a risk factor does precede the outcome. There are, however, different kinds of risk factors. An invariant risk factor cannot change or be changed. In the case of conduct disorder, gender is an invariant risk factor. Variable risk factors can change or be changed. Among these variable risk factors, however, only some have been shown to be causal risk factors, whereas others have not and could be termed *markers*. Markers are important in terms of identifying an at-risk population, but only proven causal risk factors should be the focus of intervention efforts. In the case of conduct disorder, marital discord is a proven causal risk factor, whereas low income is not and qualifies, based on current knowledge, as a marker (Offord, 1989). In the study of the etiology of emotional and behavioral problems in childhood, as one moves from correlates at one end to causal risk factors at the other, the number of qualifying variables lessens appreciably. Obviously, one of the advances that would be helpful to the prevention field is the identification, based on strong scientific evidence, of an increased number of causal risk factors.

Another issue concerning causal risk factors is their relative strength or importance. A concept of interest here is attributable risk (Lipman, Offord, & Boyle, in press; Streiner, Norman, & Munroe Blum, 1989). It indicates the maximum reduction in the incidence of a condition or disorder that could be expected if the effects of the causal risk factor could be eliminated. Relatively little data are available on the attributable risks of causal risk factors in children's mental disorders. Clearly, prevention efforts should focus on altering the effects of causal risk factors with high attributable risk. It is in this area that the contributions of developmental epidemiology to prevention efforts would be most helpful.

Trade-Offs Between Targeted
and Universal Approaches

Prevention programs are of two major types—targeted and universal. Both have advantages and disadvantages and the major ones are outlined in the following sections. A more complete discussion of this topic is available elsewhere (Offord et al., 1996).

Targeted Programs. In a targeted program, individual families (and children) do not seek help. Children can be identified for targeting in two ways: The identifying characteristics can be outside the child (e.g., family is on social assistance) or the children themselves can have distinguishing characteristics (e.g., mild antisocial behavior). In the report on prevention by the Institute of Medicine, these two types of prevention programs are termed *selective preventive interventions* and *indicated preventive interventions,* respectively (Mrazek & Haggerty, 1994). The Comprehensive Child Development Program (see Chapter 3, this volume), in which low-income families are targeted, and the programs of Kumpfer and colleagues (Chapter 11, this volume), in which the offspring of parents with drug abuse problems are the focus of the intervention, are examples in this volume of selective preventive interventions. The Fast Track Program (e.g., Chapter 4, this volume), the Coping Power Program for aggressive children (Chapter 6, this volume), the Adolescent Transitions Program (Chapter 9, this volume), and the Montreal prevention experiment (Chapter 12, this volume) are all examples of indicated preventive interventions.

There are several advantages to targeted programs. A major advantage is that they are potentially efficient in that the population of interest could be at much increased risk for the outcome. There are, of course, many disadvantages to the targeted approach. The first disadvantage is that the screening procedure itself may be expensive; furthermore, the refusal rate of participation in the collection of the screening data will be highest among those at greatest risk for disorder (Rose, 1985; Rutter, Tizard, & Whitmore, 1970). Second, the ability of screens to identify accurately a high-risk group is limited and brings with it important trade-offs. Figure 14.1 presents the different aspects of the relationship between the screen and the outcome. The ones of particular interest in this discussion are the trade-offs between the positive predictive value and the sensitivity. If the positive predictive value is low, then the screen will be identifying far more children as being at risk for the outcome than actually end up with the outcome. Large numbers of children will be misidentified and perhaps wrongly labeled or stigmatized, and the intervention will be given to large numbers of children who do not need it. On the other hand, if the results of the screen are used to increase the positive predictive value, it is likely that the sensitivity will be reduced. Although the screen more accurately identifies children who will end up with the outcome, the percentage of children with the eventual outcome identified by the screen will be relatively low. Thus, even if the intervention in the

Outcome

Positive

$$
\begin{array}{|c|c|}
\hline
a & b \\
\hline
c & d \\
\hline
\end{array}
$$

Negative

Positive predictive rate: $\dfrac{a}{a+b}$ Negative predictive rate: $\dfrac{d}{c+d}$

False positive rate: $\dfrac{b}{a+b}$ False negative rate: $\dfrac{c}{c+d}$

Sensitivity: $\dfrac{a}{a+c}$ Specificity: $\dfrac{d}{b+d}$

Prevalence of outcome: $\dfrac{a+c}{a+b+c+d}$

Figure 14.1. Relationships Between the Screening Identification Procedure and the Outcome

high-risk group is effective, the majority of children who end up with the outcome will not be in the original high-risk group. A recent publication (Lochman & Conduct Problems Prevention Research Group, 1995) on the performance of the screen in the Fast Track Program shows that the combined teacher and parent screens in kindergarten have difficulty accurately predicting problem outcomes in the fall and spring of Grade 1. The positive predictive value of the screen is 70.4%, but the sensitivity is only 50.9%. When the task is to predict disorder over longer periods of time, the accuracy of a screen is diminished. For example, in the Dunedin study, the accuracy of preschool measures at ages 3 and 5 predicting persistent antisocial behavior in late childhood is disappointing (White, Moffitt, Earls, Robins, & Silva, 1990). Here, the positive predictive value is only 15.3%, whereas the sensitivity is 64.0%. Although the strength of the relationship between the results of a screen and the identification of disorder can be statistically significant, they may have important limitations in terms of their usefulness in prevention projects.

Another disadvantage of the targeted approach is that its focus is to ameliorate the effects of risk factors that distinguish the high-risk group from the rest of the population. This approach does not usually consider as candidates for intervention causal risk factors that put the entire population at risk rather than those that put a segment of it at increased risk (Rose, 1985). For example, if a high-risk population for antisocial behavior in children is identified as the focus of a prevention program in an economically disadvantaged community, the intervention will be directed at those causal risk factors that distinguish the high-risk group from the rest of the population. No attention will be paid to communitywide causal risk factors that are responsible for the elevated rate of antisocial behavior in the entire group of children in the population. These could include variables such as lack of social organizations or civic traditions (Putnam, 1993)—all potential risk factors that apply to the population as a whole.

Universal Programs. In a universal program, all children in a geographic area or setting (e.g., a school) receive the intervention. Individual families (and their children) do not seek help and children are not singled out for the intervention. There are two types of universal programs: those that focus on particular communities or settings (e.g., a public housing complex) and those that are province- or statewide or countrywide. Better Beginnings, Better Futures (see Chapter 2, this volume), community-based parent training programs (see Chapter 7, this volume), the Life Skills Training Program for the prevention of drug abuse (see Chapter 10, this volume), and the programs Preparing for Drug (Free) Years and the Iowa Strengthening Families Program for Pre- and Early Adolescents (see Chapter 13, this volume) are all examples of universal programs.

The advantages of universal programs are several and include the absence of labeling or stigmatization, the involvement of the middle-class demands that the program will be well run, and the large potential they have for gains for the overall population even though the gains for individual members of the population will be small (Offord et al., 1996). There are also several disadvantages, including the possibility that the programs are unnecessarily expensive because the majority of children receiving them may not require them and, of course, there is a small benefit to the individual. A major potential disadvantage is that they may have their greatest effects on those at lowest risk. In the antisocial domain, the worry is that universal programs will make nice children even nicer but will have a negligible effect on those children at greatest risk for future clinically important levels of antisocial behavior.

Summary. It is important for those involved in prevention and early intervention projects to understand thoroughly the advantages and disadvantages of the general strategy they are employing. If it is a targeted approach, the cost, the rate of compliance, and accuracy of the screen become important. If it is a universal approach, the extent to which the program has beneficial effects on those children at highest risk becomes a central issue.

Descriptive Versus Experimental Epidemiology

In a seminal article on psychiatric epidemiology, Lee Robins (1978) distinguished between descriptive epidemiology and experimental epidemiology. In descriptive epidemiology, the investigator simply describes the frequency, distribution, correlates, and so on of various conditions. There are no interventions initiated by the investigator. In experimental epidemiology, on the other hand, an intervention is launched by the investigator and the results are evaluated. The Ontario Child Health Study (Offord et al., 1987) is an example of descriptive epidemiology, whereas prevention and early intervention initiatives are examples of experimental epidemiology. This distinction is clear, but what is not so evident is the extent of the contribution of descriptive epidemiology to experimental efforts. At what point is it more productive to launch intervention studies rather than continuing to fund or begin funding large-scale descriptive epidemiology studies? It has to be kept in mind that experimental studies, in addition to determining whether an intervention is effective, can provide the strongest evidence for a risk factor being causal and for its attributable risk (McMaster University Health Sciences Centre, 1981).

Dissemination and Maintenance

It is one thing to demonstrate that a prevention program has been effective but quite another to ensure that the effective program is widely disseminated and maintained in other settings. Unless this occurs, the successful program will have no effect in reducing the incidence of the problems of interest in the larger society. Why is it that successful interventions in the child mental health field are almost never disseminated successfully to other settings and, indeed, are usually not maintained in the original setting (Jones, in press)? There are a number of reasons for this.

Cost. One of the first questions asked about a program that is being considered for implementation is its cost. In many instances, the program is so expensive that it could never be widely disseminated. In all cases in this volume, except for Better Beginnings, Better Futures (Chapter 2), data on costs are never mentioned, and thus it is not known what the costs would be to apply a specific prevention program widely to the community population. It is possible, for example, that the Fast Track Program, if successful, could never be broadly disseminated in its present form because it would be far too expensive.

Feasibility. The program, to be successfully spread, must be acceptable and administratively feasible. If the prevention initiative requires special effort from the deliverers and unusually complex administrative arrangements, it is unlikely to be taken up in other settings. A current prevention project at Johns Hopkins, the "Good Behavior Game," is a case in point. A participating classroom is divided into two "teams" that compete with each other over the extent of their good behavior (Kellam & Rebok, 1992). In addition, participating classroom teachers must receive 140 hours of special instruction prior to beginning the program. Because of these demands of the program, it is possible that it will not be acceptable to school boards and teachers in the wider community and thus would not be disseminated.

Program Imposed. When a prevention initiative is launched in a setting by others who are not members of that setting, there is little guarantee that the workers in that setting will maintain the program. This is especially relevant to academics who may both supervise and evaluate a prevention program—for example, in the schools. The school may never see the program as theirs, however, and as soon as the research is completed, the schools may immediately discontinue the program. For example, Kolvin's demonstration project (Kolvin et al., 1981) in the Newcastle schools launched from an academic setting was discontinued by the school system as soon as the study itself was finished. On the other hand, the Better Beginnings, Better Futures Project, by working in partnership with the participating communities, is attempting to ensure that the program will not be seen as a university initiative imposed on them (Chapter 2, this volume).

Reliance on Exceptional People. To initiate a prevention project requires people with unusual dedication and energy and perhaps other characteristics such as charismatic personalities. Whatever these positive characteristics are, they are difficult to duplicate in other persons. The more a program is dependent on exceptional people, the less likely it will be widely disseminated.

Summary. A major problem in the prevention field is the lack of attention paid in the planning of prevention projects about how, if successful, the initiative could ever be widely disseminated. Issues such as cost and administrative feasibility must be considered up front. It is difficult to justify a large-scale prevention project in children's mental health that has little chance of ever being disseminated widely.

CONCLUSION

This volume, by bringing together not only reports of major initiatives in the child mental health prevention field but also by presenting the current thinking and concerns of principal researchers provides a unique contribution to this area. It gives the reader a comprehensive picture, in terms of accomplishments and challenges, of the state of the field at the present time.

Impressive progress has been made in designing and evaluating prevention programs to reduce the incidence of emotional and behavioral problems in children and adolescents. Gains are especially apparent in the strong designs being employed, improved models of causation guiding prevention efforts, multifaceted interventions in which the elements are clearly described, independent outcome measures, and examples of long-term follow-up and replication. Increased knowledge about the developmental epidemiology of disorders or conditions will provide much-needed data on the identification of causal risk factors and their relative importance as measured by their attributable risk. Both targeted and universal approaches will continue to be needed. Of great concern will be the determination of the effectiveness of programs that have characteristics that would suggest that the programs, if successful, could be widely disseminated. These characteristics include being relatively inexpensive, acceptable to the providers and populations of interest, and administratively feasible. There will be continued tension between studies in descriptive and experimental epidemiology, especially in these times when funding is curtailed.

The goal of the prevention field is to determine for each condition in the child mental health domain what combination of universal, targeted, and clinical programs is optimal, in cost-effective terms, to reduce the burden of suffering in large populations of children. This optimal mix will change as knowledge accumulates.

REFERENCES

American Psychiatric Association. (1980). *Diagnostic and statistical manual of mental disorders* (3rd ed.). Washington, DC: Author.

Bird, H. R., Canino, G., Rubio-Stipec, M., Gould, M. S., Ribera, J., Sesman, M., Woodbury, M., Huertas-Goldman, S., Pagan, A., Sanchez-Lacay, A., & Moscoso, M. (1988). Estimates of the prevalence of childhood maladjustment in a community survey in Puerto Rico: The use of combined measures. *Archives of General Psychiatry, 45,* 1120-1126.

Boyle, M. H., Offord, D. R., Racine, Y. A., Szatmari, P., Fleming, J. E., & Links, P. S. (1992). Predicting substance use in late adolescence: Results from the Ontario Health Study follow-up. *American Journal of Psychiatry, 149,* 761-767.

Canadian Task Force on the Periodic Health Examination. (1979). The periodic health examination. *Canadian Medical Association Journal, 121,* 3-45.

Costello, E. J. (1989). Developments in child psychiatric epidemiology. *Journal of the American Academy of Child and Adolescent Psychiatry, 28,* 836-841.

Institute of Medicine. (1989). *Research on children and adolescents with mental, behavioral and developmental disorders: Mobilizing a national initiative.* Washington, DC: National Academy Press.

John, L. H., Offord, D. R., Boyle, M. H., & Racine, Y. A. (1995). Factors predicting use of mental health and social services by children 6-16 years old: Findings from the Ontario Child Health Study. *American Journal of Orthopsychiatry, 65,* 76-86.

Jones, M. B. (in press). Undoing the effects of poverty in children: Non-economic initiatives. *Proceedings of the inaugural symposium of the Centre for Studies of Children at Risk: Improving the life quality of children; options and evidence.*

Kazdin, A. E. (1993). Treatment of conduct disorder: Progress and directions in psychotherapy research. *Development and Psychopathology, 5,* 277-310.

Kellam, S. G., & Rebok, G. W. (1992). Building developmental and etiological theory through epidemiologically based preventive intervention trials. In J. McCord & R. E. Tremblay (Eds.), *Preventing antisocial behavior: Interventions from birth through adolescence* (pp. 162-195). New York: Guilford.

Kolvin, T., Garside, R. F., Nicol, A. R., MacMillan, A., Wolstenhome, I., & Leitch, I. M. (1981). *Help starts here: The maladjusted child in the ordinary school.* New York: Tavistock.

Kraemer, H. C., Kazdin, A. E., Offord, D. R., Kessler, R. C., Jensen, P. S., & Kupfer, D. J. (1995). *The MacArthur Risk Assessment Project: Coming to terms with the terms of risk.* Manuscript submitted for publication.

Lipman, E. L., Offord, D. R., & Boyle, M. H. (in press). What if we could eliminate child poverty: The theoretical effect on child psychosocial morbidity. *Social Psychiatry and Psychiatric Epidemiology.*

Lochman, J. E., & Conduct Problems Prevention Research Group. (1995). Screening of child behavior problems for prevention programs at school entry. *Journal of Consulting and Clinical Psychology, 63,* 549-559.

McMaster University Health Sciences Centre, Department of Clinical Epidemiology and Biostatistics. (1981). How to read clinical journals: IV. To determine etiology and causation. *Journal of the Canadian Medical Association, 124,* 985-990.

Mrazek, P. J., & Haggerty, R. J. (Eds.). (1994). *Reducing risks for mental disorders: Frontiers for preventive intervention research.* Washington, DC: National Academy Press.

Offord, D. R. (1987). Prevention of behavioural and emotional disorders in children. *Journal of Child Psychology and Psychiatry, 28,* 9-19.

Offord, D. R. (1989). Conduct disorder: Risk factors and prevention. In D. Shaffer, I. Philips, & N. B. Enzer (Eds.), *Prevention of mental disorders, alcohol and other drug use in children and adolescents* (pp. 273-307). Rockville, MD: U.S. Department of Health and Human Services.

Offord, D. R., Boyle, M. H., Fleming, J. E., Munroe Blum, H., & Rae-Grant, I. (1989). Ontario Child Health Study: Summary of selected results. *Canadian Journal of Psychiatry, 34,* 483-491.

Offord, D. R., Boyle, M. H., Szatmari, P., Rae-Grant, N. I., Links, P. S., Cadman, D. T., Byles, J. A., Crawford, J. W., Munroe Blum, H., Byrne, C., Thomas, H., & Woodward, C. A. (1987). Ontario Child Health Study: Six-month prevalence of disorder and rates of service utilization. *Archives of General Psychiatry, 44,* 832-836.

Offord, D. R., & Fleming, J. E. (in press). In M. Lewis (Ed.), *Child and adolescent psychiatry: A comprehensive textbook* (2nd ed.). Thousand Oaks, CA: Sage.

Offord, D. R., Kraemer, H. C., Kazdin, A. E., Jensen, P. S., Kessler, R. C., & Kupfer, D. J. (1996). *Reducing the burden of suffering from child mental disorders: Trade-offs among clinical, targeted and universal programs.* Manuscript in preparation.

Patterson, G. R., DeBaryshe, B. D., & Ramsey, E. (1989). A developmental perspective on antisocial behavior. *American Psychologist, 44,* 329-335.

Putnam, R. D. (1993). *Making democracy work: Civic traditions in modern Italy.* Princeton, NJ: Princeton University Press.

Robins, L. N. (1966). *Deviant children grown up: A sociological and psychiatric study of sociopathic personality.* Baltimore, MD: Williams & Wilkins.

Robins, L. N. (1970). The adult development of the antisocial child. *Seminars in Psychiatry, 6,* 420-434.

Robins, L. N. (1978). Psychiatric epidemiology. *Archives of General Psychiatry, 35,* 697-702.

Rose, G. (1985). Sick individuals and sick populations. *International Journal of Epidemiology, 14,* 32-38.

Rutter, M., Tizard, J., & Whitmore, K. (1970). *Education, health and behaviour.* London: Longman.

Sanford, M. N., Offord, D. R., Boyle, M. H., Peace, A., & Racine, Y. A. (1992). Ontario Child Health Study: Social and school impairments in children aged 6 to 16 years. *Journal of the American Academy of Child and Adolescent Psychiatry, 31,* 60-67.

Streiner, D. L., Norman, G. R., & Munroe Blum, H. (1989). *Epidemiology.* Toronto, Canada: B. C. Decker.

Tugwell, P., Bennett, K. J., Sackett, D. L., & Haynes, R. B. (1985). The measurement iterative loop: A framework for the critical appraisal of need, benefits and costs of health interventions. *Journal of Chronic Disease, 38,* 339-351.

Velez, C. N., Johnson, J., & Cohen, P. (1989). A longitudinal analysis of selected risk factors for childhood psychopathology. *Journal of the American Academy of Child and Adolescent Psychiatry, 28,* 861-864.

White, J. L., Moffitt, T. E., Earls, F., Robins, L., & Silva, P. A. (1990). How early can we tell? Predictors of childhood conduct disorder and adolescent delinquency. *Criminology, 28,* 507-533.

Index

Abbott, R. D., 270, 280
Academic skills, 12
Access to high-risk population, 4
Achenbach, T. M., 68, 192, 256
Active modes of learning, 80
Adler, T., 10
Administration on Children, Youth and
    Families (ACYF), 48, 55, 56
Adnopoz, J., 145
Adolescent Transitions Program (ATP):
    assessing, 202-203
    component analysis, 190-193
    dental model framework, 185
    family interaction patterns, 193-195
    goals and interventions, 188-190
    implementation, school-based,
        198-202
    summary and future directions,
        203-210
    youth problem behaviors, 195-198
African Americans, 234-235, 249-252
Age appropriateness, 54-55, 96
Ageton, S. S., 10, 113, 304
Aggression:
    kindergarten, 270-276
    later deviant behavior linked to early,
        269-270
    peer status, 14-15, 81-82
    risk markers, 112-114

socioeconomic status, 268
    See also Montreal Prevention Experiment;
        Social-cognitive intervention with
        aggressive children
Aktan, G., 251
Alcohol use, 185-186, 215-218, 228-230,
    302-303
Alder, R. J., 7
Allen, G. J., 119
Allgood, S. M., 169
Alvarado, R., 305, 319
Ambrose, S. A., 155
Analysis of covariance (ANCOVA), 318, 320
Anastopoulos, A. D., 145
Andrews, D. W., 190, 192, 194, 202, 203,
    349
Andrews, K., 243
Anger arousal, social-cognitive model of,
    114-116
Anger Coping Program, 116-120
Anthony, J. C., 69
Armbruster, P., 162
Arthur, M. W., 244
Asarnow, J. R., 4, 10, 21, 69, 115, 244, 293,
    303, 308, 319
Asher, S. R., 66, 69, 75
Assessment:
    Adolescent Transitions Program, 193,
        202-203

About the Editors

Ray DeV. Peters, Ph.D., is Professor of Psychology at Queen's University in Kingston, Ontario, and is research director of the Better Beginnings, Better Futures Project, a large, multisite longitudinal study in Ontario on the prevention of mental health problems in young children from birth to 7 years of age. He was a visiting scientist with the Oregon Social Learning Center in 1979-1980 and with the Mental Health Division of the World Health Organization in Geneva, Switzerland, in 1986-1987. His primary research interests are in the areas of children's mental health and development psychology. Since 1982, he has served on the executive committee of the Banff International Conference on Behavioral Science.

Robert J. McMahon, Ph.D., is currently Professor and Director of the Child Clinical Psychology Program in the Department of Psychology at the University of Washington. His primary research and clinical interests concern the assessment, treatment, and prevention of conduct disorders in children. He is a principal investigator on the Fast Track project, a large, multisite collaborative study on the prevention of serious conduct problems in school-aged children. His primary responsibilities on that project concern the development and implementation of the family-based intervention components. He is also a principal investigator on the Early Parenting Project, a longitudinal study examining the development of children of adolescent mothers from infancy into elementary school. He is the author (with Rex Forehand) of *Helping the Noncompliant Child: A Clinician's Guide to Parent Training* and of a number of scientific articles, chapters, and reviews. He has also coedited (with Ray Peters and others) several volumes emanating from the Banff International Conferences on Behavioural Science.

About the Contributors

David W. Andrews, Ph.D., is Research Associate at the Oregon Social Learning Center. He has authored numerous articles on the influence of families and friends on both healthy and problematic development through childhood and adolescence. He served as Head of the Department of Human Development and Family Sciences at Oregon State University, where he received honors as a Distinguished Professor and Fulbright Scholar. Upon completion of a National Institute of Mental Health Postdoctoral Fellowship, he joined the Oregon Social Learning Center staff in developing and evaluating programs for high-risk adolescents. His recent publications include coauthored articles in *Child Development,* the *Journal of Personality and Social Psychology,* the *Journal of Consulting and Clinical Psychology,* and *Developmental Psychology.*

Karen L. Bierman, Ph.D., is Professor of Psychology at the Pennsylvania State University. Her research has focused on the exploration of factors that affect the development of adaptive peer relations, social competence, and behavioral adjustment in middle childhood and on the design and evaluation of remedial and preventive interventions for at-risk children. Previous intervention studies have been published in *Child Development* and the *Journal of Consulting and Clinical Psychology.* She is principal investigator of the rural Pennsylvania site of the Fast Track project.

Gilbert J. Botvin received his Ph.D. from Columbia University in 1977 with training in both developmental and clinical psychology. After graduate school, he spent 3 years at the American Health Foundation, first as a staff psychologist and later as Director of Child Health Behavior Research. He is currently Professor of Psychology at Cornell University Medical

College with a joint appointment in the Department of Public Health and the Department of Psychiatry. He is also the director of Cornell's Institute for Prevention Research and director of the New York Hospital-Cornell Medical Center Smoking Cessation Service, where he has been involved in the treatment of addictive behavior. He has conducted research in child and adolescent development, adolescent health behavior, and behavioral approaches to chronic disease risk reduction and is internationally known for his groundbreaking work in tobacco, alcohol, and drug abuse prevention. He has authored or coauthored more than 115 scientific papers and chapters and presented more than 100 papers at national and international conferences. He has served as a consultant to a number of state and federal agencies in the United States, including the National Cancer Institute and the National Institute on Drug Abuse.

John D. Coie, Ph.D., is a Professor of Psychology at Duke University, where he has been director of the clinical training program. He received his Ph.D. in psychology from the University of California at Berkeley. He has been the recipient of an ADAMHA Senior Research Scientist Award since 1990 and has chaired the NIMH Review Committee on Child and Adolescent Risk and Prevention Research. The primary focus of his research is on identifying early risk factors for adolescent involvement in violence and antisocial behavior. He currently directs a longitudinal study of youth from age 8 to young adulthood. He is codirector of a major comprehensive program for early prevention with children who are at high risk for adolescent violence. The Fast Track project is a four-site consortium funded by NIMH since 1990. This program addresses family, school, and child competence needs across the period of elementary school and early middle school. His recent publications deal with child aggression and peer relations, with developmental models of adolescent dysfunction and antisocial behavior, and with peer group processes that either protect against or increase the likelihood of delinquency. He has coauthored *Peer Rejection in Childhood* with Steven Asher.

Charles E. Cunningham, Ph.D., is a Professor of Psychiatry in the Faculty of Health Sciences at McMaster University and an affiliate member of the Centre for the Studies of Children at Risk, in Hamilton, Ontario. He has been involved in research on both pharmacological and behavioral interventions and has a special interest in models that increase the availability and cost efficacy of services for children with disruptive behavior disorders. He is currently involved in the development and evaluation of large-group, community-based parenting programs and student-mediated conflict resolution programs. He directs Chedoke-McMaster Hospital's Community Parent Education (COPE) Program, which provides parenting courses for families of children with disruptive behavior disorders. He is a member of the editorial board of the *ADHD Report* and the Chair of the National Professional Advisory Board of CHADD Canada. He is a principal investigator or coinvestigator on grants from the Ontario Mental Health Foundation, the Medical Research Council, and the Ministry of Education. He holds a Senior Research Fellowship from the Ontario Mental Health Foundation. Recent publications are coauthored articles in the *Journal of Consulting and Clinical Psychology* and the *Journal of Child Psychology and Psychiatry.*

Thomas J. Dishion, Ph.D., is Research Scientist at the Oregon Social Learning Center, an Adjunct Behavioral Scientist at the Oregon Research Institute, and an Associate Professor of Counseling Psychology at the University of Oregon. He is collaborating in basic research on interpersonal processes underlying the influence of peers on adolescent problem behavior. In addition, he is principal investigator on a project funded by the National Institute on Drug Abuse to evaluate preventive intervention strategies with high-risk youth. He has recently coauthored three books on theory, intervention, and assessment with child and adolescent problem behavior and a book for parents of preschool children, in addition to research publications in the *Journal of Consulting and Clinical Psychology, Development and Psychopathology, Child Development,* and *Developmental Psychology.*

Mark T. Greenberg, Ph.D., is Professor of Psychology at the University of Washington. He is coauthor of several books, including *Promoting Social and Emotional Development in Deaf Children: The PATHS Project* (1993), *The PATHS Curriculum* (1995), and *Attachment in the Preschool Years: Theory, Research and Intervention* (1990). He is one of the principal investigators of the Fast Track project and is the director of the PATHS Curriculum project (both funded by the National Institute of Mental Health). His primary interest is in the prevention of childhood psychopathology (in normal and challenged populations) through interventions that promote healthy emotion regulation and social competence.

Kate Kavanagh, Ph.D., is Developmental Psychologist and Research Associate at the Oregon Social Learning Center. She has worked with hundreds of parents, teens, and children during her 17 years at the center. This direct service has contributed to her work in the study of family variables predictive of child and adolescent adjustment problems, the development of family and school-based intervention and prevention programs, and the training of community professionals in assessment and intervention techniques. She has created video and print intervention materials for family populations, including working parents of preschoolers and elementary school children, families with at-risk and delinquent youth, and families of kindergartners at risk for conduct disorders. Currently, her research is focused on conduct disorders in females and the development of gender-sensitive intervention and assessment materials. Two recent publications have addressed cross-gender influences of parents and teachers in the identification, prediction, and remediation of problem behaviors in early adolescence.

Karol L. Kumpfer, Ph.D., is a psychologist with more than 20 years experience in alcohol and drug abuse treatment and prevention research. She is Associate Professor of Health Education at the University of Utah where she has conducted federally funded research for NIDA, NIAAA, NIMH, CSAP, DOE, FIPSE, and OJJDP on family, school, and community approaches to drug prevention. A frequent conference speaker, she is coauthor (with Ezekoye and Bukoski) of *Childhood and Chemical Abuse: Prevention and Intervention*, as well as journal articles and monographs. She has developed several family skills training programs, including a 14-session Strengthening Families Program with DeMarsh and Child, focusing on elementary-age children, and the Strengthening Families Program II with Molgaard, focusing on fifth to eighth graders. She is currently involved in research on applications of the Strengthening Families Program for different ethnic youth and their families. Recently, she completed a national search for the best family programs in the country for the Office of Juvenile Justice and Delinquency Prevention. She is an evaluation specialist, who was CO-PI on the CSAP National Evaluation of the High Risk Youth Demonstration Program and consultant on the Pregnant and Post Partum Drug Abusing Women and Infant Grantee Program. She is currently the evaluator for several CSAP-HRY and CYAP grants. She has published an evaluation book, *Measurements in Prevention*, on measurement instruments for prevention program evaluators.

John E. Lochman received his Ph.D. from the University of Connecticut. He is an Associate Professor in the Department of Psychiatry at Duke University Medical Center and an Associate Professor in the Department of Psychology: Social and Health Sciences at Duke University. He is on the editorial board for the *Journal of Consulting and Clinical Psychology* and a Fellow in the American Psychological Association. He has authored research papers and chapters on cognitive-behavioral assessment and intervention with aggressive children, on the social-cognitive dysfunctions of aggressive children and their parents, on the later adolescent adjustment of children identified as aggressive in elementary school, and on preventive interventions for conduct disorder and substance use. Recent journal articles have appeared in the *Journal of Consulting and Clinical Psychology*, the *Journal of the American Academy of Child and Adolescent Psychiatry*, *Developmental Psychology*, the *Journal of Abnormal Child Psychology*, and *Development and Psychopathology*. His research work has been funded by grants from the National Institute on Drug Abuse and the National Institute of Mental Health.

Louise C. Mâsse, Ph.D., is Assistant Professor of Behavioral Sciences at the University of Texas–Houston School of Public Health. She received her doctorate from the University of Ottawa in Measurement and Evaluation. Her background also includes a B.Sc. and M.Sc. in exercise sciences. She was a postdoctoral fellow of the Research Unit on Children's Psychosocial Maladjustment at the University of Montreal. Her research interests are in measurement and evaluation, juvenile delinquency, and violence. Her interests lie in assessing delinquency and violence, with a focus on understanding the psychosocial determinants of these behaviors. Her other research interests are in the area of physical activity and are related to the validation of instruments measuring physical activity and understanding the psychosocial determinants of physical activity.

Gloria E. Miller received her Ph.D. from the University of Wisconsin—Madison and is currently Professor of Psychology at the University of South Carolina. She is a Fellow of the Division of School and Educational Psychology in the American Psychological Association. Her research interests lie in the prevention of severe conduct disorders in children, with a particular emphasis on understanding the parental and child self-regulatory processes that contribute to antisocial outcomes. Her most recent work focuses on intervention enhancements that lead to increased engagement, compliance, and subsequent behavioral improvements in children and families. In collaboration with Ron Prinz, this work has been funded by two consecutive grants from the National Institute of Mental Health. She has coedited *Cognitive Strategy Research* (1989), and her most recent publications have appeared in *Psychological Bulletin,* the *Journal of Consulting and Clinical Psychology*, and the *Journal of Clinical Child Psychology.*

Virginia Molgaard is Associate Professor in the Department of Human Development and Family Studies at Iowa State University where she received her Ph.D. in Family Environment. She has served as State Family Life Specialist for the past 11 years for the Cooperative Extension Service. In that role she has developed curricula on topics such as building self esteem in youth and families, dealing effectively with stress, balancing work and family, and building strong families. In addition, she is presently serving as a research scientist at the Social and Behavioral Research Center for Rural Health at Iowa State University where she has served as a liaison to the extension system, developing news media releases for the public, and providing research updates for staff. In her research role, she has been involved through PROJECT FAMILY in a National Institute of Mental Health-funded project to test a preventive intervention for families, designed to reduce the risk of adolescent substance abuse and other behavior problems. In addition, she has developed a model, presented at a recent workshop sponsored by the NIMH, for involving the extension service in large-scaled intervention research projects.

David R. Offord is a child psychiatrist with major interests in epidemiology and prevention. He is Professor of Psychiatry at McMaster University and head of the Division of Child Psychiatry, research director of the Chedoke Child and Family Center. He has been director of the Child Epidemiology Unit since its inception in 1980. He is also director of the newly formed Centre for Studies of Children at Risk, which focuses on policy issues, scientific research, and training. He is a National Health Scientist and a member of the Premier's Council on Health, Well-Being, and Social Justice. He has played a leading role in the Ontario Child Health Study and the follow-up. The major goal of the initial cross-sectional study, carried out in 1983, was to obtain unbiased precise estimates of the prevalence of emotional and behavioral problems, physical health problems, and substance use among Ontario children 4 to 16 years of age. The follow-up study carried out in 1987 focused on issues of outcome, prognosis, and risk. He was principal investigator on a community intervention project in a public housing complex in Ottawa that focused on providing a first-rate nonschool skill development program for all children, 5 to 15 years of age, in the complex. The model employed in this successful demonstration project is now being replicated in two locations in Ontario. He is director of the State-of-the-Child Research Unit funded by the Laidlaw Foundation, in which the major goal is to determine what data should be collected on a regular basis on children and youth in Ontario to inform and evaluate policy. Furthermore, he has completed pilot work on two Native reserves in the area of children's health, particularly mental health, and he is the coprincipal investigator of the Tri-Ministry Project, a 6-year study aimed at determining whether adjustment problems can be prevented in children from kindergarten to Grade 3 by a combination of parent training, classwide social skills training, and academic support. In addition, he has published widely in the scientific literature.

Linda Pagani, Ph.D., is Assistant Professor Research Associate (School of Psycho-Education) and Research Associate (Research Unit on Children's Psycho-Social Maladjustment) at the University of Montreal. Her current research, which is mostly prospective in nature, focuses on the influence of family processes (marital transitions, poverty, parent-child relationships, child rearing) on children's development (academic performance and sociobehavioral adjustment). She is currently involved with several longitudinal projects, including the Montreal Longitudinal-Experimental Study of Boys and the Quebec Longitudinal Study. Some recent publications include authored and coauthored articles in the *American Journal of Orthopsychiatry*, the *American Journal of Family Therapy*, the *Journal of Consulting and Clinical Psychology*, and the *Journal of Divorce and Remarriage*.

Peter J. Pizzolongo is Research Associate at CSR, Incorporated, in Washington, D.C. Primarily, he serves as Assistant Director for Management Support for the Comprehensive Child Development Program (CCDP). The CCDP, a federally funded project of the U.S. Department of Health and Human Services, is a community-based family support and education demonstration project begun in 1988. It is designed to encourage intensive, comprehensive, integrated, and continuous services for low-income families and their children to promote economic and social self-sufficiency among participating adults and to enhance children's physical, socioemotional, and intellectual development. As management support coordinator, he oversees the monitoring of and training and technical assistance to 34 CCDP projects nationwide. Previously, he served as project director for the Head Start Home-Based Support Services Project and for the U.S. Public Health Services's HIV/AIDS Training Institute for Public Health Professionals, as the child development associate representative coordinator for the Council on Early Childhood Professional Recognition, as a child care resource and referral agency director, as a Head Start state training officer, and as a Head Start and day care center administrator and caregiver. He is coauthor of *Caring for Preschool Children*, the U.S. Department of Defense's *Child Caregiver Training Program*, *HIV/AIDS Training Cur-*

riculum for Public Health Professionals, Responding to Children Under Stress, The Head Start Home Visitor Handbook, Living and Teaching Nutrition Curriculum, and other publications.

Ronald J. Prinz obtained his B.A. at the University of California at Berkeley and received his Ph.D. from the State University of New York at Stony Brook. He is currently Carolina Research Professor in Psychology at the University of South Carolina. He has published several edited books and more than 50 research articles pertaining to problems encountered by children and families. He coedits the Advances in Clinical Child Psychology series with Thomas Ollendick. He is a Fellow of the American Psychological Association, an elected member of the Board of Directors in the Association for Advancement of Behavior Therapy, and on the editorial boards for the *Journal of Clinical Child Psychology* and the *Journal of Abnormal Child Psychology.* His research interests lie in the areas of prevention and treatment of childhood aggression and related sequlae.

Cleve Redmond, Ph.D., is Research Scientist at the Social and Behavioral Research Center for Rural Health at Iowa State University. His current research interests include the examination of factors influencing the recruitment and retention of families into preventive interventions designed to prevent teen problem behaviors, as well as the factors influencing the efficacy of such preventive interventions. His research is being conducted as part of Project Family, a series of studies evaluating factors that affect parent motivation to enhance parenting skills and the efficacy of family skills-focused interventions for the prevention of juvenile substance abuse and conduct problems (funded by the National Institute on Drug Abuse, the National Institute of Mental Health, and the Center for Substance Abuse Prevention). Among his recent publications are coauthored articles in the *Journal of Marriage and Family,* the *Journal of Family Psychology,* and *Health Education Research.*

Carol Crill Russell is Senior Research and Policy Adviser for Children's Services, Ministry of Community and Social Services, in Ontario. She monitors population based and intervention research on healthy child development funded by the ministry. The key research projects are the Ontario Child Health Study, a multiphase epidemiological study of children's mental health; the Better Beginnings, Better Futures Project, an investigation of an ecological prevention model currently demonstrated in seven disadvantaged urban neighborhoods and five First Nations; the Helping Children Adjust Project, an early intervention project in more than

50 primary schools; and a multisite investigation of intensive family preservation in child welfare. She is also working with an advisory group to design a system to identify, evaluate, and disseminate information on effective services for children in greatest need or at greatest risk. She is the past chair of the Family System Working Group for the Provincial Substance Abuse Strategy, a member of the Inter-Ministry Committee on Crime Prevention, and a member of the Expert Advisory Group for the National Longitudinal Survey of Children. She holds a B.A. in psychology, an M.S. in sociology, and an M.S.W. and Ph.D. in social work and sociology.

Nancy M. Slough, Ph.D., is Research Scientist in the Department of Psychology at the University of Washington. She is currently the Research Director and Clinical Supervisor at the Seattle site for the Fast Track Program, a national multisite collaborative study on the prevention of conduct problems in school-aged children. Her primary research and clinical interest is the prevention of conduct disorders in children with a focus on improved parenting skills and the parent-child relationship. Her other research interests include the development and assessment of attachment and peer relationships in school-aged children. Her most recent publication appeared in *New Directions for Child Development.*

Lawrence H. Soberman, Ph.D., is former Project Director for the Adolescent Transitions Program. He specializes in the assessment of and educational programming for high-risk and special education students. He has developed screening techniques for the identification of problem behavior during adolescence and was instrumental in formalizing the curriculum components of the Adolescent Transitions Program prevention trial. He is continuing to implement innovative strategies for improving learning environments in public schools.

Richard Spoth, Ph.D., is Research Scientist and Project Director for Prevention Programming and Research at the Social and Behavioral Research Center for Rural Health. Following his tenure as clinical director of a hospital-based service where he developed and evaluated preventive behavioral health programs, he obtained a grant to support the establishment of the Social and Behavioral Research Center for Rural Health with colleagues at Iowa State University in the late 1980s. His interest in interdisciplinary research led to further collaborative activity directed toward the organization of the Iowa Consortium on Substance Abuse Research and Evaluation, a consortium of universities and state agencies;